COMMITTED TO THE FLAMES

The History and Rituals of a Secret Masonic Rite

Arturo de Hoyos
P.M. McAllen Lodge No. 1110, AF&AM, Texas
Gr Archivist & Gr Historian, Supreme Council, *33°*, S.J., U.S.A.

S. Brent Morris
P.M. Patmos Lodge No. 70, AF&AM, Maryland
W.M. Quatuor Coronati Lodge No. 2076, U.G.L.E.
Managing Editor, *The Scottish Rite Journal*

Dedicated to the memory of

Ill. Robert B. Folger, 33°
Earnest Physician • Passionate Historian • Zealous Craftsman

First published 2008

ISBN (10) 085318 293 0
ISBN (13) 085318 293 1

All rights reserved. No part of this book may be reproduced or transmitted in any form or by any meand, electronic or mechanical, including photocopying, recording or by any information storage and retrieval system, without permission from the Publisher in writing.

© Arturo de Hoyos & S. Brent Morris 2008

The rights of Arturo de Hoyos and S. Brent Morris to be identified as author of this work have been asserted by them in accordance with the copyright design and patents act 1988.

Published by Lewis Masonic

an imprint of Ian Allan Publishing Ltd. Hersham, Surrey KT12 4RG
Printed in England by Ian Allan Printing Ltd. Hersham, Surrey KT12 4RG

Code 0802/B2

Visit the Lewis Masonic website at www.lewismasonic.co.uk

Contents

Chapter 1. Introduction — 7

Chapter 2. The Mystery of the Folger Manuscripts — 19

Chapter 3. The Cryptanalysis of the Folger Cipher — 35

Chapter 4. The Coadjutors of Robert B. Folger — 51

Chapter 5. The Biography of a Remarkable Freemason — 75

Chapter 6. Folger Manuscript 1 (*The Macoy Book*) — 95

Chapter 7. Folger Manuscript 2 (*The Supreme Council Book*) — 133

Chapter 8. Folger Manuscript 3 (*The Walgren Book*) — 227

Notes — 278

Index — 285

1

Introduction

THE STORY OF THE FOLGER MANUSCRIPTS IS AN INTRIGUING TALE SET IN the middle of nineteenth-century New York Freemasonry. It is almost impossible to appreciate all the influences on the manuscripts' author, Robert B. Folger, without understanding the milieu in which the story unfolds. The following paragraphs should give a sufficient overview of the Byzantine complexities of New York Freemasonry to help the reader appreciate his tale.

NEW YORK FREEMASONRY IN THE EARLY 1800S

The earliest record of Freemasonry in the United States is the account book of a "St. John's Lodge" in Philadelphia, known as "Libre B"; its first entry is dated June 24, 1731. A year earlier on June 5, 1730, Daniel Coxe had been appointed Provincial Grand Master for New York, New Jersey, and Pennsylvania, but he seems not to have exercised his authority. The first chartered lodge in the United States is First Lodge, now St. John's, of Boston, which received its charter on July 30, 1733.

The first reference to Masonry operating in New York City is an oblique notice in January 1737/38, stating the Master of a Lodge had resigned because of his removal from the city. The formal chartering of New York City lodges started with St. John's Lodge No. 2 (now No. 1) on December 7, 1757, and continued with Temple Lodge ca. 1758, La Parfait Union on November 1, 1760, and St. John's Independent Royal Arch Lodge No. 8 (now No. 2) on December 15, 1760. The Grand Lodge of New York, which governs all lodges in the state, was formed in 1787.[1]

Civic Respectability

By the early 1800s Freemasonry had become a large, influential organization throughout New York State, attracting many prominent citizens. During the War of 1812, De Witt Clinton, Mayor of New York City and Grand Master of the Grand Lodge of New York, assembled the grand officers and members of two local lodges to construct fortifications in Brooklyn that became known as "Fort Masonic." By 1826 there were 480 Lodges throughout the state and a total membership of 20,000, making it one of the largest grand lodges in the world. New York City Masonry was particularly cosmopolitan, with lodges working in several languages, including French and German.

> As an organization with the discretion to choose its members from among the applicants, Masonry was exclusive by definition. Nevertheless, the diversity of its membership suggests that neither wealth, politics, nor religion governed admission.... Men who otherwise were prominent in their communities also, though not always, tended to be rewarded for Masonic merit.... The membership seems best explained as an association of like-minded men who were attracted to Masonry because of its exotic qualities and its personal or social usefulness.[2]

Additional Degrees

Masons in New York, and particularly in New York City, had many opportunities for involvement. They first joined a lodge and received the degrees of Entered Apprentice, Fellowcraft, and Master Mason. If they sought further "light" and involvement in the fraternity, they could join a chapter of Royal Arch Masons and receive four more degrees. The first chapter was formed about 1791 and the grand chapter followed in 1798. Royal Arch Masons could join a council of Royal and Select Masters (also called Cryptic Masonry), and those who were Christian could join an Encampment (now Commandery) of Knights Templar. Cryptic Councils began in New York about 1810 and Templary started there as early as 1783. The Knights Templar became the elite of New York Masonry, not only because of their greater Masonic "knowledge" but also because of the exclusivity that came from the expense of multiple dues and initiation fees.

Providing yet another source of Masonic light was the Scottish Rite with its thirty-three degrees and two competing bodies in New York City. One grew from a consistory of the 32° established without authority by Antoine Bideaud on August 6, 1806. The other was started by Joseph Cerneau in 1807, who illegitimately extended his authority under the twenty-five degrees of the Order of the Royal Secret (also known as the Rite of Perfection) to create a consistory in New York City and later extended his degrees to thirty-three to compete with the Scottish Rite. The conflicts of these two groups plagued New York Masonry for nearly a century, at times threatening to destroy it.

SCOTTISH RITE FREEMASONRY

Like nearly every major Masonic rite, the Scottish Rite is not really sure of its earliest origins. The Scottish Rite confers thirty-three degrees—thirty beyond the first three, which are under the control of grand lodges. Its origins can be traced to the rise of *hauts grades* in England, France, and Germany, which in turn are believed to have been influenced by the celebrated oration of Chevalier Andrew Michael Ramsay in 1737 in Paris.

Ramsay's Oration

Ramsay put forward the original (and unsubstantiated) theory that the crusaders were the originators of Freemasonry. He wove a romantic story about the knightly origins of the fraternity that resonated with continental Masons, especially those in France.

> Our ancestors, the Crusaders, gathered together from all parts of Christendom in the Holy Land, desired thus to reunite into one sole Fraternity the individuals of all nations....
>
> We have secrets; they are figurative signs and sacred words, composing a language sometimes mute, sometimes very eloquent, in order to communicate with one another at the greatest distance, and to recognize our brothers of whatsoever tongue. These were words of war which the Crusaders gave each other in order to guarantee them from the surprises of the Saracens, who often crept in amongst them to lull them....
>
> The word Freemason must therefore not be taken in a literal, gross, and material sense, as if our founders had been simple workers in stone, or merely curious geniuses who wished to perfect the arts. They were not only skillful architects, desirous of consecrating their talents and goods to the construction of material temples; but also religious and warrior princes who designed to enlighten, edify, and protect the living Temples of the Most High....[3]

Apparently inspired by Ramsay, a whole succession of Masonic degrees were created on the continent. Those taking these degrees seemed most interested in discovering prestigious Masonic pedigrees for themselves. Each degree claimed to be of higher importance or authority than any other, hence the name *hauts grades*. During the eighteenth century these degrees waxed, waned, and were gathered together into "rites" or systems of interrelated ceremonies.

Stephen Morin

These rites in turn competed for influence and power in the chaotic swirl of continental Freemasonry. The Emperors of the East and West, formed in 1758, gained momentary ascendancy in the battle for control of the *hauts grades*. The most significant action of the Emperors was the 1761 deputation of Stephen Morin as a Grand Inspector in America, "authorizing and empowering him to establish perfect and sublime Masonry in all parts of the world, ... with full and entire power to create Inspectors in all places where the sublime degrees shall not already be established...."[4]

Morin lived in Saint Domingue (now Haiti) and Jamaica, where he established bodies of the "Order of the Royal Secret" (often incorrectly called the Rite of Perfection), a twenty-five-degree rite collated from the degrees he received in France. He created dozens of other Inspectors who were often itinerant degree peddlers, supplementing their incomes with the sale of Masonic titles, but they spread the rite to the United States and eventually around the world. The first American Lodge of Perfection was established in New Orleans in 1763, and then Henry Andrew Francken started one in Albany, New York, in 1767. Others soon followed in Philadelphia, Charleston, Baltimore, and New York City.

The Mother Supreme Council

On May 31, 1801, the Order of the Royal Secret was effectively replaced by the establishment of the Supreme Council, 33°, Ancient and Accepted Scottish Rite of Freemasonry. The Mother Supreme Council was created on the basis of the *Constitutions of 1786,* attributed to Frederick the Great of Prussia for reorganizing the Order of the Royal Secret. All the degrees of the older Order are contained in the Scottish Rite plus eight additional ones, including the 33°, Sovereign Grand Inspector General. It is not known when or where any of the founders of the first Supreme Council received their 33° or how they came into possession of the *Constitutions of 1786*, but the organization they created stretches around the world today.

CERNEAUISM

The Mother Supreme Council was created to bring order to the chaotic world of high-degree Masonry, but its early effects were just the opposite. The *Constitutions of 1786* authorized two Supreme Councils in the United States, and the Charleston body seemed intent on waiting until just the right moment to divide its territory and share it with a sister Supreme Council. The right moment came sooner than expected.

Opportunists in New York

In August 1806, Antoine Bideaud, a member of the Supreme Council of the "French West India Islands," visited New York City and found an opportunity to make a little extra money. He conferred the Scottish Rite degrees on J. J. J. Gourgas and four other Frenchmen for $46 each and then created a "Sublime Grand Consistory 30°; 31°; and 32°." Bideaud's authority was for the islands only and certainly did not extend into New York, which was under the jurisdiction of the Charleston Supreme Council. Principal officers of the Bideaud Supreme Council were J. J. J. Gourgas, Daniel D. Tompkins, Sampson Simson, and Richard Riker.[5]

In New York City in October 1807, Joseph Cerneau, a jeweler from Cuba, constituted a "Sovereign Grand Consistory of Sublime Princes of the Royal Secret." Cerneau was a "Deputy Grand Inspector, for the Northern part of the Island of Cuba" under the Order of the Royal Secret. His patent limited him to confer the 4° through 24° on lodge officers, and the 25° once a year. Early records are sufficiently vague that it cannot be determined if the original members of Cerneau's Sovereign Grand Consistory thought they had the 25° or the 32°. With even less authority than Bideaud, Cerneau launched his foray into high-degree Masonry in New York. Principal officers of the Cerneau Grand Consistory included Cerneau, De Witt Clinton, John W. Mulligan, and Cadwallader D. Colden.[6]

Introduction

Complicating the situation of the rival and equally illegitimate consistories were the personal, political, and Masonic rivalries of their principal officers. Tompkins as governor of New York was succeeded by Clinton, his lieutenant governor; Clinton as Grand Master of New York was followed by Tompkins. Simson and Mulligan opposed each other in Grand Lodge; Mulligan defeated Simson as Grand Treasurer in 1814, but Simson regained the office in 1815. Colden was assistant attorney general in 1798 and replaced Riker as district attorney in 1811; Riker regained the position in 1812.[7]

> Neither Clinton nor Tompkins cared one whit for the honors conferred upon him by his Supreme Council. Both of them were first, last and always, politicians, bending every effort and every agency they could to secure for themselves political preferment.... [Each was] perfectly willing to permit Freemasonry to use itself in his service.... Mulligan and Simson were adversaries in the Grand Lodge of New York. The professional paths of Colden and Riker were continually crossing and soon we find their political reactions antagonistic.[8]

Legitimacy in the North

In 1813 Emmanuel de la Motta, Grand Treasurer of the Mother Supreme Council, traveled to New York City for his health. While there he discovered the two competing Grand Consistories, each created without authorization from Charleston. He examined them and "healed" the Bideaud organization, making it legitimate. His actions were confirmed by the Mother Supreme Council on December 24, 1813, which also issued a charter creating another Supreme Council on January 7, 1815, which was ratified on May 21, 1815.

The Cerneau Grand Consistory ignored de la Motta's actions, but it was aware the competition offered thirty-two degrees.

> To the minds of Clinton and his colleagues something had to be done to put their Grand Consistory at least on the same level as the Bideaud Sublime Grand Consistory, and they wheedled Joseph Cerneau into taking a step which in all probability he otherwise would not have taken.
> In 1813 Cerneau ... claimed jurisdiction over thirty-two degrees [for his Sovereign Grand Consistory] and announced the formation of what he called a Supreme Council of Grand Inspectors General of the Thirty-third Degree for the United States of America.... In this body both Clinton and Colden were given high official posts.[9]

The two supreme councils continued side-by-side for years, usually as bitter rivals, each having its ups and downs, though the Cerneau faction had the more steady existence. Neither side was diplomatic in language, and each seemed to delight in bold, public condemnations of the other. Finally in 1867, after years of feuding, the two sides peacefully united to form the current Supreme Council, 33°, for the Northern Masonic Jurisdiction of the United States. The peace was short-lived.

The Cerneau Supreme Council(s) Revived

Harry Seymour, expelled from the Cerneau Supreme Council in 1865, started the Ancient and Primitive Rite of Freemasonry, an outgrowth of the Rite of Memphis of about ninety degrees. By 1872 Seymour had reduced the rite to thirty-three degrees and was claiming to confer Scottish Rite degrees as the only legitimate successor to Joseph Cerneau. Robert Folger and others, angered by the position of the United Supreme Council towards the old Cerneau Supreme Council, revived the Cerneau Supreme Council in 1881. Both of these Supreme Councils proudly traced their origins to Joseph Cerneau, and about this time the term *Cerneauism* was coined to describe their movement.

Cerneauism finally died when the corrosive rivalry of the groups spilled over into the activities of other Masonic organizations. Grand lodges began asserting their authority as the ultimate arbiters of Masonic regularity within their jurisdictions. Masons in state after state were forbidden to join a Cerneau body under pain of expulsion. Several suits were brought by Cerneauists challenging the authority of grand lodges to declare them forbidden, but each case eventually was lost. The Cerneau movement ended in 1919 when M. W. Bayliss died; he was the head of Folger's revived Cerneau Supreme Council and probably the last national Cerneau officer.

THE AMERICAN ANTI-MASONIC MOVEMENT

As Freemasonry grew in prestige and importance in America during the eighteenth and early nineteenth centuries, many citizens became increasingly concerned about its effect on the republic. Some disliked private meetings of wealthy and important men in lodges. Others objected to Masonic toasting, drinking, and singing after meetings, while still others found the Masonic ideal of religious tolerance blasphemous, especially when applied to non-Christians. In short, the growing respectability of Masonry was matched by the increasing suspicions of anti-Masons.

THE ABDUCTION OF WILLIAM MORGAN

In 1826 in Batavia, New York, William Morgan, a disgruntled Mason, announced plans to publish the rituals of Freemasonry. This created a great deal of excitement in the community—Masons were outraged their "secrets" would be divulged and citizens were eager to know what the Masons were hiding. Neither group seemed to be aware that nearly thirty Masonic exposés had been published in English since 1723. A fire in Morgan's printer's office was blamed on the Masons, while the Masons blamed the printer for staging a publicity stunt. On September 11, Morgan was arrested for a debt and was jailed in Canandaigua, New York. The next day four Masons appeared at the jail, discharged the debt, and escorted Morgan to an awaiting carriage. He was driven to Ft. Niagara, held in the old Powder Magazine for five days, and never seen after September 19, 1826.[10]

The public was shocked by the charges that Morgan had been murdered by the Masons. "In February, April, and August of 1827, various participants in Morgan's abduction were tried; but the choice of Masonic jurors, the silence of the local press, and the circumspection of law enforcement officers who were also Masons outraged some people. The sentences were light, ranging from a few months to two years."[11]

Introduction

The Birth of a Movement

Fueled by the outrage of Morgan's abduction and by a general sense of helplessness in the face of huge social changes of the time, many people found Masonry convenient to blame for all of society's ills.

> The Antimasons quickly developed a conspiracy theory with respect to Masonry, "suddenly" uncovering a group of unscrupulous leaders plotting to overthrow the American social order.... Many Antimasons believed that Masonic secrecy concealed the members' "unconditional loyalty" to an autonomous state, and this allegiance far exceeded any loyalty to the nation.[12]
>
> In the decade after William Morgan's disappearance, Antimasonry raged like a brushfire, spreading into politics and giving birth to the first third party in American history. It expanded from western New York in an arc that stretched from Pennsylvania to Maine. The flames of Antimasonry burned especially brightly in New England. In Vermont, Antimasons became the largest political party in the early 1830s; in Massachusetts they edged aside the Democrats to become the second strongest party; in Rhode Island they captured the balance of power between Democrats and National Republicans and ruled in coalition with the Jacksonians. In Connecticut they polled at their peak almost a quarter of the vote.[13]

The high water mark of political anti-Masonry came in the 1832 presidential election when William Wirt ran on the Anti-Masonic ticket against two Masons, Andrew Jackson and Henry Clay. The political movement soon died after Wirt's defeat, but the effects of social anti-Masonry lingered much longer.

Many churches banned Masons and argued that "unless it was destroyed, Masonry as a tool of Satan would overthrow the church and its moral code along with the American system of justice and other republican institutions. Anti-Masons, using the religious argument, therefore condemned Masonry as an evil and dealt with it as they would with any other form of 'flagrant Sin.'"[14]

New York went from 480 Lodges in 1826 to 75 in 1835; Massachusetts dropped from 108 Lodges in 1830 to 56 in 1840. The Grand Lodge of Vermont simply went out of existence. The anti-Masonic movement was strongest in the Northeast, but its effects were felt throughout all the United States. The low point for Masonry came in 1840, after which the fraternity slowly regained members and prominence. It was not until 1860 that American Freemasonry fully recovered from the Morgan Affair.[15]

A GLOSSARY OF MASONIC TERMS

A.F. & A.M.: Ancient, Free and Accepted Masons.

A. & A.S.R.: Ancient and Accepted Scottish Rite.

BLUE LODGE: The basic organizational unit of Masons. (*see* Lodge)

BROTHER: The general term applied to any Freemason.

CAPITULAR: Concerning Royal Arch Masonry.

CAPTAIN GENERAL: Third officer of a Knights Templar Encampment or Commandery, roughly corresponding to second vice-president.

CHAPTER: The basic organizational unit of Royal Arch Masons which confers the degrees of Mark Master, Past Master, Most Excellent Master, and Royal Arch Mason.

CHAPTER OF ROSE CROIX: An organizational unit of the Scottish Rite that confers the 17° and 18°, and sometimes the 15° and 16°.

COMMANDER: Presiding officer of an Encampment or Commandery of Knights Templar.

COMPANION: The general term applied to Royal Arch Masons and Royal and Select Masters.

CONSISTORY: An organizational unit of the Scottish Rite that confers the 19° through 32° degrees. It is the highest body of the Scottish Rite outside of the Supreme Council. In the Southern Jurisdiction today, consistories confer only the 31° and the 32°.

COUNCIL: The basic organizational unit of several Masonic organizations, usually Royal and Select Masters which are sometimes called Cryptic Masons. Princes of Jerusalem, 16° of the Scottish Rite, meet in a Council of Princes of Jerusalem. (A Supreme Council is the supreme governing body of the Scottish Rite, and a Grand Council is the supreme governing body of Royal and Select Masters).

CRAFT LODGE: The basic organizational unit of Masons. (*see* Lodge)

CRYPTIC: Concerning the Royal and Select Masters Degrees.

ENCAMPMENT: The basic organizational unit of Knights Templar (now known as a Commandery) which confers the orders of Knight of the Red Cross, Knight of Malta, and Knight Templar on Christian Royal Arch Masons.

EXALT: To confer the Royal Arch Mason Degree.

F. & A.M.: Free and Accepted Masons.

GENERALISSIMO: Second officer of a Knights Templar Encampment or Commandery, roughly corresponding to first vice-president.

Introduction

Grand: When used to describe a Masonic organization, it usually indicates the supreme organization for a branch of Masonry within a jurisdiction, composed of representatives from all of the subordinate bodies; Grand Officers preside over Grand Bodies.

Grand Commander: The presiding officer of a Scottish Rite Supreme Council is the Sovereign Grand Commander, the presiding officer of a Grand Encampment of Knights Templar is the Right Eminent Grand Commander.

Grand Council: The supreme organization for Cryptic Masonry, Councils of Royal and Select Masters. Not to be confused with a Supreme Council of the Scottish Rite.

Grand Lodge: The supreme Masonic organization for a jurisdiction, usually a state in the U.S.A., composed of representatives from all lodges. Since all other Masonic organizations limit their membership to Master Masons, the Grand Lodge effectively controls them by saying which groups Master Masons may or may not join. There is no national Grand Lodge in the U. S.

Grand Master: The presiding officer of a Grand Lodge.

Greet: To confer the Select Master Degree.

Hauts Grades: French term meaning "high degrees" and referring to degrees that evolved in France often with a numerical designator greater than 3°, Master Mason. Some of these degrees eventually coalesced into the Scottish Rite and other rites.

High Priest: The presiding officer of a Chapter of Royal Arch Masons in the U.S. (known as the First Principal in England).

Ineffable: Concerning the 4° through 14°of the Scottish Rite conferred in a Lodge of Perfection.

Initiate: To confer the 1° or Entered Apprentice Degree.

Inspector General: A 33° Mason and member of a Supreme Council with authority to create and govern Scottish Rite Masons and bodies of lesser degree; also Sovereign Grand Inspector General, Deputy Inspector General, etc.

Inspector General Honorary: A 33° Mason, not a member of a Supreme Council, without any special authority.

K.T.: Knights Templar.

Lodge: The basic organizational unit of all Freemasonry that confers the three fundamental degrees of Entered Apprentice, Fellowcraft, and Master Mason. These degrees are common to all Masonic rites. Sometimes called a "Symbolic Lodge," "Craft Lodge," "Ancient Craft Lodge," or "Blue Lodge."

Lodge of Perfection: An organizational unit of the Scottish Rite that confers the 4° through 14° or the ineffable degrees.

Master: The presiding officer of a lodge.

N.M.J.: Northern Masonic Jurisdiction of the Scottish Rite.

Order of the Royal Secret: A system of twenty-five degrees, originating in France that evolved into the Scottish Rite, often incorrectly called the Rite of Perfection The degrees of the Lodge are considered part of this and all other Masonic Rites.

Pass: To confer the 2° or Fellowcraft Degree.

Profane: Literally "before the temple" or one who has not yet entered the temple, hence a non-Mason.

Raise: To confer the 3° or Master Mason Degree.

R.AM.: Royal Arch Masons.

R.&S.M.: Royal and Select Masters.

Receive: To confer the Royal Master's Degree.

Rectified Scottish Rite: A system developed by J. B. Willermoz that replaced the Rite of Strict Observance in 1782. The degrees of the Lodge are considered part of this and all other Masonic Rites.

R.E.R.: Rite Ecossais Rectifié or Rectified Scottish Rite.

Rite: A system of Masonic degrees, usually with a unified theme and teachings, controlled by one central authority, *e.g.*, Scottish Rite, Rite of Perfection, York Rite, etc. The degrees of the lodge are considered part of all Masonic rites.

Rite of Perfection: *See* Order of the Royal Secret

Rose Croix: The 18° of the Scottish Rite, conferred in a Chapter of Rose Croix.

Scottish Rite: A system of thirty-three degrees, originating in France, that evolved out of the Rite of Perfection. The degrees of the lodge are considered part of this and all other Masonic Rites.

S.J.: Southern Jurisdiction of the Scottish Rite.

Sovereign Grand Commander: Presiding officer of a Scottish Rite Supreme Council.

Strict Observance: A rite of Masonic Knighthood started by Baron von Hund in Germany ca. 1750 which promoted the theory that Masonry originated with the Knights Templar. The Rite of Strict Observance was replaced by the Rectified Scottish Rite in 1782.

Supreme Council: The Supreme organization of the Scottish Rite within a jurisdiction, composed of 33 Inspectors General. Not to be confused with a Grand Council of Royal and Select Masters.

Symbolic Lodge: The basic organizational unit of Masons. (*see* Lodge)

Templar: Concerning the Orders of Masonic Knighthood conferred in an Encampment or Commandery of Knights Templar.

Wardens: Two officers of a lodge, Senior and Junior, roughly corresponding to first and second vice-presidents.

York Rite: The sequence of Masonic degrees conferred in Royal Arch Chapters, Royal and Select Councils, and Knights Templar Encampments or Commanderies. Sometimes called the American Rite. The degrees of the lodge are considered part of this and all other Masonic rites.

2

The Mystery of the Folger Manuscripts

THE RITUAL MANUSCRIPTS OF ROBERT B. FOLGER ARE CURIOUS ENIGMAS in Masonic literature. Their author, Robert Benjamin Folger, M.D., (1803–1892) lived during some of the most turbulent years of Freemasonry. He experienced the American anti-Masonic movement first hand, witnessed at least six different grand lodges for the state of New York, lived through the American Civil War, and saw more than fourteen supreme councils for the Scottish Rite come and go. Through all of this, he was seldom an idle bystander, but was actively involved in many of the controversies. He is today viewed as a schismatic, a troublemaker, and one of the most ardent proponents of the Cerneau faction of the Scottish Rite.

Among his legacies to the Craft are three small books, written in a mixture of cipher and plain text. Folger Manuscript 1 (FM1) has a plaintext preface dated July 12, 1827; the book contains the rituals for the first three degrees of the Rectified Scottish Rite from Copenhagen. The preface and bequest were subsequently revoked on September 25, 1854. Folger was a new and active Mason in 1827, having been raised to the Sublime Degree of Master Mason only seventeen months before. In the short space between his Third Degree and the dating of the manuscript, he joined additional Masonic groups, including the Chapter, Council, Commandery, and Consistory; helped found a Royal Arch Chapter; and served as charter Senior Warden of a Lodge.

Follow here the mystery of Folger's manuscripts. The reader will be shown the evidence and deductions that led to a solution. The steps for solving the mystery will include identifying the rituals, locating their source, and inferring their use. These puzzles are interesting in their own right, but solving them gives us a glimpse of early Rectified Scottish Rite workings and insight into the tumultuous world of nineteenth-century American Masonry.

SETTING THE SCENE

Robert Benjamin Folger was born on December 16, 1803 in Hudson, New York. His education began in the Quaker Schools there and then was continued at a boarding school in Lenox, Massachusetts, some thirty-five miles from Hudson. He moved to New York City and became a Master Mason on February 10, 1826, in Fireman's Lodge No. 368. Three months later, on May 25, he met Dr. Hans Burch Gram in Jerusalem Chapter No.8, R.A.M., when Gram officiated at his Exaltation, and "the acquaintance there formed soon ripened into very close intimacy...."[1]

Folger had entered the College of Physicians and Surgeons (later with Columbia University) in 1821,[2] and probably graduated in 1824; he is listed in the 1825 *New York City Directory* as a physician. His new friend, Hans Gram, son of the secretary to the Governor of the Danish West Indies, was born in Boston in 1787 and died in New York City on February 26, 1840. He began studying medicine in 1808 at the Danish Royal Academy of Surgery[3] and became a convert in 1823 to Samuel Hahnemann's theory of homeopathy, new at the time. Gram returned to America in 1825, began a medical practice, and is known today as the "Father of American Homeopathy." He and Folger became fast friends apparently because of their Masonic and medical interests, and through Gram's influence, Folger eventually converted to homeopathy.

FM1 was written in a strange hieroglyphic-like cipher in a black leather-bound book on thirty-three of eighty-eight 4¾ × 7½ inch pages. It appears to be a blank book from a stationery store, the pages are watermarked "Lathrop & Willard" with yellow fore edges, and the front and back covers are bordered in gold with a large gold cross embossed in the center. The cipher looks like Chinese ideographs, and some pages are decorated with pen sketches that have a Masonic tone. Representative illustrations include blazing stars, a cubical stone with a square resting on it, and a sketch of what seems to be the layout of a Lodge room.

The cipher is first known to have been broken in the 1950s by Wil Baden, Past Master of Henry Clay Lodge No. 277 in New York (now merged with George Washington Lodge No. 287), who had a photocopy of FM1 plus a page from Folger Manuscript 2.[4] He used the cryptanalytic technique of "matched plain and cipher" to break the code. Some thirty years later, Mr. Donald H. Bennett independently broke the cipher from a single page of FM1 using a "ciphertext only" attack. Macoy Publishing and Masonic Supply Co., Inc. of Richmond, Virginia, owns FM1, sometimes referred to as the *Macoy Book*, as well as the Baden decryption.

Beyond this basic, descriptive information lurk several intriguing mysteries. What does the cipher conceal? Why did Folger so painstakingly write this book? Who, if anyone, helped him prepare it? Where did the text originate?

IDENTIFYING THE RITUALS

Folger Manuscript 1 contains the rituals for the "Blue" Degrees of Disciple, Fellow, and Master Mason from a Masonic system unlike any widely known in the United States. It can be inferred from a note on the cover page of the Baden translation that Ward K. St. Clair (1899–1966), a noted student of Masonic Ritual, identified the manuscript as a "French Blue Lodge Ritual." A detailed examination of the text shows that it is a very good interpretation of the first three Degrees of the Rectified Scottish Rite (Rite Ecossais Rectifié or R.E.R.), whose six Degrees are Apprentice, Fellow, Master Mason, Scottish Master, Squire Novice, and Knight Beneficent of the Holy City (Chevalier Bienfaisant de la Cité Sainte or C.B.C.S.).

In fact, FM1 is the earliest evidence of the R.E.R. in the United States. While the R.E.R. is active in several other countries, including France, Belgium, and Switzerland, the R.E.R. has never been a significant force in American Masonry, though it has surfaced at least two other times. On May 16, 1900, the Great Priory of Helvetia granted Belgian-born Edouard Blitz a charter to establish the R.E.R. in the United States. The American Metropolitan College of the Grand Professed was founded on June 16, 1901, in Pentwater, Michigan, with Blitz as Great Prior of America. There were few members, and it was active only a short time.[5] Then William Moseley Brown (1894–1966) and J. Raymond Shute II (1909–1988) reestablished the rite on August 8, 1934, in Raleigh, North Carolina, again with a Swiss Charter; it continues today as an exclusive group with an annual meeting and a limit of eighty-one members.

An *hauts grades* connection is suggested within FM1 by several references to what could be the R.E.R. Fourth Degree, Scottish Master. "Vow of the Anc[ient] Scotch Master: I promise" appears on page 83 (with the rest of the page maddeningly blank). Page 16 has the "Obligation for all members, also all candidates for Scots Ritus, and visiting Masons"; and the "Covenant before entering a Scotch Lodge" is on page 86.

This could support a connection with the Ancient and Accepted Scottish Rite as well as the Rectified Scottish Rite; but when Folger was Grand Secretary General and Henry C. Atwood was Grand Commander of the Cerneau Supreme Council, they sought Scottish Rite rituals for the first three degrees. In a letter of ca. July 1853, to James Foulhouze, Grand Commander of the clandestine Supreme Grand Council for the Sovereign and Independent State of Louisiana, Atwood requested assistance for his Supreme Council.

> And now my brother permit me to remind you of some things about which we conversed while together.... We should be glad to obtain the Scottish ritual of the 3 first or symbolic Degrees in English—or if not possible—then French, as I can get them translated....
>
> The above are sufficient to trouble you with & you can reply to them as you may find leisure, as there is no pressing haste in the case.[6]

Whatever origin Folger may have ascribed to his Masonic rituals, he obviously did not think they were from the Scottish Rite, else he wouldn't have offered them to his Supreme Council.

Emblems of the Degrees

The strongest connection to the R.E.R. is given by certain emblems of the three degrees, unique since about 1782 to that Rite. For the First Degree, the following question and Answer appear on FM1:8.5: "Q: What is the emblem of a Disciple? A: A broken pillar with the inscription *Ad hoc* [*sic*] *stat*." The Ritual of the Belgian R.E.R. requires among the "Decorations and Accessories Particular to the First Grade, ... a picture representing a column ruined and broken, but standing on its base, with the motto: *Adhuc stat* [Thus far it stands]."[7]

Further evidence comes from the Second Degree. The Fellow's Catechism, FM1:10.28-29, has the following question and answer: "Q: What is the symbol of a Fellow? A: The square stone with the inscription DO." Then on the right side of FM1:11, which has the heading "Fellow," is a drawing of a square stone on which is resting a Mason's square with D O (□ ⌐) written in cipher. The decorations of the Lodge for the R.E.R. Second Degree include "a picture of a cubical stone, on which is resting a square, with the motto: *Dirigit Obliqua* [He makes the crooked straight]."[8]

The cubical stone from FM1:11.

Finally, on FM1:77 there is a pencil sketch of a ship with its three masts broken off. This researcher initially identified this as a drawing made by a child sometime after Folger finished the manuscript; there was no apparent connection to Masonry. However, part of the decorations for the R.E.R. Third Degree is "a picture representing a dismasted vessel, without sails and without oars, tranquil on a calm sea, with the motto: *In silentio et spe fortitudo mea* [In silence and hope is my strength]."[9]

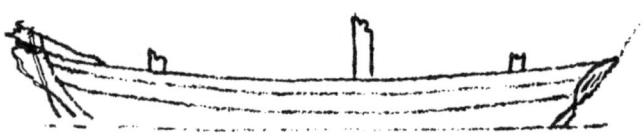

The dismasted ship from FM1:77, originally misidentified as a child's drawing.

These emblems are also found in the first three Degrees of Baron von Hund's Rite of Strict Observance, but a succession of Masonic congresses, Kohlo in 1772, Lyons in 1773, and finally Wilhelmsbad in 1782, modified its organization and ceremonies to produce the Rectified Scottish Rite. For all practical purposes, the Strict Observance ceased to exist after the Congress of Wilhelmsbad when its transformation into the R.E.R. was completed. Other evidence, discussed later, leaves little possibility that Folger's rituals are from the Strict Observance, and thus the R.E.R. remains the major candidate as the ultimate source.

On FM1:19 of the manuscript a triangular monument is drawn, carrying an inscription (in very poor Latin): *Tria formant alienum deponent et ascendit in unum*

The emblems of the first three degrees in the Strict Observance. Ferdinand Runkel, *Geschichte der Freimaurerei in Deutschland* (1932).

[Three things form an alien thing, they set it aside, and it rises into one(?)]. Curiously, FM2:120.15 & 16 has two unidentified lines that appear to be attempted translations of this poor Latin: "Three strange recumbent shapes in one arose." and "Three strange and different shapes laid down, and arose in one." However the motto is translated, the monument and inscription are very similar to a decoration of the R.E.R. Third Degree.

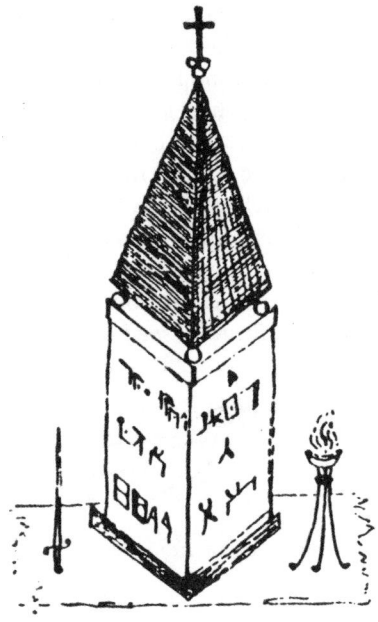

A picture representing a triangular mausoleum sitting on three steps. At each of the three corners of the mausoleum are shown three small balls, colored yellow or gold, joined together, for a total of nine balls. The mausoleum is topped by a funeral urn, over which is a blazing flame detached from the opening of the urn. The picture has the following mottoes, on the upper part: "Deponens aliena ascendit unus" [Setting aside alien things, he rises as one] and on the lower part: "Ternario formatur, novenario dissolvitur" [It is formed by three, dissolved by nine].[10]

The triangular monument from FM1:19.

On FM1:13.2–5, the candidate for the Fellow's Grade draws aside a veil over a mirror to behold his reflection and is then told, "Know thyself." It is important to note that Lachmann, in his *Geschichte und Gebrauche*, claims the R.E.R. was the first system to use the mirror in the Second Degree, not the Strict Observance.[11] Today this ceremony is still in the Rectified Scottish Rite as well as the Scottish Rite and the French Modern Rite.

The entire substance and tone of Folger's work harmonizes with the R.E.R. work, from the introduction of the candidate, through the broad flow of the ceremonies, to the closing of the Lodge. It certainly is not a translation of contemporary Rectified Scottish Rite rituals, differing as it does in so many places, but it is a very good interpretation, preserving the substance of the R.E.R. with some variations.

Plan of the Lodge

A pencil sketch of the symbolic floor plan of a Lodge is on FM1:25, but for some reason it was not finished with ink. The drawing has a large rectangle in the center composed of four Mason's squares with a knotted cord bordering the interior. Inside the top or east of the rectangle is a sun, a blazing star, and a moon with stars. In the center are seven steps surmounted by a large locked door, possibly with a curtain across the bottom step. At the bottom is a rough stone, an opened book, and a square stone. At the top of the large rectangle is a smaller one, representing the Master's seat with two seats on either side for other officers, perhaps the Secretary and Orator. In the center of these three stations is what appears to be a draped rectangle, probably the Altar; at the bottom or west are the Wardens' seats. This seating arrangement follows several eighteenth century French exposés and is used today in the Scottish Rite, the French Modern Rite, and the R.E.R. Three small circles, probably representing candles, are at the northwestern, southwestern, and southeastern corners of the central rectangle, and two small double circles, perhaps representing more candles, are at the north and south of the central rectangle.

This layout is similar to plans for Apprentice-Fellow Lodges found in eighteenth century French exposes: *Catéchisme des Francs-Maçons*, 1744; *L'Ordre des Francs-Maçons Trahi*, 1746; *Les Francs-Maçons Ecrasés*, 1747; *La Desolation des Entrepreneurs Modernes*, 1747; and *Le-Maçon Démasqué*, 1751. All of these plans show "Steps of the Temple," and *Les Francs-Maçons Ecrasés* and *L'Ordre des Francs-Maçons Trahi* show locked doors at the top of their steps. The placement of the officers is also supported by these texts. The only features prominent in the other plans and left out by Folger are the pillars Boaz and Jachin. Folger's plan, however, seems to be an unfinished pencil sketch (perhaps being prepared for redrawing in ink), and what may be a pillar is partially drawn to the right of the steps.

More significant, Folger's floor plan is nearly identical to the Tracing Board of the Second Degree from the Belgian R.E.R. The Belgian design shows no officers' positions nor candles and has a drawing of the forty-seventh problem of Euclid in place of Folger's open book. The only major difference is the absence of pillars, as noted above. Allowing for these few variations, perhaps from more than 150 years between the interpretations, the drawings are the same.

History of Freemasonry

On pages 81 and 82, Folger has written (or paraphrased or transcribed) a curiously distorted history of Freemasonry, virtually unknown in English Masonic literature. Part of it explains that Oliver Cromwell altered the doctrines of Masonry to suit "his

Redrawn lodge floor plan from FM1:25.

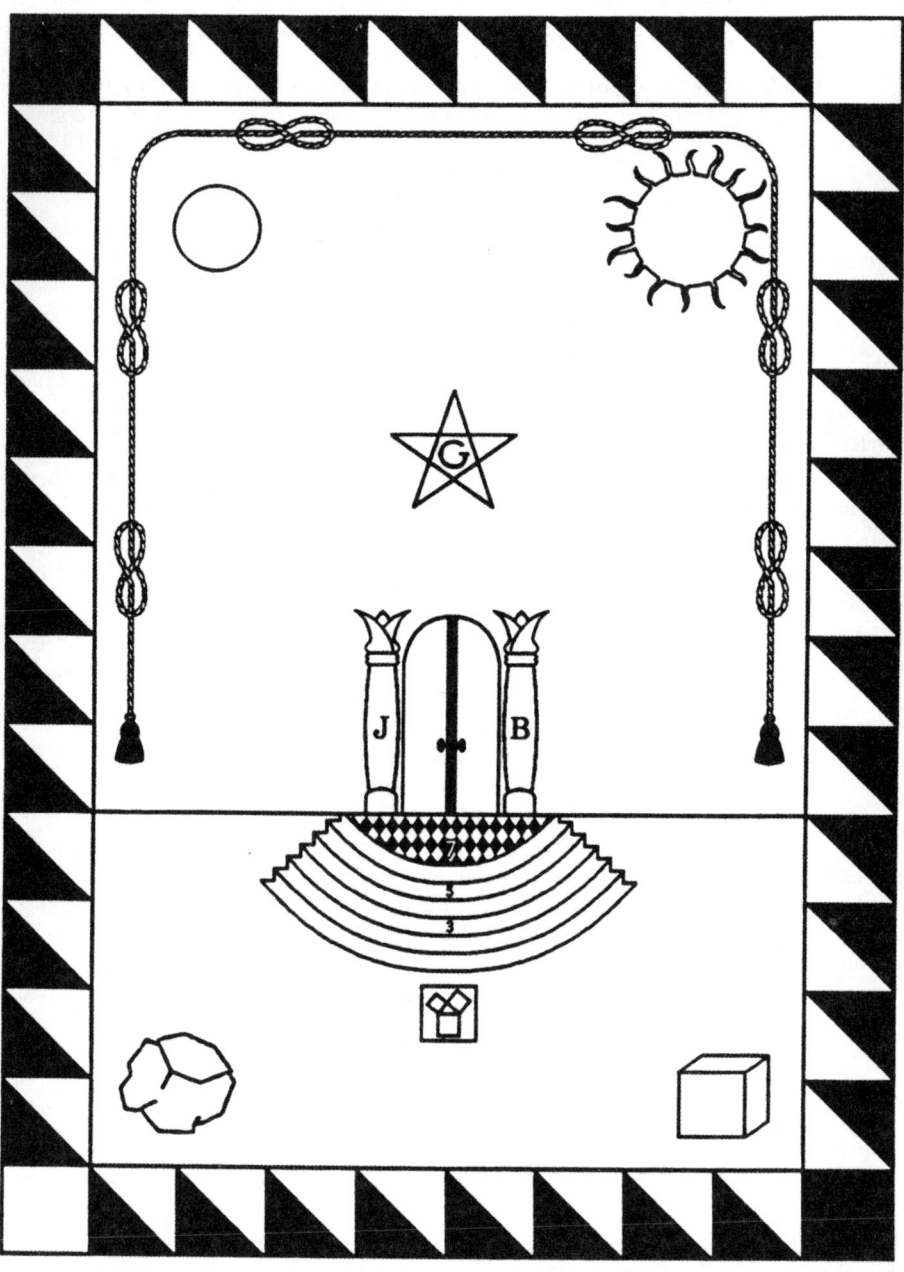

Second Degree Belgian R.E.R. Tracing Board. *Ritual de Loge de Saint-Jean 2ᵉ Grade* (Brussels: Grand Loge Régulière de Belgique, N.d.), p. 9.

republican and later despotical views." Albert Mackey wrote about the Cromwell theory in his *History of Freemasonry*:

> The theory that Freemasonry was instituted by Oliver Cromwell was ... the invention of a single mind and was first made public in the year 1746 [sic], by the Abbé Larudan, who presented his views in a work entitled *Les Francs-Maçons Ecrasés*—a book which [George B.] Kloß, the bibliographer, says is the armory from which all the enemies of Masonry have since derived their weapons of abuse.
>
> The propositions of Larudan are distinguished for their absolute independence of all historical authority and for the bold assumptions which are presented to the reader in place of facts.[12]

Although Larudan was the first writer to present this bizarre theory, it was later translated into German and used as introductory material to Carl Friedich Eber's exposure, *Sarsena oder der vollkommene Baumeister* (1817).[13] Eber's exposure purported to unveil Johann Wilhelm Kellner von Zinnendorf's "Große Landesloge" rituals, a German version of the Swedish System of Freemasonry. Because both the Swedish System and the R.E.R. descended from the Strict Observance, the two rites shared commonalities, primarily in the Craft Degrees.

Folger's history on page 82, lines 17 to 31, seems to have come directly from *Sarsena*. These lines are printed below beside the appropriate text and its translation. Because Folger understood German,[14] but not French,[15] it is more likely that he borrowed from *Sarsena* than from *Les Francs-Maçons Ecrasés*.

FOLGER	SARSENA	TRANSLATION
In England about this time, the Order had many names one after the other as Freemasons—**Nivelleurs**—then members of the 5th Monarchy and finally were again Called Freemasons	Der Orden, oder vielmehr diese neugestifte Gesellschaft veränderte in den ersten Jahren oft ihren Namen. Zuerst nannte sich die Gesellschaft Freimaurer; hernach wurden ihre Mitglieder Nivelleurs (Messer mit der Wasserwage,) dann solche: die der Polizei nicht unterworfen waren, hernach Mitglieder der fünften Monarchie genannt; und endlich nahmen sie wieder ihren ersten namen Freimaurer an.	The Order, or rather this newly-founded society, changed its name often in the first years. At first it called itself the society of Freemasons; afterwards its members became Nivelleurs (measurers with the levels): those which were not subject to the police were then called members of the Fifth Monarchy; and finally they again took their first name of Freemasons.

The translator (likely Folger) may not have known the meaning of *Nivelleurs* or thought this was actually an accepted name for the Levelers, one of a group of radicals arising in the Parliamentary army during the English Civil War and advocating a program of constitutional reform.

Folger	Sarsena	Translation
Cromwell appointed [priests] for Secretaries for the four Quarters of the Globe, etc. **General Rainsborough** was the Master of the Nivelleurs.	Von allen diesen verschiedenen Benennungen gaben sie einen scheinbaren Grund an. Der name Nivelleurs sollte ihren Vorsatz andeuten, alle Glieder in eine gewisse Gleichheit zu setzen, ihr Haupt (Meister) war General Rainsborough, ein großer Freund Cromwells.	All these different designations indicated one apparent purpose. The name Nivelleurs should suggest their resolve to place all members in a certain equality; their head (Master) was General Rainsborough, a great friend of Cromwell.

Folger wrote that "Cromwell appointed † for Secretaries for the 4 Quarters of the Globe, etc.," with the cross probably meaning priests; this passage does not occur in either Larudan or Eber. Thomas Rainborow or Rainsborough (?–1648) was an English soldier, a leader of the republican officers, and a supporter of the Leveler document, *Agreement of the People*, which called for manhood suffrage and religious toleration.

Folger	Sarsena	Translation
They had the form of a flag with a lion sleeping with this motto—"Who will wake him?"	Sie hatten eine Fahne, worauf ein schlafender Löwe mit den Worten: wer wird ihn aufwecken? gemalt war.	They had a flag, on which was painted a sleeping lion with the words: who will wake him up?

This is further evidence that the text came from the secondary German text rather than the original French. Although Larudan uses the word *couchant*, which derives from the verb *coucher*, meaning to sleep, it has a specific heraldic meaning: lying down with the head up. *Sarsena*, on the other hand, uses the words "ein schlafender Löwe," a sleeping lion. Clearly, the French text is more appropriate when describing a device on a flag.

LOCATING THE SOURCE

Folger had been a Master Mason only seventeen months when he dated his manuscript, and the ceremonies seem too sophisticated and too much at variance with standard American workings to have been created by so recent a Mason without guidance or inspiration. It is possible that he was inspired by the ceremonies of some New York lodge working a French or R.E.R. Ritual. In his "Recollections of a Masonic Veteran," Folger wrote about visiting Lodge L'Union Française during his early years in the Craft.

> The Lodge was a French Lodge, their members were French, the usages were French, as also the language.... [During the reception of a Profane] the Nature of Fire, Air, Earth, and Water were fully demonstrated and developed.... [T]he French recipient would, though perspiring at every pore, view the whole with the most perfect nonchalance, and bow with a gracious smile, with the hand upon the breast, when it was finished, although it had taken the whole of two or three hours to pass the rugged way.[16]

The ceremony "demonstrating" the four elements and the length of the degree are enough to eliminate L'Union Française. Folger's first Degree is a rather straightforward ceremony that might last an hour or so, but nothing like the grueling two or three hours at L'Union Française which left the candidate "perspiring at every pore." Ceremonies with fire, air, earth, and water are characteristic of the French Rite and Scottish Rite Craft Degrees, but most other distinctive Scottish Rite features are completely absent from the manuscript.[17] While the possibility of some local Lodge serving as the source cannot be eliminated, a much more satisfying solution can be found.

The solution to this mystery begins on the first page, Folger's dedication or bequest (underling in original).

>Dr. Hans B. Gram, No. 296 Pearl St.
>Mr. Ferdinand L. Wilsey, Fulton Slip near Fulton Bank. *R.B.F.*
>
>New York July 12th 1827.
>
>It is my earnest prayer that this book, if it be found among my earthly remains after my decease, may be handed over to my dearly beloved Friend and Brother, Dr. Hans B. Gram to whom I bequeath it with my thanks for the constant and untired kindness which he has shewed me from the first hour of my acquaintance with him to the present—to whom I feel that I never can be too grateful and whose good will I desire to seek to my latest breath. If he is not in America at the time of my dissolution—it may be given to Mr. Ferdinand L. Wilsey who will know what it contains and also how to preserve the substance in his mind while he commits the manuscript to the <u>flames</u>. This he will do for the sake of one who loves him with a Brothers [sic] love and who has desired during his life to merit his esteem.
>
>*Robert B. Folger*

The critical piece of the puzzle comes in September 1826, four months after Folger's Exaltation in Jerusalem Chapter. The following event was detailed in 1871 in *The New England Medical Gazette* by Henry M. Smith, M.D., (emphasis added).

>From conversations with Drs. Wilsey, … , Folger, … and others, I have obtained many of the facts herein mentioned.… In September, 1826, Dr. Gram was introduced to Mr. Ferdinand L. Wilsey by Dr. Folger, who had made his acquaintance the year before. Mr. Wilsey, then a merchant and comb-manufacturer, was a master of a masonic Lodge, and Dr. Folger having received from Dr. Gram some important information in Masonry, desired that his friend should also receive the benefit of it.[18]

Folger dated his manuscript on July 12, 1827, ten months after he introduced Gram to Wilsey for the purpose of sharing "important information in Masonry." On November 3, 1819, while living in Copenhagen, Hans Gram had entered one of the predecessor Lodges of Zerubbabel and Frederick of the Crowned Hope.[19] Belonging to this Lodge in Copenhagen from 1819 to 1826, Gram must have been familiar with the R.E.R. rituals, and his presiding over Jerusalem Chapter in New York shortly after returning to America indicates more than a passing enthusiasm for Masonry.

The solution is now at hand! Hans Gram joined a Danish Lodge working the R.E.R., and a familiarity with its rituals would be consistent with his Masonic activity in New York in 1826. In May of that year he met fellow physician Robert Folger, and sometime after this Folger received "important information in Masonry" from Gram. In September 1826 Folger introduced Gram to Ferdinand Wilsey so that he too could benefit from this information, and ten months later the manuscript with R.E.R. rituals was prepared. The timing of these events, the reason for Wilsey's introduction to Gram, and the dedication page strongly point to the scholarly and worldly Gram as the source, to the established and successful Wilsey as a participant, and to the young and eager Folger as the scribe.

INFERRING ITS USE

The meticulously prepared cipher manuscript shows an intent to preserve information of great value, but there is no direct evidence that it was ever used. There is only one clue pointing to a definite use of the ritual, and a few hints as to other places it may have been employed. Internal, textual evidence indicates strongly that FM1 was the original manuscript and FM2 and FM3 were copies from it.

Elmira Consistory

The only indication of a direct use comes from February 26, 1883, fifty-six years after the manuscript was dated. Folger, then eighty years old, was at a Scottish Rite Reunion of 200 candidates at Elmira Consistory, New York, a Cerneau body. He was introduced as the oldest American 33° Mason, having received the degree in 1827. At the end of his talk, recorded in the Elmira *Daily Advertiser* for February 27, 1883, he proposed a toast that must have been taken from FM2:120.

Our Institution	Folger's Toast
Though adverse circumstances have likened it to the broken pillar of our Order with its beautiful capital buried at its base, it is consolatory to us to know that it is not entirely cast down or destroyed. As by the remnant of the pillar that is yet standing we can ascertain to what order it belongs, and determine what its proportions [and] ornaments were, when it was entire may we be enabled by diligence and perseverance to form another pillar in the likeness of the broken one, more perfect and beautiful than that which adverse circumstances has destroyed. (*Anonymous*) FM2:120	And now, in closing, let me offer this toast: Our Institution Though adverse circumstances have likened it to the broken pillar of our order with its beautiful capital buried at its base, it is consolatory to us to know that it is not entirely cast down or destroyed. As by the remnant of the pillar that is yet standing we can ascertain to what order it belongs, and determine what its proportions and ornaments were when it was entire, may we be enabled by diligence and perseverance to form another pillar in the likeness of the broken one, more perfect and beautiful than that which adverse circumstances have destroyed.

Folger could have been reviewing his manuscript before the Elmira meeting, but the difficulty in reading the cipher, even for someone familiar with it, makes this seem remote. It is more likely he memorized portions of the Ritual earlier in his Masonic career and called on them when needed.

ZOROBABEL LODGE

Other possible uses of the rituals by Folger are more speculative. On June 8, 1827, one month before the manuscript was dated, a charter was granted to Zorobabel Lodge No. 498 of New York City with Hans B. Gram, Master; Robert B. Folger, Senior Warden; and Lewis Saynisch, Junior Warden.[20] The Lodge had a brief existence and then apparently closed during the anti-Masonic excitement. Beyond the presence of Gram and Folger as the top two officers, the name of the lodge is significant to the mystery.

Dr. Gram is listed in the 1871 register of the Copenhagen Lodge Zerubbabel and Frederick of the Crowned Hope [Zorobabel og Frederik til det kronede Håb] as having entered November 3, 1819. Zerubbabel and Frederick Lodge was formed in 1855 by the merger of two Lodges, Zerubbabel of the North Star [Zorobabel til Nordstjernen] and Frederick of the Crowned Hope.[21] The 1871 register does not indicate in which Gram was Initiated, but it is a striking coincidence that the Lodge over which he presided in 1827 chose the name Zorobabel, selecting the Greek form of the name used by the Danish Lodge.

Perhaps Gram was Initiated in Zorobabel til Nordstjernen and honored his Mother Lodge in naming the new Lodge, and perhaps Zorobabel Lodge No. 498 worked the R.E.R. Degrees? Certainly the dating of the manuscript on July 12 coincides nicely with the chartering of the Lodge on June 8. Masonic Ritual in New York at that time was in a state of flux, and the Grand Lodge exercised little control. There were German and French Lodges, and the ritual system taught by Jeremy Ladd Cross (now nearly universal in the United States) was just beginning to challenge the "old style" of work. Thus one more Lodge working one more variant of the degrees would not have caused particular notice. However, Folger had just learned the Cross system from Henry C. Atwood during his first classes in 1826, and it is also possible Zorobabel joined those Lodges working this version of the Ritual, which Folger said were "overrun with candidates and members."[22]

JOHN THE FORERUNNER LODGE

A much better candidate for use of the rituals comes from the Cerneau faction of the Scottish Rite, of which Folger was a lifelong, ardent supporter. Around 1853 the Supreme Council in and for the Sovereign and Independent State of New York, with Henry C. Atwood as Grand Commander and Folger as Grand Secretary General, began plans to charter symbolic Lodges in New York City, which is the exclusive right of the Grand Lodge. The minutes for March 8, 1853, detail the only two such charters.

> The Ill∴ Bro∴ Folger then proceeded to lay before the Council the following Petitions for the constituting and establishing Symbolic Lodges of the Ancient Free and Accepted Scottish Rite.

> From Bro. Robert B. Folger and others for a Lodge of St∴ John by the distinctive title of "John the Fore-runner" and by Number 1 (See document on file) which petition was granted and the Patent ordered to be made and executed bearing date March 8th 1853 of the Christian Era.
> From Bro. Deszelus, Roullier, Vatet, Ploquin & others, in all 14, for a Lodge of St. John, the ritual &c in the French Language, by the distinctive title of "La Sincérité," and by number 2 (see documents in French and English on file) which petition was granted and the Patent ordered to be made out and executed, bearing date March 8th 1853 of the Christian Era.[23]

Twenty-one years later in 1874 Folger gave some details on this ultimately unsuccessful action, unprecedented by an American Supreme Council (emphasis added).

> The petition for [a charter for John the Forerunner Lodge] is believed to have been the first effort made in this country to establish the French system in the English language. *And for this purpose a very beautiful and minute translation of the French ritual into the English, together with the consecration, the installation, and the table rituals and ceremonials, with abundant and minute directions, had been procured,* and everything was in readiness to go forward. But at this juncture there was some misgivings on the part of the founders although the ritual was entirely and essentially different from the York Rite—so much so that it could not be taken for Masonry, as practiced at the present day; yet there were certain things about it which led to the determination, on the part of the founders, to abandon the project altogether and it proved to be a wise course. The lodge was never constituted, and *the rituals, etc., are now in our possession.*[24]

Recall that around July, 1853, a few months after chartering John the Forerunner and La Sincérité Lodges, Henry Atwood wrote to James Foulhouze requesting "the Scottish Ritual of the 3 first or Symbolic Degrees in English." The founders of La Sincérité Lodge apparently had no written Ritual then, even though they had been members of the French Scottish Rite.[25] Foulhouze was told to reply as he found leisure, "as there [was] no pressing haste in the case" (see page 3). FM2 has the ceremony for the consecration of a lodge, installation of officers, and a Masonic banquet.

Five years later on September 14, 1858, Atwood wrote again to Foulhouze repeating his request for rituals of the first three Degrees (emphasis added). "We find ourselves embarrassed with the Scottish rituals that we have; *they are translations teeming with considerable variations.* If you have at your disposal an English copy of the Ritual of these Degrees such as you work, I beg of you to send it to me so that we can compare them."[26] Atwood gave a perfect description of FM2 in this letter: a translation that varies considerably from Scottish Rite rituals. Here is yet further circumstantial evidence that Folger offered Gram's R.E.R. rituals for use in Scottish Rite Blue Lodges.

Gram may have thought Rectified Scottish Rite rituals were the same as those of the Ancient and Accepted Scottish Rite. He may have told Folger these rituals were French, and Folger could have preferred them for Scottish Rite Blue Lodges as more exotic than the work seen in L'Union Française or La Sincérité. In any event, Folger apparently still had the rituals of John the Forerunner in 1874, just nine years before he spoke at Elmira Consistory.

Folger Manuscript 2 must be the "beautiful and minute translation" to which Folger alluded. Indeed, if it is not, we must conclude that Folger possessed yet another ritual, likewise translated from the French and appropriate for use in a Scottish Rite Blue Lodge which has vanished without trace. This, surely, is asking too much of coincidence.

Revocation of the Preface

One tantalizing clue remains unexplained: the revocation of the preface to FM1. In the swirl of clandestine activity by his Supreme Council, Folger managed to get himself expelled from the Grand Lodge of New York, but not for chartering a Scottish Rite Symbolic Lodge! (Which supports Atwood's contention that his lodges only exemplified the work to Master Masons.) Folger took violent exception to the election of Reuben H. Walworth as Grand Master in 1853 and argued for the reactivation of St. John's Grand Lodge, which had been formed by a schism in 1837 and had just reunited with the regular Grand Lodge in 1850. The charges brought before the Grand Stewards' Lodge and his response, however, ignored his activity with John the Forerunner Lodge. On September 27, 1853, he was expelled by the Grand Stewards' Lodge, and a year later on September 25, 1854, he revoked the preface to his manuscript, taking great pains to obliterate almost completely the name of Ferdinand L. Wilsey, who was to receive the cipher Ritual after Folger died if Hans Gram were not available. Gram's name is untouched in the preface, he having died in 1840. We can only speculate about whether Wilsey was involved with Folger's expulsion from Grand Lodge or with the failure of his Supreme Council's foray into Symbolic Masonry or with some other activity.

REVIEWING THE SOLUTION

Shortly after receiving his M.D. and starting his medical practice, Robert Benjamin Folger was raised a Master Mason on February 10, 1826, in Fireman's Lodge No. 368 in New York City; he then began a most remarkable Masonic career. On May 25, 1826, he became a Royal Arch Mason in Jerusalem Chapter No. 8, with Hans B. Gram presiding. Gram had recently returned to America after a successful medical career in Copenhagen and while there had joined Zerubbabel of the North Star Lodge [Zorobabel til Nordstjernen].

Gram and Folger soon became fast friends, with Gram advising Folger on several patients and eventually converting him to Samuel Hahnemann's then new theory of homeopathy. During their growing professional and Masonic friendship, Gram taught Folger the Rectified Scottish Rite rituals of his Lodge in Copenhagen and initiated him at least through the Fourth Degree of Scottish Master. In September 1826, four months after their first meeting, Folger introduced Gram to Ferdinand L. Wilsey, a merchant and Master of Minerva Lodge No. 371. Gram in turn introduced Wilsey to the "French" work of the R.E.R.

The three friends made plans to establish a lodge in New York City working the Rectified Scottish Rite, and on June 8, 1827, Zorobabel Lodge No. 498, named after

Gram's mother lodge, was chartered with Gram as Master, Folger as Senior Warden, and Lewis Saynisch as Junior Warden. Folger enciphered the R.E.R. rituals for Zorobabel Lodge into FM2, also called the *Supreme Council Book*. On July 12 he started but didn't finish another copy, FM1, owned today by Macoy Masonic Publishing and Supply Co. Included in FM1 is a bizarre history of Masonry, attributing much of Masonic philosophy to Oliver Cromwell. This portion of the history is taken from Abbé Larudan's 1747 *Les Franc-Maçons Ecrasés* through some intermediate text. Folger's cipher is similar to other Masonic ciphers of the period but unique in the nonlinear way the characters were "stacked." Zorobabel Lodge closed shortly after it opened due to the anti-Masonic movement in New York.

Some thirty years later, Folger planned to use his R.E.R. rituals to exemplify French work in John the Forerunner Lodge, chartered March 8, 1853, by the Cerneau Scottish Rite, but it was dissolved before holding any meetings. On September 25, 1854, Folger revoked the preface to his ritual book and almost completely obliterated the name of Ferdinand L. Wilsey. On February 26, 1881, at the reunion of Elmira Consistory in Elmira, New York, Folger proposed a toast using a paragraph from his manuscript. From 1881 to his death in 1892, Folger served as Grand Secretary General of the Cerneau Supreme Council. His offices were at the same address as the Masonic Publishing Co., 63 Bleeker St., one of the predecessor firms of Macoy Co. On his death, at least one of the R.E.R. ritual books, FM1, came to the Masonic Publishing Co. and eventually to Macoy where it is still today.

Most of the major questions about the Folger Manuscripts are now answered, though a few small issues remain.

- Did Hans Gram reproduce the R.E.R. rituals from memory, or was there a book or manuscript, perhaps in French?
- Were the rituals ever actually used in a lodge?
- Where did Folger get his cipher?
- What is the origin of the odd history of Masonry?
- Why are portions of FM1 unfinished?
- Why didn't he include more of the secret work for the degrees?
- What happened to make Folger revoke his preface and nearly obliterate the name of Ferdinand L. Wilsey?

Much of the satisfaction in studying the Folger Manuscripts has come from the digging required to locate answers rather than from the answers themselves. These open questions are left for better investigators with greater patience so that they too can gain satisfaction in studying the Folger Manuscripts.

3

The Cryptanalysis of the Folger Cipher

ONE CHILLY DAY IN 1955, WIL BADEN RETURNED TO HIS NEW YORK HOUSE and fixed some hot lemonade. He then sat down and opened an envelope from Harold Voorhis, Master of the American Lodge of Research, containing about ten pages photocopied from Robert Folger's cipher writing. Baden earlier had deciphered *Mnemonics*, the ritual book of Rob Morris's Conservators of Symbolic Masonry, and Voorhis had found out about his cryptanalytic abilities. Macoy Publishing and Masonic Supply Co., Inc. owned a copy of the FM1, and Voorhis wanted to see the cipher broken—both as a Vice-President of Macoy and as a student of Masonry. He had, in fact, already published a paper in the 1952 *Proceedings of the Ohio Chapter of Research*, entitled "Masonic Alphabets," illustrated with two pages from FM1.

As Baden studied the pages, his initial enthusiasm turned to dismay. The cipher had no readily identifiable characters and appeared impregnable. Two of the pages were laid out similarly, with some of the same text written in plain English on each. However, one had portions encrypted where the other had plain text. Hoping for the best, he carefully compared the phrase "contains great treasures" on one page with the matching cipher on the other and discovered he could read the manuscript!

In less than thirty minutes Folger's "impregnable" encryption had fallen to the cryptanalytic technique of "matched plain and cipher." Baden then translated the entire manuscript but never published his solution. The enciphered phrase essential to his solution was from page 84 of FM1 (figure 1), and the page with the key phrase

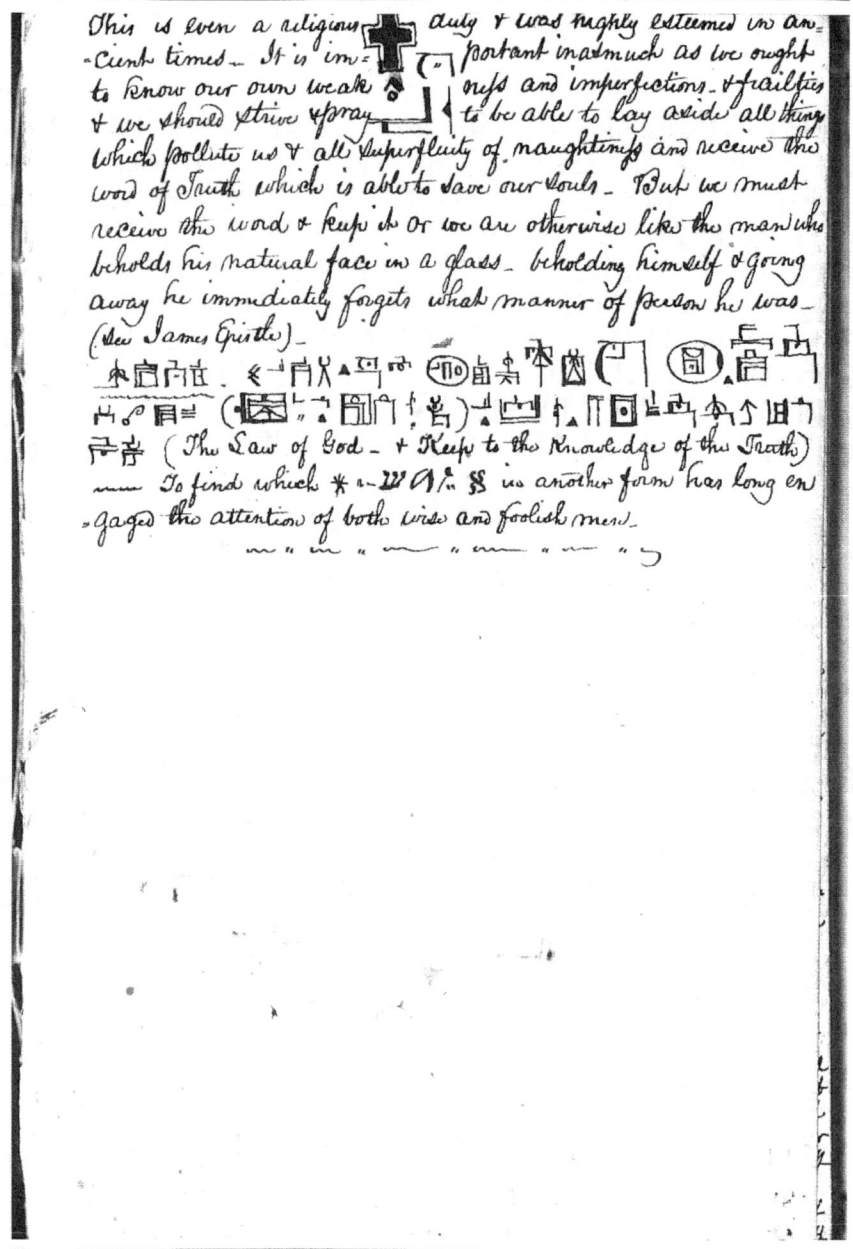

Figure 1. Page 84 of FM1 (the *Macoy Book*). Four and five lines from the bottom, just before "(The Law of God …),", is the encrypted phrase "contains great treasure."

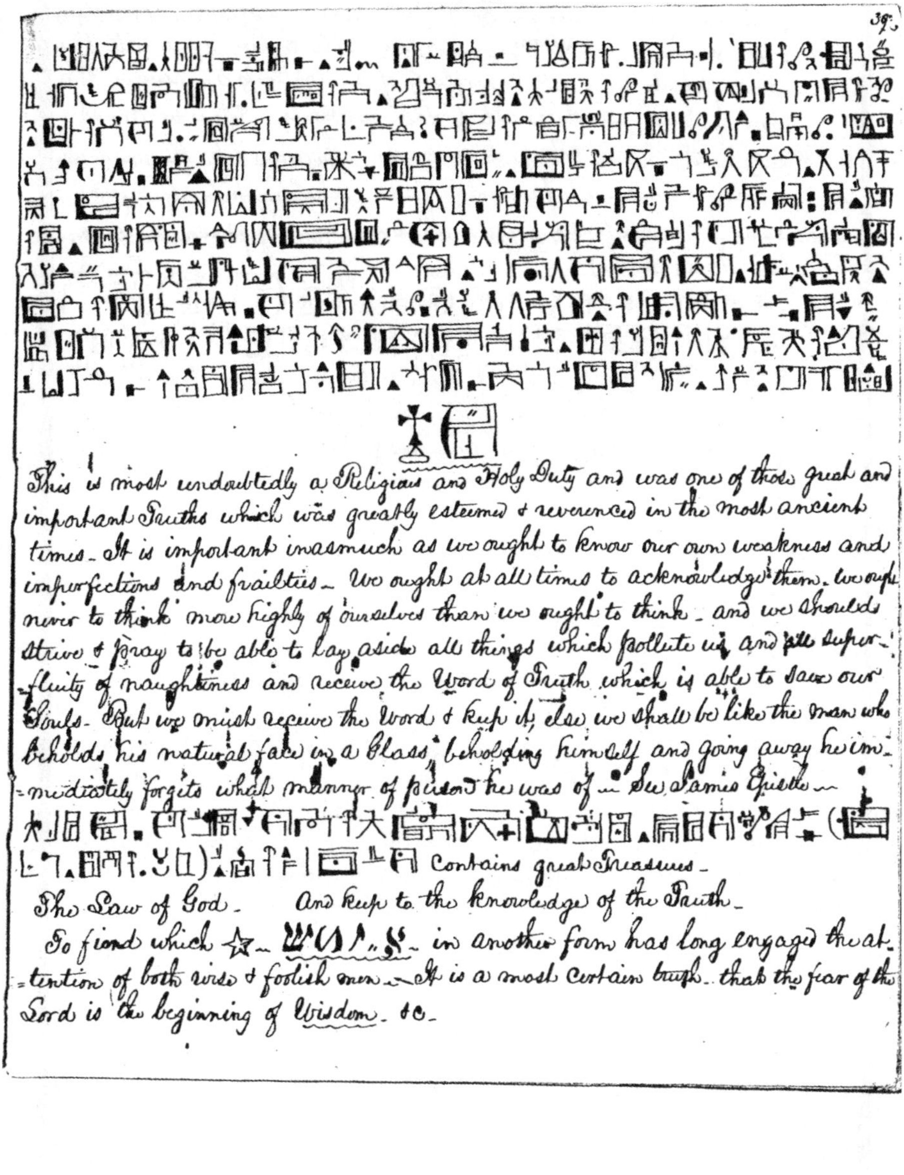

Figure 2. Page 39 of FM2 (the *Supreme Council Book*). Five lines from the bottom, just before "The Law of God," is the plaintext phrase, "Contains great Treasures."

written in plain English came from page 39 of FM2 (figure 2). Both phrases are shown side-by-side for comparison in figure 3.

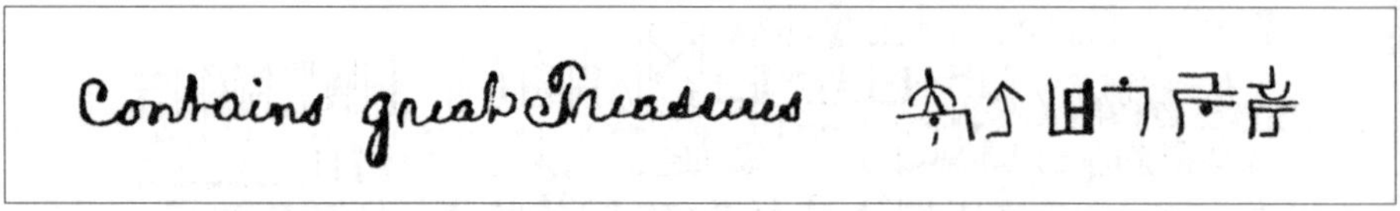

Figure 3. Matched plain and cipher phrases used by Wil Baden to solve the Folger cipher.

In 1982, Donald H. Bennett sat down at his computer and started a lengthy program. While it was running he read Brent Morris's article, "Fraternal Cryptography," which showed page 21 (figure 4) of FM1 as an example of an exotic, unbroken, possibly Masonic cipher (Baden's solution was unknown then to Morris or Bennett). The unsolved puzzle challenged Mr. Bennett, and he set about applying classical cryptanalytic techniques. In a few hours he had independently broken the cipher as it yielded to his "cipher text only" attack. Bennett published his results as "An Unsolved Puzzle Solved" in *Cryptologia* magazine, and his work forms the basis for the discussion that follows.

ASSUMPTIONS

Before beginning the cryptanalysis of an unknown message like page 21 (figure 4), certain fundamental assumptions must be made. Little was known to Mr. Bennett, except that the document was composed by Robert B. Folger, M.D. in 1827. Because of his Masonic membership, the cipher was assumed to conceal some message relating to Masonry. A number of words commonly used by Masons, such as *grand*, *lodge*, *council*, *brother*, *companion*, or *Freemason* had been suggested in Morris's article. Each group or cluster of cipher symbols was suspected to represent a syllable or word. There were other theories and speculations advanced regarding the Folger cipher, but after more than 150 years its solution was unknown to the public.

Some of the assumptions are given below with their reasons.

• *The underlying language is English.* This follows from the author living in New York and having an English sounding surname.

• *The orientation of the page is correct as shown.* The cipher reads from left to right and top to bottom. A paragraph seems to end in the middle of the second line, and a new paragraph, indicated by the illumination of its first few characters, starts on the next line. This one ends on line 8, and another paragraph starts on the next line, indicated by a slight indentation.

• *The cipher is homogeneous throughout.* That is, the same method of encryption is used in all parts of the text. Cipher symbols are repeated throughout the text and are not limited to one part of the page.

Figure 4. Page 21 of FM1 reproduced in S. Brent Morris's "Fraternal Cryptography" and used by Donald Bennett to break the Folger cipher by a "cipher text only" attack.

• *Clusters of symbols represent words.* If clusters represent only letters, then each cluster must contain many meaningless strokes, because hundreds of discrete clusters can be identified. These clusters are referred to as cipher words.

• *There is no transposition of the order of letters within a cipher word.* If rearranging the order of symbols were part of the enciphering process, then repeats of longer words would be rare, but exact repeats of many words do occur.

• *The order of the symbols within a cipher word is from top to bottom and/or from left to right.* This corresponds to the order of normal English writing.

• *A discrete set of about twenty-six cipher symbols represent English letters.*

• *Minor artistic variations in individual cipher symbols is immaterial.* Dark shading of certain strokes may have special meaning.

ANALYSIS

Folger disguised his cipher symbols well; little can be gained from examining the individual characters. The symbols are angular, a characteristic of most Masonic ciphers, and only a few curved strokes can be found, each of which might be an elemental symbol (figure 5). Nine other symbols which showed up repeatedly in the text are also shown. The last three symbols, which occurred less frequently than the first six, are assumed to be infrequent letters, the first six to be frequent ones.

Boxed-In Symbols

The only other useful information gained from individual characters is the observation that many words are surrounded by boxes (figure 6). The box-like character is

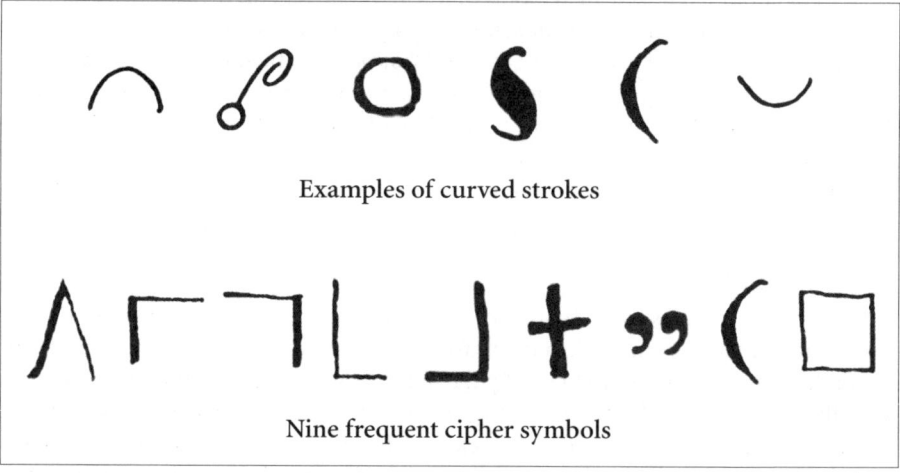

Figure 5. Possible elemental cipher symbols.

The Cryptanalysis of the Folger Cipher

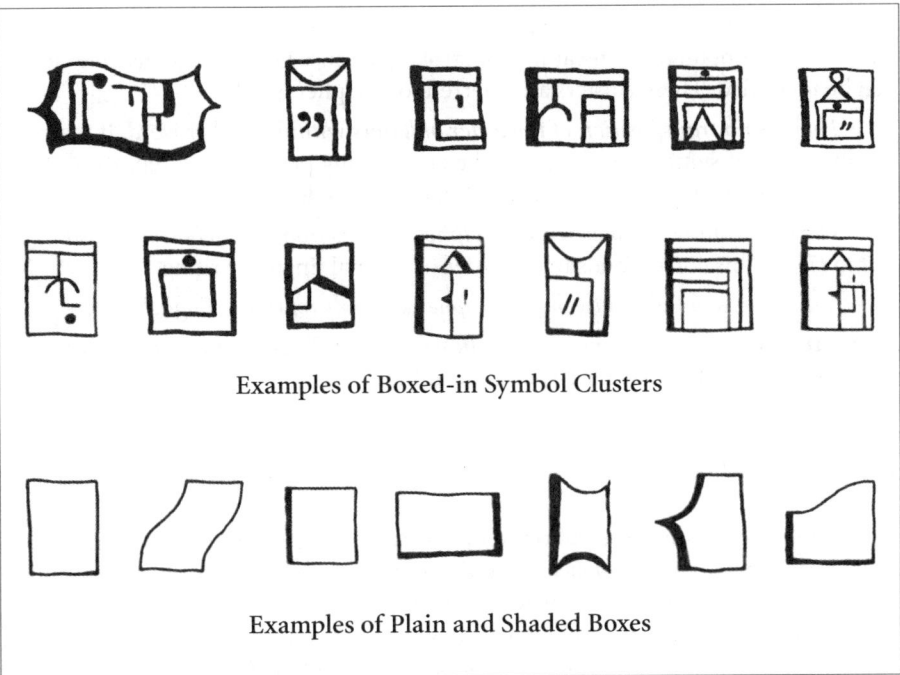

Figure 6. A sample from about 150 boxed-in symbols.

probably the first letter, with the rest of the word inside the box. The dark shading on the sides of some boxes may or may not be significant.

Out of about 150 boxed-in symbols on the page, no less than 42, or 28%, contain a horizontal stroke just inside the box, near the top (e.g., in figure 5, row 1, words 3 and 4, and row 2, words 1, 2, 4, 6, and 7); the stroke appears to be the second letter.

The most frequent letter in English is *e* and it most often occurs as the second letter of a word. The horizontal stroke ⁻ could be the symbol for the letter *e*! This symbol occurs throughout the text but is relatively inconspicuous, a desirable feature for a cipher character representing a high frequency letter. However, it is too soon to firmly identify cipher symbols.

The Mystery Digraph

The analysis continues by searching for digraphs or pairs of symbols with noticeable positional limitations. In English the most striking example of a positional limitation is *qu*: the letter *q* is always followed by the letter *u*. A pronounced limitation is found with the *crescent moon*, (, and *backward gamma*, ⁊: the *crescent moon* is always followed by the *backward gamma*, ⊓, without exception! The *backward gamma*, however, is preceded only occasionally by the *crescent moon*. Next, all cipher words containing this "mystery digraph" are listed (figure 7). It appears twenty-three times in thirteen dif-

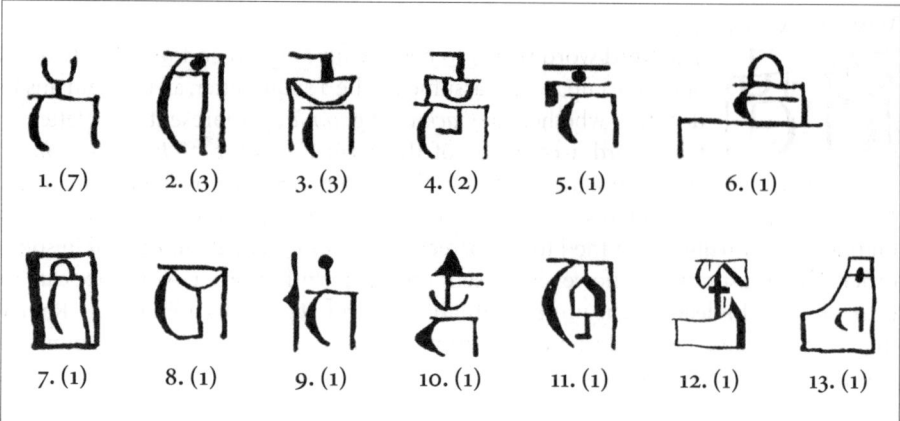

Figure 7. The thirteen words with the mystery digraph and their frequencies in the text.

ferent words. The first word on the list occurs seven times, the second and third three times each, and all others only once. The first three words should be fairly common, consisting of perhaps three to five letters each.

The most distinctive feature of the digraph is that it occurs as the last two letters in fifteen times out of twenty-three, and as the first two letters six times. Only twice (in words 4 and 6) does it occur within a word, and word 4 appears to be the same as word 3 with a suffix added. The *crescent moon* is probably an infrequent letter and the *backward gamma* a common one, and, if so, then what is the mystery digraph? Certainly not *qu*, because *qu* cannot occur at the end of words. It is most likely the letters *th*, with the *backward gamma* as *t* and the *crescent moon* as *h*.

WORD 1

Testing this hypothesis proves interesting and fruitful. Word 1 has *th* or *ht* as its last two letters, with either one or two letters preceding. Since no three-letter English word fits this format, it must be a four-letter word, such as *both*, *with*, *hath*, or *doth* (taking into consideration that verb forms such as *hath*, *doth*, *goeth*, *doeth*, and so on, might occur more often in English written in 1827). There's no use guessing which four-letter word this might be, but if the other cipher symbols represent two letters of plain text, then the most logical way to split this combination is into a cup, ⌣, and a short, vertical line, ⎮.

WORD 2

Word 2 is a short word starting with *th* (an *ht* start is impossible). Since the *backward gamma* is assumed to be *t*, Word 2 must have the form *th - t*. Only one word fits this format—the word *that*—which implies the *dot*, ·, stands for *a*. Before substituting an *a* for every ·, however, it's best to analyze the mystery digraph words further.

Words 3 and 4

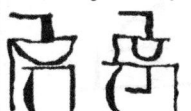

The third word seems to begin with *t* and to end in either *th* or *ht*. Since the cup, ⌣, was assumed to be a single letter, all that remains to decide is whether the *backward gamma*, ⅂, represents one letter or two. Word 3 could be of the form *t - - th, t - - ht, t - - - th*, or *t - - - ht*, with ⌣ representing the third from the last letter. Some possibilities are *tenth, troth, taketh*, or *taught*, but *truth* is just the sort of word a Mason might use three times on one page. If *truth* is assumed to be correct, then ⌈ and ⌣ equate to *r* and *u* in some order. These assumptions however, present problems with Word 4, which appears to be *truths*, but this leads to the unlikely situation where ⌈ represents both *r* and *s*. Rather than reject earlier, seemingly sound assumptions, Word 4 is put aside for the moment and the analysis continues.

Word 5

Word 5 has five letters, four of which have been tentatively identified. Its form is *- arth* or *- auth*, depending on whether ⌈ is *r* or *u*. the only candidate is *earth*, which confirms the earlier idea of the horizontal stroke as *e* and clearly indicates that ⌈ stands for *r*. At this point, the following cipher letters have been tentatively identified: *a, e, h, r, t,* and *u* (figure 7).

Figure 7. Six tentatively identified cipher characters: *a, e, h, r, t,* and *u*.

Words 6 and 7

An upper semicircle, ⌢, begins Word 6 followed by *ther*. This suggests *other*; the only alternative, *ether*, begins with *e*, a horizontal stroke, –. Thus ⌢ is probably identified as *o*. The seventh word contains ⌢ followed by *th*. It seems to be a short word of the form *- oth*, like *doth*, or *both*, but there is not enough information to decide. Word 7 does neither proves nor disproves ⌢ as *o*.

Synthesis

The ⌢ symbol does not occur again in the word list, so a different approach is needed to continue its analysis. The answer is to synthesize a short, common word containing *o* and then to look for it in the cipher text. The symbols for *a, e, h, o, r, t,* and *u* have been tentatively identified, which allows (among other possibilities) the construction of the words *to* and *or* (figure 8). The first possibility for *to* occurs seventeen times in the message and the first possibility for *or* three times, which confirms ⌢ as *o*.

Committed to the Flames

Figure 8. Synthesizing short words: *to* and *or*.

Words 8

Returning to the list brings up Word 8, which is of the form *thu – or thu – –*. The word must be *thus*, but the last cipher symbol is difficult to distinguish because it seems to merge with the bottom of the crescent moon. Thus, the symbol for *s* could be either | or ⌐|, and more analysis is required. Words 9 through 12 are too long or have too many unknown symbols for good assumptions.

Word 13

Word 13, however, lends itself to partial analysis. It is one of the boxed-in words, and, if the box is the first letter, it has the form *– eath* or *– – eath*. This could be a five-letter word such as *death* or a six-letter word like *breath* if the box is a combination of two symbols. A final decision must wait. It is important to note a missing "bite" from the upper left corner of the box. Is this just an artistic variation of a plain box, or is it significant?

Other Interesting Words

Word 13 exhausts the list of words with the mystery digraph, but analysis can continue by looking for "interesting" words in which most of the symbols have been tentatively identified. Such a word ends FM1:21.25. It begins with *ru*, followed by three to five additional letters, one of which is *e*. The last character may be *s*, if the analysis of word 8 was correct. The word is of the form *ru – es* or *ru – ees*, depending on whether the symbol L represents one letter or two. Some possibilities are *rules, runes, ruses,* or *rupees*. The most likely word is *rules*, which goes nicely with the earlier recovery of the word *truths*. This means the symbol for *l* is, of all things, a capital *l*—very poor cryptographic practice!

Another interesting word occurs in the middle of FM1:21.17. It starts with *e*, followed by a repeated letter, and then ends with *orts: e – – orts*. The obvious choice is *efforts*, which provides additional confirmation of the *backward gamma*, ⊣, as *s* and establishes the *half-mast flag*, ᛉ, as *f*.

The Solution

From this point on, the rest of the alphabet can be recovered using the ten known letters: *a, e, f, h, l, o, r, s, t,* and *u*. Only *z* cannot be recovered from page 21, because it was not used. Folger seemed to have used FM1:11 for practice and to have copied the entire alphabet there (figure 9).

The Cryptanalysis of the Folger Cipher

Figure 9. Row 1: Folger's cipher alphabet from FM1:11; rows 2 & 3: cipher alphabet redrawn.

Note that the cipher symbol ∪ is used for the letters *u*, *v*, and *w*. Thus word 1 from the list of those with the mystery digraph is *with*, even though the symbol ∪ was originally recovered as *u*. The letter *h* is represented by either of two symbols: the standard symbol is ⊓ but a variant symbol, ⸦, is used sometimes after *t*. When Folger began writing his manuscript he used the standard *h* exclusively. About FM1:15, however, he started using the variant more and more often after *t*. This variant could have been for ease of writing, but the *th* digraph ⊓ looks like the Hebrew letter *tauv*, ת, and Folger may have tried to introduce Hebrew into his cipher.

Folger's Cipher

Some of Folger's cipher symbols are similar to those found in other Masonic ciphers from the seventeenth and early eighteenth. (This, however, is not surprising because of the small number of possible simple geometric shapes.) It almost seemed as if each new degree (particularly the *hauts grades* from the continent) had its own cipher of twenty-six symbols. The basic "Masonic cipher" consists of a tic-tac-toe grid with nine cells and an *x* with four cells. Each cell stands for a letter, and adding one or sometimes two dots makes a cell represent a different letter. It has been published many times as a secret of the Masons since at least *Le Sceau Rompu* and *L'Ordre des Francs-Maçons Trahi* of 1745.

The grid and *x* cipher is also known in Kabbalah as Aiq Beker and was first published by Heinrich Cornelius Agrippa in his *Three Books of Occult Philosophy* (*Libri tres de occulta philosophia*) in 1531, centuries before it was associated with Freemasonry. The name Aiq Beker comes from reading the Hebrew letters in the first two cells (from right to left): Aleph (א), Yod (י), Qoph (ק), and Beth (ב), Kaph (כ), Resh (ר). The cipher next appeared in print a few decades later in Johannes Balthasar Friderici's *Cryptographia* of 1684.

Despite the availability of several published Masonic ciphers in 1827, Folger seems to have invented his own. The strength of his system comes not from the symbols he chose to represent letters, but from his non-linear method of writing (figure 14).

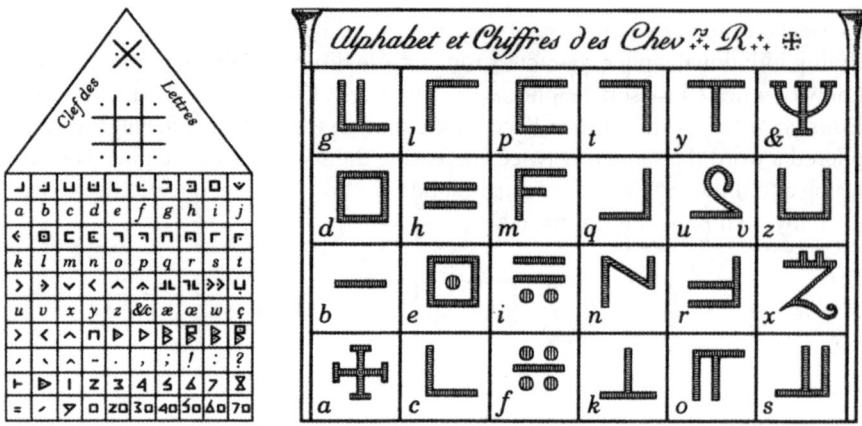

Figure 10. Representative Masonic ciphers. Left from Antoine Guillaume Chérau, *Explication de la Pierre Cubique* ([Paris]: 1806);, tipped in engraving, right from Chérau, *Explication de la Croix Philosophique* ([Paris]: 1806), p. 22.

Figure 11. The Aiq Beker cipher from Heinrich Cornelius Agrippa's *Three Books of Occult Philosophy* (1531), book 3, chapter 30.

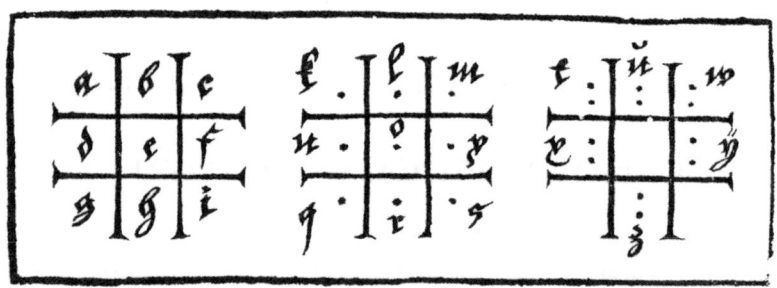

Figure 12. The "grid" cipher from Johannes Balthasar Friderici's *Cryptographia* (1684), p. 230.

He stacked and nested his symbols, probably to conserve space, but it also made identifying individual cipher characters much more difficult. The only other example we know of a nested Masonic cipher is the title page of Jean-Pierre-Louis Beyerlé's 1788 *Essai sur la Franc-Maçonnerie*. Except for common words like *with*, Folger rarely enciphered a word the same way twice, increasing the security of his cipher. His neat lettering and uniform-sized words suggest he transcribed his text from a draft; there are virtually no misspellings or mistakes.

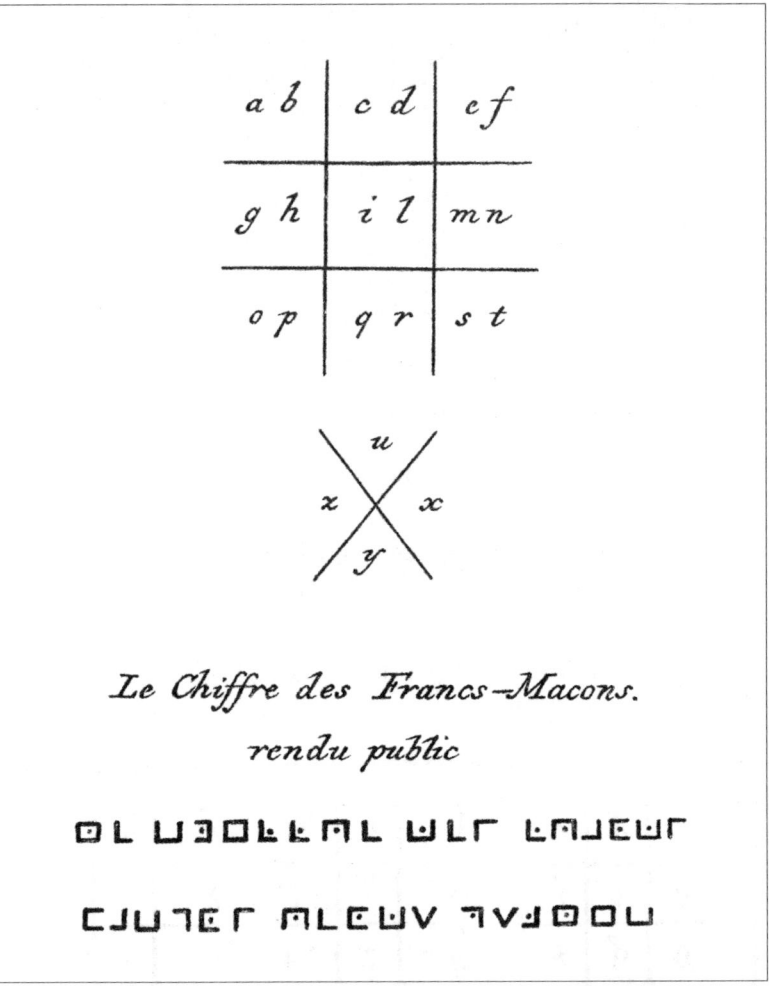

Figure 13. "The cipher of the Freemasons made public." *L'Ordre des Francs-Maçons Trahi* (1745) from Harry Carr, *The Early French Exposures* (London: Quatuor Coronati Lodge No. 2076, 1971), p. 271.

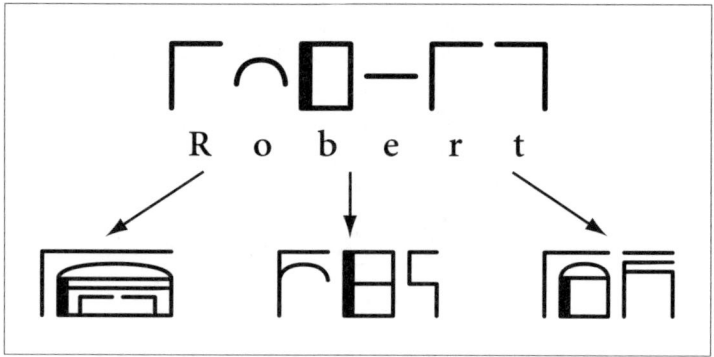

Figure 14. Possible encipherings of the word *Robert* showing the non-linearity of Folger's cipher.

SUMMARY

Folger's cipher alphabet and his method of writing are unlike any other Masonic cipher. Based on the mixture of good and bad cryptographic practices and on the evolving nature of the cipher throughout the manuscript, we conclude that Folger was a self-taught amateur who stumbled on a rather good cipher.

Breaking this cipher and reading the text solves only part of the puzzle. Some important questions are still unanswered: who was Robert Folger and what kind of a person was he? Several interesting conclusions can be reached from studying the *Macoy Book*, many of which are confirmed in chapter 5.

• *Robert Folger was a well-educated man.* His grammar, syntax, and spelling are quite good. He was a meticulous draftsman; his characters are well-defined and precise so that there is little ambiguity in the deciphering process. There are virtually no errors on FM1:21; the few misspelled words, such as *hapy* and *intereresting*, could be clerical errors in encryption, while words like *beautifull* probably reflect the spelling of the day. Using one cipher character for *u*, *v*, and *w* and interchanging the symbols for *i* and *j* in the text hint at a knowledge of Latin. The use of Hebrew letters elsewhere shows a crude knowledge of that alphabet.

• *Robert Folger was an experienced speaker.* The address on the Bible on FM1:21 shows careful, simple wording of complex ideas, suitable for a general audience.

• *Robert Folger was an enthusiastic Mason.* Many hours were devoted to writing and decorating the manuscript, showing an intense interest in Masonry.

• *Robert Folger was a man of strong passions.* The almost complete obliteration of Ferdinand L. Wilsey's name in the preface goes well beyond the simple revocation in the margin.

Figure 15. Note the nested Masonic cipher symbols on the title page of Jean-Pierre-Louis Beyerlé's 1788 *Essai sur la Franc-Maçonnerie*.

4

The Coadjutors of Robert B. Folger

ROBERT FOLGER DID NOT WORK IN A VACUUM WHILE PREPARING AND using his cipher manuscripts. He was helped and influenced by several people, including Hans Burch Gram, Ferdinand Little Wilsey, and Henry Clinton Atwood. Gram was the source of the rituals and a major influence on Folger's medical career. Wilsey was involved in some way with the manuscripts, was a fellow pioneer of homeopathy with Folger, and served with Folger as a Knights Templar officer. Atwood had a profound effect on Folger's Masonic career and led him to use the rituals in a clandestine Scottish Rite lodge. While there were others who influenced Folger's Masonic and medical careers, these three had the most direct effect on Folger's manuscripts.

HANS BURCH GRAM

DR. HANS BURCH GRAM was the pioneer of homeopathic medicine in America. Homeopathy is a medical theory, developed in the early nineteenth century by Dr. Samuel Hahnemenn in Germany, that treats a disease with minute doses of a substance that in a healthy person would produce symptoms of the disease. Thus a patient suffering from a fever is given a fever-inducing drug. Homeopathy has been largely discarded by medical schools, but it was a radical advance in its day, largely because of its gentle, holistic methods. In contrast, standard medical practice of the early 1800s relied heavily on purgatives, bleedings, and other harsh and largely ineffective techniques.

From Boston to Copenhagen

Hans Burch Gram was born in Boston on July 13, 1786 or 1787. After the death of his grandfather in Denmark in 1802, Hans Burch's father prepared to sail for Copenhagen the next year to take care of the estate but died just before setting sail. Hans Burch's mother died two years later when he was barely eighteen, and he soon thereafter sailed for Copenhagen to claim his father's inheritance. His father, Mr. Hans Gram, had been secretary to the Governor of Santa Cruz Island in the Danish West Indies before settling in Boston after marrying a Miss Burdick.[1]

Arriving in Copenhagen in 1806 or 1807, Hans Burch Gram was admitted to the Royal Academy of Surgery with the help of his uncle, Dr. Fenger, physician in ordinary to the King. Within a year Gram was appointed Assistant Surgeon in a large military hospital, where he remained during the last seven years of the Napoleonic Wars. In 1814 he resigned his post in the military hospital, having attained the rank of Surgeon. He graduated from the Academy with the degree of C.M.L. and began a private practice in Copenhagen. For several years he was secretary to his uncle, Dr. Fenger, then the State Medical Counselor. During the years 1823 and 1824, Gram studied and applied the principles of homeopathy in his medical practice.[2]

Zerubbabel Lodge

While in Copenhagen Gram became a Freemason, which later provided him important contacts in New York City. The 1871 register of the Copenhagen lodge Zerubbabel and Frederick of the Crowned Hope [Zorobabel og Frederik tel det kronede Håb] has the following entry: Hans Benjamin Gram, practicing doctor of medicine, born in Boston July 13th, 1787, entered the lodge November 3rd, 1819. Zerubbabel and Frederick Lodge was formed in 1855 by the merger of two lodges, Zerubbabel of the North Star [Zorobabel tel Nordstjernen] and Frederick of the Crowned Hope [Frederik tel det kronede Håb], both working the Rectified Scottish Rite or R.E.R. Circumstantial evidence indicates that Gram joined Zerubbabel of the North Star Lodge (see Chapter 1) and was initiated through at least the R.E.R. Fourth Degree, Scottish Master.[3]

From Copenhagen to New York City

In 1824, after a financially successful medical career in Copenhagen, Gram decided to return to his homeland and to enjoy his retirement. He sailed from Stockholm on the ship *William Penn* and landed at Mount Desert, Maine, where he stayed for some time. He finally arrived in New York City in 1825 and lived with his brother, Neils B. Gram, at 431 Broome St. Hans Gram soon lost his fortune by co-signing loans for his brother and was compelled to enter again the practice of medicine.[4]

By 1826 Gram had proved himself well enough in the Masonic establishment of New York City to be officiating at the conferral of degrees. On May 25 of that year in Jerusalem Chapter No. 8, R.A.M. he presided at the Royal Arch Degree of a young Mason and physician, Robert B. Folger. Folger had become a Master Mason only three months before and recently had established a medical practice. Common Masonic and medical interests fueled a lasting friendship between Gram and Folger after their

Hans Burch Gram, M.D., pioneer of homeopathic medicine in America. From *United States Medical and Surgical Journal*, vol. 2, July 1867, facing p. 449.

initial meeting in Jerusalem Chapter, and "the acquaintance there formed soon ripened into very close intimacy...."5

FOLGER AND WILSEY

Four months after Gram met Folger, Folger introduced him to Ferdinand Wilsey, a successful merchant and Master of Minerva Lodge No. 371. "Dr. Folger having received from Dr. Gram some important information in Masonry, desired that [Wilsey] should also receive the benefit of it." This "important information in Masonry" was Initiation into the Rectified Scottish Rite through at least the Fourth Degree, Scottish Master. The meeting had significant Masonic and professional implications for Gram. He translated the Rituals into English (whether from memory or a manuscript is not known), and Folger enciphered them into three or more small books. One of the volumes, FM1, dated July 12, 1827, has instructions that Gram or Wilsey were to receive the book upon Folger's death. On June 8, 1827, one month before the FM1 was dated, a charter was granted to Zorobabel Lodge No. 498 of New York City with Hans B. Gram, Master; Robert B. Folger, Senior Warden; and Lewis Saynisch, Junior Warden. The rituals may have been used by the lodge, but it had a brief existence and then closed during the anti-Masonic excitement.6

PROFESSIONAL ACTIVITIES

Gram later used homeopathic methods to successfully treat Wilsey for dyspepsia, and Wilsey's enthusiastic endorsements helped him establish a thriving medical practice. From 1826 to 1828 Folger studied homeopathy with Gram as his only student and assistant. Gram attempted to bring the tenets of homeopathy to the attention of the medical profession by publishing a translation of Hahnemann's *Spirit of Homeopathic Healing Laws* [Geist der Homöopathischen Heillehre]. The booklet was addressed to Dr. Hosack, President of the College of Physicians and Surgeons in New York City, but was not well received among the medical profession because of its radical departure from accepted theory. Two years after receiving his copy Dr. Hosack had yet to read it. "Unhappily for [Gram], the medical doctrines which he taught and practiced were so lightly esteemed, that his acquaintance was rather shunned than sought," and he published nothing more on homeopathy. Gram was elected to the New York Medical and Philosophical Society in February 1828 and was elected its President in July, 1829. In January 1828 Folger traveled to Charlotte, North Carolina, for his health, and Gram made plans to join him there in the fall of 1828 to open a joint practice. However, business problems forced Folger to move from Charlotte, and Gram abandoned his medical plans with Folger.7

The last few years of Gram's life must have been disappointing. While his medical practice flourished, he was largely unsuccessful in getting the theories of homeopathy accepted; many in the New York medical establishment considered him a quack. His brother Neil went insane and eventually died, and, just as homeopathy began to be accepted among medical practitioners, he suffered a paralyzing stroke in May, 1839, and died on February 26, 1840. Gram was a member of the Church of the New

Jerusalem (Swedenborgians) and was buried in St. Mark's Burial Ground on Second St. in New York City. A plate on his coffin read: HANS B. GRAM, M.D., a Knight of the Order of St. John, died Feb. 18, 1840, aged 53. On September 4, 1862, his remains were removed to Greenwood Cemetery where they rest today. His marble tombstone still stands in Greenwood Cemetery.[8]

```
H. B. GRAM, C.M.L.
HAFNIAE • PIONEER
OF HOMEOPATHY,
IN AMERICA.
DIED 1840,
AET. 54.
```

FERDINAND LITTLE WILSEY

FERDINAND LITTLE WILSEY was born in New York City, on June 23, 1797. In February 1822 he was "admitted" to Hiram Lodge No.10 after paying an initiation fee of $1.25. Fifteen months later on May 6, 1823, he withdrew from Hiram Lodge to become the charter Senior Warden of Silentia Lodge No. 198. Then ten months later on March 16, 1824, he withdrew from Silentia Lodge and on March 25 became the first Master of Minerva Lodge No. 371. In 1825 he was Captain General of Morton Commandery, No. 4, Knights Templar. A year later, in 1826, he was again Master of Minerva Lodge, served as Generalissimo of Morton Commandery, and was listed in Longworth's *New York City Directory* as a comb manufacturer at 33 Fulton St.[9]

FOLGER AND GRAM

In September 1826, while serving his second term as Master of Minerva Lodge, Wilsey was introduced to Hans Gram by Robert Folger, whom he had met the year before. "Dr. Folger having received from Dr. Gram some important information in Masonry, desired that [Wilsey] should also receive the benefit of it."[10] This "important information in Masonry" was initiation into the Rectified Scottish Rite through at least the Fourth Degree, Scottish Master. Folger enciphered or coied the rituals in at least three small books with instructions dated July 12, 1827, in FM1 that Gram or Wilsey were to receive the book upon Folger's death.

Another motive may have led Folger to introduce Gram and Wilsey: medical care. Dr. John F. Gray had been treating Wilsey unsuccessfully for dyspepsia, and, after meeting Gram, Wilsey turned to him for care. Wilsey thus became the first patient in

America to be treated by homeopathy when Gram used these techniques to cure him. Wilsey was so enthusiastic about homeopathy that he convinced Dr. Gray to study the subject and induced his friends to turn to Dr. Gram for medical treatment. Wilsey's enthusiasm for Gram and homeopathy was responsible for much of the early spread of this medical theory throughout the United States.[11]

In September 1826 when Wilsey met Gram, William Morgan was removed by Masons from the jail in Canandaigua, New York, and disappeared, supposedly murdered because he planned to publish secret Masonic rituals. The anti-Masonic frenzy produced by these lurid allegations produced the first major third political party in the United States, the Antimasonic Party, and caused a social upheaval of amazing intensity. Anti-Masonic excitement gripped New York and the country from about 1826–1840 and resulted in the closing of eighty percent of the lodges in New York. Throughout this difficult period Wilsey remained a staunch Mason. He maintained his membership in Minerva Lodge until it surrendered its charter in 1836, and he served as an officer of Morton Commandery for eight of the years from 1827–1841. His acquaintance with Robert Folger must have continued, as Folger was an officer of Morton Commandery for three of those years, and in 1845 Wilsey was Generalissimo while Folger was Captain General.[12]

From Manufacturing to Medicine

Sometime after his favorable introduction to homeopathy, Wilsey began studying medicine under Gram until he acquired the title of "Doctor." Wilsey established a medical practice but only treated friends gratis. He remained in the comb-manufacturing business until 1837, when financial reverses nearly ruined him. In 1841 he took a position with the Custom House, and in 1844 he was graduated with an M.D. from the College of Physicians and Surgeons (later the medical school of Columbia University). About 1845 or 1846 he joined a copper mining company in Cuba and moved there to superintend the operations. This venture proved disastrous because in less than a year his health failed and he was forced to return to New York City where he commenced the public practice of medicine. In 1850 he was listed in Longworth's *New York City Directory* as a physician at 588 Houston St.[13]

On September 25, 1854, Folger revoked the preface to FM1, almost completely obliterating Wilsey's name. It is not clear what Wilsey did, if anything, to cause Folger's reaction; as recently as 1845 they had served together as officers in Morton Commandery. Folger had had troubles with the Grand Lodge of New York, which had led to his suspension on September 27, 1853, and his Supreme Council was getting more deeply embroiled in controversies at this time. It is most likely that Wilsey spoke out against one of Folger's Scottish Rite schemes, but no evidence of any specific action by Wilsey can be found.

In 1856 or 1857 Wilsey had a severe, protracted illness, which left him weakened and often confined to bed. He would resume his activities when his strength returned, but finally about 1858 he turned over his practice to his successor, Dr. Forbes, and moved with his family to Bergen, New Jersey, where he died May 11, 1860.[14]

HENRY CLINTON ATWOOD

HENRY CLINTON ATWOOD was a Mason who had a great impact on the fraternity in New York State and on the Masonic career of Robert Folger. Atwood was born on March 13, 1801, in Woodbury, Connecticut, to Elijah and Abigail Atwood. He started his Masonic activities on March 25, 1823, when he was initiated an Entered Apprentice in Morning Star Lodge No. 47 in Oxford, Connecticut; on April 22 he received the Second and Third Degrees. He then took the Capitular Degrees in Solomon Chapter No. 3, Royal Arch Masons, in Denby, Connecticut: Mark Master, Past Master, and Most Excellent Master on October 9, and Royal Arch on December 17. His first year in Masonry was completed with his appointment as Senior Deacon of Morning Star for 1824. In 1825 Morning Star Lodge elected Atwood Junior Warden, and on March 25 he was Received and Greeted in Harmony Council No. 8, Royal and Select Masters. Then on November 22 he moved to New York City and was "declared off" (withdrawn) by Morning Star Lodge.[15]

MYSTIC LODGE AND THE CROSS WORK

Atwood began working in New York City as a journeyman hatter and wasted no time in getting involved in Masonry. On March 10, 1826, he was the charter Master of Mystic Lodge No. 389, and on May 25 he joined Rising Sun Chapter No. 16, R.A.M. Mystic Lodge met in St. John's Hall on Frankfort St. and caused quite a stir within the Fraternity with its rituals. In Connecticut Atwood had studied under Jeremy L. Cross, the Masonic ritualist. As Master of Mystic Lodge, Atwood introduced the "Cross work" (Masonic Ritual as organized and taught by Cross who learned it from Thomas Smith Webb) into New York Lodges, whose Grand Lodge had earlier rejected it. This introduction was different, though, because from 1823–27 New York suffered from a schism between the "City Grand Lodge" and the "Country Grand Lodge." While both bodies undoubtedly were opposed to Cross's innovations, their dispute kept them from taking much notice of Atwood and Mystic Lodge. However, the Masons of New York City noticed, "and hundreds flocked to the place every meeting night to see the spectacle." Cross visited the lodge on September 18 and exemplified the first two degrees.[16]

There was such interest in the Cross work that Atwood established classes of twenty Masons each to learn the new style of Ritual. Robert Folger was in the first class, all of whom were young and eager to excel, and which met from 2:00 to 6:00 P.M. twice a week. Atwood converted many individual Masons to this style of working as well as a few lodges; "the few lodges which [espoused] Bro. Atwood's [style] were overrun with candidates and members, drawn there by a love of decoration, finery and new things." During a meeting of Atwood's first class the Ineffable or Scottish Rite Degrees came up. The information was scant, as the bodies were quite secretive and selective; the Gourgas or regular Supreme Council was unknown to the class and the fees of the Cerneau Supreme Council were prohibitive. However, Atwood found in one Abraham Jacobs a cut-rate source of the Ineffable Degrees.[17]

Henry Clinton Atwood From Henry C. Atwood, *The Master Workman* (New York: Simons and Macoy, 1850), frontispiece.

Abraham Jacobs and the 32°

Abraham Jacobs was a one of a small number of itinerant "degree peddlers" who helped spread Masonry in North America. He taught Hebrew for a living and supplemented his income by conferring various Masonic degrees on interested Brethren. While today such entrepreneurs are viewed with disdain, they were considered a legal if not honorable source of "advanced Degrees" in the late 1700s and early 1800s, and Jacobs seemed scrupulous in requiring his clients to obtain charters for their subsequent activities.

On November 9, 1790, Jacobs had been advanced by Moses Cohen to Knight of the Sun, 23° in Morin's twenty-five degree "Order of the Royal Secret." Then on November 24, 1809, Jacobs was promoted to 32° by John Gabriel Tardy, Deputy Inspector General of the Scottish Rite of thirty-three degrees, the successor to Morin's rite. This final promotion presumably was made in return for Jacobs' submission to the authority of the Scottish Rite. After falling on hard times, however, Jacobs began again to confer degrees to supplement his income. Oliver Lowndes, 33°, Sheriff of New York County, and member of the Cerneau Supreme Council, offered Jacobs a clerkship in the Sheriff's Office in return for his agreement to not confer any Scottish Rite Degrees within forty miles of New York State. It was after this point that Henry Atwood met with Jacobs to negotiate the site, time, and fees for conferring the degrees on his class.[18]

Trenton, New Jersey, was selected as the site, and in late winter 1826 Jacobs Initiated the class, including Atwood and Folger, through the 32° of the Scottish Rite for an unreported fee. "The members of the class were well-satisfied,"[19] but they had been misled—Jacobs' patent from Tardy gave no authority to confer degrees. This type of situation was not uncommon in the early, chaotic days of the Scottish Rite, and most of the class members were probably legitimized by joining some regularly chartered Scottish Rite Body.

James Cushman and the 33°

In 1827 Atwood traveled again to Trenton to meet with James Cushman, his friend and a fellow student of Cross. Cushman had an honorary 33° from the Southern Supreme Council with no authority to confer any degrees, especially in the jurisdiction of the Northern Supreme Council. Undeterred, Cushman conferred the 33° on Atwood in the fall of 1827. In 1828 Atwood was High Priest of Rising Sun Chapter and represented it at the meeting of the Grand Chapter of Royal Arch Masons in Albany on February 5–7. While there, he called on Governor De Witt Clinton, 33°, Sovereign Grand Commander of the Cerneau Supreme Council, who "approved" Atwood's patent on February 7, 1828, four days before dying. Atwood must have considered the legitimacy of his Scottish Rite Degrees adequately certified, regardless of their origin.[20]

On November 17, 1828, Atwood withdrew from Mystic Lodge and returned to Oxford, Connecticut. He was restored to membership in Morning Star Lodge No. 47 in late 1829 or early 1830, and on December 27, 1830, was elected and installed Master of the lodge. He was reelected in 1831 when he also served Eureka Chapter No. 22, R.A.M., in Oxford as High Priest. Atwood was clearly a staunch supporter of Freemasonry, because in 1832 he signed the "Declaration of Principles" which had been prepared by Massachusetts Masons in response to the anti-Masonic fervor. Defiance in the face of overwhelming opposition was a characteristic Atwood would demonstrate over and over in his Masonic activities. He was again High Priest of Eureka Chapter in 1832 and Master of Morning Star Lodge in 1833. In 1835 he returned to New York City and was admitted a member of York Lodge No. 367 (now No.197).[21]

The St. John's Day Parade

When the rumors of William Morgan's abduction and murder were first heard in 1826, the Grand Lodge of New York had 480 lodges on its rolls; by 1835 only 75 remained. The Grand Lodge took a very conservative approach towards bringing attention to Masonry in those days and issued an edict "forbidding all public processions and public displays." In 1836 Atwood's lodge, York No. 367, tried to get Grand Lodge permission to openly celebrate St. John's Day, but failed to get an exception to the edict. The next year York Lodge pressed the issue again by calling a meeting of Masons to discuss the propriety of a public celebration of St. John's Day. James Herring, Grand Secretary, cautioned the meeting that the edict was still in full effect, but he was reminded that he himself had violated the edict by having a Masonic banner flown outside the offices of the grand lodge. After a raucous debate, York Lodge succeeded in convincing Benevolent, Silentia, and Hibernia Lodges to join in their plans for the celebration.[22]

On June 24, 1837, St. John's Day, several hundred Masons assembled at Warren Hall to celebrate the feast day of one of their patron Saints. Just before the festivities began, James Van Benschoten, Deputy Grand Master, and James Herring appeared and once again warned the participants against defying a grand lodge edict. The warnings were ignored, and the Masons showed their firm attachment to their ancient, honorable fraternity. Their brave public display in the face of recent vicious attacks attracted positive interest in the Craft and, many believed, helped restore the health of the grand lodge.

> They marched several hours up one street and down another, through the length and breadth of the metropolis, reaching the City Hall Park late in the afternoon, where they marched and countermarched, the music playing sweetly to the amusement and satisfaction of the throng of spectators…. The church where the exercises were held was completely thronged, everything passed off remarkably well, and all were well pleased with the demonstration. The brethren were dismissed, and retired to finish up the whole with a sumptuous dinner, which proved a very pleasant affair.[23]

Even though the parade seemed to leave a positive impression on citizens of New York, the grand lodge was unwilling to let such open flaunting of its authority go unpunished. A special meeting of the grand lodge was called on July 12 for the purpose of preferring charges against Atwood and his fellow conspirators. Some of the enthusiasm for pursuing this case seems to have stemmed from the longstanding dislike of James Herring for Atwood. Herring strongly objected to Atwood's promotion of the Cross work, referring derisively to its changes as "wooden nutmegs and horn gunflints, imported fresh from Connecticut." Atwood's defiance of the grand lodge edict gave Herring an opportunity to discipline someone who had dared question the Masonic status quo.[24]

Atwood and William F. Piatt were charged at the special meeting, but the members would not agree with the grand officers on how to prosecute the charges. After a great deal of parliamentary maneuvering and after losing two votes, the Deputy Grand Master declared a resolution against Atwood adopted over strenuous protestations, and the meeting was adjourned. The Grand Steward's Lodge (dominated by Herring and other grand officers) expelled Atwood and Piatt on August 26, 1837, and the grand lodge confirmed their punishment at its quarterly meeting on September 11, 1837. Further, all who marched in the parade were expelled and the charters of the participating lodges were annulled. It is ironic that, as an economic depression spread through New York State and as anti-Masons continued their fierce opposition, the grand lodge was most concerned with internal conformity.[25]

ST. JOHN'S GRAND LODGE

The expulsions of Atwood and the others did nothing to solve the problems of the Grand Lodge of New York but rather exacerbated them. The immediate result was a schism and the establishment of St. John's Grand Lodge. Atwood was not the founder or a grand officer, but he became the major force driving the institution—a charismatic opponent to reckon with. Folger described Atwood as "one of the most noisy and disputatious men which that grand lodge contained, and withal, when excited, very abusive. He was a man ... obstinate in his prejudices and preconceived opinions, very easily excited, and slowly appeased." Atwood was "never content unless engaged in some way in the promotion [of Masonry].... Contention and argument were his 'forte,' accompanied with wild loud and boisterous declamations. On this account he always managed to draw after him the crowd, while his nature was so genial that his followers became strongly bound to him."[26]

York Lodge changed its allegiance to St. John's Grand Lodge, and Atwood served as its Master in 1838 and 1840. Atwood devoted his considerable energy on the new grand lodge and "rigorously promoted the cause of Masonry as he saw it. From 1841 to 1847 he was Master of Independent Lodge No. 7 (now No. 185), in 1847 and 1848 he was High Priest of Orient Chapter No. 1 (now No.128), R.A.M., and about this time he was Commander of Palestine Commandery No. 1 (now No. 18), K.T. For ten years, 1838–1848, Atwood served as Deputy Grand Master, and for 1849 and 1850 he was Grand Master. In this capacity he presided at the "Great Union" on December 27, 1850, when St. John's Grand Lodge reunited with the Grand Lodge of the State of New York. This union was eased by the fact that there had been yet another schism in 1849, and James Herring, Atwood's nemesis, had abandoned the grand lodge to become Grand Secretary of the new breakaway group. When Atwood returned to the grand lodge, he brought with him twenty-five lodges and 3,000 members, and he was recognized with the full honors of a Past Grand Master.[27]

The Cerneau Supreme Council Revived
Atwood's triumphant return was not without its dark side. The opponents of St. John's Grand Lodge persecuted its members, with Atwood at the center of their efforts; "he was literally 'hounded down' in his business affairs, until he was reduced to abject poverty, and was, at one time without a place which he could call a home for his family." By 1841 many of the members of St. John's Grand Lodge despaired of their isolation from all other Masonic contact and were ready to return to the regular grand lodge on whatever terms might be offered. Atwood would hear nothing of this and kept St. John's going by force of his personality. He started Independent Lodge No. 7 and oversaw ritual instruction for his grand lodge, demanding strict uniformity and perfection. In 1842 St. John's reduced the fees for its degrees to attract candidates.[28]

On October 27, 1846, the Cerneau Supreme Council had divided its funds among its four remaining members and disbanded. Atwood and others from St. John's Grand Lodge stepped into this breach and revived the Supreme Council on May 15, 1849, on the theory that Scottish Rite authority reverted to the 33° Inspectors General with the dissolution of the Supreme Council. Atwood was elected Grand Commander. Folger later claimed the revival was in 1846, but this could hardly be so as all except Atwood received their 33° the summer of 1848.[29]

The revolt of St. John's Grand Lodge had resulted in its members being shut out of most of the Masonic activities in New York State. Atwood tried to address this by using his position in the revived Cerneau Supreme Council to reward St. John's members with the 33°. He also had the warrant of the suspended and dissolved Lafayette Chapter of Rose Croix, a Cerneau body. Later comments by Atwood indicate that he apparently believed that any use of the warrant was justified if it promoted his grand lodge.

> The warrant of that body has done us good service, inasmuch as it served its purpose for the document founding and establishing Orient Chapter of Royal Arch Masons and Palestine Encampment of Knights Templar. It was shifted over from one body to the other at every meeting, as occasion required, and was never called in question. It had plenty of large seals in silver cases, it passed off admirably, and no one knew the difference. If any brother made any objections after receiving the degrees of the chapter or encampment, I always threw myself upon my patent as a Sov. Grand Inspector-General, 33°, and last degree, which gave me full power to establish lodges, chapters, councils, and other bodies, at my pleasure.[30]

When the Great Union occurred, Orient Chapter and Palestine Encampment, both created by the "full power" of Atwood's 33° patent, were welcomed into their respective Grand Bodies. Atwood's bitter treatment must have led him to these desperate, autocratic actions that, however, established a later pattern of authoritarian rule.

The Supreme Council for the Northern Hemisphere
After seeing his grand lodge restored to legitimacy and himself increased in prestige, Atwood seemed to have set his sights on building up "his" Supreme Council. If he had had as much success with the Scottish Rite as with St. John's Grand Lodge, his influ-

ence would have been magnified even more. Further, he would have had the control of honors with which to reward his friends and the power to punish his enemies—specially J. J. J. Gourgas, Grand Commander of the Northern Supreme Council, who had vigorously and regularly denounced the Cerneau Supreme Council for years. Comments by Atwood indicate that this rivalry provided some of the motive for the revival of the Cerneau Supreme Council.

> By all means [the Supreme Council] will be continued, but must undergo a complete and full reorganization. This is rendered the more imperative by a movement which has been set on foot by a few members of our jurisdiction who have called in question my authority, and have gone to Bro. J. J. J. Gourgas.... We cannot stand idly by, and see this intrusion succeed without making some effort to stop it.

Atwood "was really a very difficult man to get along with. Sensitive in the highest degree from the slightest provocation, he would go off like a rocket...." He was "never content unless engaged in some way in the promotion [of Masonry] ...," and the Scottish Rite was now his cause.[31]

In early January 1851, a few weeks after the Great Union, Folger called on Atwood to find out about the Masonic papers of Abraham Jacobs that had been given to Atwood just before Jacobs' death in 1834. Atwood asked Folger to join him in reviving the Supreme Council, and Folger agreed, taking on the task of locating a new Grand Commander. He wanted to find someone "who had not been mixed up with past troubles, and who would carry a strong influence as a Mason." Jeremy Cross the Masonic lecturer, then a merchant in New York City, was just that person.[32]

Cross received his 33° and joined the Southern Supreme Council on June 24, 1824, but never exercised his authorities nor participated in its activities. Folger convinced him to serve as Grand Commander, but not without some conditions from Cross. Cross had spent his life promoting and propagating the York or American Rite, which consisted of the Symbolic Lodge, Royal Arch Chapter, Royal and Select Council, and Knights Templar Commandery. He insisted on these conditions: 1) the Supreme Council would not charter Symbolic Lodges; 2) only Royal Arch Masons could join the Scottish Rite; and 3) only Knights Templar could advance beyond the 14°. In essence the Scottish Rite would be subservient to the York Rite. Atwood and Folger were willing to agree to anything, at least for a time, to bring to their Supreme Council the respectability of Cross and the authority of his patent. Their blatant cynicism was made clear in later comments by Folger.

"While the propositions made by Bro. Cross seemed to be fatal to the interests of the Sup. Council, on the other hand it was deemed necessary to secure an establishment of the body, knowing well that Bro Cross would not long remain the Commander on account of the infirmities of age."[33] "It became the duty of the members [of the Supreme Council] to select from personal friends such persons as ... [probably] would accede to the proposals of forming a new Council in the place of the then local body." To be blunt, Atwood "stacked the deck" to insure approval of the changes demanded by Cross. In April 1851 a meeting was held of this expanded Supreme

Council, consisting of Atwood, Folger, and three others, and they agreed to Cross's conditions. On May 29, 1851, the "Supreme Council for the Northern Hemisphere" was organized with Cross as Grand Commander, Atwood as Grand Master of Ceremonies, and Folger as Grand Treasurer General.[34]

The organizers appointed prominent Masons from around the country as officers. Their zeal to select influential Masons led them to make at least one appointment without regard for the officer's interest or membership in the Scottish Rite. Nathan B. Haswell, Grand High Priest of Vermont, was listed in their proclamation in the June 20, 1851, *New York Herald* as Grand Keeper of the Forest of Lebanon. On July 14, 1851, Haswell responded to his appointment as follows (emphasis added).

> I received a letter from J. L. Cross, of New York, under date of the 18th of June, last, saying that he has ventured to put my name on the list of officers of a General Consistory of the Gen . Grand Council of the 33d Degree of Masonry in New York, without consulting me, and requesting my acceptance of the appointment. At the time of my receiving this letter, which was on the 21st or 22d of June, I deemed it Masonic and proper, *having, myself, never taken those degrees,* to make the necessary inquiries respecting the organization of a body of whose correct and regular standing I had doubts.[35]

On August 16, 1851, Atwood began publishing the *Masonic Sentinel*, a weekly journal with the purpose of advancing the position of the Cross Supreme Council; the belligerent tone of the *Sentinel* reflected the style of its editor. Atwood tried to present the history of the Cerneau Supreme Councils in the most favorable possible light, but his writing demonstrates either his ignorance, his lack of access to records, or his willingness to rewrite history to suite his ends. The *Masonic Sentinel*'s life was brief; it ceased publication on February 7, 1852, after only twenty-six issues. Cross's tenure as Grand Commander was also brief, as well as inconsequential. After a serious illness, he resigned on April 29, 1852, and retired to Haverhill, New Hampshire, where he passed away in 1861. Atwood resumed the helm as Acting Grand Commander.[36]

The Supreme Council for the State of New York

Atwood's resumption of control of the Supreme Council was contrary to the regulations of the Supreme Council. He advanced over two more senior officers, William H. Ellis, Minister of State, and Rev. Salem Town, Grand Keeper of Seals. Ostensibly this was done because both Ellis and Town were from Connecticut and could not tend to the business of the Supreme Council in New York. More likely this was done because Atwood had remained the power behind the throne during Cross's short term in office.[37]

On October 28, 1852, six months after Cross's resignation, Atwood reorganized again and created the "Supreme Council for the Sovereign, Free, and Independent State of New York," appointing Robert Folger as Grand Secretary General. He was influenced in this change of territorial control by James Foulhouze, Grand Commander of the "Louisiana State Supreme Council, Scottish Rite." It was Foulhouze's goal to have a Supreme Council in every state in control of both the higher degrees and the Scottish Rite symbolic degrees, and New York was the first state to sign on to this program.[38]

Radically reorganizing the Supreme Council and ignoring its regulations disturbed some of the members. In fact John Simons, Grand Secretary General of the Cross Supreme Council and later Grand Master of the Grand Lodge of New York, apparently was not consulted at all about either the reorganization or his replacement by Folger. Simons was so outraged that he issued an edict in 1853 as "Acting Grand Commander," condemning Atwood's autocratic actions (emphasis in original).

> Now, therefore, be it known that ... inasmuch as the various other subordinate officers, myself excepted, have *strayed* from the TRUE FOLD to parts unknown, therefore, by virtue of the constitution and regulations of the Order, as herein before set forth, the power and authority devolve on me, and I hereby accept them, and duly notify all Chapters and Councils ... that all bodies of Scottish Masons held in contravention of this, *my edict*, and the authority of the Supreme Grand Council, of which I am the *sole representative*, are irregular, clandestine, and spurious ....[39]

Simons was mollified somehow and withdrew his objections, giving further testimony to Atwood's strength of personality. Later events, though, hint that Simons did not forget his summary replacement.

SCOTTISH RITE SYMBOLIC LODGES

On December 23, 1852, James Foulhouze was received by the Supreme Council for the State of New York, and he installed Atwood and the other officers. Under the influence of Foulhouze's theories of Masonic authority, Atwood's activities took a fateful turn. Foulhouze convinced Atwood that the Scottish Rite had the inherent authority to control Craft lodges, and Atwood decided to exert this prerogative for his Supreme Council. This radical change in jurisdiction was surprising, not only because Atwood was a Past Grand Master, but also because it flew in the face of earlier pronouncements by his Supreme Council.[40]

In 1851 the Grand Master of the Grand Lodge of Louisiana was faced with the problem of the Supreme Council of that state chartering Craft lodges. He addressed a circular letter to the other grand lodges seeking their advice. His letter produced a presumably authoritative edict from the first Atwood Supreme Council on April 14, 1851, signed by John W. Simons, Lieutenant Grand Commander, Daniel Sickels, Grand Secretary General, and George E. Marshall, Grand Treasurer General. After a lengthy discussion of the facts, the edict reached three conclusions.

> *First.*—That the creation of symbolic Lodges by the Grand Council of La∴ in that State, is unjust and an unwarrantable assumption of power, and a direct interference with the established usages of the Order, and the recognized authority of the regular Grand Lodge.
> *Secondly.*—That being constituted under the Scottish Rite, they are not "York or Ancient Craft Masons."
> *Thirdly.*—That being constituted in open defiance of the lawful authority of the State, they are illegal and unconstitutional, and of course cannot be recognized as regular, nor be permitted to communicate with or visit the Grand Lodge or its constituents.[41]

In 1852, when the Supreme Council reorganized according to Cross's dictates, it reaffirmed its earlier position in a public notice in the *New York Herald* on June 20, 1852, (emphasis added).

> This body is formed for the purpose of conferring the ineffable degrees, ... and for that purpose branch councils will be established in the various States comprising the jurisdiction, as fast as applications are made, all of which will be governed in their work by an order issued from this Grand East, *forbidding the initiatory degrees to be conferred at all.*... This Supreme Council and Branches will acknowledge, and, to the extent of their jurisdiction, cause to be respected, the rights of all regularly established organizations in the several branches of the order, as Grand Lodges, G∴ Chapters, and Grand Encampments, with their general heads in this country.... By Order,
>
> JOHN W. SIMONS, G∴ Secretary

In spite of these solemn pronouncements, Atwood reversed the position of his Supreme Council. His motivation was probably power—to have complete control over all of Masonry from 1° to 33°, but he genuinely may have been convinced by Foulhouze that the Scottish Rite had abdicated its responsibility to govern the Craft. In any event Atwood persuaded the Supreme Council to change its position, and on March 8, 1853, the minutes clearly record the chartering of two Craft lodges (underlining in original).

> The Ill∴ Bro∴ Folger then proceeded to lay before the Council the following Petitions for the constituting and establishing Symbolic Lodges of the Ancient Free and Accepted Scottish Rite.
> From Bro Robert B. Folger and others for a Lodge of St∴ John by the distinctive title of "John the Fore-runner" and by Number 1 (see document on file) which petition was granted and the Patent ordered to be made out and executed bearing date March 8th 1853 of the Christian Era.
> From Bro Deszelus, Roullier, Vatet, Ploquin & others, in all 14, for a Lodge of St. John, the ritual etc. in the French Language, by the distinctive title of "La Sincerite" and by number 2 (see documents in French and English on file) which petition was granted and $he Patent ordered to be made out and executed, bearing date March 8th, 1853 of the Christian Era....
>
> Attest,
>
> *Robt. B. Folger*, G∴C∴G∴ Secy of the H∴E∴ [42]

Twenty-one years later Folger tried to temper the appearance of the actions of his Supreme Council with a revisionist interpretation of the events. "Although the powers [then] assumed, not only over the Ancient Accepted Rite, but over all other Rites, were unlimited, there was a conservative stand taken by the minority [of the Supreme Council], which would always prevent any overt act on the part of the majority...."[43] It is hard to imagine a more overt act than the chartering of Craft lodges, and Masonic authorities of the day seemed to agree.

The response to this usurpation of power from the grand lodge was swift. On June 7, 1853, Grand Master Nelson Randall reported in his address to the Grand Lodge of New York that he was "informed that one or more [lodges], in the Scotch Rite, have been established within the last few months in the city of New York, under the patronage and countenance, or assumed authority of a distinguished Past Grand Master in this Grand [Lodge]...." A special committee was appointed, considered the evidence, and reported back on June 10. They deemed "the fact of the establishment of such lodges an invasion of the jurisdictional rights of [the Grand Lodge of New York]." The committee concluded that "[a] Grand Lodge has, of undoubted right, supreme control over the Symbolic degrees within its temporal jurisdiction.... This body, therefore, cannot, in self-respect, or in the protection of her undoubted rights of supremacy do less than to resist this invasion of its authority."[44]

St. John's Grand Lodge Revived

While the controversy over Atwood's Scottish Rite Craft lodges was growing, yet another crisis in New York Masonry developed with Atwood and Folger in the lead. On June 9, 1853, Reuben H. Walworth, Chancellor (now Governor) of New York, was elected Grand Master of the grand lodge. His election caused an uproar because Atwood and others alleged that during the anti-Masonic period (ca. 1826–1840) Chancellor Walworth had publicly denounced Masonry; Atwood stated he would not sit in grand lodge with Walworth. On June 13 a meeting of Masons opposed to Walworth was held in Tollerton Hall where Robert Folger and others spoke against the election. A committee of three, including Folger, was appointed to consider grievances against the grand lodge and reported back on June 20, urging the reestablishment of St. John's Grand Lodge until Chancellor Walworth's term as Grand Master expired. "Whereupon, all present came forward, and pledged themselves to the form support of the same." St. John's Grand Lodge was revived formally on June 24 when Henry Atwood installed the new grand officers.[45]

On August 12, 1853, Deputy Grand Master Joseph D. Evans issued an edict to all New York lodges. In it he declared St. John's Grand Lodge clandestine and further noted "that the Lodges instituted by Henry C. Atwood, to work in the Scottish Rite, have conferred those degrees upon persons who are not Masons...." Evans forbade all Masonic communication with St. John's Grand Lodge and with Atwood's Scottish Rite lodges. In grand lodge on September 6, 1853, charges of unmasonic conduct were preferred against Folger and others for reactivating St. John's Grand Lodge. Atwood was summoned to appear before the grand lodge officers to explain his actions, but he refused "in very abusive and unbecoming language." He was expelled from Masonry on September 27, 1853.[46]

Responding to the charges brought against him, Folger wrote to James M. Austin, Grand Secretary, on September 26, 1853. While Atwood's reply with its "abusive and unbecoming language" has been lost, Folger's reply has not. It indicates the level of the passion these issues generated.

> I assure you Sir that my expulsion from that body will prove ... but very little mortification to me, but rather an honour.... It strikes me that it would have been more proper on the part of the body to which you belong to have selected some member from my own Lodge to have preferred these charges ... but like all other filthy pro-

ceedings of that Grand Body, I suppose they were unable to find a man who was acquainted with me, who would so far debase himself, as to brings these charges, based upon falsehood, against me....[47]

Folger was expelled from Masonry by the Grand Steward's Lodge on September 27, 1853.

THE GRAND PLAN

The rebirth of St. John's Grand Lodge seemed to play right into Atwood's grand plan. "It was supposed that on the withdrawal of the lodges from the grand lodge, they would seek the protection of the Supreme Council, and work under its jurisdiction." If this indeed had happened, Atwood would have quickly had an organized power base from which to carry forward his design of building up his Supreme Council. Such a plan of expansion easily fit Atwood's demonstrated character, but it seemed to be too much for some members of his Supreme Council, even though they had just chartered two Craft lodges. "The conservative feelings of the Council, however, [were] sufficiently strong to prevent any such step, and the whole matter was referred back to the lodges, with the expressed wish that they would conclude to remain as individual lodges, and proceed with Masonic work, or revive for the time being the old St. John's Grand Lodge...."[48]

Atwood's decision to brazenly challenge the authority of the Grand Lodge of New York proved ruinous for him and ultimately led to disaster for his Supreme Council, as the stigma of chartering Craft lodges plagued it for another fifty years until its final demise. Atwood tried to gain power for his Supreme Council by trying to play the various grand lodge factions in the state against themselves. He laid out this bold strategy to his mentor and fellow agitator, James Foulhouze of the Supreme Council of Louisiana, in a letter written sometime shortly after St. John's Grand Lodge had been revived. Atwood explained that the "Phillips Grand Lodge," the Past Masters' faction, was trying to split New York State into eastern and western grand lodges, and "failing in this, they will continue their present organization, charter all the lodges they can of the York Rite—cheap—offer to us a 'Chamber' in their Grand Lodge, giving us the exclusive control of the Scottish Rite & any union after that is done will never be brought about."[49]

Atwood was confident his Supreme Council would survive because both the Phillips Grand Lodge and the Grand Lodge of New York, or Willard Grand Lodge, were courting him, or so he wrote to Foulhouze. Having sustained one grand body, St. John's Grand Lodge, in the face of fierce opposition, Atwood believed he could do it again with his Supreme Council—at least until his goals were achieved. He wanted a grand lodge organized along the lines of the Grand Orient of France: his Supreme Council would have official recognition, a legislative chamber, and exclusive control of the Scottish Rite from 1° to 33°. These grandiose plans apparently grew from a desire for power or revenge and Atwood's new beliefs of the inherent authority of Supreme Councils (emphasis in the original).

> [W]e are a Supreme Council yet & must either have a chamber in the <u>Grand Lodge proper</u> & be acknowledged or we hold the balance of power now & will shiver them

into fragments & ride over the ruins. We do not want a Chamber now, until the <u>Union</u> takes place or else a <u>Break up</u>. If the former, we shall have the Chamber, that is understood, & being still in full communion with the Willard party we labour diligently to bring about the same, but if the latter, viz. a break up, then we have a Chamber, & thus control both Rites and draw with us a large body of the Lodges of their side....

But one of two things will take place, 1st there will be a grand Union in which the Scottish Rite will participate, maintaining at the some time all its powers & its prerogatives & thus killing the [J. J. J.] Gourgas, [Charles W.] Moore & [Albert] Mackey imposition effectually in this country by giving us the acknowledgement & power, or 2d there will be 5 distinct powers in the State of New York, viz. the Willard Power, the Phillips Power, the St. Johns Grand Lodge renewed power, the Pythagoras or Hamburg power, & ourselves as the Scottish Rite. We are prepared for either event, & shall so endeavour to conduct ourselves as to get the best part of the victory if we can."[50]

The idea of establishing Scottish Rite lodges and extending the authority of the Supreme Council seemed to have been plotted for some time by Folger and Atwood. Folger hinted at some of their plans in a letter to Dr. Barthe of Foulhouze's Louisiana Supreme Council, dated May 26, 1852, nine months before the chartering of John the Forerunner and La Sincérité Lodges. "All Lodges having intercourse with each other in this country must be York. It is easy to have our Lodges nominally York secretly Scottish. This gives us the advantage over them. We can visit them as York Masonry, while they will be entirely ignorant of our Scottish Rite. This we can easily arrange."[51]

The Crumbling Empire

If Atwood's separation from the grand lodge had been based solely on his complaint against Reuben Walworth, he may have once more emerged from the battle a hero. However the notion of Supreme Council autonomy, if not superiority, was simply too much to be accepted by American Masons. Atwood's empire began crumbling almost as soon as he decreed it.

The Grand Lodge of New York, the "Willard Faction," sent letters to its sister grand lodges explaining the situation in New York. The response was almost immediate condemnation of Atwood's Supreme Council. For example in December, 1853, only six months after the chartering of John the Forerunner and La Sincérité Lodges, the Grand Master of Alabama denounced Atwood and his Supreme Council. "Disobeying and setting at naught the mandates of the Grand Lodge of [New York], Henry C. Atwood has claimed and exercised the same right and power to grant charters to subordinate Lodges in New York to work the Scotch Rite, which the Supreme Council of the 33d degree for the valley of New Orleans does in Louisiana."[52]

Atwood was St. John's Grand Master from June 1854 to June 1855, during which time defections from his cause, both big and small, began to mount. On June 10, 1854, Atwood Lodge No. 208 of the Grand Lodge of New York changed its name to Cyrus Lodge. Five months later on November 30, 1854, Atwood changed the name of his Supreme Council back to "The Supreme Council for the United States of America, their Territories and Dependencies" and resumed its "ancient jurisdiction."[53]

General Tomás Cipriano de Mosquera, Past Grand Commander of the Supreme Council for and former president of New Grenada (now Colombia), made a grand visit to the Supreme Council on April 4, 1853; some time after this Andres Cassard, his private secretary was proposed for the 33°. This met with great opposition from the French members of the Supreme Council, and after two or three hours of debate the proposal was tabled. "... Some months after the proposition had been disposed of by the Supreme Council, a peremptory official order came to [Folger] requiring ... [him] to confer the 33° upon [Cassard] forthwith." Folger tried to dissuade Atwood from thwarting the will of the Supreme Council, but Atwood was adamant. Ever the faithful servant, Folger eventually communicated the 33° to General de Mosquera's private secretary, but this action alienated La Sincérité Lodge which had stopped meeting in early 1854.[54]

The members of La Sincérité Lodge seemed to have had enough of Atwood's autocratic rule and on February 20, 1855, petitioned the Grand Lodge of New York for a charter. Their letter to the Grand Master says much about their frustrations and Atwood's apparent promises of eventual recognition by regular Masonry.

> When we made an application to the Supreme Council whose rite is so congenial with our manners and habits, it was with the hope that within a short time a fraternal fusion of the two rites would take place, and allow us to become members of the great Masonical [sic] order of the United States.
>
> Without expanding upon the motives which incite us to place ourselves under your authority, we will only mention that long since our expectations such as we cherished them, have never been realised, and after being constituted two whole years, we still remain at the same point from which we started.[55]

No meetings of the Supreme Council are recorded from April 4, 1853 until March 1, 1855, when the members of La Sincérité Lodge resigned their positions in the Supreme Council. These were Eugene Vatet, Deputy Grand Commander, and Deszelus, Lt. Grand Commander. Also resigning that day was Edward Unkart, Grand Treasurer and a member of the illegally chartered Pythagoras Lodge, who had resigned under pressure from the Grand Lodge of Hamburg. Unkart seemed to tire of controversy and turned to the Grand Lodge of New York to reestablish Pythagoras Lodge with a legitimate charter. Despite alienating firm supporters, losing La Sincérité Lodge, and having four of his principal officers resign, Atwood kept stubbornly on his course.[56]

> A complete line of demarcation had been formed between the supporters of Ill. Bro. Atwood, and his opponents, in this controversy, and so far did this feeling extend, that it was not thought proper to continue the meetings of the body until a better feeling on both sides was manifest.... At the next meeting after the resignations were received and acted upon, Ill. Bro. Atwood, as Sov. Grand Commander—filled all the offices of the Supreme Council by appointment, and determined to go forward, notwithstanding the existing bad feeling....
>
> Among those who remained [in the Supreme Council] there were not such hearty good feelings manifested toward the interests of the Council as there might have been. The prospect was discouraging, and Bro. Atwood not at all inclined to pacify

the discontented by the offer of concessions of any kind. As a natural consequence there was but little interest felt in the meetings and business of the Council was transacted by Bro. Atwood himself.[57]

By 1856 Atwood's health began to fail, "on account of repeated attacks of neuralgic disease, attended with many complications," and he began to look for some place to retire where he could end his days in peace. Still a believer in his absolute power as Sovereign Grand Commander, Atwood appointed Edmund Hays Deputy Grand Commander on November 19, 1857, and on May 14, 1858, named Hays to succeed him upon his death.[58]

Atwood's preference of Hays and eventual appointment of him as Deputy Grand Commander, was too much for even the faithful Folger, who resigned as Grand Secretary General. Atwood had succeeded in driving away another of his supporters. Folger's great dislike of Hays and his reasons for leaving the Supreme Council were made clear in a letter to Enoch Terry Carson in 1881.

> Hays was an infidel in opinion, but exceedingly ignorant and uncultured, & being the pet of Henry C. Atwood, was named by him as his successor.... Like all uncultured men he was a worshiper of Albert Pike, & never rested until he had completely transferred the Rituals & Degrees into the blasphemous languages & doctrines of that plausible deceiver.
>
> In consequence of their perversion of the Truth I have never been at one of their meetings, or associated with them in their bodies, although I loved the order, & wished it well....[59]

Even though Folger was expelled from the Grand Lodge of New York for "aiding and assisting in the formation and organization of a Body, claiming to be a Grand Lodge...,"[60] it's not entirely clear that he ever joined one of St. John's Lodges. On the heels of his fiery response on September 26, 1853, to the charges of unmasonic conduct, Folger meekly requested restoration of membership on June 2, 1857, which was granted June 6. Folger went out like a lion and came back in like a lamb.

The Final Years

Atwood doggedly pressed ahead with Foulhouze's notion of a Supreme Council in every state, even though on November 30, 1854, he had readopted the name "Supreme Council for the United States, their Territories and Dependencies." On March 8, 1858, he conferred the 33° on his nephew, Edward Washington Atwood of Bridgeport, Connecticut, who went on to become Grand Commander of a short-lived and ineffectual Supreme Council for that state. Henry Atwood bought property in Seymour, Connecticut, for his final years and, after selling his business on October 21, 1858, moved back to his home state. He had worked in the New York Custom House under Presidents Jackson and Van Buren. Afterwards he ran for Sheriff of New York County and lost and then served as Surveyor of the Port of New York under President Tyler. In late 1845 he became proprietor of a hotel, the Hermitage Hall on the corner of Allen and Houston streets. In 1855 he is listed in Trow's *New York City Directory* as proprietor of the Keystone Hotel at Division and Christie streets. The scant evidence indicates it was this business he sold before moving to Connecticut.[61]

On November 1, 1858, the Phillips Grand Lodge and the Grand Lodge of New York rejoined on terms honorable to both parties, but they now had no interest in dealing with either St. John's Grand Lodge or Atwood's Supreme Council. Atwood still sounded optimistic on September 14, 1858, just before he left New York.

> We have not yet made much progress as far as regards the first three degrees of the Scottish Rite, but our preparations are good. We have fourteen Lodges in New York which are under the jurisdiction of the Grand Lodge of St. John, and each of these numbers about a hundred members, of which the greater number wish to receive the first three degrees of Scotticism [*sic*].[62]

John Simons was Grand Master of New York at this time; when Grand Secretary General of the Cross Supreme Council in 1862 he had been summarily replaced by Atwood. It was now Simons' turn to issue decrees: no treaty of any sort would be made with St. John's Grand Lodge; its members would be subject to balloting, fees, and initiation like any other non-Mason; and its lodges, if they chose to continue, would have to pay the Grand Lodge of New York the normal fees to receive new charters. There was a lining of generosity in these harsh terms—the St. John's Lodges that joined the Grand Lodge of New York had their fees and their members' fees returned to their treasuries. By 1859 St. John's Grand Lodge had been reabsorbed with barely a whimper.[63]

The last hurrah of Atwood as a schismatic Scottish Rite Mason seems to have occurred on April 11, 1859, when he, Hays, and the other officers of his Supreme Council issued a manifesto. He railed against the Grand Lodge of New York and tried to justify the positions taken by his Supreme Council (emphasis in original): "The Grand Lodge of the State of New York Commits a *monstrous error*, and endeavors to USURP POWER, in arrogating to herself the exclusive administration of the *first three degrees*."[64] Compromise or conciliation were foreign to Atwood's personality.

On Thursday, September 20, 1860, Henry Clinton Atwood was called from labor. His body was returned to New York City where he lay in state in his son Charles' home. On Saturday evening, a meeting was held at the Masonic Temple to pay tribute to Atwood's memory. A committee chaired by John Simons prepared resolutions of respect that were presented to Atwood's family. On Sunday an "immense concourse" attended the religious services and accompanied the body to Greenwood cemetery. Because he was still an expelled Mason, Atwood did not receive a Masonic burial service, but members of his Supreme Council acted as pallbearers and provided a Scottish Rite service.[65]

A memorial published in *The Masonic Messenger* nicely summarized Atwood's turbulent relationship with Masonry.

> His whole life has been enthusiastically devoted, right or wrong, to the Institution [of Masonry].... Whatever of difficulties may have arisen between our lamented friend and the Craft at large, have been solely on matters of governmental policy; we do assert the esoteric duties of a craftsman were always conscientiously performed,

that the call of duty or the cry of distress were ever promptly responded to, and that the arcana of the institution were never committed to more trustworthy hands....

Though of an impulsive nature, and firm in what he deemed to be right, no warmer or more generous friend ever existed.[66]

Nine months later his friends in the Grand Lodge of New York, with whom he had feuded for so many years, set about to ensure that history knew they forgave their errant Brother. On June 6, 1861, the grand lodge paid its final tribute to Atwood. "*Resolved*, that, as far as within the power of this Grand Lodge so to do, the memory of HENRY C. ATWOOD be, and is hereby relieved from censure, and his name be restored to our roll as one of the Past Grand Masters of this Grand Lodge."[67]

5

The Biography of a Remarkable Freemason

May you live in interesting times.
Ancient Chinese Curse

IT IS INSTRUCTIVE TO SEE WHO IS REMEMBERED BY HISTORY, WHO IS forgotten, and who is vilified. Among those who have figured prominently in American Masonry, George Washington has been remembered (and deified), Joseph Cerneau has been vilified, and Robert Folger has been forgotten. Anything Washington did has taken on mythical proportions, and his every involvement with the Craft has been carefully preserved. Cerneau unwittingly lent his name to a movement that almost fractured the harmony of American Freemasonry, and he is now an exemplar of unmasonic cupidity and ambition. Folger's effect on American Masonry was negative. He has earned well-deserved condemnation for reestablishing the Cerneau Supreme Council in 1881 and for the years of turmoil that action produced, but to be completely forgotten seems too harsh a punishment. He was a complex man and dedicated Mason; his life is an interesting study in the sometimes consuming passions of Freemasonry.

Folger lived during times that can be best described as very "interesting." He experienced the anti-Masonic movement first hand, witnessed at least six different Grand Lodges for the state of New York, lived through the American Civil War, and saw more than a dozen Supreme Councils of the Scottish Rite. Through all of this he was seldom an idle bystander, but was actively involved in many of the controversies. He is today

ROBERT B. FOLGER,
Gr∴Sec∴Gen∴H∴E∴

Robert Benjamin Folger, M.D., 33°, Grand Secretary General of the Holy Empire. From *Masonic Chronicle*, vol. 6, no. 10 (Sept. 1884)

viewed as a schismatic, a troublemaker, and one of the most ardent proponents of Cerneauism ever seen. While his Masonic career is perhaps as checkered as the ground floor of King Solomon's Temple, one cannot study his life without feeling that he was indeed a remarkable Freemason.

EARLY LIFE

Robert Benjamin Folger was born on December 16, 1803, in Hudson, New York, a city in Columbia County that had been settled earlier by Quakers. His education began in the Quaker schools and then was continued at a boarding school in Lenox, Massachusetts, some thirty-five miles from Hudson. He returned to Hudson with the intention of completing his preparatory education, but was unable to enter college and moved to New York City in 1817.[1]

After a year in New York, he decided to become a physician and was apprenticed in a wholesale drug store. His apprenticeship lasted a year, following which he took the position of a druggist in an apothecary and entered the College of Physicians and Surgeons Cater with Columbia University) in 1821. He graduated from medical school, probably in 1824, with the M.D. degree and is listed in the 1825 *New York Directory* as a physician living at 39 Harrison Street.[2]

Light in Masonry

In 1824 he was initiated in Fireman's Lodge No. 368 (which later became New York Lodge) at the Old City Hotel in Broadway; this Lodge was a daughter of Independent Royal Arch Lodge No. 2. On February 10, 1826, he was raised to the Sublime Degree of Master Mason, and then began a period of extensive Masonic labors. According to Folger, the Lodges meeting in the Old City Hotel had a "rule in those days for every member to come 'in full dress' ... the ordinary gentleman's dress for dinner, or an evening party. (Black was the rule, with white vests and gloves, etc.)" Refreshments were just as important then as any Lodge ceremony, and members were assessed from $8 to $10 per year (about $160–200 in 2005) for the food. After the first hour or so of a typical meeting, a Lodge would "call off" from about 9:00 to 9:30 to enjoy a half hour of light refreshments: "cold boiled ham, tongue, bread, cheese, wines, liquors, etc." After another hour or so of work, Lodges would close and prepare for supper, which was provided by the hotel for $14 per night (about $280 in 2005), with "the Lodge furnishing its own liquors, cigars, etc." "The supper was always plain and substantial, but varied according to the season," and would be completed by midnight.[3]

New York was quite a cosmopolitan town and offered a great variety of Masonic experiences; Folger indulged in many of these. Though not speaking French, he visited L'Union Français Lodge, which also met in the Old City Hotel, and there witnessed their lengthy initiations in which "the nature of Fire, Air, Earth, and Water were fully demonstrated and developed." (This would imply by today's ritual practices that L'Union Français worked French Modern or Scottish Rite rituals.) Folger also attended their elaborate, quarterly table lodges. He did speak German and regularly visited German Union Lodge, especially during the anti-Masonic period, as it seemed unaffected by the excitement.[4]

More Light in Masonry
Folger's thirst for Masonic knowledge seemed unquenchable. On May 25, 1826, three months after becoming a Master Mason, he became a Royal Arch Mason in Jerusalem Chapter No. 8, R.A.M. Dr. Hans B. Gram presided at his exaltation, and "the acquaintance there formed soon ripened into very close intimacy...." Later he joined Columbia Council No. 1, R.&S.M., with the noted Masonic lecturers James Cushman and John Barker officiating. On June 23, he was made a Red Cross Knight at a joint ceremony of Columbian Encampment No. 1 and Morton No. 4, and on June 30 he was created a Knight Templar by James Herring and joined Morton No. 4. Folger joined the first class organized by Henry C. Atwood to teach the "Cross work" (Masonic Ritual as organized and taught by Jeremy L. Cross). There were twenty Masons in this class, which met from 2:00 to 6:00 P.M. twice a week. On August 23, Folger resigned from Jerusalem Chapter to help form Temple Chapter, which later closed during the anti-Masonic period. Its members (including Folger, presumably) consolidated with Ancient Chapter No. 1, which also closed for the same reason.[5]

Further Light in Masonry
The event to have the most lasting impact on Folger's Masonic career came in the winter of 1826, at the end of a busy Masonic year for him. Folger, Atwood, and the Cross class were initiated through the 32° of the Scottish Rite by Abraham Jacobs for an unreported fee. Trenton, New Jersey, was the site because Jacobs had agreed to stop selling the degrees within forty miles of New York City. "The members of the class were well-satisfied," but they had been misled— Jacobs' patent gave him no authority to confer the degrees! Nonetheless, Folger and Atwood returned to New York content that they were 32° Scottish Rite Masons and joined Lafayette Chapter of Rose Croix, operating under the Cerneau Sovereign Grand Consistory.[6]

Abraham Jacobs moved from New York to Georgia and supplemented his income selling Masonic degrees. While he was willing to stretch his Masonic prerogatives, he did appear scrupulous in requiring his newly elevated Brothers to obtain charters from proper Masonic authorities. Though Folger and Atwood received their degrees in all good faith, their honorable intentions did not save them or the Craft from later controversy and dissension.

It is ironic that some sixty years after receiving the Scottish Rite degrees Folger, at the cost of questioning the regularity of his own degrees, expressed the utmost contempt for Jacobs and his activities. Jacobs had thrown in his lot with the Bideaud Supreme Council, and Folger, ever the faithful defender of Cerneauism, could not allow even a shadow of respectability for anyone who had opposed his beloved movement.

> Jacobs was a Jew peddler of the degrees of the Ancient Accepted Rite, up to the year of his death, 1840. He was not connected with any legitimate body of that Rite,

but was arrayed against them all, by being a peddler and selling the degrees for what he could get from any one who would take them. He had no Masonic standing here whatever, and the introduction of his name in connection with the Ancient Accepted Rite in a favorable manner displays ... ignorance and folly.[7]

In 1824 James Cushman, a well-known American Masonic itinerant lecturer, was made a 33° Inspector General Honorary. From this distance in time it cannot be known if he fully understood the limitations of being an honorary member of the Supreme Council. In any event, whether through ignorance or opportunism, Cushman assumed the prerogatives of an active Inspector General and on November 9, 1827, elevated Henry C. Atwood, his friend and a fellow student of Jeremy L. Cross, to the 33°. Atwood in turn conferred the 33° upon Folger sometime later that year. Folger's reception of all the Scottish Rite degrees, from 4° to 33°, was irregular and illegitimate. When he was eighty-one, it was claimed he was a member of the Supreme Council for the Western Hemisphere during Elias Hicks's term as Grand Commander (ca. 1832–1846). Baynard found no connection of Folger with any Supreme Council prior to 1851, and Folger, in testimony in 1889, only claimed active membership from 1850.[8]

Medicine and Masonry from Denmark

Folger's friendship with Hans B. Gram had a great effect on his medical and Masonic career. Gram is known as the Father of American homeopathy, and shortly after exalting Folger in Jerusalem Chapter, Gram introduced this then new theory of medicine to him. Folger originally dismissed homeopathy, but in August 1826, Gram successfully treated several patients that Folger had deemed incurable. At this point Folger became Gram's student and assistant in order to learn homeopathy.[9]

While living in Copenhagen, Gram had joined Zerubbabel of the North Star Lodge, which worked the rituals of the Rectified Scottish Rite or R.E.R. (Rite Écossais Rectifié). In addition to teaching Folger the theories of homeopathy, Gram apparently taught him the workings of the R.E.R. through at least the Fourth Degree, Scottish Master. In September, 1826, Folger introduced Dr. Gram to his friend Ferdinand L. Wilsey, Master of Minerva Lodge. "Dr. Folger having received from Dr. Gram some important information in Masonry, desired that his friend should also receive the benefit of it." This "important information in Masonry" was initiation through at least the Fourth Degree of the Rectified Scottish Rite. Gram, Folger, and Wilsey then made plans to start a Lodge in New York working the R.E.R. rituals.[10]

The Cipher Manuscripts

Folger took on the task of preserving the R.E.R. ceremonies. He created a remarkably secure cipher in which he wrote the rituals in at least three blank books. Folger Manuscript 1 (FM1), also known as the *Macoy Book* and owned today by the Macoy Publishing and Masonic Supply Co., Inc., of Richmond, Virginia, was dated July 12, 1827. It was copied into Folger Manuscript 2 (FM2), formerly known as the *Supreme Council Book*, now in a private collection. The close involvement of Folger, Gram, and Wilsey in the project is shown on the dedication or bequest page. (Underlining in original.)

> It is my earnest prayer that this book, if it be found among my earthly remains after my decease may be handed over to my dearly beloved Friend and Brother Dr. Hans B. Gram to whom I bequeath it with my thanks for the constant and untired kindness which he has shewed me from the first hour of my acquaintance with him to the present.... If he is not in America at the time of my dissolution—it may be given to Mr. Ferdinand L. Wilsey who will know what it contains and also how to preserve the substance in his mind while he commits the manuscript to the <u>flames</u>.[14]

On June 8, 1827, nine months after Wilsey received the benefit of Gram's "important information in Masonry" and a month before FM1 was dated, a charter was granted to Zorobabel Lodge No. 498 in New York City. Hans B. Gram was the Master; Robert B. Folger, Senior Warden; and Lewis Saynisch, Junior Warden. The Lodge most likely was named to honor Gram's mother Lodge in Copenhagen and must have worked the Rectified Scottish rituals transcribed by Folger. Zorobabel Lodge closed shortly after opening, probably due to the anti-Masonic fever sweeping New York.

In January 1828, Folger moved to North Carolina for his health, and made plans for Gram to join him in the fall in Charlotte to establish a joint practice. Business reverses prevented Gram from coming south and starting a partnership with Folger. Folger became involved in mining and seemed to abandon the practice of medicine. He did not return to New York City until 1835.[12]

RETURN TO NEW YORK

A brief biography of Folger was published during his lifetime in the article, "Homeopathic Directory: New York Historical Sketch," by Henry M. Smith, M.D., in *The New England Medical Gazette*, vol. 6, no. 2 (February 1871). Smith stated that "from conversations with Drs. Wilsey, ... , Folger, ... and others, I have obtained many of the facts herein mentioned." According to Smith, Folger "returned to this city in 1835, was for some time connected with a patent medicine, subsequently retired from the practice of his profession, and gave his attention to mercantile pursuits." William Gardner's *Historical Reminiscences of Morton Commandery No. 4*, however, indicates that Folger returned earlier, as it showed he served as Captain General in 1833. There were no entries for Folger in any New York City directories from 1830–1838. Apparently in 1871, at sixty-eight, Folger's memory had him returning to New York two years after he actually moved.

It is not known if Folger joined or visited any Masonic Lodges while in North Carolina, but he wasted no time in becoming active upon his return to New York City. He was Captain General of Morton No. 4 in 1833. In 1835, New York Lodge No. 368 surrendered its charter, and Folger affiliated with Independent Royal Arch Lodge No. 2 on November 9, 1835, where his advancement was rather rapid. He was Junior Warden in 1836, Senior Warden in 1837, and Master in 1838, 1839, and 1840. In 1838 while serving his first term as Master of I.R.A. No. 2 he was Commander of Morton No. 4. In 1840 he is recorded as attending Grand Lodge twice: on September 2 when he served as

Junior Grand Warden and on December 2 when he served as Grand Standard Bearer, both times with William Willis, Deputy Grand Master, sitting as Grand Master.[13]

The Dutcher Affair

On February 3, 1841, Folger assumed the East at the Shakespeare Hotel for Benjamin C. Dutcher, Master of I.R.A. No. 2, and held an extra meeting under a dispensation from Deputy Grand Master William Willis, also a member of No. 2. A Mr. Page was initiated that evening. During the course of the meeting Folger permitted some "informality" in the proceedings.

Willis visited I.R.A. No. 2 on February 8, 1841, discovered there was no record of the extra meeting, and pointed out Folger's errors. Folger stated that he had the minutes of the meeting, attempted to justify his actions (whatever they were), and held that he would repeat the act under similar circumstances. Willis then apparently bullied the Lodge into unanimously disapproving the proceedings of the earlier meeting. We may infer Folger's actions from the resolution offered by Richard Pennell: "Resolved, That this Lodge consider it improper to bring any Candidate to light until he has taken the usual obligations, and invoked the penalties attached thereto."[14]

Suspended from Masonry

Folger later made a statement to the Grand Lodge, and the affair was referred to a special committee. He asked to speak before the committee with counsel and was denied. The committee then summoned him to appear before them. Folger responded with a letter which was deemed improper to be read, and it was destroyed by the Grand Secretary. On June 4 Folger was suspended until he acknowledged his error. He answered that afternoon with a letter that was also unsatisfactory as it did "not contain an acknowledgment of his error in unequivocal language, nor a satisfactory apology for the indignity offered the Grand Lodge...."[15]

Folger withdrew from Masonry on June 28, 1841, apparently in response to his suspension, though on September 6 and 8 he presided at extra meetings of No. 2. Three weeks later, on September 27, he applied as an adjoining member of Independent Royal Arch, and on November 8 his application was rejected by the lodge. The episode ended on December 13 for Folger when the Master, by authority of Deputy Grand Master Willis, declared Folger a member and ruled his withdrawal invalid because of some technicality. (It is worth adding that during the course of this dispute, Dutcher withdrew from the Lodge, took the Charter to his house, and made arrangements for it to be buried with him!)[16]

Folger had the last word thirty-three years later when he alluded to his case before the Grand lodge and had the opportunity to describe Willis for his readers:

> All [of Willis's] education was of a business kind. Being of limited intellect, as a natural consequence, he was a very superficial man. All that he knew about Masonry was what he had heard and witnessed; research and study were matters that never entered his mind.... He never felt his own incompetence more than when, in the absence of the M.W. Grand Master, he occupied his chair, and he verily believed his

decisions, while there, partook more of the fiat of a monarch than the expression of the opinion of a simple member of the fraternity.

We cite only one instance among many equally striking. A brother who was under accusation, and who demanded an open trial by his peers, with counsel to conduct his case, in preference to going before the Grand Stewards' Lodge, made a motion to that effect before the Grand Lodge. At first, his application was bluntly rejected by him as being out of order and unmasonic, but finding that a majority of the body were largely in its favor, he stated, "that he was entirely and utterly opposed to the proposed course, because he believed it not only contrary to the constitution by which we were governed, but also contrary to the whole spirit of Masonry—still, as he had a great respect for his constituents, he would in the face of his own convictions, put the motion." Strange to say, the vote appeared as unanimous in favor of an open trial, which to him was more than a common disappointment.[17]

Masonic, Medical, and Mercantile Pursuits

A circular in 1843 listed Folger as a member of a committee to form a Freemasons' Hall and Asylum Fund. In 1844 he was again Master of No. 2. He served briefly as Secretary of No. 2 and Trustee of the Asylum Fund in 1845, resigning from each on April 28, 1845. He and Ferdinand Wilsey served together as officers of Morton No. 4 in 1845, Wilsey as Generalissimo and Folger as Captain General; Folger repeated this office in 1846. He tried to start another Lodge in 1847, but for reasons unknown it never was instituted, as the *Proceedings* for 1847 indicate. "The Warrant granted to W. Brother Folger and others, under the name of 'Andrew in the East,' has not been taken up; it is now for the Grand Lodge to say if it should be given, if applied for; no fee has been paid." At a special meeting of Grand Lodge on April 28, 1851, to dedicate the Masonic hall at the corner of Broome and Crosby Streets, Folger participated as Grand Marshal.[18]

Dr. Smith's biography of Folger said he "returned to [New York] city in 1835, was for some time connected with a patent medicine, subsequently retired from the practice of his profession, and gave his attention to mercantile pursuits." Folger's later mercantile pursuits are unknown, but an advertising booklet was published in 1845 entitled *Folger's Hygeiangelos*, which described "Dr. Folger's Olosaonian or All-Healing Balsam." The medicine was claimed to be an effective remedy for consumption, dyspeptic consumption, and asthma, with as little as half a bottle effecting a cure; the testimonials were effusive in their praise. Folger's advertising did not claim any homeopathic origin for his miraculous elixir, but his training with Dr. Gram must have influenced the recipe.[19]

Though Smith's biography said Folger retired from medicine after returning to New York, various city directories showed otherwise. New York City directories from 1839–60 and Brooklyn directories from 1860–67 have Folger listed as a physician, usually with separate addresses for his home and for his practice. It is hard to reconcile Dr. Smith's biography, written in consultation with Folger, with the record of the city directories. Perhaps Folger continued to call himself a "physician" for either professional or social prestige but pursued some medically related business? He did serve in the New York State Assembly in 1849, representing the thirteenth ward of the eleventh district of New York County, so any prestige could also have had political value.[20]

THE REVIVAL OF CERNEAU'S SUPREME COUNCIL

Up to 1850 Folger's Masonic activities had been entirely local to New York City. His only involvement with the Grand Lodge of New York had been to challenge its authority, though he was unwilling to go so far as to join with the schismatic St. John's Grand Lodge (1837–1850). After the "Great Union" of the two Grand Lodges in December 1850, Folger sought out his old Masonic friend, Henry C. Atwood. "We had commenced, in a measure, our Masonic life under his tuition, we had worked together for years, the separation which took place in 1837 had estranged us from each other as Masons for thirteen years, and we now felt a strong desire to have a familiar interview with him, in order to talk over the past."[21]

At their reunion in January 1851, Atwood and Folger discussed their Supreme Council and its future. For largely personal reasons Atwood was insistent the Supreme Council be restored to health with him again in power. (See Chapter 3.) Atwood was hampered by being widely recognized as the force behind the schismatic St. John's Grand Lodge, recently reunited with the regular Grand Lodge. He had served as St. John's Grand Master during its last two years. Folger agreed to help locate a new Grand Commander "who had not been mixed up with past troubles, and who would carry a strong influence as a Mason." Jeremy Cross, the Masonic lecturer, then a merchant in New York City, was just that person.[22]

Cross agreed to help revive the Supreme Council, but insisted on these conditions: 1) the Supreme Council would not charter Craft lodges; 2) only Royal Arch Masons could join the Scottish Rite; and 3) only Knights Templar could advance beyond the 14°. Atwood and Folger agreed to this subservience of the Scottish Rite to the York Rite, in order to use the reputation of Cross to revive their Supreme Council. Their ready agreement, however, was carefully calculated to advance their cause and was not intended to be permanent, as revealed by later comments of Folger. "While the propositions made by Bro. Cross seemed to be fatal to the interests of the Sup. Council, on the other hand it was deemed necessary to secure an establishment of the body, knowing well that Bro. Cross would not long remain the Commander on account of the infirmities of age."[23]

The Supreme Council for the Northern Hemisphere was organized on May 29, 1851, with Cross as Grand Commander, Atwood as Grand Master of Ceremonies, and Folger as Grand Treasurer General. Cross served briefly and resigned in April 1852 because of his health. In October 1852 Atwood resumed the Grand Commandership and reorganized the Supreme Council again, now restricting its jurisdiction to the State of New York. He appointed Folger as Grand Secretary General.

SCOTTISH RITE CRAFT LODGES

In 1853 Atwood made the fateful decision to have his Supreme Council charter Craft lodges, which is the exclusive right of Grand Lodges, and Folger agreed to serve as Master of one of them. The Cerneau Supreme Council's decision plagued it for another fifty years until its final demise. Atwood's motivation was probably power—to have complete control over all of Masonry from 1° to 33°. Folger's motivation is more difficult to understand. He could have been a faithful officer doing everything to support the Grand Commander, regardless of whether he agreed with him. He may have wanted to finally use Gram's R.E.R. rituals, believing them to be for the *Ancient and Accepted* Scottish Rite, not the *Rectified* Scottish Rite. The minutes for March 8, 1853, confirm the deed. "From Bro. Robert B. Folger and others for a Lodge of St. John by the Distinctive title of 'John the Fore-runner' and by Number 1 (See document on file) which petition was granted and the Patent ordered to be made and executed bearing date March 8th 1853 of the Christian Era." The other officers were Charles W. Willets, Senior Warden, and George L. Osborne, Junior Warden.[24]

In 1874, over twenty years after the event, Folger revealed his thoughts on the Lodge and gave a clue that it intended to use Gram's R.E.R. rituals (emphasis added):

> The petition [to charter John the Forerunner Lodge] is believed to have been the first effort made in this country to establish the French system in the English language. *And for this purpose a very beautiful and minute translation of the French ritual into the English, together with the consecration, the installation, and the table rituals and ceremonials, with abundant and minute directions,* had been procured, and everything was in readiness to go forward. But at this juncture there was some misgivings on the part of the founders—although the ritual was entirely and essentially different from the York Rite so much so that it could not be taken for Masonry, as practiced at the present day; yet there were certain things about it which led to the determination, on the part of the founders, to abandon the project altogether—and it proved to be a wise course. The lodge was never constituted, and *the rituals, etc., are now in our possession.*[25]

Whatever Folger's motivation, the Grand Lodge of New York reacted forcefully. A committee was appointed on June 7, 1853, to investigate the matter; it reported back on June 10. They deemed "the fact of the establishment of such Lodges an invasion of the jurisdictional rights of [the Grand Lodge of New York]." Folger, Atwood, and their Supreme Council were on a collision course with the Grand Lodge of New York.[26]

FURTHER CONTROVERSY

While the controversy over the Scottish Rite Craft lodges was growing, yet another crisis in New York Masonry developed with Atwood and Folger in the lead. On June 9, 1853, Reuben H. Walworth, Chancellor (now Governor) of New York, was elected Grand Master of the Grand Lodge. His election caused an uproar because Atwood and others alleged that during the anti-Masonic period (ca. 1826–1840) Chancellor Walworth had publicly denounced Masonry. Atwood stated he would not sit in Grand Lodge with Walworth. On June 13 a meeting of Masons opposed to Walworth was held in Tollerton Hall where Robert Folger and others spoke against the election. A committee of three, including Folger, was appointed to consider grievances against the Grand Lodge and reported back on June 20, urging the reestablishment of St. John's Grand Lodge until Chancellor Walworth's term as Grand Master expired. "Whereupon, all present came forward, and pledged themselves to the firm support of the same." St. John's Grand Lodge was revived formally on June 24, 1853, when Henry Atwood installed the new Grand Officers.[27]

Suspended Again from Masonry

Fitz Gerald Tisdall, a Past Master of St. John's Lodge No. 1, brought charges against Folger for his activity with the revived St. John's Grand Lodge. The Scottish Rite lodges must have become a non-issue, as they were not mentioned in the charges against Folger.

> Charge 1st. **Unmasonic Conduct** ... For aiding and assisting in the formation and organization of a Body, claiming to be a Grand Lodge....
>
> Charge 2nd. For exciting by inflammatory appeals a spirit of revolt against the Grand Lodge and its Officers, amongst a portion of the fraternity of the City and State.[28]

Folger answered these charges with a strongly worded letter, no doubt similar to his 1841 letter to the Grand Lodge, which had been deemed "unproper to be read" (underlining in original):

> It strikes me that it would have been more proper on the part of the body to which you belong to have selected some member of my own Lodge to have preferred these charges, or any others, against me.... But like all other filthy proceedings of that Grand Body, I suppose they were unable to find a man who was acquainted with me, who would so far debase himself, as to bring these charges, based upon falsehood, against me, & so they used the most fitting tool they had at hand—I will not sully this paper by mentioning his name....
>
> The "aiding & assisting in the formation & organization of a Grand Lodge" in accordance with the spirit of the institution, was not an invasion of the rights of the body now styled by yourself & others "The Most Worshipful Grand Lodge"—For if the malappropriation of the monies in its treasury was not sufficient cause to deprive it of its name & power, the election of Reuben H. Walworth to the office of Grand Master was so humiliating to the friends & advocated of the true principles of Masonry, that it gave rise to a feeling of utter contempt toward those who participated in the deed....
>
> I demand of you & the body which you represent, that if my Expulsion is published this answer (of which I have an attested copy) together with the whole proceedings, be published—in full—
>
> And further—hereby notify you & through you, the body which you represent, that any publication of my name with a view to injure my character or reputation
>
> Or in any way so that the full proceedings are not published & made known—Will be met on my part with all the redress which the Law gives me
>
> Besides which, if you do not publish the full proceedings I will publish them for you & take excellent care that they have an honest circulation.
>
> Respectfully,
>
> *Robt. B. Folger*[29]

He was suspended on September 27, 1853, by the Grand Lodge of New York for refusing to appear at Grand Lodge and for an unmasonic communication. It is not known if the root cause was organizing a schismatic Grand Lodge, chartering a clandestine Lodge, or perhaps some other offense. On December 9, 1853, he was suspended by Morton Encampment.

Revocation of the Preface

Folger revoked the preface and bequest contained in FM1 on September 25, 1854. An X was drawn through the page, and the name of Ferdinand L. Wilsey was almost totally obliterated. Hans Gram's name was untouched, but he had died in 1840. No reason for the revocation was given, but tenuous circumstantial evidence points to events surrounding Folger's recent expulsion from Grand Lodge.

It is clear from his blistering letter of September 26, 1853, to Grand Lodge that Folger did not like Fitz Gerald Tisdall. Tisdall was a member of Morton Encampment No. 4, Folger's Encampment, and had served as Generalissimo in 1852. After preferring charges against Folger in September 1853, Tisdall had charges of unmasonic conduct brought against him on December 6, 1853, and was expelled from his Lodge on March 9, 1854. Tisdall also was expelled from Morton No. 4, and tried to fight that by claiming "the alleged offense was committed before he (Tisdall) became attached to this branch of the Order; therefore, Morton Encampment [should have] no jurisdiction." On June 8 Tisdall's expulsion from Grand Lodge was rescinded, and his case referred back to his Lodge, St. John's No. 1. During all this legal maneuvering, Morton No. 4 held a meeting on September 23, 1854, the day before Folger revoked the preface of FM1.[30]

Neither Folger, Wilsey, nor Tisdall are shown as members of Morton No. 4 in 1854. The minutes do not show any of them attending the meeting on September 23 nor do they record any discussion relating to any of them. But the issue of Tisdall and Folger could have been discussed after the meeting. What if Wilsey had spoken favorably of Tisdall's appeal, either as an unrecorded attendee or shortly after the meeting? What if Folger heard of Wilsey's support of Tisdall's position? Perhaps this would have been enough to set off the fiery-tempered Folger and to cause him to obliterate Wilsey's name from the preface? In the absence of more evidence, this flimsy but possible explanation is all that is available.

Return to the Fold

St. John's Grand Lodge eventually was abandoned about 1859. Folger clearly states that he never participated in its activities, even though he was expelled for advocating its reestablishment. "We were not one of their number, nor did we ever visit one of their lodges. We were intimately connected with Ill. Bro. Atwood, in the Supreme Grand Council, and from him received all the leading matters which have been published concerning St. John's Grand Lodge of 1853."[31]

Shortly before June 2, 1857, Folger petitioned the Grand Lodge of New York to restore his membership. His mildly worded request is an ironic contrast to his earlier answer to the charges of unmasonic conduct; Folger left like a lion and returned like a lamb.

> To the Most Worshipful Grand Lodge of the State of New York
>
> The undersigned would respectfully present the following request.
>
> At a Communication of the Grand Stewards Lodge in 1853 he was expelled by that body for Contempt. The expulsion was confirmed by the Grand lodge. He asks that the said expulsion may be rescinded and he be restored.

> New York - July 12th 1825.
>
> It is my earnest Prayer, that this book if it be found among my earthly remains after my decease may be handed over to my dearly beloved Friend and Brother Dr Hans B Gram to whom I bequeath it with my thanks for the Constant and untired kindness which he has shewed me from the first hour of my acquaintance with him to the present — to whom I feel that I never can be too gratefull — and whose good will I desire to seek to my latest breath. If he is not in America at the time of my dissolution - it may be given to ~~————~~ who will know what it Contains and also how to preserve the substance in his mind while he Commits the manuscript to the flames. This he will do for the sake of one who loves him with a Brothers love and who has desired during his life to merit his esteem.
>
> Robert B Folger

Revoked Sept 25th 1854

The preface to Folger Manuscript 1, revoked on September 25, 1854.

Being one of the oldest living members of Independent Royal Arch Lodge No. 2 and having served her faithfully for a long series of years, he desires to be placed in a position by which he can constitutionally commute and pay his dues to his Lodge.

He is not now, nor has he been, a member in any other Lodge nor is he in any manner connected with any other subordinate Lodge of any kind.

A warm attachment to the Masonic Institution and the principles which it inculcates has prompted this request.

Respectfully submitted,

Robt. B. Folger[32]

He was restored to membership on June 6, 1857, with the Committee on Grievances noting that "he was expelled for words used in the heat of debate, and not for 'any violation of the moral law or the fundamental principles of Masonry' as required by ... the present Constitution...." There is no record that he actually rejoined Independent Royal Arch Lodge No. 2 or any of the other bodies in which he had been active.[33]

With his 1841 suspension overturned on a technicality and his 1853 expulsion rescinded because he had not violated any "fundamental principle of Masonry," Folger was able to say in 1884 with a clear conscience (and perhaps a selective memory). "No charges have ever been preferred against me by the Fraternity, nor have I ever been expelled (except by the '*Highest Prerogatives of the Northern Jurisdiction*,' without charges or specifications, without a Summons to answer, without a Trial or Conviction) and this I consider an HONOR rather than a DISGRACE."

RESIGNATION AS GRAND SECRETARY GENERAL

In 1856 Henry Atwood's health began to fail "on account of repeated attacks of neuralgic disease, attended with many complications," and he made plans for a transfer of power in his Supreme Council. He appointed Edmund Hays Deputy Grand Commander on November 19, 1857, and on May 14, 1858, named Hays to succeed him upon his death. Atwood's appointment of Hays as Deputy Grand Commander was too much for even the faithful Folger, who resigned as Grand Secretary General at the same meeting.[35]

Folger's published reasons for his resignation reflect only credit upon his beloved Supreme Council:

> In consequence of the removal of Bro. Atwood from New York City, the Grand Secretary General thought proper to tender his resignation. He had served four years under the direction of Ill. Bro. Atwood, during which he had labored hard, and "had done what he could" to promote the interests of the body. The calls of business had very much increased upon him during the then recent panic, beside which he was engaged in collecting documents and collating a history of the Rite.

Further, he expected to be absent from the city for several months for unspecified reasons, though there is no evidence he ever left.[36]

In a letter to Enoch Terry Carson in 1881, Folger revealed his great dislike for Hays, which doubtless was the real reason for his resignation.

Hays was an infidel in opinion, but exceedingly ignorant and uncultured, he being the pet of Henry C. Atwood, was named by him as his successor.... Like all uncultured men he was a worshiper of Albert Pike, & never rested until he had completely transferred the Rituals & Degrees into the blasphemous languages and & doctrines of that plausible deceiver.

In consequence of their perversion of the Truth I have never been at one of their meetings, or associated with them in their bodies, although I loved the order, & wished it well....[37]

LATER YEARS

With his resignation as Grand Secretary General, Folger changed the nature of his involvement with Masonry. He became a historian and writer of the gentle craft, even as he continued his strong opinions and sharp words. In 1862 he published his notorious book, *The Ancient and Accepted Scottish Rite in Thirty-Three Degrees*, which was the most rigorous defense of Cerneauism ever seen. It formed the foundation for all later claims of legitimacy for Cerneauism. While he claimed no partiality in his history, a casual reading contradicts this.

Defending the Cerneau Supreme Council

Enoch T. Carson summarized the strengths and weaknesses of Folger's book:

> Mr. Folger belonged to what was known as the "Cerneau Supreme Council," and his history throughout reveals a strong bias towards his party.
>
> The history proper, in that work, [is] the first part of the volume, ... and in view of the author's well developed prejudice, this part of the work may be taken *cum grano salis*.
>
> The "Documents" ... form the second and by far the more valuable portion of the work, for they are authentic, and many of them are printed for the first time from the original manuscripts, or reprinted in many cases from the excessively rare original pamphlets.[38]

Among other things, Folger claimed "the whole proceedings of Stephen Morin and his successors, from the beginning, have been illegal and unmasonic...." Folger attacked the Mother Supreme Council for admitting Jews to the 17° through the 32°, claiming these teach Christian doctrines and should be reserved for Christians:

> These degrees, or at least some of them, are founded upon, and promulgate the peculiar doctrines of Christianity, more especially, the Divinity, Death, Resurrection and Ascension of the Messiah, our common Lord. The right of possession to all the degrees of Masonry, up to the Sixteenth of the Ancient and Accepted Rite, is claimed by all sects of people alike, because they are not based upon, and have no direct allusion to these doctrines. But the Statutes of the Order, as well as the moral sense of the members of the institution require that a Jew should go no further in these mysteries, because he is not a believer in the doctrines which they assume to teach.[39]

Finally he claimed the Ancient and Accepted Scottish Rite did not originate in Charleston in 1801, but had begun earlier in France where it eventually was taken over by the Grand Orient of France. Thus all authority for the Scottish Rite emanated from the Grand Orient. His theory was that

> the Count de Grasse ... established a Sup. Gr. Council in Paris in 1804. That Council was in existence just 44 days, when ... it merged into, or united with, the Gr. Orient of France. Thus the Grand Orient came into possession of all that Sup. Gr. Council had in the way of degrees, although that was not much of an acquisition, as the Grand Orient had possessed all the degrees for Forty years before the Union [of the Cerneau and Northern Supreme Councils] took place.[40]

He went on to explain that the Grand Orient of France "regularized" Cerneau's Sovereign Grand Consistory in New York in 1813. In short, Folger's history at times confuses the Scottish Rite and the Order of the Royal Secret (often called the Rite of Perfection) and is at odds with what can be accepted and verified today. Whether he willfully invented some of his "history" or was misled by others is not known. He seems to have interpreted the evidence to suit his prejudices.

THE UNION OF 1867 AND TEMPORARY PEACE

The Cerneau and regular Supreme Councils united in 1867 to form the current Supreme Council, 33°, for the Northern Masonic Jurisdiction. Folger seemed happy to see the union, which ended the bitter factionalism tearing at the Scottish Rite. "We now behold the fruits of these negotiations in the forming of one, united, and undivided Supreme Council, under the old banner of 'Union Toleration Power,' and we believe it to be the sincere desire of every brother of our beautiful Rite, that this union may continue for all time 'one and indivisible.'"[41]

These words would become sadly ironic in 1881 when he and others withdrew from the united Supreme Council to reestablish the Cerneau Supreme Council. Folger signed an Oath of Fealty to the new Supreme Council and then seemed to have slowed his Masonic labors even more. His son, Robert Benjamin Folger, Jr., was born in 1868 when Folger was sixty-eight.

In 1872 he wrote to Josiah H. Drummond, Sovereign Grand Commander, N.M.J., and proposed rewriting and republishing his history, with the hope that the proceeds might benefit his family. This may have been an indication of financial difficulties for Folger. Drummond did not accept his offer. Still hoping to have the Supreme Council republish his book, Folger wrote to Enoch T. Carson, Lieutenant Grand Commander, in 1873. Folger explained about his book "that it was written at a time when party spirit in Masonic matters ran high, & being an old member of the Cerneau body, devotedly attached to that section & all its interests, indulged largely in sharp words & many expressions which would now be deemed objectionable in the highest degree. 8ut the true history of the Rite is not marred."

This is perhaps Folger's indirect confession to some historical inaccuracies in the book. The Supreme Council finally purchased the manuscript from him for $500, though the book was never published. Its full title is "A History of the Ancient Accepted Scottish Rite in the United States: More Especially as Connected with the Operations of the So-Called Cerneau Supreme Council from its Organization in New York in 1807, to its Final Absorption into the Supreme Council of the Northern Jurisdiction of the U.S. in 1867."[42]

Much of the material is taken from a series of forty-three "Recollections of a Masonic Veteran," published by Folger from April 20, 1873, to September 20, 1874, in the *New York Dispatch*. These articles provide a fascinating glimpse into early New York Masonry and the many controversies that swirled around the fraternity. Folger's writing is peaceful and polite, even about those with whom he clashed. It is easy to conclude he thought this would be one of the last things he wrote, so he reviewed his career in Masonry through rose-colored glasses. He still maintained his partisanship for the Cerneau Supreme Councils but managed a few kind words for their opponents.

The Reprinted History

In 1876 Folger attended the only Supreme Council session after he signed the Oath of Fealty in 1867. By this time Harry Seymour's Ancient and Primitive Rite of about ninety degrees had condensed itself to a rite of thirty-three degrees and was claiming to be the only legitimate Supreme Council in the U.S. as the successor to Joseph Cerneau. In June 1880 Seymour resigned as Grand Commander in favor of William H. Peckham. (Peckham actually had bought the Grand Commandership from Seymour for several hundred dollars!) Peckham sought to put his Supreme Council on firmer footings and turned to Folger for help. Peckham contracted with Folger to reprint his history of 1862 with a supplement to bring it up to 1881. Five hundred copies were to be printed, and the Peckham Supreme Council paid $700 in advance for 175 copies. What happened next is confused.[43]

The second edition of Folger's history was printed in 1881 with the update, but pages 99–104 of the supplement emphatically argued that the Peckham Supreme Council was the only legitimate Scottish Rite body in the United States. Folger claimed his good name had been used dishonestly to advance the Peckham cause because these pages had been written by someone else and had been inserted without his knowledge. For a while Folger sold copies of the history with pages 99–104 cut out; later he kept the book intact but pasted in a note disclaiming authorship of the offending pages. His motives in disclaiming the pages were obscured when he soon thereafter revived yet another Cerneau Supreme Council, it too claiming to be the only legitimate source for the Scottish Rite. The pages in question were harmful to Folger's new cause as they argued against the legitimacy of any Supreme Council except Peckham's. Folger's detractors point to the deceptive reasoning of the supplement as an example of his unreliability as a historian and his willingness to prostitute himself.

The Final Controversy

At its September 1881 session the Supreme Council, N.M.J., voted to publish a series of articles by Charles T. McClenachan. These were a condensed history of Scottish Rite

Supreme Councils which contradicted much of Folger's writings. In particular McClenachan questioned Cerneau's possession of the 33°, the sine qua non of his authority to establish a Supreme Council. McClenachan said, "It has been asserted that prior to the year 1822, at least, Joseph Cerneau had not regularly received the 33d degree, and those whose greatest interest it was to prove the contrary have failed in response." On September 20 at the same session Albert Pike, Grand Commander, S.J., addressed the Supreme Council. In Folger's words, Pike, for the "twenty-five years past, with all the polite bitterness he was capable of expressing, and all the malice he could politely bring to bear, Denounced, Defamed, & Spit at every man that loved the name of Joseph Cerneau, and every Masonic organization that manifested the least proclivity towards the doctrines taught by his bodies or himself."[44]

McClenachan's history of Scottish Rite Supreme Councils was an assault, albeit in polite, scholarly terms, on Folger's crowning achievement as a historian. Albert Pike's mere presence was an assault on any Cerneau Mason, and it is not known what Pike may have said about Cerneau when he addressed the Supreme Council. On top of these indirect attacks on Folger, charges of unmasonic conduct had been preferred against him for the claims of legitimacy for the Peckham Supreme Council in the supplement of his recently reprinted history. Folger submitted his resignation from the Supreme Council, but it was refused on September 22 until the charges of unmasonic conduct could be resolved.[45]

On September 27, 1881, Folger began his last fight against the Masonic status quo. He, Hopkins Thompson, and several other old Cerneau men resigned their honorary memberships in the Supreme Council, withdrew their Oaths of Fealty, and revived the Cerneau Supreme Council! All this came less than eight months after Folger had printed in his history that "he [disclaimed] any partiality for either of the parties, having long since withdrawn his connection with the 'High Degrees.' " In the reborn Cerneau Supreme Council, Thompson became Sovereign Grand Commander and Folger resumed his old office of Grand Secretary General. This body had an uneven existence and died out about thirty years later. Charges were preferred against Folger and the other seceders on December 19, 1881, by the Supreme Council, N.M.J., and they were expelled at the September 1882 session.[46]

Folger tried to provide a rationale for his discordant actions. He claimed the union of the Supreme Councils in 1867 was fatally flawed because of irregularities at the meeting of the Cerneau Supreme Council that planned it. Edward W. Atwood neatly captured the spirit of the union of 1867, "I got the impression that they thought that although they might not have done what was right in every respect, they had done what they thought was for the best." Folger's arguments (and those of Cerneau supporters that followed him) are intricate and legalistic, as if they were arguing a point of constitutional law or religious doctrine. It was not enough that the Supreme Councils had put their differences behind them and joined to work for the common good. If the united Supreme Council would not acknowledge Joseph Cerneau as the only origin of authentic Scottish Rite Masonry in the United States, then Folger and his colleagues would not participate.[47]

Folger worked faithfully to establish the "Ancient Council" as a Masonic power. His efforts were remarkably successful and probably tell more about organizational weaknesses of the Supreme Council, N.M.J., than about Joseph Cerneau's authorities. Folger later took on the less strenuous job of Corresponding Grand Secretary in 1885 and on July 23, 1892, made a "long journey of over six miles" from Brooklyn to New York City to attend an informal meeting of Sovereign Grand Inspectors General where he made a speech. This was his last recorded Masonic activity, for on September 13, 1892, at eighty-nine years of age, he was called from labor at his home. On September 16, 1892, Masonic services were conducted at his residence by Silentia Lodge No. 198, and he was buried the next day in the family plot in Oak Wood Cemetery at Nyack-on-the-Hudson. He left a wife, Anna C., and a son, Robert B., Jr. His wife survived him by only a few months, passing away on November 19, 1892.[48]

Thus ended the career of a zealous Craftsman. Folger's life and activities indicated a passion for the gentle Craft that was at times overwhelming in its intensity. He did not fear challenging established authority, whether the medical community, the Grand Lodge, or the Supreme Council. In almost all cases he acted in a manner that can be viewed as honorable and certainly in a manner that he felt was in the best interests of Freemasonry. Whether he is viewed as a rogue and a charlatan or a sincere Craftsman whose error was to choose the losing sides of several battles, it is easily agreed that he was indeed a remarkable Mason.

6

Folger Manuscript 1

HIS CIPHER MANUSCRIPT, ALSO KNOWN AS THE *MACOY BOOK*, WAS THE first of at least three books of Masonic ritual that Robert B. Folger prepared. The preface is dated July 12, 1827, which probably is the date he started or stopped writing. The preface and bequest were subsequently revoked on September 25, 1854. It was written in a strange hieroglyphic-like cipher in a black leather-bound book on thirty-three of eighty-eight 4¾ × 7½ inch pages. It appears to be a blank book from a stationery store, the pages are watermarked "Lathrop & Willard" with yellow fore edges, and the front and back covers are bordered in gold with a large gold cross embossed in the center.

From 1881 to his death in 1892, Folger served as Grand Secretary General of the Cerneau Supreme Council. His offices were at the same address as the Masonic Publishing Co., 63 Bleeker St., New York City, one of the predecessor firms of Macoy Publishing and Masonic Supply Co. On his death, at least this one of the ritual books came to the Masonic Publishing Co. and eventually to Macoy Co. where it is still today.

Harold Van Buren Voorhis, Vice-President of Macoy Co., used 2 pages from FM1 to illustrate his article, "Masonic Alphabets" in the 1952 *Proceedings of the Ohio Chapter of Research*. The book lay forgotten in Macoy's archives until the early 1990s when Brent Morris started researching Folger's cipher rituals. Mrs. Vee Hanson of Macoy generously opened their archives to him, gave him a copy of the book, and encouraged him to publish his research. His analysis of FM1 was the 1993 volume of the Masonic Book Club, *The Folger Manuscript: The Cryptanalysis and Interpretation of an American Masonic Manuscript*.

Folger Manuscript 1

(4.1)DISCIPULUS

[First Section]

[The candidate is conducted to the Chamber of Preparation[1] where he is seated.]

Introductor.[2]   Hither we have come. Let us now rest for a short time. I beg you to abstract yourself from all worldly thoughts for a short space of time and to devote this time to the consideration of yourself and such things as may here occur to you.

[*Shows cross*][3] To the place of which this is a symbol we must all sooner or later come. (86.26)It is dark, black, separated from the world. (4.3)The rules of our Order have made me bring you here. Let me make you acquainted with these things.

[*Shows hourglass*] The hourglass, an emblem of time. Turns it. Behold how rapidly the particles of sand run. It will soon run out, and then, if no external power set it in motion again, its movements will never be renewed. Forget this not.

Here is water for your refreshment.

[*Shows skull*[4]] Here is an image of death and an emblem of mortality. No human philosophy or thinking can divine what lies on the other side of this veil or what shall happen to us there, yet it is certain we shall all thence, and it is certain that duration beyond the grave, in comparison to the period of human life, is infinite. This subject is interesting then.

[*Shows bible*[5]] See, here is the only light by which we can learn how to enter the grave so as to enjoy happiness hereafter. It is the book of wisdom and contains a revelation of the Divine will.

(2.1)Question First: Do you believe in the existence of a God, perfect and good,[6] the creator of all things?

Second: Do you believe in the immortality of the soul?

Third: What do you believe is your duty toward God, your neighbor, and yourself?

Here it is proper for a Deputy to return to the Master the aspirant's answer.

(3.1)**Introductor.** The Lodge have commanded me to inform you respecting some of our customs and to prepare you in a proper manner to be brought to the Lodge in order to be accepted a Disciple. Permit me to advise you: I would encourage you to exercise fortitude in the trials you are about to endure and to place confidence in those

---

1. The phrase "Chamber of Preparation" does not appear here, but it is at FM1:9.21–22.
2. The speaker is not identified, but the text which follows this on FM1:3.1, begins, "Introductor: The Lodge have commanded me...." Thus the Introductor seems to be an officer of the Lodge responsible for conducting candidates to the Chamber of Preparation.
3. No object is identified, but on FM1:11.29, is written, "✝ When thou has passed to the place of which this is a symbol, thy destiny will be fixed forever."
4. No object is identified.
5. No object is identified.
6. The manuscript reads, "in the xstnce of a *j*, perft and good." The letter *j* can represent the word *God*, FM:2.38.3.

who shall conduct you on the way in which you have concluded to enter upon. The first sign of your ready determination to join us is to deliver me your hat and sword.

[*Speaking to the Deputy*] Brother, please deliver this to the Lodge and return hither to me again.

Sir, will you please to lay from you all money, jewels, metal, and other signs of distinction; uncover your left breast and expose the knee; tread down the left shoe. Now, Sir, you are externally prepared to be presented to the Lodge, and it is pleasing to me to believe that your heart and thoughts correspond with this external preparation, and that you have taken, and will continue to take, all possible pains to eradicate all prejudices and emotions of the mind which militate against your proper duties as a man.

But Sir, you must be convinced that a (5.1)man who is stripped of all sensual and false decorations and ornaments and coverings of vanity cannot be known and distinguished from others but by righteousness and virtue. It is absolutely necessary that you henceforth be convinced of your own weakness and that it is impossible to go forward toward the Temple of Truth without help and guidance.

In order to give us a plain token of your want of confidence in yourself, you must permit us to deprive you of the light. It is an emblem of the false views which are the lot of that man who is left to his own guidance.

Bandage [*is placed over candidate's eyes*].

Tell me, can you see any thing? On your honour? Be careful not to use deception with him who shall guide you. You will else presently certainly repent.

You are now in darkness, but fear not. Those who guide you go in light and will not lead you astray. Hold your hands before you and guard against the hindrances that can meet you. You are now left alone. Strive to go forward, but use the utmost prudence in order to avoid surrounding danger.

[*The candidate*] *takes three steps forward.*

I acknowledge you as one who seeks. I mark well your serious desire, but in thick darkness and alone you would undoubtedly go astray.

[*The Introductor*] *takes his left hand and says:*

As such I will bring you to the Lodge. I pray, be constant and confident, learn to suffer with patience and abstinence, and thereby make yourself worthy to obtain in time what at present you ask for. Follow me. Fear not.

Three knocks [*at the door*][7]

DEACON.[8] Who comes here?
INTRODUCTOR. One in darkness who seeks light and wishes to be accepted.
DEACON. His name? Age? Father's name? Where born? Profession? Religion? And has

---

7. FM1:5.12. Three gavels are drawn in the text, which are translated here as knocks. Later translations as knocks or gavels are mate without further comment.

8. FM1:5.12. The manuscript reads, "D. Who cms h."

he made any vow that forbids his joining the Masonic fraternity? Enter, Sir.

INTRODUCTOR. Here I have brought you. My task is now finished. You are in safe hands, even with them who deserve your perfect confidence.

When in the west and the Guide[9] has left him Master says:

W.M. Thus, Sir, you have sought (2.4)to be received among us. This your request we have seriously attended to, and from the good opinion we have conceived of your character, and as one of our Brethren has pledged himself for you in a solemn manner, and he who I sent to inquire as to your motives in joining us and your opinion of our institution has reported so favorably of you, we have therefore sent you a Guide who has opened our door to you, and now you are in the midst of us in a state fit for trials which you must endure and which everyone who wishes to be received among us must endure, remembering that the present is a state of trial.

But, Sir, before we can proceed further, I have some questions to ask to you which I must require an audible and unequivocal answer. But first, Sir, I must state to you that there is nothing in our Order which is incompatible with religion or with civil or moral duties. For the truth of this we pledge you our honour.

And I now ask you if you are prompted to join us by a desire of being charitable and useful to your fellow man?

Second, are you prompted to join us by a desire of the knowledge of truth and to be associated with those who profess to promulgate it and encourage virtue and laudable pursuits?

Third, will you conform to the regulations of the Freemasons and do you voluntarily request to be made a Mason?

Well then, your request shall be granted you. God give at some future day it may serve to make you happy. You are about to be going on a mysterious journey, and, although you cannot see the way, yet confiding in him who leads you, go forward with firmness, yet with caution, and rest assured that your guide will not bring you in paths where you should not go.

Three gavels

GUIDE. Sir, the naked sword pointing to your heart is but a weak symbol of the dangers which surround one who wanders in darkness, put your trust in God and fear not. Come with me.

First Round

(4.12)Man was created in the image of God, but who can know him when he deforms himself?

Second Round

He who is ashamed of religion and of truth is unfit for and unworthy of fraternity.

---

9. FM1:5.15. The manuscript reads, "and the G has left him."

Third Round

      That man whose ear is deaf to the cries and the distresses of his fellow man is a monster in the assembly of the Brethren.

W.M. Let him now ascend the three first mysterious steps leading to the Temple to try his strength, and then bring him to the East to make his vow.

      Sir, your patience has enabled you to reach an altar at which, by the rules of our Order, you are required to make a solemn and irrevocable oath or covenant never unlawfully to reveal any of the secrets, symbols, signs, or ceremonies belonging to the Order of Free and Accepted Masons. You have already been assured that the Order does not contain anything contrary to our duties toward God, our country, our neighbors, or ourselves. This assurance I now repeat to you and ask you if you are willing to make the oath or covenant required? What do you answer?

      But, Sir, before you can make a covenant, it is necessary that you be well acquainted with its tenure, we holding it to be wrong to make a covenant with any unless they be well acquainted with its conditions. Therefore, you will please to kneel on the left knee on the square and let your right hand rest upon the Bible, on which lies the square and compasses covered with a sword. Sir, the book on which your hand now rests is the Holy Bible opened at the first chapter of St. John and the fifth verse where there is written, "And the light shineth in darkness; and the darkness comprehended it not."

      Do you believe that your hand thus rests upon the Bible? And why do you believe it? Thus you conceive that a man, upon the serious assurance, can believe the thing of which he has no other evidence than this assurance?

      Now, I desire you to be attentive to the voice of the Senior Warden who will repeat to you the covenant which you are required to make, even in the presence of the Supreme Architect of the Universe, and which, when made, can not be recalled.

[*The Disciple's Obligation follows, but later, for reasons unknown, Folger encrypted another, nearly identical version, which is printed with the first for comparison.*]

[DISCIPLE'S] (6.1)OBLIGATION	(16.20)DISCIPLE'S VOW IN FULL FORM
S.W. I do promise, solemnly and sincerely, in the presence of God and this Lodge of Freemasons, that I will be faithful and true to the holy Christian religion and to the government of the country in which I live, and that I will strive to gain the esteem and love of my fellow man by practicing virtue and shunning vice, and by encourag-	**S.W.** I do promise, faithfully and sincerely, in the presence of God and this Lodge, that I will be faithful and true to the holy Christian religion and to the government of the country in which I live, and that I will strive to gain the love and esteem of my fellow men by practicing virtue and shunning vice and by encouraging others

ing others so to do. And I promise that I will, as far as I can, help the distressed, and that I will conceal from everyone who is not a Free and Accepted Mason all the secrets, signs, symbols, and usages of this Order and every part thereof, and I will not unlawfully reveal any of these things, nor write them on anything, or make them legible so that the secrets of our Order can thereby be unlawfully revealed. And I will strive to cherish and love all worthy and good Brethren Free and Accepted Masons as Brothers, and should I violate this oath, the keeping of which I solemnly promise, I am willing to be looked upon by all honest and good men and all Freemasons as a man without honour and every praiseworthy quality and deserving their contempt and disdain. And I now repeat my wish to be made a Mason. So help me God.

so to do. And I promise that I will, as far as I can, help the distressed. I also promise that I will conceal from everyone who is not a Mason all the secrets, symbols, signs, and usages of this Order and every part thereof, and I will not reveal unlawfully any of these things, nor write these on anything, nor make them legible to others whereby the things and matters or secrets or usages shall be unlawfully revealed. And I will skive to cherish and love all worthy and good Brethren of the Order as Brothers, and should I violate this oath, the keeping of which I solemnly promise, I am willing to be looked upon by all honest (17.1) and good men and all Masons as a man without honour and every praiseworthy quality and deserving their contempt and disdain. And I now repeat my wish to be made a Mason. So help me God.

W.M. (6.11)Have you heard and rightly understood this solemn covenant? Are you willing to make it and to sanction it according to the customs of our Order? I ask you for the last time.

One gavel.

In order Brethren, and while this man makes this covenant, let us give a token of our accordance with it.

[*The candidate repeats the covenant.*]

You are now bound to us and we to you by this your oath, but the trial of your sincerity, which is the hardest trial, is now at hand. You have said that you would sanction this covenant according to the customs of the Order. Are you willing to sanction it with your blood if it should be required of you?

(3.11)Then I accept you as a Disciple in Masonry, to the honour of almighty God, in the name of fraternity,[10] and by virtue of the power vested in me, Amen.

Response [*by the candidate*]

---

10. FM1:3.11. The manuscript reads, "N the nme of F." This is the same formula as used in the opening of a Disciple's Lodge, where *fraternity* is spelled out.

W.M. Arise.

This last trial, your being willing to sanction your vows with your blood, is convincing of your sincerity and I now salute you by the name of Brother, but forget not under what conditions you obtained this name. Brother Wardens, bear him to the West, there to come to light.

S.W. He is prepared.

One gavel.

[*The new Disciple's blindfold is removed, and in dim light he sees several Brothers apparently threatening him with their drawn swords.*]

W.M. However weak the present light that flames before you may be, yet my Brother it is sufficient to show you our weapons turned against you, threatening you with shame and disdain if ever you should unhappily betray the trust we have reposed in you. Let him be veiled again.

One gavel. [*After the Brethren with swords retire the light is restored, and the blindfold is removed again.*]

Sic Transit Gloria Mundi! For a moment since, you saw our weapons turned against you, apparently hostile. Look at us now, armed for your defense and welfare. Yes, my Brother, the Order will not and shall not forsake you as long as you are faithfully doing your duty and keeping your covenants.

Brother Master of Ceremonies, let our new Brother be clothed and return with him to the Lodge.

[Second Section]

[**Deacon.**][11]   Worshipful Master, one knocks.
W.M.   (7.1)See who it is, and, if a Brother, let him enter.
[**Deacon.**]   It is our new made Brother.
W.M.   Bring him to the East by the new way.

My Brother, permit me to clothe you with this lambskin, and in the name of the Order I present you with these white gloves. The white clothing you are now decorated with is emblematic of purity and innocence. Worn honorably it is a very honorable badge. Preserve them from stains. Wear them and never appear without them in the Lodge.

The Order for good reasons does not permit women to its assemblies, yet we profess and cherish esteem for the virtues and good among the other sex. In token of this, I present you with these gloves, which you can give to such a one as merits your esteem.

Here is your money. Take them, my Brother. In giving you back these, we would admonish you to bear in mind that it is a most certain truth that the love of gold,

---
11. No officer is identified here.

silver, and the like has produced more evils than anything else in this world. Yes. Covetousness and avarice have led men much astray, have induced them to commit the meanest acts of cowardice and most atrocious acts of injustice and oppression and violence. Acts so mean and so atrocious as to excite disdain and horror in every honest and feeling man. Acts which cause the sign of sorrow to burst from the breasts of the really pious, and which, alas, it is to be feared, have brought down the thunder of damnation on the heads of the guilty perpetrators. Therefore, respecting the pernicious influence of these things, we should watch.

Here is your hat. In delivering it to you I must remark that none except they be Masters[12] sit covered in Lodge.

Take your sword, use it carefully when called upon by your country for its defense, but bear in mind that a man of blood is deemed unfit to build a temple to the name of God, and never forget His commandment, who gave law to man in order to make them happy, saying, "Thou shalt not kill."

I will now learn you the tests of this degree.

Go to the Wardens and make yourself known (9.1)to them and to the Brother who pledged himself in your behalf, as a Mason. Afterwards, the Senior Warden will teach you the symbolic work upon the rough stone.

S.W.   My Brother, the rough stone, an emblem of which you here see, is a symbol of man deformed by prejudices and passions. To eradicate and to subdue them is the duty and the work of every Mason.

The gavel is symbolical of power. It is used by hewers of stone to strike off the asperities of the ashlar and to reduce it to the form which the Master has prescribed it should have. And we are reminded by it to strive to subdue our passions and eradicate our prejudices to fit ourselves for that spiritual temple, not made with hands, eternal in the heavens. In token of your willingness to do this work, which the Great Master has ordained we should do, stoop humbly down toward the earth and strike the rough stone as I do.

Three gavels

Continue constantly in the work you there began to do, that the Supreme Architect may not be displeased with your labors and that you may strive to merit reward: His approbation. Now, let the first work you do as a Mason be a good work. Do a deed of charity, give a pittance to help the distressed.

Turn around, (9.11)be attentive to a recitation of the rite of initiation which now is ended.

---

12. This probably means *Master Masons* rather than *Masters of Lodges*. In the Belgian R.E.R., a new Master Mason has his hat returned to him, and is told, "From now on you will always be covered in Lodge, to indicate the superiority that this Degree gives you over Apprentices and Fellows." (*Ritual de Loge de Saint-Jean, 3ᵉ Grade* [Brussels: Grand Loge Règuliére de Belgique, n.d.]:41.) In the Amez-Droz translation of the ritual of the Lodge Union des Couers, a new Master Mason is told, "In future you are empowered to don it in Lodge to mark the authority your rank gives you over the Apprentices and Companions." (F. Amez Droz trans, "Ritual of the Third degree [Master Mason], Decreed at the Convent General of the Order in 1782," n.d.:23, Archives, Iowa Masonic Library, Cedar Rapids.)

[LECTURE]

W.M.   The symbols, usages, and customs of our order are intended to lead the mind to the contemplation of things of the greatest importance to that man who is wishful to learn, and to meditate upon that which may promote his welfare. You was first led into a dark and narrow chamber where you was separated from the world and from your friend who brought you there. Although this separation was but short, yet the things there led you to meditate upon subjects however common, yet of a very serious nature.

Your meditations were disturbed by the coming of a Brother who inquired of you your motives for joining our Order, for none but those actuated by right motives should be admitted among us. He who was deputed to guide you hither in company with your friend caused you to be divested of all money, jewels, and the like, and otherwise prepared you for introduction into our Lodge, that you might know that worldly distinctions can not give rank and must not create differences among Masons. In the Lodge we all meet upon the level. In fact, among the good and impartial, nothing but virtue and mental acquirements can give preeminence among men in the world, and nothing else can distinguish Brethren in the Lodge.

In the Chamber of Preparation, it is hoped you spent the time profitably. You was abstracted from the world and, for a moment perhaps, was engaged in the consideration of yourself and, that external objects might not entirely engage your attention or disturb the impression which you there received and that you should shew confidence in your guide, you was deprived of the light and thus led to the door of the Lodge where you was received by the Warden. He demanded your religion, name, age, and other particulars, for none but a professor of religion, and one who is free, and who we know a man arrived at the years of real manhood, can be admitted to our Lodge.

The three blows on the door of the Lodge should remind you that for him who seeks with constancy, who seeks with humility, and who knocks rightly, the door of the Temple of Fraternity and Peace shall be opened. You was conducted to the care of the Warden and stood then upon the threshold of the Lodge, your former guide leaving you with assurances that you were in the hands of those who would not mislead you. But before you could, by the assistance of your new conductor, proceed on your way, the Master addressed you, and your motives for coming here were acknowledged to the Brother by him who best could inform us thereof, by yourself.

[28]Then we, reciprocating the confidence you had hitherto placed in us, believed you, and you commenced a journey on which you learned from the East some truths on which the tenets of our Order in a great measure rest. You then ascended the mysterious steps of the Temple, and was brought to the altar to make a very serious promise. On the whole of this journey reciprocal confidence supported you. Confidence between you and us, for if you had not had confidence in us you would have refused to follow our directions and, if we had not have believed you to have been upright, we would not have received you among us.

You was joined to us by a solemn tie, and afterwards you saw a blazing and unsteady light which was only sufficient to discover surrounding apparent dangers. Finally, the veil was removed wholly, and you saw the light. You beheld Brethren armed for your defense and welfare. All hostile appearances were done away, and everything bore appearances of love. Those scenes are emblematical of the different states of man.

The unenlightened state, in which man makes sacrifices and oblations for obtaining favours from heaven or for the atonement of atrocious deeds he may have committed. In which state nearly all the objects he perceives were hostile in appearance, and his fellows seemed strangers to him, and their arms appeared to threaten him, their power to place him in danger. He shuns, fears, or even hates them, but, in a more enlightened state, he perceives that heaven rather accepts a sincere and contrite heart than burnt offerings and oblations. He then acknowledges his fellow men as his Brethren, and he looks upon their power as means for his own defense and welfare. He joins them, relies upon them, and loves them. You was invested with the badges of innocence and purity and admonished by good conduct to keep them unsullied.

(8.14)And then you received the tests of this Degree, by which you can make yourself known to Brother Masons. Do not, my Brother, be among those who strive to publish to the world that they are Masons. Neither countenance anything tending to this end, for the honour and usefulness of the Order are much more extended by concealment and by an intimate acquaintance with the exalted aim of our labours and the probable extent of their influence upon the welfare of the human race. You will be assured that silence and circumspection tend to give our Order force.

The carpet[13] before you, containing the principle symbols of our Order deserves your attention. The Border, including the whole, is a representation of Mason work, and this is the covering to all the other symbols and should remind us of that concealment of which we have already spoken.

The Rough Stone and Square Stone are symbols. The one of the raw and uncultivated man, the other of him which has subjected himself to the discipline of truth and virtue.

The Trestle Board should admonish us carefully to study and to follow the plans of the Master.

You see the Sun and Moon. They are here represented to remind us of application to our duties day and night, for this is all a man can do without erring.

There are the different instruments used by Masons as plumb, level, and square and so forth. They are adopted as hieroglyphs by us, and therefore are (4.32)here represented.

And in the center is the Blazing Star, which we view with reverential silence.

And finally, the Cord. It is here in remembrance of the cord which (3.21)the veil of the tabernacle was drawn aside with, and it is emblematical of the tie which unites all good men and Masons, and we should remember ever that silence is the veil which keeps our sanctuary in safety.

---

13. This probably refers to the drawing on page 25.

Close before you is the Mosaic Pavement, which in Solomon's Temple covered the courts and on which the sanctuary stood. It is emblematical of the foundation which we seek in those we accept among us. They should be men of a firm and fair character, fit for surrounding and supporting a sanctuary.

On the left you see a Pillar with the initial of the word of your degree. Bear in mind the meaning of the word: "In him is strength."[14] You ascended those three first steps of the Temple, but, as your time was not yet come, the door remained shut and you was led back again, and it is recommended to you to wait with patience and to labour diligently yet with meekness, that when the door of the Temple shall be opened to you, you may hope, yes believe, to enter into the inner apartments with great joy.

END

---

14. The word *Boaz* in Hebrew means "In him is strength."

[15]Opening the Disciple's Lodge

W.M. Brother Warden, are you a Disciple?
S.W. I am.
W.M. Brother Senior and Junior, what is the first duty of every good Mason and, in the Lodge, particularly of the Brother Wardens?
S.W. To see (5.16)that the profane are removed and the hall in safety.
W.M. Please to perform that office. The profane are removed and so on.
   Since the profane and so on are removed, we will pursue that path of duty which is pointed out to us and strive to consummate our work.

Three [gavels]

S.W. Brethren, look toward the East. It was there the light arose by which we are enabled to work. Let us be prepared to continue our labours at the signal of the Master.

One [gavel]

W.M. In order.

[*The three tapers in the East are lit.*][16]

   May the clearest light shine for us during our labours.

Prayer by the Master as follows:

   Thou Creator God of Heaven and Earth the thickest darkness hides not from thy sight. In mercy view and purify our hearts. Bless us that we may learn and do thy will. Wisdom itself, Almighty King, is Thine and Thou alone hast strength, others are weak, in all thy works beauty effulgent shines. We humbly pray thee in this hall of peace, send down thy blessing on our labours here that we may be wise, beautiful and strong.
W.M. Brother Junior, what is the time?
J.W. It is past high twelve.
W.M. Brother Senior, is it the right time to begin to work?
S.W. It is.
W.M. Then assist me, Brethren to open this Disciples' Lodge. Let us live together in unity, to the honour of God. In the name of fraternity and by virtue of the power of my office, I declare this Disciples' Lodge opened.
   Brethren, be attentive to the work.

One [gavel]. The work now proceeds in the usual form. The candidate is introduced.

---

15. FM1:3.30. The manuscript reads, "Opning the Dscples ☐." Folger sometimes used the box symbol, ☐, to stand for *Lodge*, but ☐ is also the symbol for the letter *d*, and thus the line could be read as either "Opening the Disciple's Lodge" or "Opening the Disciple's Degree." The next line reads, "Br W are you a ☐?", and clearly the proper interpretation here is *Disciple*, while in the next line, ☐ should be interpreted as *Lodge*. The translation of ☐ for *Lodge* or *Degree* or possibly *Disciple* will not be elaborated in most later decisions.

16. Only a drawing of a three branched candlestick appears in the text, but the Master's comments let us infer the Master's action.

(5.31)Closing [the Disciple's Lodge]

W.M. Brother Junior, what is the time?
J.W. Toward low twelve.
W.M. Brother Senior, is the labour finished?
S.W. It is.
W.M. Have any of the Brothers anything to offer, as the labour is finished?
(7.17)Brother Almoner, please perform your duty.

One [gavel]

In order Brethren. Before we part, Brethren, let us form a tie of fraternal union and offer up our dutiful acknowledgments to the great Master whose goodness has enabled us thus far to do the work of Masonry and supplicate his blessing.

Here the Brethren all join hands and the Master prays thus:

O Thou Great Master on the throne of Heaven. Thy word from nothing did call forth the whole. Thy view perceiveth every thing that is, and thou pervadest all in Heaven and Earth. Look down in mercy from thy holy Heaven on us, the creatures of thy gracious Will. Grant wisdom, we are ignorant and blind. Grant strength, without thy aid our toils are vain. And with thy blessing, beautify our Souls. And to thy Honour may our work be done, the Brethren live in peace teaching good will, and may our Brother tie continue strong.

Brethren, assist me to close this Lodge. Let us be unanimous.

I declare this Disciples' Lodge closed to the honour of Jehovah, in the name of fraternity, and by virtue of my office. Brothers be attentive.

[Three tapers in the East are extinguished.]

[17]Thus vanisheth the splendor of the world, like a flame kindled suddenly before your eyes and suddenly extinguished when you seek for it, nor a vestige of it is to be found. Notwithstanding its apparent splendour, it shall utterly vanish. Brother, when you look for light,[18] remember it is only to be found in the East.

(7.34)That light which shined during our labours cannot be seen by the profane. Brethren, when you seek for light wherewith you would perfect your works, remember that that light is in the East and only there to be found.

Dismiss.

---

17. FM1:86.27. This brief statement, standing alone in the manuscript, seems to describe the extinguishing of a candle and is thus placed here.

18. FM1:86.29. A unique symbol is used that looks like a flame, which is interpreted as the word *light*.

[Disciple's Catechism]

Q: (6.17)Brother Senior, are you a Disciple?
A: I am.
Q: From whence come the Disciples?
A: From the West.
Q: And whither are they going?
A: Toward the East.
Q: Why?
A: In search of light.
Q: What are your duties as a Disciple?
A: To continue diligently the work I did begin as commanded by the Master on the rough stone.
Q: With what did you work?
A: With the symbol of power.
Q: Why?
A: To shew the proper use of the power with which I was intrusted
Q: How is a Mason to be known?
A: By signs, words, and grips.
Q: How so?
A: His manners must be gentle and unassuming, his conversation, prudent and discreet. He being rather a hearer than a speaker, being willing to hear, yet apt to teach, and shunning foolish disputes. He disdains to pollute himself by doing any mean, fraudulent, or criminal act. He discountenances libertinism, commends and practices virtue. He encourages benevolence and charity by precept and example.
Q: Where do the Disciples labour?
A: In the outer court of the Temple.
Q: Have you received your wages?
A: Yes.
Q: What are they?
A: I got food and raiment and many other things.
Q: Where do you receive your pay?
A: At the entrance of the Temple.
Q: Who pays you?
A: The Master.
Q: Are you satisfied with your wages?
A: I am well satisfied and know the word.
Q: What time do you begin to work?
A: Past high twelve.
Q: When is the time of rest?
A: Toward midnight.
Q: What are the dimensions of your Lodge?
A: Its length is and so forth.

Q: Why this extent?
A: Because Masonry includes all things; it is unlimited.
Q: What do the three tapers represent?
A: The sun and moon and the Master of the Lodge, and as the sun and moon regularly dispense light and life[19] to the earth, (8.4)so does the Master dispense knowledge and discipline to the Lodge, and all Masters of Lodges should strive so to do.
Q: What is the emblem of a Disciple?
A: A broken pillar with the inscription "Adhuc stat."[20]
Q: How is it explained?
A: As by the remnant of the pillar that is yet standing we can ascertain to what order it belongs and determine what its proportions and ornaments were when it was entire, and thus be enabled to form another pillar in likeness of the broken one, so from what we know relative to man we hope and believe that he may be restored to a state approaching to that first pristine purity and happiness.
Q: Why is Solomon's Temple used emblematically in Freemasonry?
A: It was a highly finished and splendid building and the first Temple erected by man publicly sacred to the name of the only wise and true God, and Freemasonry teaches us to be built up living temples as perfect and beautiful as the Solomonic Temple was to the service and to the honour of the Supreme Architect of Heaven and Earth.

Close of the Catechism

---

19. FM1:6.31. The manuscript reads "Lght and ~~heat~~ and lfe".

20. FM1:8.5. The manuscript reads "Ad hoc stat," but this is probably a misspelling or misunderstanding of the motto of the R.E.R. First Degree, "Adhuc stat."

FELLOW'S GRADE (88.4)

[First Section]

[The candidate is conducted to the Chamber of Preparation by the Introductor, and then asked the] (86.1)*Preparation Questions.*

INTRODUCTOR. Man was originally pure, undefiled, happy. How comes it then that he wars with his own welfare and often makes himself miserable? This is a subject which undoubtedly demands our highest attention, in as much as we ought to study to avoid unhappiness.

SECOND, The fool wanders his whole life through without considering or knowing from whence he came or whither he went. Brother, the wise man studies to know what he is about. And considering every step, its end and intention, and, by closely pursuing the objects of happiness, he avoids all that can stop him in his way. And knowing his own weakness and ignorance, he receives with humility the doctrines that are given him and with gratitude proffered support when he is wrong, and when his own strength would not bear him farther.

GUIDE.[21] Masonry is progressive. It is necessary, in every pursuit of knowledge, gradually to advance in order to understand things aright. Wherefore you was not all at once made acquainted with all the arts of our order, but are advanced gradually through them, and, indeed, as nearly everything in our rites is symbolical, it requires previous preparation to understand them and to make them useful to ourselves.

Permit me to ask you what is your opinion of the tendency of our Order?

This degree is to be considered partly as a recompense for your labours past, but principally as tending to prepare you for the Master's degree. I can assure you, my Brother, that your constancy and fortitude in this degree must stand very serious tests. If you are determined and fixed to go forward, then follow me like a man, but if you waver then I advise you rather to remain in the degree of Disciple until you, by the easier duties required in the degree you have taken, have become strong.

Now, Brother, decide. Yet do not deceive yourself. Will you follow me?

[Candidate answers and, if affirmative, gives] three knocks.

DEACON. Who knocks?
GUIDE. It is a Disciple who wishes to be accepted as a Fellow.
DEACON. His name?
GUIDE. He has laboured in the outer court of the Temple on the rough stone.
DEACON. Pass.
GUIDE. Hither I have brought you, as you desired, to the place whither you durst not approach. My work is now finished. Try to find yourself a new guide.
W.M. Brother you are welcome. *One gavel*

---

21. The text clearly shows the Guide begins speaking here, which seems to indicate that another officer, perhaps the Introductor as in the Disciple's Grade, brought the candidate to the Chamber of Preparation.

(12.1) ADDRESS FROM THE MASTER

The Fellows and Masters present have given their unanimous consent to your being accepted as a Fellow, and I am well satisfied that in the character of a Fellow you will use your best endeavours to discharge your duties as such. Yet it is my duty to inform you that the work of a Fellow not only requires good application, but that it is difficult, yet it undoubtedly has its reward.

You are from henceforth carefully to inspect the work done already on the rough stone and strive to complete it according to the designs of the Master Great Architect, that they may happily never be deemed unfit for the Temple. We are prepared and willing to assist you with advice and rules for your work, but the work you must do yourself. No man can do it for you. And we desire ever that your honest endeavours will meet a reward.

Formerly on your symbolic Journey, you was blindfolded, you was in darkness. At the present time you wander in the light. Yet, my Brother, you would undoubtedly go astray unless you were assisted by a guide who knew the way and is willing to shew it to you.

If you will go to our Brother Second Overseer, he will conduct you in paths on which you can learn things relative to the duty of a Fellow. His hand holding yours, and by which you will be lead forward, should remind you that a Brother should assist another in good and laudable pursuits, while the sword resting on your breast should impress you with a sense of the irregularity and precipitancy in the striving to consummate our views at the same time it teaches one of the important duties of a Fellow, viz. that of checking all imprudent hastiness, but especially when he is going upon a way where he is a stranger.

One gavel. Guide makes the first round.

FIRST ROUND[22]

2ND O.   Man was originally pure, upright, undefiled, happy. How comes it then that he so often wars with his own welfare and makes himself miserable? His passions lead him astray, and sensual enjoyments entice him from the garden of happiness into the wilderness of vice and into the labyrinth of error. But present, often, alas too late it is feared, he is undeceived or, what is worse, he is satiated. A feeling of duty or of shame rouses him to view his present state and he sees with remorse that he is far from where he should be, but the ways he has wandered through are so winding and intricate that he can perhaps never retrace his steps. And he stands like the fool man, not knowing from whence he came or whither he went.

Two gavels

SECOND ROUND
2ND O.   *One gavel.* He who has begun to go forward in the path of wisdom and virtue

---

22. Immediately after this in the text, FM1:12.17, is a drawing of a temple and a man facing a looped cord. Inside the cord is a skull, a sprig, two crossed swords, a cross, and a blazing star (see chapter 3, figure 4).

and turns back is a thousand times more deplorable

One gavel

than he who never went that way, for he never knew what duty was nor did he take the pleasures arising from virtuous actions. Such a man has brought a dangerous enemy to war (13.1)against his welfare, viz. Himself—his own self.

One gavel

Third Round

2nd O.   *One gavel.* Brother, we believe that you are willing and ready to undertake the task of the Fellow. The subject on which you are to labour is deserving of your attention, and you ought never to neglect it.

W.M.   Brother Warden, lead the Brother to the image of the pillar of beauty, and let him consider it well that he forget it not.

Warden.   If you desire to view the object of your labours then draw the veil aside. See yourself.

See emblem. [A curtain is pulled aside to reveal a mirror.]

[23]Know thyself. This is even a religious duty and was highly esteemed in ancient times. It is important, inasmuch as we ought to know our own weaknesses and imperfections and frailties, and we should strive and pray to be able to lay aside all things which pollute us and all superfluity of naughtiness and receive the word of Truth, which is able to save our souls. But we must receive the word and keep it, or we are otherwise like the man who beholds his natural face in a glass, beholding himself and going away, he immediately forgets what manner of person he was. (See James' Epistle.[24])

Consider thyself. This is shewn and that thou shouldst often think upon this duty and remember that what you here see (apparently at the bottom of a vault) is the image of the receptacle that contains great treasures (the Law of God—and keeps to the knowledge of the truth), to find which, in another form, has long engaged the attention of both wise and foolish men.

W.M.   (13.5)Brother, the Fellows are generally well pleased with their own work, but if they behold them with the eye of the Master, they would be astonished to see how imperfect that is which they think so finished, and they would be very much alarmed on beholding how much yet remains to be done in order that they may not be rejected by Him who is appointed to inspect them and Who will dispose of them according to their merits. Even the most finished work a man who follows his own thoughts of perfection can produce will, perhaps, be found very imperfect and full

---

23. FM1:84.1. This text stands alone in the manuscript, with no indication where it goes or who speaks it. The text of the Fellow's Grade contains the unexplained instruction "See emblem," but the R.E.R. has a similar mirror ceremony in its Second Degree (see p. 8).

24. "For if any be a hearer of the word, and not a doer, he is like unto a man beholding his natural face in a glass: For he beholdeth himself, and goeth his way, and straightway forgetteth what manner of man he was." James 1:23–24.

of error and deemed unfit and unuseful, yet it is a consolation to know that a good artist is able to make of the most unfinished block of rough stone an indisputable likeness of one of the most beautiful and perfect creatures, but in order to do this he must be well instructed by and must follow the rules of a great and good Master.

Brother Senior, let our Brother ascend the five first steps of the Temple that he may from thence behold an emblem of the light which guided wise men, and from thence conduct him to the East to make his vow.

W.M.   Brother when you were before at this altar, although blindfolded, you had so much confidence in us that you did not hesitate to give your consent to a covenant, the tenure of which you was unacquainted with. But before you took it, it was wholly made known to you. Now you are in light, and you have in some measure become acquainted with us and with the Order. Therefore we can expect more confidence of you than when you was the stranger among us. Wherefore I ask of you if you are willing to make the covenant belonging to this degree?

[*The candidate gives his*] *answer*.

W.M.   My Brother, we expected of you this expression of confidence and thank you for it, but Brother take our admonition in good part: never consent to a serious engagement without first having heard its contents and without having understood them. Brother Senior, please read the covenant to our Brother.

[*The Fellow's Obligation follows, but later, for reasons unknown, Folger encrypted another, nearly identical version, which is printed with the first for comparison.*]

[FELLOW'S] (14.3)COVENANT   (17.3)FELLOW'S VOW

S.W. I do voluntary and without deceit, in addition to my former covenant, most seriously promise and vow never to reveal to anyone whatever, not even to a Brother Disciple, any of the secrets, symbols, or anything appertaining to the Degree of a Fellow which I am now receiving, except it should be in a just and legal Lodge of Fellows such as I am now in. And I vow carefully to conceal all things belonging to this Degree from everyone, except I am convinced, after strict trial, inquiry, and examination, that he or they are entitled to receive the same, and that I can, without a breach of covenant in the least degree, communicate respecting these things, he or	S.W. I do voluntarily and without any deceit, in addition to my former covenant, most solemnly promise never to reveal to anyone whatever, not even to a Brother Disciple, any of the secrets, symbols, mysteries, or anything appertaining to this Degree of a Fellow which I am now receiving, excepting it should be in a legal Lodge of Fellows such as I am now in. And I promise carefully to conceal all things belonging to this Lodge from everyone, except I am convinced after strict trial, inquiry, and examination that he or they are entitled to the same, he or they having been accepted as a Disciple and Fellow in a just and perfect Lodge such as this I am now in, and that I can, with-

they having been accepted as a Fellow in a just and perfect Lodge of Fellows such as I am now in. And as a token of my sincerity I pledge my heart.

Then proceed as in Disciple's vow.

out a breach of covenant in the least degree, communicate respecting the things with each person. I likewise promise that I will aid and assist, to the best of my ability, all worthy Fellows who may claim my help and to be faithful. With the exceptions above mentioned, I promise to keep the secrets of this Lodge enclosed in my heart, and, as a pledge of my sincerity, I declare that I will have my heart torn from my breast, rather than violate this vow I now make. So help me God. Amen.

W.M. (13.21 Brother, have you heard this covenant and are you willing to take it?

[*The candidate answers.*]

W.M. Kneel then on the square and hold the square to your breast. Now read it yourself. Brethren, while our Brother reads the oath, let us give a signal of our accordance.

Covenant is here taken.

W.M. We hail you as a Fellow!

Open book

I present you with this blue ribbon which you will hereafter wear. It denotes constancy and is the colour of the heavens.

Learns the grip, sign, and word.

One gavel

This sign is a pledge of constancy and good faith. It is like pledging the heart. Thus, in pledging our words as Fellows, we point at the heart as the thing pledged for the sincerity of what we say. Now make yourself known to the Wardens and to our Fellow (14.1)who has pledged himself in your behalf.

S.W. Are you a Fellow?

Answer [of the new Fellow]

S.W. By what shall I know you.

Answer [of the new Fellow]

S.W. As often as you make this sign, remember that you pledged your heart, your life for the truth of what you say.

Salutes him.

Lecture

W.M. The well instructed guide who brought you to the door of the Lodge and properly prepared you for your entrance here, and assurance that you had laboured diligently procured you admission and the welcome of the Master. You came to the West. Your guide might follow you no longer. You was then to seek another guide, and the address from the East must have convinced you how necessary directions and instructions are in things to which we are strangers. You could not possibly guess at what was intended to be done or how you were to be disposed of.

Yet, your believing that they wished to do well toward you prompted you to follow the directions given you. Thus when they believe in the good intentions of fellow beings, they are easy, and they willingly enter into their views that, although experience and reason teach us that men are very frail and feeble creatures, if they were perfect, how much more easily, willingly should they follow them.

You went again on a symbolic journey, and you learned on the way the causes of much of the unhappiness and misery to which man could be subjected. Your attention was called to one who could become your most dangerous enemy. You was made acquainted with the error which could make him such. Finally, the subject on which you was to labour with constancy and care was presented to you, and the imperfection of human works taught was the rule for removing those imperfections.

From a more elevated situation than you before had, you could view an emblem of the guide of the wise. My dear Brother, let me persuade you to retain that emblem in your memory, and, if unhappily passion should tempt you from the path of duty, may the remembrance of what was seen serve to lead you from error. If unhappily avarice or ambition should stop you on your way,[25] and the recollection of that bright emblem should happily arouse you again to pursue your journey, oh return not to the vicious, betray not the good. At the altar you made a voluntary vow and received the tests of this degree. We hope you will often call these things to mind with pleasure.

Our Order has, as you already know, adopted the implements of operative masons as hieroglyphs. Such (15.1)instruments were used in erecting the Temple in Jerusalem, which was sacred to the name of deity, and they have been moralized. Those peculiar to this degree are the square, plumb, and level. By help of these, the rough stone becomes a good square stone. If a stone be so wrought that by neither of these instruments defects can be found, it is fitted for the builder's use.

But the square is applied to two sides at once, but it will not rest evenly on the superficies if the stone is defective. Hence it is called the symbol of truth and discoverer of error, and we hail the love of truth as one of the greatest virtues.

The plumb admonishes us to righteousness. See its unerring line. It directs from Earth to Heaven and from the Heavens to the Earth.

The level is only applicable to the upper superficies of the stone when placed on the building. By it, undue eminences or depressions are discovered which require

---

25. FM1:14.25. The manuscript reads "you on your ~~journey~~ way."

the gavel's use to be removed. Hence it is taken as a symbol to remind us of that equality which should exist among all good Masons.

The builders of the holy Temples in the days that are past were well acquainted with the proportions necessary to the constructing of these beautiful and well contrived edifices, and hence they ought not to be unacquainted with the dimensions and proportions of architecture, and it is certain that in the places where wisdom, beauty, and strength characterize the buildings, there we not only find science cultivated and the social virtues encouraged but heaven born charity is there extending the hand to the assistance of the needy.

The Doric, Ionic, and Corinthian orders are those which in our times are generally esteemed originals. They are here in the Lodge, instead of our more ancient pillars, as monuments of human genius and of the high degree of taste and love of splendour which already existed among the people of the old world. But most of the magnificent monuments of antiquity are destroyed or ruined. Sic transit gloria mundi.

The liberal arts and sciences deserve our attention and encouragement. These distinguish a polite people from savages, and the capacity for acquiring a knowledge of them leads man to contemplate upon the works and perfections of Deity and enables them to lead others from many pernicious errors and to shun them himself.

On both sides at the entrance of the Temple you see two pillars, the one formed and ornamented like the other. These stood before the entrance of the sanctuary, and no one could enter therein without passing them. Boaz and Jakin is the name of the two pillars. The meaning of the word he shall establish it. These pillars were taken from the Temple by Nebuchadnezzar. They were cast by Hiram, the widow's son, of brass, were hollow, eighteen cubits high, and four cubits thick. They stood here ornamented with the symbols of peace, wealth, and plenty, like twins—no difference in them but their names.

My Brother, if you will meditate upon these things and upon the mysteries of this Lodge, you will find a wide field for the exercise of the mind. The subjects are useful in a high degree and full of interest, and particularly those relating to yourself. These demand your most serious attention.

HERE ENDS THE LECTURE OF THE FELLOW LODGE

Three gavels.

(10.1) Opening of the Fellow's Lodge[26]

Senior [Warden.] Calls to order.

W.M. In order Brethren.

Brother Wardens, what is the duty of all good Masons before the Temple is opened?

S.W. To see that the profane are removed and the Temple in safety.

W.M. You will please to perform that duty.

S.W. The profane are removed and the Temple in safety.

Then follows the lighting as in the Disciple's Grade, with the address. Then the exhibition of the blazing star.

W.M. Brethren, behold an emblem of the guide of the wise. Let me persuade you to retain this emblem in your memory, and, if unhappily passion should tempt you from the path of duty, may a remembrance of what was seen serve to lead you from error. If unhappily avarice or ambition should stop you on your way, and a recollection of that bright emblem should happily arouse you again to pursue your journey. Oh return not to the vicious, betray not the good.

W.M. Brother Senior, what is your order's name?

S.W. Giblem.

W.M. Brother Junior what time is it?

J.W. Toward low twelve.

W.M. Brother Senior, is it right time to begin the work?

S.W. It is.

W.M. Then please to be in order. Assist me in opening.

One gavel.

Sign. Prayer.

One gavel

Be seated.

W.M. Brother Senior, for what purpose are we here assembled?

S.W. To learn to know ourselves, and to inspect work done already on the rough stone, and to strive to complete it according to the designs of the Master, and to make farther progress in Masonry.

W.M. My Brother, let us strive deeply to impress upon our minds that it is highly important to labor diligently in order to complete the work according to the designs of the Master. Let us henceforth abstain from all foolish and vain pursuits and use the time allotted to us here to labor in discharge of our duty that happily we may be deemed fit for the Temple and not be rejected, and that we may hope to meet the reward, remembering that time flies swiftly away and is irrecoverable for mortals, but, to the view of the Great Master on high, the past, the present, and the future are all open. He perceives all the actions of men and knows all their thoughts.

---

26. The immediately previous text, FM1:8.12–13, reads "Next follows the catechism work," even though the text has the opening and closing of a Fellow's Lodge. Most of the dialogue could comprise the catechism.

[*Folger has two nearly identical passages for the closing of a Fellows' Lodge that are printed together for comparison.*]

(10.19) FELLOW'S LODGE CLOSING	(16.1) CLOSING OF THE FELLOW'S GRADE
W.M. Brother Senior, are you a Fellow?	W.M. *One gavel.* Brother Senior, are you a Fellow?
S.W. I have been accepted as such.	S.W. I have been accepted as such.
W.M. Where?	W.M. Where?
S.W. In a perfect Lodge of Fellows.	S.W. In a perfect Lodge of Fellows.
W.M. Who accepted you?	W.M. Who accepted you?
S.W. The Master.	S.W. The Master.
W.M. How shall I know you to be a Fellow?	W.M. How shall I know you to be a Fellow?
S.W. By the sign.	S.W. By the sign.
W.M. What is the work of the Fellow?	W.M. What is the work of the Fellow?
S.W. On the square stone and the rough stone, and to finish it according to the Master's designs.	S.W. To square the smooth stone and to finish it according to the Master's designs.
W.M. Where have you worked as a Fellow?	W.M. Where have you worked as a Fellow?
S.W. In the Temple.	S.W. In the Temple.
W.M. Why was you accepted as a Fellow?	W.M. Why was you accepted as a Fellow?
S.W. To learn the letter *G*.	S.W. To learn the letter *G*.
W.M. What did you perceive in the Fellow's Degree that you had not before seen?	W.M. What did you perceive in the Fellow's Degree that you did not before see?
S.W. The blazing star.	S.W. The blazing star.
W.M. What did it represent?	W.M. What is it?
S.W. It is a symbol of the guide of the wise and faithful.	S.W. The guide to the wise and faithful.
W.M. Where did it arise?	W.M. Where did it rise?
S.W. In the East.	S.W. In the East.
W.M. From whence did you see it?	W.M. From whence did you see it?
S.W. From the steps of the Temple.	S.W. From the steps of the Temple.
W.M. Did you go toward it?	W.M. Did you go towards it?
S.W. Yes, I was brought toward it.	S.W. Yes, I was brought towards it.
W.M. Whither did it guide your steps?	W.M. Whither did it guide your steps?
S.W. Towards the Master.	S.W. Towards the Master.
W.M. What else did you perceive?	W.M. What else did you perceive?
S.W. The letter *G*.	S.W. The letter *G*.
W.M. What does it signify?	W.M. What does it signify?
S.W. I know but little about it, but it has	S.W. I know but little about it, but it has

been said to me to signify geometry.
W.M. Was anything else shewn to you?
S.W. Yes, one of the subjects on which I was to labour.
W.M. Have you commenced your labours?
S.W. I have.
W.M. Can you complete them?
S.W. Yes.
W.M. How?
S.W. By following the directions given by the Master and by his assistance.
W.M. When will your labours as a Fellow cease?
S.W. When I am admitted to the Masters' Lodge and have passed through the inner chamber.
W.M. Have you received wages?
S.W. Yes, at the pillar Jakin I have met with encouragement and the promise of ample reward.
W.M. What is the symbol of a Fellow?
S.W. The square stone with the inscription "D O."
W.M. What is the meaning of this symbol?
S.W. That the Master discovers and points out the defects of the work and has given us the means of rectifying these, and it should remind us of our duty to strive to conform to the rules given us, thereby endeavouring to fit ourselves for a place in the Temple.
W.M. Brother Senior, when does the work end?

been said to me to signify geometry.
W.M. Was anything else shewn you?
S.W. Yes, one of the subjects on which I was to labour.
W.M. Have you commenced your labours?
S.W. I have.
W.M. Can you complete them?
S.W. Yes.
W.M. How?
S.W. By following the doctrines given me by the Master and by his assistance.
W.M. When will your labours as a Fellow cease?
S.W. When I am admitted to the Masters' Lodge and have passed to the inner chamber.
W.M. Have you received wages?
S.W. Yes, at the pillar Jakin I have met with encouragement and the promise of ample reward.
W.M. What is the symbol of a Fellow?
S.W. A square stone with "D O" engraved on it.
W.M. What is the meaning of this symbol?
S.W. That the Master discovers and points out the defects of the work and has given us the means of rectifying them, and it should remind us of our duty to strive to conform to the rules given us, thereby endeavouring to fit ourselves for a place in the Temple.
W.M. Brother Senior, when does the work end?
S.W. At midnight.

Here follow closing as in the Disciples' Lodge, exhibiting star with the address, then questions as in opening of Fellows' Lodge.

Three gavels

[MASTER'S GRADE]

(18.1)PREPARATION FOR THE MASTER'S GRADE

INTRODUCTOR.[27]   We should, while we live, prepare for death, and we should constantly be at this work because we know not when we shall die. But it is certain we shall die, and we shall give up our bodies to the dust from whence they came. Our souls die not, they are to exist forever. But how shall this existence be—miserable, unhappy? Could we determine it, we should choose the happy state, but then we ought to be prepared for its enjoyment.

And what is necessary to prepare the soul for its happy state, and what will make it fit for its enjoyments? Whoever saw the vicious happy? Even in this gross bodily state they are not. So they can clothe themselves in purple, they can live in palaces, they can own piles of gold, they eat of dainties and become drunk of rich wines, but is this happiness or is it not rather the source of unhappiness? If deprived of these things, would they not be miserable? In the grave, none of these things follow with them. If they think but on death and futurity, it is agony to them. What then would realization be?

INTRODUCTOR. (18.12)Brother, you wish to be accepted as a Master. Come, follow me.

Five raps at the door.

DEACON.   Who is here?
INTRODUCTOR.   A Fellow who wishes to be accepted as a Master.

Gives the pass: [Giblem].

INTRODUCTOR. He is over five years old and has worked in the inner court of the Temple on the polished stone. He has served his time and his Master is well pleased with him.

DEACON.   *Admits him and says::* Are you worthy to wear this badge?[28]

Takes it from him and places him in the west.

[29]My Brother, in times of old it was ordained, even by God, that those who entered the sanctuary should wash themselves, cleansing themselves from uncleanness. It was a symbol and it impressed upon the mind the necessity of holiness in those who went into the sanctuary. My Brother, it is a token of your sincere wish and intention henceforth to live undefiled. Wash your hands and remember, God is a witness to the performance of his ordinances.

---

27. No officer is indicated as speaker here, but the Introductor is continued as in the Disciple's and Fellow's Grades.

28. Probably an apron, though no object is identified.

29. FM1:83.1. This passage stands alone, with no indication of where it goes or who speaks it. However, the salutation, "My Brother," seems to eliminate the Disciple's Grade, where the candidate would be addressed as "Sir," and it does appear to come prior to entering the "sanctuary."

(18.16) Address from the Master

W.M. Brother, you are now brought to the inner chamber.

[*Exhibits a cross*] When you are passed to a place of which this is an emblem,[30] there no art nor deception can hide any error or any imperfection. The Judge who there presides views the hearts of men and knows their most hidden secrets. Wherefore, in reverence to these solemn truths, be sincere.

My Brother, we are here assembled to commemorate and to lament the death of our Grand Master. His loss we may justly sorrow for, and as justly deplore the cause of his death, and, deploring them, shun them. He was killed by unfaithful Fellows. No guile was in his heart nor evil in his ways, yet they set his goodness at nought and their ruffian hands murdered him.

Brother Warden, shew our Fellow the horrid spectacle before us and watch him well and see if he appears to be one of the conspirators against the Grand Master.

Warden. Our Fellow does not appear to be among the guilty, and he is moved, we believe, at this sight.

W.M. We are glad that you do not appear greatly concerned in this work of death, and we hope you never will join those who are guilty. Bring him on the Master's path for instruction, that he can join us in seeking the Master.

Symbolic Journey

(19.1) First Round

Warden. Remember Death. *One gavel*

That man who has a sense of his own frailty and who has learned to observe his own imperfections has made the first step toward the light.

(19.3) Second Round

Warden. Remember Death. It is unavoidable.

How dangerous it is to venture upon the far distant journey without a knowledge of the way we are going. How foolish to refuse to attend to the infallible doctrines which point out the way. Would one who thus ventures and thus refuses not easily err and not find the city he sought, but instead thereof faint among the sands of the desert where there is no water to allay burning thirst and bread to keep from starving?

Remember Death. *Two gavels*

(19.9) Third Round

Warden. Remember Death. It is unavoidable.

It may be very near; perhaps it is near at hand. Let us incline our hearts to instruction and our minds to understanding and learn the way to the habitation of rest and comfort. Let us seek the way thither with earnestness. Let us knock at its door with confidence and with all humility. Let us ask alms for our wants of the

---

30. No object is identified, but on FM1:11.29, is written "☦ When thou has passed to the place of which this is a symbol, thy destiny will be fixed forever."

good Master of the house, and, believe me, He will not reject our prayer and will even grant us much more than we expected and more than we can dispose of.

W.M.   Let him now ascend the seven steps of the Temple, and bring him with Master's steps to the East.

W.M.   (19.15)My Brother, before you can be accepted as a Master, it is required of you to make a solemn covenant with us.

The Warden reads it.

W.M.   Now, Brother, you are to receive the word and grip of this degree, and in future when you use these things, call to mind the situation you were in just before you received them.

One gavel

Brother Warden, lead our Fellow[31] to the place where we shall all assemble.

Accepts him. Hymn and procession.

W.M.   (19.20)Behold, Brethren, the pall covers. The coffin contains a Brother. God give you may henceforth be dead to sin, and ever may you bear in mind that you shall die. May you have firm hope of being raised from the Fellow to the Master, from darkness to light, from dust to heaven, from mortality to eternal life, and may this hope cheer you and make you faithful.

Brethren, let us seek to find our Master who was slain.

Pass once round the grave.

Lord help us children of the dust. Here is acacia sprig, and this has the appearance of a grave. Let us look into this.

W.M.   (20.1)Brother, as the word was lost at the death of our Master, let us now agree that, when the body is raised, the first spoken shall hereafter be considered as the Master's word.

The flesh is corrupt. [Five Points of Fellowship] Raises the body.[32]

(20.3)LECTURE AND INSTRUCTIONS

W.M.   Your being advanced to this degree, the objects can no longer be strange to you. But permit me to call your attention to some of the things which are inculcated by our symbols and ceremonies, independent of your obligations. Your mind was, at an early period of your connection with our institution, called upon to consider the very important and interesting subjects, viz. time, death, and immortality. And our aim in the course of initiation has been, symbolically and directly, to point subjects for meditation which could lead men to live virtuously and happily,

---

31. FM1:19.18. The manuscript reads, "lead our F to the blace." This could be *fratre*, but it makes more sense for the candidate to be considered still a Fellow until he is raised.

32. FM1:20.2. The manuscript reads, "The flesh is corrupt.   Raises the body."

to meet death with serenity, and to cheer this hope of a blissful futurity.

(20.15) The necessity of mutual confidence in each other must be apparent to all who have wandered from the court of the Temple to its inner chamber, who would follow on in strange paths blind or in darkness or seeing where the sword point rests against the naked breast, except he had confidence in the directions of those with whom he went, and who would conduct any to the sanctuary of fraternity and make an indissolvable covenant of friendship with him unless he had confidence in his honesty and was convinced that he would betray not and would not be come an enemy.

(20.26) Confidence grows, however, out of the good opinions we may have conceived of others, either arising from a knowledge of those good principles or our observation of their good acts. Thus if we know men who live blameless lives, who shun covetousness and other vices, and who encourage truth and virtue, who protect innocence, and who do good, then we should certainly have confidence in these.

If they, at the same time, strive to propagate rules of life or doctrines tending professedly to make men happier than they otherwise would be, then, considering the character of these, men should at least examine the things they hold out to us. And if we even will not readily admit them, we ought not to neglect trying with them, and if upon a fair trial and proper examination they be found to be useful, as having a salutary effect upon individuals and upon society in general, if they are in unison with the truth, if they answer the great ends of making men better qualified for the discharge of duties, if they make men really happier, then it would undoubtedly be very contrary to our ideas of duty, if not very foolish, to reject them or even to neglect them. And that, if even they should be a little at variance with our customary thoughts or be somew(21,1)hat inconvenient because of our habits, such men and such rules or doctrines as I have alluded to are to be found, and it is believed that everyone who has strove to do his task as a Disciple and Fellow will seek and find them.

[Address on the Bible]

W.M.   This great light of Masonry is ever open in a proper Lodge, to that end that we should be reminded of the duty, that of learning and practicing the excellent precepts it contains. And if we, as far as we can, scrupulously examine both the character of those who gave the precepts and the influences they have had upon society and still have upon it, if we examine the great ends and views of the doctrines here written, and thus become acquainted with this volume, we shall experience that this volume is an inestimable treasure and should be viewed as such by all good men. It is in fact the book that contains the rules of life pointing out to man his whole duty. This volume is of great antiquity, and splendid monuments of the ancients have decayed and nations who peopled the countries where these things were written have vanished or are scattered over the face of the earth, their former places of abode are desolate, the languages the book was written in are dead, yet the book survives.

And the enemies of order and opposers of the good precepts this volume contains have sought with astonishing obduracy and unwearied pains, with jests, with philosophy falsely so-called, with misapplied learning, with every effort of their genius to bring this volume into contempt. But they have been engaged in a foolish work. All their pains have been taken in vain. It stands deservedly now in higher estimation than ever.

Considering the character of the writers for this volume and finding them to be good, even inimitably so, examining the doctrines contained in this volume, and observing their unison with truth and their beneficent influence upon society and upon individuals, thinking upon the great antiquity of these writings and the many revolutions which they have survived and their complete victory over the efforts of enemies, therewith continually increasing in the estimation of the world at large of the friends of good order and of truth, then it can be said, even if there were no other reasons for so saying, that this volume is not to be neglected, but, on the contrary, that it ought to be examined and should be made the subject of our attention and study.

And see how correct is its philosophy, how interesting the history, how sublime and beautiful the poetry, how acceptable the doctrines of religion and morality contained in this volume. It is calculated in every point of view to engage our attention, and, if attended to, the truths it contains make men better, wiser, and happier, and the benefits arising from these sacred truths are not limited to the period of human life. They point not forward to the grave as the boundary of our existence, as the place where men shall cease to be.

No, the thick gloom of death is dissipated by divine truth. A ray of sacred light makes visible to the eye of faith a state of existence beyond the grave, a state of existence, at the approach of which all must fear. For it lasts to all eternity, for it is a state of rewards and punishments, for it is dependent upon Divine mercy, for no man can claim a place there. Happy indeed is the man who has strove to subdue his passions and to lay aside his prejudices, and thus is fitted for the task of the Fellow.

And studying and executing the designs and rules of the Master, by contemplating upon the image of the pillar of beauty, he may have observed his own weakness and his own inability to make his work according to the pattern given him by the Master. If he is sensible of his own incapacity and imperfections, (22.1)he has in truth made the first step toward the light and has thus become more susceptible of the truth than he was. Then he will have the trestleboard in his hands and use all proper means for becoming acquainted with the designs which are drawn, and no doubt he will not only direct others how to exert them, but he will participate in the labour in the erection of the truly noble edifice—a Temple sacred to the name of God.

And in this work he will use the implements of the Master. The compasses will remind him to set proper limits to his duties, desires, and actions, not to be eccentric in behavior, but to preserve any even line of conduct without irregularities.

We should, by example and persuasion, try to exact and encourage fraternal love. This is the very cement of the Temple. If it is wanting the whole becomes a heap of rubbish and is of no worth, but on the contrary is an obstacle to those who pass where it lies and nuisance to those who may have a habitation near it. Where fraternal love is not, there must be many evils. There the ruffian passions are enthroned and virtue is driven out or spurned with contempt or bound with thorns. There folly derides wisdom, and truth is obliged to hide her fair face. There religion or morality can not be found. There all is but mockery.

Time we cannot recall, but we can and we ought to use that aright which is to come. [*Exhibits hourglass.*] See the sand. The particles run rapidly, and, for aught we know, with the passing of one of them you or I shall die. It is uncertain. We should not then neglect a moment, but from henceforth do all we can do to the great end of being really happy. For we shall die, and in the grave there is no working. There is no device, no knowledge, no pardon there.

[*Exhibits skull*] See this emblem, this monitor. It is silent vacant dead yet it speaks to our minds. The good hear a sound that even make them tremble. To some it can be a great cause of terror. It reminds all to remember death. We have crowned it with a green sprig, for we hope, in partaking of immortality, immortality and happiness through faith in the giver of every good and perfect gift, and by an earnest striving to do His will.

Remembering that man was created in His image and, although much deformed, can be again restored to his pristine state, be made fit for blissful enjoyments. Remembering that we should not be ashamed of truth and religion, for that would make us unfit for fraternity on earth and disqualify us utterly for the enjoyments of a future state, where love is the most essential requisite. Remembering that we should be charitable and sensible of the wants of our fellow men, for else we are monsters even here, as although associated as Brethren, and therefore would be hereafter unfit for lasting joys.

We must have hope to be restored to pristine purity. We must have faith. We must confess the truth. We must exercise love and charity with all our might. These are the rounds of the mysterious ladder that reaches from earth to heaven, and charity is the upper round.

[Opening or Closing of the Master's Lodge][33]

W.M. (22.26)*Salutation and so forth.*
   Brother Senior Warden, are you a Master Mason?
S.W. Yes, I know the acacia sprig.
W.M. Where do Master Masons hold their Lodges?
S.W. In the inner chamber.
W.M. What is that place?
S.W. A place of perfect silence.
W.M. Where is it situated?
S.W. In a deep valley.

Furniture, jewels, ornaments, symbols, 3 tapers, numbers, colors, signs, grips,[34] and words in each Degree same as in the others.

(23.1)**W.M.** From whence come the Masters and how do they journey?
S.W. From the East.
W.M. Why?
S.W. To dispense light and truth.
W.M. When one of our Brethren is missing, where shall we hope to find him?
S.W. Between the compass and square.[35]

---

33. The following questions and answers appear in the text without any heading and end abruptly, followed by a prayer. As the dialogue is between the Master and the Senior Warden, it is assumed to be the Opening or Closing rather than the Master's Catechism.

34. FM1:22.28. The manuscript reads, "furniture jewels ornaments symbols {3-branched candelabra} numbers colours signs gs, and words."

35. The "Wilkinson Manuscript" of ca. 1730–90 has "Q. If a Mason be lost where is he to be found? A. Between the Square & the Compass." Douglas Knoop, et al., *The Early Masonic Catechisms*, 2nd ed., Harry Carr, ed., (London: Quatuor Coronati Lodge, No. 2076, 1975), p. 138. *Le Maçon Démasqué* of 1751 has on its title page "D. Si un Franc-Maçon se perdoit, ou le trouveriéz vous? R. Entre l'équerre, & le Compas." Harry Carr, ed., *The Early French Exposures*, p. 417.

[PRAYERS]

[The prayer on the left, written in the clear, follows the previous questions (with three intervening lines of special symbols). Later Folger wrote a similar version, marked "Opening," which is printed with the first for comparison; it could be used to open any degree. Below the later opening prayer is a prayer marked "Closing."]

[PRAYER]

(23.6)Thy word is truth and we shall surely die. From dust we came, to dust we shall return, but Thou hast given us the fond desire, the hope, belief of life, even after death. For as Thy mighty word formed us of dust, so canst Thou raise us from the grave again and place us in a paradise divine or drive us out to sorrow and to pain. But how can we, Almighty King, obtain Thy blessing, or eternal life and joy? Lead us from evil, Lord, or else we err. Shield us from danger, Lord, or else we fall. Lead us to learn and do Thy holy will. Save us from perishing, or else we're lost, Thou King of Mercies, Great, Almighty God.

(85.1)OPENING [PRAYER]

Thou King of Mercies, great Almighty God, Thy word is truth and we shall surely die. From dust we came, to dust we shall return. Yet Thou hast given us the fond desire, the hope, belief of life, even after death. And as thy mighty word formed us of dust, so canst thou raise us from the grave again and place us in a paradise divine or drive us out to sorrow and to pain. But how shall we, Almighty King, obtain Thy blessing or eternal life and joy. Lead us from evil, Lord, or else we err. Shield us from danger, Lord, or else we fall. Lead us to learn and do Thy holy will. Save us from perishing, or we are lost.

CLOSING [PRAYER]

[9](85.17)Father of every good and perfect gift, humbly we offer Thee our feeble thanks for Thy great mercies to us sinful men for our desire, our hopes, our faith in life, blissful, eternal in the realms of light. Guide us and keep us in the way of truth, give us firm faith in Thee and in Thy word, and grant that we may live and die in love.

SCOTTISH OBLIGATIONS

[*The following "Scottish" obligations stand alone in the text.*]

(86.19)COVENANT BEFORE ENTERING A SCOTCH LODGE

I solemnly promise and vow that I will not converse about, so as in any manner to communicate or reveal to any person whatever, not even to a Free and accepted Mason, any of the forms, doctrines, symbols, or ceremonies, or any other things practiced or done in the Scotch Degree, excepting it be to a member of the same, or to such as are members of a Lodge acknowledged by the Master or his successors to be working according to the work done here, unless our Master or his successors grant me permission so to do. Nor will I reveal the time and place of meeting to any but members of the same. Amen.

(16.3)OBLIGATION FOR ALL MEMBERS ALSO ALL CANDIDATES FOR THE SCOTS RITUS AND VISITING MASONS

I promise and swear, sincerely and without deceit, that I will not reveal, speak about, or communicate in any manner whatever to any person in the world, not even to any Free and Accepted Mason, any of the forms, symbols, doctrines, or ceremonies, or any other things practiced in this body, excepting to such as are members of the same or of a Lodge acknowledged by the Master of this body to be working according to the work done in this Lodge, unless the Master of this body grant me permission so to do as far as it respects any Free and Accepted Mason. And I will not suffer the works to be altered, neither will I do the work which is practiced here in any other Lodge, or cause or allow it to be done, unless I have the consent of the Master for so doing, or the permission of the present Grand Master of the Grand Lodge.[36] So help me God, amen.

---

36. The manuscript uses a unique symbol here. Since the covenant refers to the *G M*, the consistent interpretation of the symbol is *Grand Lodge*. However, this is the covenant for the "Scots Ritus," and perhaps the special symbol stands for *Supreme Council*, or *Grand Consistory*.

[THE HISTORY]

(82.1)The regular formation of {? ? ?}[37] was undoubtedly affected by Cromwell[38] and at his time, but this was {? ? ? ? ?} and no other and in_____. The first regular {Lodge} was undoubtedly formed in {Europe} not in other places as in {? ? ? ? ?} , etc.

{? ? ?} was born 1590—lived 61 years. (In Cromwell's time Charles I was likened upon figuratively[39] by the courtiers as the murdered master—his mother was yet living as a widow and his Masonic subjects called themselves her children, etc., etc.) During Cromwell's time there were many Lodges in England, Ireland, and Scotland, and Masonry was generally adopted and flourishing throughout these kingdoms but also in other places. Yet out of England, Masonry was something also in form and object, and in these places it was not popular and connected with wrong speculations.

Cromwell's Lodges admitted all kinds of people without respect to Religion, Morality, or Cultivation, and it appears that he only used the Order as a means by which he expected to effect some certain more political views. He pretended to advocate Equality and Freedom, but this appears to have been all a sham. He found the doctrines of Masonry convenient with a little feeble alterations to his republican and afterwards to his despotical views. The rebuilding of the Temple was made a figure in all its parts subservient to the circumstances and to the political views of many of his English coadjutors.

In England about this time, the Order had many names one after the other as Free Masons-then Nivelleurs-then members of the Fifth Monarchy and finally were again called Free Masons. Cromwell appointed priests[40] for Secretaries for the four Quarters of the Globe etc. General Rainsborough was the Master of the Nivelleurs. Some of his Companions were concerned in the death of the King. Their ostensible object was as a society to the establishment of Freedom, etc. Harrington was Master of the Fifth Monarchy and a friend and connection of Cromwell. Their professed object was freedom and equality and not to acknowledge any other Regent than {Jesus} . They had the form of a flag with a Lion sleeping with this motto—"Who will wake him?" They conspired however against Cromwell and were persecuted afterwards by him.

Hereafter Cromwell sought to give to Free Masonry in England a more religious tendency that it had before had in that land, and it is said that the oath now has received quite another form and a more political one than before. And several Nivelleurs were during this alteration severely punished, even with death (see Parchard's *History*, 1736, when the Order had got a more fearsome[41] oath, etc.). It is however to be

---

37. In many places, Folger used Hebrew letters to spell phonetically certain words, indicated here by braces. When his intentions are not clear, braces containing question marks are used, one question mark for each Hebrew letter. In a few places in the text, large blanks appear, as if Folger was intending to later fill in some word or characters. These blanks are indicated by underlining in the text.
38. The manuscript has an ill-formed *beth*, ב, or *kaph*, כ, but later a *kaph* is deduced to stand for *Cromwell*, because of the similarities to *Sarsena* (see chapter 1). Therefore all occurrences of the *kaph/beth*, כ/ב, letter are interpreted as *Cromwell*.
39. FM1:82.4. The manuscript reads, "C I was likened upon fig.y."
40. FM1:82.19. The manuscript reads, "כ appointed   for Secretaries."
41. FM1:82. 30–31. The manuscript reads, "the order dad got a more *f* oath &c."

remarked that Williberts Architects and Masons Societies (in 600) was one of the first formular appearances of Free Masonry in Europe, and it thereafter a short time got the name of Free and Accepted Masons.

The murdering of Charles of England gave the society another form. The flight of James II produced the higher degrees. Here is the secret of the Dagger with which the Usurper should be killed.

{? ? ? ?} and this {?}'s arrival in {? ?} and the institution thereabouts of an order is a subject much connected with the Masons' History, yet it is certain that several hundred years before this time in which {? ? ?} institution existed that there was an order established or introduced on one of the western Isles and flourished there prior to 1118. Masonry was not denominated any such thing as Masonry but was the real Masonry, which altho now but little known among Masons but is known to some few. On the restoration of the Royal family after the republic {?} was adopted instead of other things {? ? ? ? ? ?} and Knight.

(81.1)(Mons) was erected in {? ? ? ?} , etc. The monks joined the order and the _____ of the Templars originated. Now the statutes were published in England, and the English Lodges (1705) formed a Grand Lodge and usurped the Supremacy, etc. The Jesuits—Mystics—Illuminati—joined the order and by entirely influencing, altering, and adding to it, it got to the shape is now has. And the most of those who tried the in essentially and entirely different from what it originally was in the same kingdom as other places.

Before the inquiry by {Rome} , from a short time after the crucifixion,[42] there remained in {Jerusalem} several of the Brethren, among them {? ? ?} . He and they, a short time before the destruction, retired to Ephesus. At Jerusalem they taught the sublime doctrines of Christ[43] and joined to them several {? ? ? ?} who were in possession of the rites of the Temple. They had assembled and introduced many Christians into the mysteries-these serving rather as an exaltation of knowledge and shewing that the real doctrines of Christ had long been known and cultivated in the world even from very ancient times.

But Justin the High Priest and many of the Jews were opposed to the doctrines of the Cross and had got a wrong impression as to the mysteries and these and all who were not Christians were not admitted among the Brethren. From Ephesus many went into Greece, and to Achaia. In particular were they taught Christianity,[44] and in some places they privately learned the Brethren the Mysteries. Shewing them who were acquainted with these things that the new doctrine did not contradict but rather confirmed the Mysteries and the precepts of Life which these contained.

But soon after the destruction by Titus some of the dispersed Brethren returned to {Jerusalem}and their keeping to landmarks of the holy places in view, and many of them were desirous to search the vaults of the Temple and the graves of the Kings, thinking not only that it was possible that there were treasures there, but that they

---

42. FM1:81.9. The manuscript reads, "a short time after the ✗."
43. FM1:81.11. The manuscript reads, "sublime doctrines of C."
44. FM1:81.18. The manuscript reads, "were they taught C."

should in time be able to find some things belonging to the Temple of which only tradition existed and which were deposited by Zerubabel[45] according to their account. But the Roman Soldiers and many uninvited Jews and Infidels being generally present hindered them in their researches.

And as the Infidel Jews in the year 105 made a kind of revolution, Adrian utterly destroyed the buildings which had been repaired in {Jerusalem} and the three towers, and the Brethren fled. But they were well acquainted with the landmarks _____ and a description of this and of the Temple, etc. formed hereafter a part of the mysterious instruction. In the second century (121–130) many Brethren retired with associates and devoted themselves to acts of Piety, dwelling in secret places and praying, fasting, and doing acts of charity of which there was much new. But they also kept communion with each other and as far as circumstances would permit propagated the mysteries.

However many of the church were opposed to these things and the Brethren were obliged to be very discreet, and their number sometimes was very small. Yet in other parts of the world there appear to have been numerous assemblies of the same kind tho under different denominations, as in Greece. In 613 there were many in {? ? ?} , and many persons in 613–680 joined them. Buildings were now built in the holy places, one of which was called Solomon's Temple, being a church built on the foundation of the Temple's Sanctuary with flat roofs on the West side, and a kind of shelter with a stone wall and steep roof on the East side. By these buildings the place of the Sanctuary was afterwards found.—times

[*Folger Manuscript 1 abruptly ends here.*]

---

45. FM1:81.26. The manuscript reads, "deposited by Z."

7

Folger Manuscript 2

HIS CIPHER MANUSCRIPT WAS FORMERLY REFERRED TO AS THE *Supreme Council Book*. It was written in a half leather book, decorated with green and brown oil-board, measuring 6¼ × 7¼ inches. It is watermarked by "De Erven D. Blauw," a family of Dutch papermakers. Other pages bear the watermark of a double rimmed and crowned circle with bearing the motto *Liberate Pro Patria Eivsque*. Within the circle is a lion standing on a dais labeled VRYHEIT. The first 36 pages are almost completely in plain text, with very few words in cipher text. Pages 36–64 are, for the most part, an equal combination of plain text and cipher text, with occasional whole pages in one or the other; pages [65–90] are again almost wholly plain text; [91–112] are blank, and [113–120] are plain text.

Harold Voorhis, who once owned FM1 (the Macoy copy) had also seen FM2, and wrote to Brent Morris in 1979, "The first one of the code books I found in an ancient safe in 1946. The second I found in the library of the Supreme Council (S.J.) a dozen or more years ago." This explains why it was known as the *Supreme Council Book*. When Brent Morris began his research into FM1 in 1978, he searched the Library and Archives of the Supreme Council, S.J. to no avail. Subsequent searches by the library staff and others likewise yielded no results. However, early the year 2002, the missing manuscript resurfaced in a private collection on the West Coast, and the mystery was solved. Pasted on the front board was a bookplate reading: "Secrets of the Egyptian Priest ceremonies. Loaned to Wm. Boyden, Library of Supreme Council SMJ Washington D.C. To be returned to M. Clay or heirs by Jan. 1965." The book, which had been loaned to the Supreme Council, had been returned to its owner, who had been involved with irregular Masonry. Following his death the manuscript passed to a relative who was unaware of its Masonic significance, but was interested in the book as a curiosity. The book was subsequently sold to a private party who has allowed us to reproduce the work herein.

We believe the title, "Secrets of the Egyptian Priest ceremonies," refers to the pseudo-Egyptian "Ancient Mysteries" translated by Folger (FM2:66.1), which appeared in the mysterious book *Crata Repoa, Oder Einweihungen in der alten geheimen Gesellschaft der Egyptischen Priester* (Crata Repoa, or Initiations into the Ancient Secret Society of Egyptian Priests), first published in 1770.

CRATA REPOA.

Oder

Einweihungen

in

der alten geheimen Gesellschaft

der

Egyptischen Priester.

Berlin, 1778.

Bey Christian Ludewig Stahlbaum.

Folger Manuscript 2

[DISCIPLE]

(62.1)Preparation Room

It should be a small dark room painted black. He entered by three steps down. There must be a table covered with black, two chairs, also black coffin, and Bible open at the first Chapter of John, a skull and hour glass, a pitcher of water, and the tablets, a light and other things connected with the grave.[1]

In the Second and Third Degree these things are arranged differently. Each degree has different tablets. The Lodge of Disciples and Fellows is blue, and Masters, black.

The emblem of a Disciple is the broken pillar and cap laying; at the bottom, inscription: Adhoc Stat.[2]

Second Degree, a spare stone with a spare hanging on second is inscription: Deregere Obliquitas.

Third, a dismasted ship. These are painted on silk and hung on the Masters table. The aprons are plain and in the Third, the Masters wear their hats and long black robes.

(39.1)*The guide introduces the Candidate, seats him and says*: Hither we have come. Let us now rest for a short time. I beg of you to abstract yourself from all worldly thoughts for a little period of time and to devote this season to the consideration of yourself and those things which may here occur to you. To the place of which this is a symbol we must all sooner or later come. The rules of order have made me bring you hither. Let me make you acquainted with these things.

[*Exhibits*] *hourglass.* Here is the emblem of time. Turns it. Behold how rapidly the particles of sand run. It will soon run out and then if no external power set it in motion again its movements will never be renewed. Forget this not.

[*Draws attention to the pitcher.*] Here is water for your refreshment.

[*Exhibits skull.*] Here is the image of death and emblem of mortality. No human philosophy or thinking can devise what lies on the other side of this veil or what shall happen to us there, yet it is certain we shall all go thither to return no more and it is certain that duration beyond the grave in comparison to the period of human life is infinite. This subject then is to you, is to us all an interesting one and of great moment.

[*Exhibits Bible.*] See. Here is the only light by which we can learn how to enter the grave so as to enjoy happiness hereafter. It is the book of wisdom and contains a revelation of the divine will.

---

1. FM2:38.16 describes the room thus: "The Chamber should represent a tomb. There should be a coffin, table, chairs, Bible, skull, hourglass, pitcher of water, tumbler, and other things, all black."

2. This is a misspelling or misunderstanding of the motto of the R.E.R. First Degree, *Adhuc stat* (Thus far it stands).

[Preliminary Obligation]

³*This obligation may be given in the first, second or third grade.*

I solemnly pledge my word of honor and promise that I will not reveal in any manner or form whatever the secrets, mysteries, doctrines, ceremonies or any other thing whatever, concerning that degree which I am now about receiving, to any human being in the world, excepting, etc., who is properly qualified according to the rules of this holy and solemn Order.

Tablets

(39.10)*Goes out. The Candidate here studies the tablets, and so forth.*
[*The following three questions appear on one of the tablets.*]⁴

Question First: Do you believe in the existence of a God, perfect and good, the Creator of all things?⁵
Second: Do you believe in the immortality of the soul?
Third: If so, what do you believe to be your duty toward God your neighbor and yourself?

(39.10)*Then it is proper to carry the answer to the Master by the guide.*
[*In the absence of the guide, the Candidate reads the following from a set of tablets in the room.*]⁶

Know Thyself. This is most undoubtedly a religious and holy duty and was one of those great and important truths which was greatly esteemed and reverenced in the most ancient times. It is important inasmuch as we ought to know our own weakness and imperfections and frailties. We ought at all times to acknowledge them, we ought never to think more highly of ourselves than we ought to think, and we should strive to pray to be able to lay aside all things which pollute us and all superfluity of naughtiness and receive the word of truth which is able to save our souls. But we must receive the word and keep it, else we shall be like the man who beholds his natural face in a glass, beholding himself and going away he

---

3. FM2:38.8. In the R.E.R. a preliminary obligation (*engagement préliminaire*) is delivered prior to any ceremony. See *Rituel de Loge de Sainte-Jean, 1ᵉʳ Grade* (Brussels: Grand Loge Régulière de Belgique, n.d.), p. 18; *Rituel de Grade d'Apprenti, Rite Ecossais Rectifiè* (Toulouse: Grand Loge Nationale Française, n.d.), p. 28.

4. Compare *Rituel de Loge de Sainte-Jean, 1ᵉʳ Grade* (Brussels: Grand Loge Régulière de Belgique, n.d.), pp. 13-14.

5. FM2:38.14 reads, "n the xstnc of a J perfect and gd." As the manuscript explains on FM2:38.3, the character J signifies God.

6. Several versions of the R.E.R. ritual employ additional tablets in the Chamber of Reflection, which contain brief instructions for the Candidate (See *Rituel de Grade d'Apprenti, Rite Ecossais Rectifiè* [Toulouse: Grand Loge Nationale Française, n.d.], p. 9). All three of Folger's Revised R.E.R. degrees likewise employ the use of such tablets.

immediately forgets what manner of person he was of (See James's Epistle).

CONSIDER THYSELF. This is showed and that thou often shouldest think upon that duty and remember that which you here see (apparently at the bottom of a vault)[7] is the image of the receptacle that contains great treasures. The Law of God, and to keep the knowledge of the Truth, to find which in another form has long engaged the attention of both wise and foolish men. It is a most certain truth that the fear of the Lord is the beginning of Wisdom, *etc.*

After a proper time the guide returns and says: The Lodge have commanded me to inform you respecting some of our ceremonies and customs and to prepare you in a proper manner to be presented or brought to the Lodge in order to be accepted a Disciple.

Permit me to advise you. Allow me to encourage you to the exercise of fortitude in the trials you are about to endure. Place confidence in those who shall conduct you in the way you are inclined to enter upon. As the first sign of your ready determination to join us, please to deliver me your hat and sword.

[8][*Speaking to an unidentified Brother*] Brother please deliver them to the Master and return hither to me again.

[*Once again addressing the Candidate*] Sir, will you please to lay from you all money and all external signs of distinction. Uncover your left breast. Expose the left knee. Tread down the left shoe. Now, my dear friend, you are certainly and properly prepared to be presented to the Lodge, and it is pleasing to me to believe that your heart and thoughts correspond with this external preparation, and that you are inclined to take all possible pains to eradicate all prejudices and emotions of the mind which militate against your proper duties as a man.

But Sir, you must be convinced that a man who is stripped of all sensual and false decorations and ornaments and coverings of vanity cannot be known or distinguished from others but by righteousness and virtue. It is absolutely necessary that you be informed of your own weakness and that it is impossible to go forward toward the Temple of Truth without help and guidance. In order to give us a plain token of your want of confidence in yourself you must permit us to deprive you of the light. It is an emblem of the false views which are the lot of that man who is left to his own guidance.

Band[age is placed over Candidate's eyes].

Tell me can you see any thing? On your honor? Be careful not to use deception with him who shall guide you. You will else presently most certainly repent.

You are now in darkness, but fear not. Those who guide you go in light and will not let you go astray. Hold your hands before you and guard against the hindrances you may meet with. You are now left alone. Strive to go forward. Put your trust in providence in order to avoid surrounding danger.

[*The Candidate*] *takes three steps forward.*

---

7. *Apparently at the bottom of a vault.* This refers to the Chamber of Preparation, which should be "three steps down."

8. FM1 indicates he is addressing a deputy.

I acknowledge you as one who manifests a strong desire to go forward in the proper way I mark well your strong desire but in thick darkness and alone you would undoubtedly go astray.

Takes his left hand and says: As such I will bring you to the Lodge.

Goes forward.

I pray you be instructed and learn to follow and to suffer with patience and abstinence and thereby make yourself worthy to obtain in time what you at present ask for. Follow me. Fear not.

Gavel three [times] at the door of the Temple.

Deacon Who comes here?

Guide One in darkness who seeks light and wishes to be accepted. His name. Age. His Christian name? Where born? His occupation? His he made any vow which forbids him from becoming one of us?

Guide then says: Sir, having brought you here my task is finished. You are now in safe hands, even with them who deserve your perfect confidence.

Guide takes him to the West and leaves him. Gavel.

W.M. Thus, Sir, you have sought to be accepted among us. This your request shall be strictly attended to, and from the good opinion we have formed of your character, and as one of our Brethren has pledged himself for you in a solemn manner, and he who I sent to inquire as to your motives in joining and in regard to your opinion of our instruction has reported so favorably of you, we have therefore sent a guide who has opened our door to you, and you are in the midst of us and in a state fit for the trials which you must endure, and which everyone who wishes to be accepted among us must pass through, remembering that the present is a state of [trial].[9]

But, Sir, before we can precede further I have some questions to ask you and must request of you a decided and unequivocal answer. But first, Sir, I must state to you that there is not any thing in our rites doctrines or ceremonies which militate against your religion or moral duties for the truth of this we pledge you our honor, and ask if you are now prepared or prompted to join us by a desire of being charitable and useful to your fellow man?

Second, are you prompted to join us by a desire for the knowledge of truth and to be associated with those who profess to promulgate it and encourage virtues and laudable pursuits?

Third, will you conform yourself to the regulations of the fraternity and do you sincerely truly and ardently desire and request to be made a Mason?

Well then, your request shall be granted you. May God, the giver and benefactor, grant that at some future day it may serve to make you happy. You are about going on a mysterious journey, dangerous and rough. The way you cannot see, yet

---

9. FM2 ends abruptly at "a state of" but the word "trial" is present in FM1.

confiding in him who leads you. Go forward with firmness, yet with caution, and rest assured that your guide will not bring you in paths where you should not go.

GUIDE   Sir, the naked sword pointing to your breast is but a weak symbol of the dangers which surrounded you as one who wanders in darkness but you trust in God and fear not. Come with me.

Travels three rounds.

FIRST ROUND
Man was created in the image of God. But who can know him when he deforms himself?

[*Here is a picture of a seated man, perhaps indicating seated officer.*] Gavel.

SECOND [ROUND]
He who is ashamed of religion and of truth is unfit for and unworthy of fraternity.

THIRD ROUND
That man whose ear is deaf to the cries and distresses of his fellow men is a monster in the assembly of the Brethren.

[10]W.M.   Let him now ascend the three first steps of the Temple mysterious to try his strength, then bring him the East to make his vow.

Sir, your patience has enabled you to reach an altar at which, by the rules of our Order, you are required to make a solemn and irrevocable oath never under any consideration whatever to reveal any of the secrets, symbols, signs, or ceremonies belonging to the Order of Masonry, and you have already been assured that the Order does not contain any thing contrary to our duties toward God, our neighbors or ourselves. This assurance I now repeat to you and ask you if you are now willing to make the oath or covenant required of you? What do you answer?

But, Sir, before you can make a covenant, it is necessary that you be acquainted with its tenure, we holding it to be wrong to make a covenant with any unless they be well acquainted with its conditions. Therefore, you will please to kneel on the left knee upon the square and let your right hand rest upon the Bible, on which lies the square and compass covered with a sword. Sir, the book on which your hand now rests is the Holy Bible opened at the first chapter of John and fifth verse where there is written, and so forth.[11]

Do you believe that your hand rests upon the Bible and (43.1)why do you believe it? Thus you discover that a man can believe a thing of which he has no evidence but the serious assurance of another.

Now I address you to be attentive to the voice of the Senior [Warden], who will repeat to you the covenant which you are required to take, even in the presence of the Great Architect of the Universe, and which once made cannot be recalled:

---

10. The speaker is not identified.
11. FM1.1 reads, "where there is written, 'And the light shineth in the darkness; and the darkness comprehendeth it not.'"

[Disciple's Obligation]

That I will be faithful to the Religion of the Gospel, Holy and true, and to the Government of the country in which I live, will strive to gain the love of my fellow men by practicing virtue, shunning vice and encouraging others so to do; to the best of my ability will help the distressed, that I will conceal from every one who is not a member of this order, etc., the privileges of this holy Order and will strive to love all who are worthy and good brethren of this degree.

Penalty: contempt without honor, despised cast out from all, and hereby repeat my wish to be made a Mason.

W.M. Have you heard distinctly and properly understood this covenant? Are you willing to take it and assent to it according to the customs of our order? I ask you for the last time.

In order, Brethren. While this man makes his covenant let us give him a token of our accordance with it.

[The Candidate repeats the covenant.]

You are now bound to us and we to you by this your oath, but the trial of your sincerity which is the hardest trial is now at hand. You have said that you would sanction this covenant according to the customs of the order. Are you willing to sanction it with your blood if it should be required of you?

It is done.[12]

Then I accept you as a Disciple in Masonry, to the honor of God[13] the Almighty, in the name of fraternity, and by virtue of the power vested in me, Amen.

Response.

That last trial, your being willing to sanction your oath with your blood is convincing of your sincerity and I now salute you by the name of Brother but forget not under what condition you obtained this name. Brother Warden, bear him to the West, there to come to light.

[14]**S.W.** He is prepared.

[15]**W.M.** However weak the present light may be which flashes[16] before you, yet my Brother it is sufficient to show you our weapons turned against you, threatening you with shame and disdain if ever you should unguardedly betray the trust we have reposed in you. Let him be veiled again.

---

12. There were several variants of this test. In some, the Candidate's willingness was sufficient evidence of his sincerity, while in others he was mock bled by being bandaged and having his arm lightly scratched; after which tepid water was poured on his arm.
13. FM2:43.12 The manuscript reads, "to [the] honour of J [the] Almighty."
14. The speaker is not identified, but is in FM1.
15. The speaker is not identified.
16. FM2:43.14 The manuscript reads, "wh flashes bfore [you]." FM1 reads, "that flms bfre you." Perhaps the *Urtext* read *fl*, which may be read either *flashes* or *flames*.

[*The bandage is again removed from the Candidate's eyes as a flame is made to flash before him.*]

Sic transit gloria mundi! For a moment since you saw our weapons turned against you threatening you with shame and disdain if ever you should unguardedly betray the trust we have reposed in you.

We were apparently hostile. Look at us now armed for your defense and welfare yes my Brother the order will not and shall not forsake you as long as you are faithfully doing your duty and keeping your covenants.[17]

Brother Master of Ceremonies, let our new Brother be clothed and return with him to the Lodge.

End Of Section One.

Proceed With The Second Section.

[18]**Deacon**   One knocks.
[19]**W.M.**   See who it is, and if a Brother, let him enter.
Deacon   It is our new made Brother.
W.M.   Bring him to the East by the new way.

[*The manuscript includes two versions of the apron and glove presentation, which are here presented side by side for comparison.*]

Address

(43.20)My Brother, permit me to clothe you with this new badge and emblem of our Order. I present you with these white gloves. The white clothing you are now decorated with is emblematic of purity. Worn worthily it is a very hon-	(13.1)Permit me now, my Brother, as the ceremony of Initiation is over, to clothe you in this White Leather Apron. It is the badge of our Order. It should be a lamb skin, pure and white. It is a very ancient decoration, and is the emblem of innocence. You should

---

17. This artifact is a carryover from the Rite of Strict Observance. "*At this moment* Pulv. Seminis Lycopodii [powdered lycopodium spores] *are blown through the flame from both sides, so that at the removal of the hoodwink, when he opens his eyes, a flash appears before his face without doing him any harm. All the Brethren stand holding their swords erect pointing upwards, and they shout together:* Sic transit gloria Mundi ["Thus passes the glory of the world"]. *The Master continues:* Just as our hands were armed, a moment ago, to punish a misdeed, you now behold Brethren who are ready to sacrifice their blood and lives in your defense." See Arturo de Hoyos and Alain Bernheim, "Introduction to the Rituals of the Rite of Strict Observance," *Heredom*, vol. 14 (2006), p. 72.

18. No officer is identified here.

19. No officer is identified here.

orable badge. Preserve them from stains and never appear without them in the Lodge.

The Order for good reasons does not admit women to its assemblies yet we profess and cherish esteem for the virtuous and good among the other sex. In token of this I present you with these gloves which you can give to such an one as merits your esteem.

keep it unspotted, and as often as you put it on or look upon it, it should remind you of the purity of life it is necessary you should lead, in order that you bring no reproach upon the society which has received you. It is your duty always to appear with it in the Lodge and carefully preserve it from stains of any kind.

I also present you with two pair of gloves. Those intended for yourself are always to be worn in the Lodge as a part of your clothing. The other pair is intended for the lady upon whom your affections may be placed and who becomes the partner of your pilgrimage.

The Order for good reasons does not allow women by they are nevertheless to be highly esteemed and cherished. They should fill the place in the affections of the man, occupy the station and receive the kind and tender treatment which was intended by their and our Creator. Let your conversation, while in her company, be discreet, your actions toward her gentle, and your conduct be altogether marked with courteousness and respect.

Here is your money, and so forth. Take them, my Brother. In giving you these we would admonish you to bear in mind that it is a most certain truth that the love of gold, silver and the like has been productive of more evils than any thing else in this world. Yes, covetousness and war have led men astray, have induced them to commit the meanest acts of cowardice, the most atrocious acts of injustice and oppression and violence. Acts so mean and so atrocious as to excite horror and disdain in every honest and feeling man. Acts which cause the sigh of sorrow to burst from the breasts of the really pious and which, alas, it is to be feared have brought down the thunder of damnation on the heads of the guilty perpetrators. Therefore, against the pernicious influence of these things we should watch.

Here is your hat. In returning it to you I must remark that none except they be Masters should be covered in the Lodge.[20]

---

20. FM2:16.7–8 expands, "The privilege of sitting with the Hat on being only given to the Master in the East."

Take your sword. Use it carefully when called upon by your country for its defense, but bear in mind that a man of blood is deemed unfit to build a Temple to the name of God, and never forget this commandment which gave law to man in order to make them happy, saying, "Thou shalt not kill."

I will now learn you the tests of this degree.

Go to the Warden and make your signs of acknowledgment to him and to your Brother who pledged himself in your behalf.

The Warden then takes him to the rough stone and says: Please step one step forward so will I teach you your work upon the rough stone.

[*The Warden taps*] three [*times on the rough stone with the gavel*].

S.W.   Kneel humbly down, *and so forth.*[21]

(14.1)*Explanation of the Working Tools*

W.M.   As you are yet but theoretically a Mason and have never yet commenced your work it becomes my duty as the Master of the Lodge to teach you the work you are to perform and to witness your commencement.

The place in which all Apprentices labor is in the vestibule or outer court of the Temple, and the subject upon they are to labor is the rough stone. Their instrument with which the work is accomplished is the common gavel.

The rough stone is emblematic of man in his rude and unpolished state. He was created pure and upright but he has deformed himself. He was created but little lower than the angels but he has fallen from his high estate and became a child of dust. Though he is much deformed and fallen we believe he may be restored to his pristine beauty and elevated to his former purity. Yet this is an arduous undertaking requiring all the time and pains you can bestow, and all the patience you can exercise while thus engaged.

The gavel is a symbol of power. While operative Masons use it for the purpose of breaking off the corners and rough edges of stones in order that the more experienced workmen may have less trouble in completing their labors, we use it symbolically to break off the aspirates caused upon the mind by the influence of prejudice and passion, to the end that the rough symbolic stone may become a smooth and polished one, fit for the builder's use. And as it is impossible for any laborers to pursue his work aright without proper instructions.

I here point out to you the Trestle Board of the Master, which is always open for your inspection. It contains all the perfect designs of the Master so that you never need be at a loss in the undertaking which you have before you. It will not only show you what man once was, and from what he has fallen, what man is and how completely he is alienated from the Master whom he ought to serve, but it will also show you the manner in which he is to be labored with his low estate, warned of his danger, brought in from his wanderings, and prepared for the enjoyment of the pleasures which he has cast away.

---

20. The Candidate is obliged to imitate the Warden's instruction.

In future then, forget not this guide to your labors. And now, having pointed out these things it remains for you to commence your work. Continue ever thus to labor and may the Master who beholds your diligence and your earnest endeavors crown them with success and approbation, and so assist you not only with physical strength, but also with spiritual enlightenment as to enable you to form out of the rough stone a polished one in every part, not only beautiful to be looked upon here, but one altogether fitted to form a component part of that spiritual Temple in the heavens. Give diligence to your work and let nothing turn you aside from its completion.

(44.30)Now let the first work you do as a Mason be a good work. Do a deed of charity. Give a pittance to help the distressed.

The bag is presented.
Shows the Warrant with Explanation.

Address [or Lecture]

[*There are two distinct lectures which account for the ceremonies of this degree. They are here presented side by side for comparison. That on the left is similar to FM1, while the other borrows from the Webb work. Contextually, the latter could be inserted between the earlier 'Address' and the 'Explanation of the Working Tools,' but it also provides an alternate ending for the degree.*]

(44.31)Be attentive to the explanation of the rite of initiation now ended.

The symbols, usages, and customs of our Order when well attended to lead the mind to the contemplation of things of the greatest importance to that man who is desirous to come to a knowledge of truth, and to meditate upon that which will promote his welfare. You was first led into a dark and narrow chamber where you was separated from the world and from the friend who brought you there. Although this separation was short, yet the things there led you to meditate upon subjects however common, yet of a very serious nature.

(16.1)I will now endeavor to give you some reasons for and explanations of some ceremonies through which you have passed.

[22]Your Hat was taken from you to be returned to you again with the instruction that in open Lodge you are always to remain uncovered. The privilege of sitting with the Hat on being only given to the Master in the East.

Likewise your sword, for you was about to be introduced to the assembly of the Brethren who profess and ought to be men of peace. Whatever may be the views of customs of men of the world, the contrary of the spirit of peace can find no entrance in this

---

22. The following three paragraphs were already given, almost verbatim, by the W.M. prior to commencing the explanation of the working tools.

Your meditations were disturbed by the coming of a Brother who inquired of you your motives for joining our Order, for none but those actuated by right motives should be admitted among us. He who was deputized to guide you hither in company with your friend caused you to be divested of all money, jewels, and the like, and otherwise prepared you for introduction into our Lodge, that you might know that worldly [distinctions][25] cannot give rank and must not create differences among men. In the Lodge we all meet upon the level. In fact, among the good and impartial, nothing but virtue and mental acquirements can give preeminence in the world among men, and nothing else can distinguish Brethren in the Lodge.

In the Chamber of Preparation it is hoped you spent the time profitably. You was abstracted from the world and, for a moment perhaps, was engaged in the consideration of yourself and, that other objects might not engage your attention or disturb the impressions which you there might receive and that you should show confidence in your guide, you was deprived of the light and thus led to the door of the Lodge where you was received by the Warden. He demanded of you your religion, name, age, and other particulars, for none but a professor of religion and one who is free, and who we know as a man arrived at the years of manhood, can be a admitted to our fraternity as a Mason.

The three blows on the door of the Lodge should remind you that from sacred asylum. We would endeavor to encourage each other in a labor of love, bearing each others burdens, and render what assistance we may to our Brother travelers in the rough pilgrimage of life. Take it back, then, but with this friendly admonition: to use it bravely for the defense of the country in which you live, for the safety of your home and fireside, for the protection of your person when in imminent peril. But remember that it is written, "Thou shalt not kill," and that a man of blood is deemed unfit to labor and unworthy of being associated with those who would erect a Temple sacred to the name and worship of the living God.

Sword is here laid away.

Here is your money. In giving it back to you we would admonish you to bear in mind that it is a most certain truth that the love of gold, silver and the like has been productive of more evils than any thing else in this world. Covetousness, as well as war, has led many men astray and induced them to commit the meanest acts of cowardice, the most atrocious as to excite horror and disdain in every honest and feeling man, which cause the sigh of sorrow to burst from the breasts of the really pious and which it is to be feared has brought down the thunder of damnation on the heads of the guilty perpetrators. Therefore, against the pernicious influence of this thing we solemnly caution you to watch.

You was divested not only of all money, jewels and the like, but also of

---

23. FM3:45.5. The word "distinctions" is lacking, but present in FM1.

him[24] who seeks with constancy who asks with humility, and who knocks rightly at the door of the Temple of fraternity and peace, it shall be opened. You was conducted to the care of the Warden and stood upon the threshold of the Lodge, your former guide leaving you with assurances that you were in the hands of those who would not mislead you. But before you could, by the assistance of you new conductor, proceed on your way, the Master addressed you, and your motives for coming here were made known by him who best could inform us, namely by yourself.

Then, reciting the confidence you had hitherto placed in us, we believed you, and then you commenced a journey on which you learned from the East some truths on which the tenets of our Order rest. You then ascended the mysterious steps of the Temple, and was brought to the altar to make a very serious promise. On the whole of this journey reciprocal confidence supported you. Confidence between you and us, for if you had not had confidence in us you would have refused to follow our directions and, if we had not believed you to have been upright we would not have received you among us.

You was joined to us by a solemn tie, and afterwards you saw a blazing and unsteady light which was only sufficient to discover apparent surrounding dangers. Finally, the veil was removed wholly. You saw the light. You beheld Brethren armed for your defense and welfare. All hostile appearances were done away and all metallic substances with your external clothing. Of your clothing, to ascertain that you was a man. For the Order, although it cherishes the virtuous and the good among the other sex, does not admit them among its numbers. Of your money and jewels, that you might know that worldly distinctions cannot give rank and must not create differences among men. In the Lodge we all meet upon the level. In fact, among the good and impartial nothing but virtue and mental acquirements can give preeminence among men in the world, and nothing less can distinguish Brethren in the Lodge. Of all metallic substances, as a matter of usage. For at the building of the Temple there was not heard the sound of an ax or hammer or any tool of iron. As the timber was hewed in the forests of Lebanon the stones were squared in the quarries of Zeredatha, were all conveyed to Jerusalem where they were adjusted to their several places without noise of any kind. It may remind you that your work is not to be done with instruments of metal or of wood, but that the preparation is of a spiritual nature and which if done aright will fit you as a living stone to be placed in that Temple on high.

You was neither naked nor clothed, barefoot nor shod. The instruction which you have already received at the altar will remind you farther of the reason of this proceeding.

You was then deprived of the Light. For this we will give you many reasons. And first: that you might be insensible to any thing but the voice of the Master.

---

24. FM2:45.11 reads "from him." FM1 more properly reads "for him."

everything bore the appearance of love. Those scenes are emblematical of the different states of man.

The unenlightened state, in which man makes sacrifices and oblations for obtaining favors from heaven or for the atonement of atrocious deeds he may have committed. In which state nearly all the objects he perceives were hostile in appearance, and his fellows, strength.[25] Their arms appeared to threaten him, their power to place him in danger. He shuns, fears, or even hates them, but, in a more enlightened state he perceives that heaven rather accepts a sincere and contrite heart than burnt offering and oblations. He then acknowledges his fellow men as his Brethren, and he looks upon their power as means for his own defense and welfare. He joins them, relies upon them, and loves them. You was invested with the badges of innocence and purity and admonished by good conduct to keep them unsullied.

And then you received the tests of this degree, by which you were enabled to make yourself known to Brother Masons. Do not, my Brother, be among those who strive to publish to the world that they are Masons. Nether countenance anything tending to this end, for the honor and usefulness of the Order are much more extended by concealment and by an acquaintance which the exalted aim of our labors and the probable extent of their influence upon the welfare of the world. You will be assured that silence and circumspection tend to give our Order force.

[*Turns him.*][26]

You were about to make an advance toward the Temple and all who would come within its sacred enclosure must lay aside every thing of a worldly nature, must forget the follies, the pleasures, the allurements and the gaudy trappings of the world, and listen only to the pleading of that voice which, though small and still, will be heard above the tempest or the blast, and if heard aright will guide into all truth. Second: although you had pledged yourself to submit to our usages, yet if you thought proper to alter your mind it was done in order that you be returned again to the world without being able to discern the beauties of the place or the faces of the persons who composed the assemblage.

The alarm given at the door may remind you of the passage of Holy Writ which declares, "Seek and ye shall find, knock and it shall be opened to you. Ask and ye shall receive." The person deputed by the Master questioned you, and your answers proving satisfactory you was admitted within the Lodge. When, after passing around the same for the examination of the Brethren, you completed your symbolic Journey and was conducted to the East. When, after answering the questions propounded to you in a satisfactory manner, you was requested to kneel for the benefit of prayer.

As the Institution which has just received you acknowledges and believes in the existence and guidance of the living God, whose all-seeing eye

---

25. FM2:45.22 reads "fellows strngh." FM1 more properly reads "his fellows seemed strangers to him."
26. FM2:45.29 shows the symbol for "him," which is turned around.

The Carpet before you, containing the principle symbols of our Order deserves your attention. The border, including the whole, is a representation of Mason work. This is the covering to all the other symbols and should remind us of that concealment of which we have already spoken.

The Rough and Polished Ashlars are symbols. The first, of the raw and uncultivated man, the other of him who has subjected himself to the discipline of truth.

The Trestle Board admonish[27] us carefully to study and follow the plans of the Master.

You see the Sun and Moon. They are here represented to remind us of application to our duties by day and by night, for this is all a man can do without erring.

There are the different instruments used by Masons as the Plumb, Level, and Square and so forth. They are adopted as hieroglyphs by us, they are here therefore represented.

And in the center is the Blazing Star, which we view with reverential silence.

And finally, the cord, or tie. It is here in remembrance of the cord which the veil of the tabernacle was drawn aside with, and it is emblematical of the tie which unites all good men and Masons, and we should remember ever that silence is the veil which keeps our sanctuary in safety.

Close before you is the Mosaic pavement which in Solomon's Temple covered the courts and on which the sanctuary stood. It is emblematical of the foundation which we seek in those we is ever upon them and from which searching glance no secret can be hidden or concealed, so do we believe that it is not proper at any time to enter upon any important undertaking without first invoking His assistance and His blessing. For my Brother, be assured His blessing maketh rich indeed and addeth no sorrow and He is always more ready to give than we are to receive. It is the first lesson you received among us, and we hope you will not forget it, but on the contrary make it a rule of life. For the destiny of man is in His hands. He turneth them as the rivers of water are turned. He exalteth him upon thrones. He causeth him in his prosperity to stretch forth his arms like a green bay tree. He changeth his countenance and sendeth him away. Therefore, call upon Him and He will answer you, and forget not that although you see Him not, He sees you and is well acquainted with all your thoughts. On being assured that your faith was properly placed you was told to arise and proceed on your way. You departed, and after a season arrived at an altar where you made, in the sight of heaven and the Brethren who surrounded you, an irrevocable vow which united you to us and the Brethren to you for ever. And it is hoped that you may never be tempted to break it. For it is a serious thing to vow and not perform.

You was then admitted to the light when the lights of the institution were explained to you and several important lessons given, which I trust you

---

27. FM2:47.1. This, perhaps, ought to read as FM1, "The Trestle Board should admonish."

Figure 1. A diagram of the Disciple's Lodge reconstructed from Folger's description.

accept among us. They should be men of a firm and fair character, fit for surrounding and supporting a sanctuary.

On the left you see a Pillar with the initial of the Word of your degree. Bear in mind the meaning of the word: "In him is strength." You ascended the three first steps of the Temple, but, as your time was not yet come, the door remained shut and you was led back again, and it is recommended you to wait with patience and to labor diligently yet with meekness, that when the door of the Temple shall be opened to you, you may hope, yes believe, to enter into the inner apartments with great joy.

END.

will remember without a repetition. You was then put in possession of the Sign, Grip and Word of the degree and the ceremonial was finished.

Be attentive now to the explanation of the carpet of your Lodge. It is to be regretted that the representation of the symbols of each degree has so generally fallen into disuse. It was the custom of ancient times to have the floor of each degree decorated in a proper manner, and every initiate was instructed in the emblems and told the reasons why they were there placed.

A Lodge is constituted by three, five or seven Brethren with a warrant from some regularly constituted body empowering them to hold meetings for the purpose of forwarding Masonic work or labor. It is not material at what place the Lodge is assembled, so that it is held in a sure place of retirement and secrecy, and all access guarded against by faithful watchers. Our Ancient Brethren selected for their place of meeting a high hill or low valley, in order that the approach of the profane could be the better observed. Of late years custom has made it a law that all regular Lodges shall he held in a room or place properly consecrated and set apart for the purpose. But the dimensions of a Lodge are very great. They extend from the North to the South and from East to West. In other words, the whole surface of the earth constitutes the field for the beneficent labors of the Brethren. Its covering is the clouded canopy or starry decked heaven, and the supports of this great canopy are three great pillars which are named Wisdom, Strength and

Beauty. For Infinite Wisdom could alone contrive so noble an edifice. Infinite Strength could alone support, and Divine Beauty could alone adorn this glorious and stupendous piece of Architecture. The material light given to this edifice you see represented before you, viz., the sun to rule the day and the moon and stars to govern the night. It is by the medium of these shining lights that man is enabled to pursue his labors. Although the Master is in heaven and we are upon the earth, although there appears to be and is in fact a separation between the two, yet by the symbolic ladder which you there see represented, and which is emblematic of that ladder which Jacob saw in the visions of the night ascending up to heaven from the Earth—by the aid of that ladder we may hope to ascend into the immediate presence of the Master like the angels of God. For the rounds of that ladder are but three, and are named Faith Hope and Charity. By constantly keeping our faith fixed upon God and a firm belief in the commands which he has declared we must keep, by the constant exercise of charity or love to the whole family of mankind, we may hope when this tabernacle of flesh is laid aside to ascend up on high and dwell with Him for ever more.

The furniture of this Lodge is the Holy Bible the Compass and the Square. The Holy Bible, or the Sacred Scriptures, is the revealed will of God and is His inestimable gift to man. It contains all that is important for a man to know. For it shows us our miserable condition by nature, and the manner in which that misery many find a remedy. It reveals to us the Avenger[28] of all sin and the immediate dispenser of all our blessings. It calls upon us for reverence and gratitude in our low estate and not only points out the path that leads to happiness here but also to a home beyond the skies.

The Square is the emblem proper of the Master. It should not only remind him of the duty he owes to the Lodge over which he is called to preside but it should teach all Masons to regulate their conduct by the principles of mortality and virtue.

The Compass may teach you to limit your desires to every station and to set a boundary to passion, for by means of this man is often made to err. By reflecting often upon these things you will be kept in the path of duty and walk in a manner becoming the Order which has just received you, but if you lose sight of them you will most surely fall.

The ornaments of the Lodge are the Mosaic pavement, the indented tessel and the Blazing Star. The mosaic pavement is a representation of the ground floor of King Solomon's Temple. It is emblematic of human life, checkered with good and evil; the beautiful border which surrounds it, those blessings and comforts man constantly enjoys, and the blazing star which appears in the center may remind you that in every situation of life in which you may be placed, whether groaning under the hand of affliction or living in prosperity and comfort, whether tried by temptations of various kinds or led astray by prej-

---

28. The word *punisher* is here superscripted

udice and passion, a firm reliance upon and constantly looking to Him of whom this star is but an Emblem will so lead you to improve under His chastening and disciplinary hand, as not only to afford you peace and satisfaction here, but and assurance of another and a better rest.

Here the moveable and immovable jewels are explained, which are the rough ashlar and the smooth ashlar, and the trestle board; after which the Pillar (also read from Monitor, Brotherly Love, Relief and Truth; also Temperance, Fortitude, Prudence, Justice) when the Acceptation follows.

Then the charge, then Salutation.

Close ceremonials by the chain of union. Salut! Saut! Salut!

The name of this degree is called "Faith."

(47.12) Form of Opening the Lodge in the First Degree, or Disciple

W.M.   Brother Warden, are you a Disciple?
S.W.   I am.
W.M.   Brother Warden, what is the first duty of every good Mason and, in a Lodge, particularly of the Brothers Wardens?
S.W.   To see that the profane are removed and the hall in safety.
W.M.   Please to perform that office.
S.W.   The profane are removed and the sanctuary in silence.
W.M.   Since the profane are removed, and the sanctuary in silence, we will pursue that path of our duty pointed out to us, and strive to consummate our work.

Three knocks.

S.W.   Brethren, look toward the East. It was there the light arose by which we are enabled to work. Let us be prepared to commence our labors at the signal of the Master.
W.M.   One k[nock]. In order, Brethren.

Lights the [three-branched] candle in the East.

    May the clearest light shine for us during our labors.

Lights the two three-branched candlesticks. Then pray.

W.M.   Brother Junior, what is the time?
J.W.   It is past high twelve.
W.M.   Brother Senior, is it the right time to begin to work?
S.W.   It is.
W.M.   Then assist me, Brethren, to open this Disciples' Lodge. Let us live together in unity. To the honor of God, in the name of fraternity, and by virtue of the power of my office, I declare this Disciples' Lodge opened.
    Brethren, be attentive to the work.

[*The work proceeds in the*] *usual form and then the Candidate is introduced.*

Closing [the Disciples' Lodge]

W.M. Brother Junior, what is the time?
J.W. Toward low twelve.
W.M. Brother Senior, is the labor finished?
S.W. It is.
W.M. Have any of the Brethren any thing to offer as the labor is closed?
Br almoner please perform your duty.
In order Brethren. Before we part let us form a tie of fraternal union and offer up our dutiful acknowledgments to the Great Master whose goodness has enabled us thus far to do the work of my and supplicate His blessing.

[*Prayer*]

Brethren assist me to close this Lodge let us be united. To the honor of God, and so forth.
Brethren, be attentive.

Master blows out his candle.

That light which shined during our labor cannot be seen by the profane. Brethren when you seek for light wherewith would perfect your work remember this that light is in the East and only there to be found.

[Disciples' Catechism]

Q: Brother Senior, are you a Disciple?
A: I am.
Q: From whence came you and Disciples?
A: From the West.
Q: And whither are they going?
A: Toward the East.
Q: Why?
A: In search of light.
Q: What are your duties as a Disciple?
A: To continue diligently the work I did begin, as commanded by the Master on the rough stone.
Q: With what did you work?
A: With the symbol of power.
Q: Why?
A: To show the proper use of the power with which I was entrusted.
Q: How is a Mason to be known?
A: By signs, words, and grips.
Q: How so?
A: His manners must be gentle and unassuming, his conversation prudent and discreet. He being rather a hearer than a speaker, being willing to hear, yet apt to teach and shunning foolish disputes. He disdains to pollute himself by doing any fraudulent act or criminal, he discountenances libertinism, commends and practices virtue. He encourages benevolence and charity by precept and example.
Q: Where do Disciples labor?
A: In the outer court of the Temple.
Q: Have you received your wages?
A: Yes.
Q: What are they?
A: I get food and raiment and many other things.
Q: Where did you receive your pay?
A: At the entrance to the Temple.
Q: Who pays you?
A: The Master.
Q: Are you satisfied with your wages?
A: I am well satisfied and know the Word.
Q: What time do you design(48.5) to work?
A: Past high twelve.
Q: When is the time to rest?
A: Towards midnight.
Q: What are the dimensions of your Lodge?
A: Its length, and so forth.

Q: Why this extent?
A: Because Masonry includes all things; it is unlimited.
Q: What do the three candlesticks represent?
A: The sun and moon and the Master of the Lodge, and as the sun and moon regularly dispense light and life to the earth, so does the Master dispense knowledge and discipline to the Lodge, and all Masters of Lodges should strive so to do.
Q: Wt is the emblem of a Disciple?
A: A broken pillar with the inscription "Adhuc stat."[29]
Q: How is it explained?
A: As by the remnant of the pillar that is yet standing we can ascertain to what order it belongs and determine what its proportions and ornaments were when it was entire, and thus be enabled to form another pillar in the likeness of the broken one, so from what we know relative to man we hope and believe he may be restored to a state approaching to that first pristine purity and happiness.
Q: Why is Solomon's Temple used as an emblem in Masonry?
A: It was a highly finished and splendid building and the first Temple erected by man publicly sacred to the name of the only wise and true God, and Masonry teaches us to be built up living Temples as perfect and beautiful as the Solomonic Temple was to the service and to the honor of the Supreme Architect of the Universe.

END OF THE RITUAL.[30]

---

29. FM2:48.8–9 is a misspelling or misunderstanding of the motto of the R.E.R. First Degree, *Adhuc stat*.
30. FM2:48.15. A note following this reads, "The prayers are in the black covered book."

(49.1)FELLOW

Opening

Begin the same as in the Disciple and proceeds until he come to lighting. Then address as in the Disciple, then:

W.M.   What is your Order's name?
S.W.   Boaz.[31]
W.M.   Brother Senior, for what purpose are we here assembled?
S.W.   To learn to know ourselves, and to inspect the work already done on the rough stone, *and so forth, as in the Disciple.*
W.M.   Brethren, let us strive deeply to impress it upon our minds that it is highly important to labor diligently in order to complete the work according to the designs of the Master. Let us henceforth abstain from all foolish and vain pursuits and use the time allotted us to labor in the discharge of our duty that haply we may be deemed fit for the Temple and not be rejected, and that we may hope to meet a reward, remembering that time flies swiftly away and is irrecoverable for mortals, but, to the view of the Great Master on high, the past, the present, and the future are all alike open. He perceives the actions of men and knows their thoughts.

The candles should be lit and placed behind the blazing star.
Gavel.

---

31. FM1 reads, "*Giblem.*" The word of the Fellows' degree (*Le Mot du Grade*) is *Boaz* or *Booz*, while the word of recognition (*Parole de reconnaissance*) is *Giblim*. See *Rituel de Loge de Sainte-Jean, 2ᵉ Grade* (Brussels: Grand Loge Régulière de Belgique, n.d.), p. 30.

(49.9)Rite of Initiation [in the Fellow's Grade]
Preparation of Candidate

Tablets

First [Tablet]: Man was originally pure, undefiled, happy. How comes it then that he wars with his own welfare and often makes himself miserable? This is a subject which undoubtedly demands our highest attention inasmuch as we ought to study to avoid unhappiness.

Second [Tablet]: The fool wanders his whole life through without considering or knowing from whence he came or whither he is going. But the wise man strives to know what he is about. And considering every step, its end and its intention, and, by constantly pursuing the objects of happiness, he avoids all that can stop him in his way. And knowing his own weakness and ignorance, he receives with humility the doctrines that are given him and with gratitude proffered support when he is weary,[32] and when his own strength would not bear him further.

These tablets are placed on the table in the Chamber which, in other respects, is the same as the Disciples'.
The guide enters and delivers the following

Address

[There are two versions of the address, here presented side-by-side for comparison.]

(49.21)My Brother, Masonry is progressive. It is necessary, in every pursuit of knowledge, gradually to advance in order to understand things aright, wherefore, you was not all at once made a acquainted with all the rites of our Order, but are advanced gradually through them. And indeed, as nearly every thing in our rites is symbolical, it requires previous preparation to understand them and to make them useful to ourselves. Permit me to ask you, what is your	(24.2)Masonry is progressive. It is necessary in every pursuit of knowledge gradually to advance in order to understand things aright, wherefore, you was not all at once made acquainted with all the rites of our Order but are advanced gradually through them. And indeed, as nearly every thing in our rites is symbolical it requires previous preparation to understand, and to make them useful to ourselves. The degree which you are now taking may be considered partly as a rec-

---

32. FM1 reads, "when he is wrong." This suggests evidence of an earlier cipher text, which likely read, "when he s wr."

opinion of the tendency of our Order?

[*Candidate responds.*]

This degree is to be considered partly as a recompense for your labors past, but principally as tending to prepare you for the Masters'. I can assure you, my Brother, that your constancy and your fortitude in this degree must stand very serious tests. If you are determined and fixed to go forward, then follow me like a man, but if you waver then I advise you rather to remain in the degree of Disciple until you, by the easier duties required in the degree you have taken, have become strong.

ompense for labors past, but more particularly as a introduction to the Masters Degree.

The former degree is well calculated to impress upon the mind the duties of morality, and imprint on the memory the noblest principles which adorn the human mind.

The working tools of this degree are the plumb, square and level. They are made use of by operative masons to raise perpendiculars, lay horizontals, and to square their work. Our Order has, as you already know, adopted the implements of operative masons as Hieroglyphs. Such instruments were used in erecting the Temple at Jerusalem, which was sacred to the name of Deity, and they have been moralized.

The plumb admonishes us to walk uprightly in our several stations before God and man. See its unerring line. It directs from earth to heaven, and from heaven to earth.

The square may teach us to square our actions with all mankind.

It is the symbol of Truth, the discoverer of error, and we hail the love of truth as one of the greatest virtues.

The level may remind us of that equality which ought to exist among all good Masons, remembering that with God there is no respect to persons, and that together, as he has placed us, we are all traveling in the level of time, to that undiscovered country from whose bourne no traveler returns.

(49.29)Now Brother, decide, yet do not deceive yourself. Will you follow me?

[*The Candidate knocks at the Lodge door.*]

Deacon   Who knocks?
Guide   It is a Disciple who wishes to be accepted as a Fellow.

[*The guide gives*] *his name, his age, and so forth.*

Guide He has labored in the outer court of the Temple on the rough stone.
Deacon Pass.
Guide Brother, I have assisted you as you desired. I have brought you to the place whither you durst not approach. My work is now finished. Try and find yourself a new guide.
W.M. Brother, you are welcome.

[Address from the Master]

The Fellows and Masters present have given their unanimous consent to your being accepted as a Fellow, and I am well satisfied that in the character of a Fellow you will use your best endeavor and discharge your duties as such. Yet it is my duty to inform you that the work of a Fellow not only requires good application, but that it is difficult yet it undoubtedly has its reward.

You are from henceforth carefully to inspect the work already done on the rough stone and strive to complete it according to the designs of the Great Architect, that they may happily not be deemed unfit for the Temple. We are prepared and willing to assist you with advice and rules for your work, but the work you must do yourself. No man can do it for you. You must perform it yourself, and we desire that your honest endeavors may meet a reward.

Formerly on your symbolic journey, you was blindfolded, you was in darkness. At the present time you wander in the light. Yet, my Brother, you would undoubtedly go astray unless you were assisted by a guide who knew the way and is willing to show it to you.

If you will go to our Brother Junior Warden he will conduct you in paths on which you can learn things relative to the duty of a Fellow. His hand holding yours, and by which you will be led forward, should remind you that a Brother must assist another in good and laudable pursuits, while the sword resting on your breast should impress you with a sense of the danger of irregularity and precipitancy in the striving to consummate our views at the same time it teaches one of the important duties of the Fellow, viz., that of checking all imprudent hastiness, but especially when he is going upon a way where he is a stranger.

First Round.

One knock.

(53.1)Man was originally pure, undefiled, happy. How comes it then that he so often wars with his own welfare and makes himself miserable? His passions lead him astray, and sensual enjoyments entice him from the garden of happiness into the wilderness of vice and into the labyrinth or error. But presently, often, alas too late, it is feared he is undeceived, or what is worse, he is satiated. A feeling of duty or of shame rouses him to view his present state and he sees with remorse that he is far from where he should be, but the ways he has wandered through are so winding and intricate that he can perhaps never retrace his steps. And he stands like a fool, not knowing from whence he came or whither he went.

SECOND ROUND

Two knocks.

He who has began to forward in the path of wisdom and virtue and turns back is a thousand times more deplorable than he who never went that way, for he never knew what duty was, nor did he taste the pleasures arising from virtuous actions. Such a man has brought a dangerous enemy to war against his welfare, viz., his own self.

(50.11)**THIRD ROUND**

Brother, we believe that you are willing and ready to undertake the task of a Fellow. The subject on which you are to labor is deserving of your attention, and you ought never to neglect it.

W.M.   Brother Warden, lead the Brother to the image of the pillar of beauty, and let him consider it well that he forget it not.

S.W.   If you desire to view the object of your labors then draw the veil aside. See yourself.

[*The veil is drawn aside to reveal a mirror.*]

And the light shineth, *and so forth.*

Knock.

W.M.   (53.16)Brother, the Fellows are generally well content with their own works, but if they behold them with the eye of the Master, they would be astonished to see how imperfect that is which they think so finished, and they would be very much alarmed on beholding how much yet remains to be done in order that they may not be rejected by Him who is appointed to inspect them and who will dispose of them according to their merits. Even the most finished work a man, who follows his own thoughts of perfection, can produce will perhaps be found very imperfect and full of errors and be deemed unfit and unuseful. Yet it is a consolation to know that a good artist is able to make of the most uncouth block of rough stone, an indisputable likeness of one of the most beautiful and perfect creatures. But in order to do this he must be well instructed by and he must follow the rules of a great and good Master.

[33]Brother, when you were before at this altar, although blindfolded you had so much confidence in us that you did not hesitate to give your consent to a covenant, the tenure of which you was unacquainted with. But before you took it, it was fully made known to you. Now you are in light and you have in some measure become acquainted with us and with the Order. Therefore we can expect more confidence

---

33. FM2:50.13. FM1:12.12–13 here has the candidate ascend five steps, when he beholds the Blazing Star. It appears that this has been accidentally omitted from FM2, as the catechism states that the candidate saw this emblem "from the steps of the Temple."

of you than when you was a stranger among us. Wherefore I ask you if you are willing to make the covenant belonging to this degree?

[*The Candidate gives his*] *answer.*

We expected of you this expression of confidence and thank you for it, but Brother, take our admonition in good part. Never consent to a serious engagement without first having heard its contents and without having understood them.

Brother Senior, please to read the covenant to our Brother.

Covenant

(53.26)I do promise faithfully and sincerely in the presence of God and this Lodge that I will be faithful and true to the holy Christian religion[34] and the government of the country in which I live, and that I will strive to gain the love and esteem of my fellow men by practicing virtue and shunning vice and by encouraging others so to do, and that I will as far as I can, help the distressed.

I also promise that I will conceal from everyone, who is not a Fellow, all the signs, secrets, symbols and usages of this Order and every part thereof.

And I will not reveal unlawfully any of these things, nor write them on anything, nor make them legible to others whereby the things and matters or secrets or usages shall be unlawfully revealed.

And I will strive to cherish and love all worthy and good Brethren of the Order as Brethren.

And should I violate this oath, the keeping of which I solemnly promise, I am willing to be looked upon by all honest and good men and all Brethren as a man without honor, and every praise worthy quality, and deserving their contempt and disdain.

And I now repeat my wish to be made a Fellow. So help me God.

W.M. (50.22)Brother, have you heard this oath, and are you willing to take it?

[*The Candidate answers.*]

W.M. Kneel, then, on the square and hold the square on your breast. Now read it yourself.

Brethren, while our Brother reads this oath let us give a signal of our accordance.

[*The Candidate reads the oath.*]

W.M. We hail you as a Fellow!

I present you with this blue ribbon which you will hereafter wear. It denotes constancy. It is the color of the heavens.

Learns the Grip and Word, and then the Sign.

---

34. *holy Xn religion.*

This Sign is a pledge of constancy and good faith. It is like pledging the heart. Thus, in pledging our word as Fellows, we point at the heart as the thing pledged for the sincerity of what we say. Now make yourself known to the Wardens and to our Fellow who pledged himself in your behalf.

He goes and gives the Sign, Word and Grip of a Fellow.

S.W. Are you a Fellow?

[*Answers.*]

S.W. By what shall I know you?

[*Answers.*]

S.W. As often as you make this Sign, remember that you pledge, your heart your life for the truth of what you say.

Salutes him.

Lecture

W.M. (52.7) The well instructed guide who brought you to the door of the Lodge had properly prepared you for your entrance here, and assured that you had labored diligently, procured you admission and the welcome of the Master. You came to the West and your guide might follow you no longer. You was then to seek another guide, and the address from the East must have convinced you how necessary directions and instructions are in things to which we are strangers.

(52.11) You could not possibly guess at what was intended to be done or how you were to be disposed of. Yet, your believing that we wished to do well toward you prompted you to follow the directions given you. Thus when we believe in the good intentions of fellow beings, we are easy and we willingly enter into their views, and that although experience and reason teach us that men are frail and feeble creatures. If they were perfect how much more easily, willingly should we follow them.

You went again on a symbolic journey, and you learned on the way the causes of much of the unhappiness and misery to which man could be subjected. Your attention was called to one who could become your most dangerous enemy, and you was made acquainted with the error which could make him such. Finally the subject on which you was to labor with constancy and care was presented to you, and the imperfection of human works was taught, and the rule for removing those imperfections.

From a more elevated situation than you before had, you could view an emblem of the guide of the wise. My dear Brother, let me persuade you to retain that emblem in your memory and if unhappily passion should tempt you firm the path of duty may a remembrance of what was seen serve to lead you from error. If unhappily avarice or ambition should stop you on your way, and a recollection of that bright emblem should happily arouse you again to pursue your journey, oh, return not to the vicious betray not the good. At the altar you made a voluntary vow and received the tests of this degree.

We hope you will often call these thing to mind with pleasure. Our Order has, as you already know, adopted the implements of operative masons as hieroglyphics. Such instruments were used in erecting the Temple in Jerusalem, which was sacred to the name of deity, and they have been moralized. Those peculiar to this degree are the square, plumb, and level. By help of these, the rough stones become good, smooth, polished and square stones. If a stone be so wrought that by neither of these instruments defects can be found, it is fitted for the builder's use.

But the square is applied to two sides at once. But it will not rest evenly on the superficies if the stone is defective. Hence it is called the symbol of truth and discoverer of error, and we hail the love of truth as one of the greatest virtues.

The plumb admonishes to righteousness. See its unerring line. It directs from earth to heaven and from heaven to earth.

The level is only applicable to the upper superficies of the stone when placed on the building. By it undo eminences or depressions are discovered and which require the gavel's use to be removed hence it is (54.1)taken as a symbol to remind us of that equality which should exist among all good Masons.

The builders of the holy Temples in the days that are passed were well acquainted with the proportions necessary to the constructing of these beautiful and well contrived structures and edifices, and hence we ought not to be unacquainted with the dimensions and proportions of architecture, and it is certain that in the places where wisdom, beauty and strength characterize the buildings, there we not only find science cultivated and the social virtues encouraged, but heaven born charity is there extending the hand to the assistance of the needy.

The Doric, Ionic and Corinthian orders are those which in our times are generally esteemed originals. They are here in the Lodge, instead of our more ancient pillars. They stand as monuments of human genius and of the high degree of taste and love of splendor which already existed among the people of the old world. But most of the magnificent monuments of antiquity are destroyed or ruined. Sic transit gloria mundi.

The liberal arts and sciences deserve our attention and encouragement. These distinguish a polite people from savages, and the capacity for acquiring a knowledge of them leans men to contemplate upon the works and perfections of deity, and enables them to lead others from many pernicious errors and to shun them himself.

On both sides at the entrance of the Temple you see two pillars, the one formed and ornamented like the other. These stood before the entrance of the sanctuary and no one could enter therein without passing them. Jachin and Boaz is the name of the two pillars. The meaning of the Word: "He shall establish it." And these pillars were taken from the Temple by Nebuchadnezar. They were cast by Hiram, the widow's son, of brass were hollow, eighteen cubits high, and four cubits thick. They stood here ornamented with the symbols of peace, wealth and plenty like twins— no difference in them but their names.

My Brother, if you will meditate upon the mysteries of this degree, you will find a wide field for the exercise of the mind. The subjects are useful in a high degree and full of interest, and particularly those relating to yourself. These demand your most serious attention.

Closing Fellows' Lodge

W.M. Brother Senior, are you a Fellow?
S.W. I have been accepted as such.
W.M. Where?
S.W. In a perfect Lodge.
W.M. How shall I know you to be a Fellow?
S.W. By the Sign.
W.M. What is the work of a Fellow?
S.W. To square the smooth and rough stone, and to finish them according to the direction of the Master.
W.M. Where have you worked as a Fellow?
S.W. In the Temple.
W.M. Why was you accepted as a Fellow?
S.W. To learn the letter G.
W.M. Who could accept you?
S.W. The Master.
W.M. What did you perceive in the Fellow's Degree that you have not before known?
S.W. The Blazing Star.
W.M. What is it?
S.W. The guide of the wise and faithful.
W.M. Where did it rise?
S.W. In the East.
W.M. From whence did you see it?
S.W. From the steps of the Temple.
W.M. Did you go toward it?
S.W. Yes, I was brought towards it.
W.M. Whither did it guide your steps?
S.W. Toward the Master.
W.M. What is the letter G?
S.W. I know but little about it, but it has been said to signify geometry.
W.M. Was there any thing else shown you?
S.W. Yes, a likeness of the subject on which I was to labor.
W.M. Have you commenced your labors?
S.W. I have.
W.M. Can you complete them?
S.W. Yes.
W.M. How?
S.W. By following the directions given me by the Master and by his assistance.
W.M. When will your labors cease?
S.W. When I am admitted to the Masters' Lodge and have passed through the inner chamber.

[*Near the front of FM2, Folger included a lecture which is similar to the "second section" of the Fellow Craft degree, according to the Webb work. As such, it has but little in common with the Revised R.E.R. work, but it is here reproduced in full.*]

(25.1)[MIDDLE CHAMBER] LECTURE

Brother, we are now about to pass symbolically into the middle chamber of King Solomon's Temple. And previous to our so doing it is necessary that some further explanation of ceremonies should be given, in order that you may properly understand the nature of our ritual. The Temple, strictly speaking, was composed of only two rooms, viz., the sacred place where the children of Israel met to worship and to hear the laws of the Most High proclaimed, and the Sanctum Sanctorum, or Holy of Holies, which was a place of deposit for the Ark of the Testimony, which contained the divine writings, the mercy seat and the cherubim, where the Lord manifested Himself and into which place the High Priest went but once a year, and then to make atonement for the sins of the people.

In front of this Temple stood the porch, vestibule, or outer court. Here all indiscriminately assembled, but no entrance was found to the called middle chamber[35] unless through the porch or vestibule. And those who entered from the vestibule must undergo a preparation before they could find admittance there. For it was a place set apart for the service of the Most High, and to the meditation upon subjects which would have a tendency to purify the heart. Hence, no one who would not undergo the preparation was deemed fit for a place there.

The degree of Entered Apprentice, which you have already taken, is emblematic of the primary stage of human life, or its vestibule, and the doctrine of that degree, the course of preparation necessary to pass to the middle stage, with acceptance to the Author of your being. You have there been taught the necessity of eradicating from your heart all prejudices and passions, which were contrary to the divine law, and encouraged to cultivate all proper dispositions. You have been warned against troublesome and evil dispositions, and persuaded to court a life of peace. You have been instructed that charity, which is love, is the doctrine not only to be first learned, but also practiced in all after life, and many other doctrines of an important nature have been held up to your view. If you have learned these things aright and are, daily and hourly, trying to profit by them, you have undergone the preparation necessary for entering the middle chamber, and I will endeavor, as your guide, symbolically to conduct you there.

You have been instructed that it is necessary to rest a part of your time from worldly labor, and to devote that time to the service of your Great Benefactor, the Most High God. For in six days God created the heavens and the earth, and all that

---

35. FM2:25.20 reads, "to the so called middle chamber."

in them is, but He rested on the seventh, and hallowed it. In all ages of the world, and among all the people whom He has enlightened, that day has been consecrated and rigidly observed. His bounty permits you to spend six days of the week in worldly labor, during which He surrounds you with blessings of the richest kind, and guards you and preserves you, by day and by night, in the house and by the way. How reasonable then, that the seventh part of time should be spent in bringing Him the offering of a grateful heart, and rendering unto Him adoration for all His mercies. And the proper observance of this day of rest will fit you for the proper service of Him in the six days that are to come. Learn then, at the very entrance of the sacred Temple, to observe the ordinances which He has given, and bear it in mind, that is not well pleased with him who walks contrary to His commands.

At the door of the entrance of the middle chamber stood two brazen pillars—the one on the right, the other on the left. They were alike in each other in all respects. The name of the one was Jachin, the other Boaz, signifying, "In strength shall it be established for ever." They were cast by Hiram, the widow's son, on the banks of the river Jordan, in the clay grounds between Succoth and Zeredatha, in common with all the other holy vessels. They were hollow, of molten brass,[36] and were eighteen cubits high. They were adorned with two large chapiters, ornamented with net work, lily work, and pomegranates. They also had two large globes—the one celestial, the other terrestrial, which contain on their convex surfaces maps, charts, etc., of the celestial and terrestrial bodies.

These pillars stand at the very entrance of the Temple and, by their uprightness and beauty, admonish us of the character we ought to bear, the integrity which should fill all our purposes, the regularity of life[37] we should lead, and peacefulness of disposition we should cultivate in order to stand as a pillar in the assembly of the Brethren. They are fixed upon a firm foundation, they stand uprightly, and their beauties could be seen afar off. The chapiters, adorned with lily work, net work and pomegranates, denote purity of thought, and unity of purpose, in order to be filled with the abundance of plenty which the Master will bestow on all who cultivate heavenly dispositions.

My Brother, let us disdain the performance of any mean and criminal act, let us discountenance libertinism and all excess, let us encourage charity and benevolence, let us from henceforth abstain from all foolish and vain pursuits, and use the time allotted to us, to labor here with diligence, remembering that time flies swiftly, and is irrecoverable, and that we are traveling on to the Master, from whom we hope to receive a reward.

Three, five and seven steps.

The three first steps are emblematic of the Wisdom, which we should constantly seek from above to guide us in all our ways. And without which we shall most cer-

---

36. FM2:27.8–9 reads, "They were hollow ~~and~~ of Molten Brass."
37. FM2:27.15 reads, "~~and~~ the regularity of life."

tainly go astray; the Strength, which we should constantly pray for to support us in all our trials and sufferings in life, and prevent us from murmuring against the beneficent dispensations of Him, who does all things well, in order that our walk and conversation among the Brethren and the world may be adorned with the Beauty of holiness in every part.

The five steps[38] are emblematic of the five different orders of architecture, viz., the Tuscan, Doric, Ionic, Corinthian and Composite (*see Monitor*). Also, to the five different senses, viz., hearing, seeing, feeling, tasting, smelling (*see Monitor*).

The seven steps[39] allude to the seven liberal arts and sciences, viz., grammar, rhetoric, logic, arithmetic, geometry, music, astronomy (*see Monitor*).

In conclusion of this part of the instruction, let me say to you that the liberal arts and sciences deserve our encouragement and attention, as these distinguish a polite people from savages, and the capacity for acquiring a knowledge of them leads men to contemplate upon the works and perfections of Deity, and enables them to lead others from many pernicious errors, and to shun them off himself. And the study of these things belongs not to the vestibule, of early life, for then first principles occupy the mind. They belong not to the latter period, that should be spent in reflection and improvement. Here is the time and place, viz., the middle age, when the man is clear and vigorous and the body fit to undergo the fatigue accompanying the labor of acquirement, before[40] the golden be broken or the silver cord be loosed, before the wheel be broken at the cistern, and the dust return to the dust.

We will now salute the Junior Warden.

Sign, Word and explanation. Word means "Plenty." Represented by a sheaf of wheat and a waterfall. History of the Word .
We will now salute the Senior Warden.
Sign and lesson (hypocrisy).

W.M. My Brother, you are now symbolically admitted to the middle chamber, on account of that which ought to attract your earnest attention. It is the letter G, and alludes to the name of the Deity. Though unseen by mortal eye, His eye is ever upon us. He is intimately acquainted with all our actions, even our most secret thoughts. With Him there is no beginning of days or end of life. He is immutable, unchangeable, past finding out. Yet he is our wise and glorious benefactor, and supplies all our wants. He will guide us in life, and keep us in all our ways, and deserves at our hands constantly the tribute of grateful acknowledgment. Acquaint now thyself with Him, and be at peace. Worship and adore Him, for He is worthy of all thy praise.

Clothing and Charge.

---

38. FM2:28.9 reads, "The 5 x."
39. FM2:28.13 reads, "The 7 x."
40. FM2:28.24 reads, " ~~and~~ before the golden."

(56.21)Masters Grade

Black clothing and decorations.
Tablets in the preparation room:

[First Tablet] We should, while we live, prepare for Death. And we should constantly be at this work because we know not when we shall die. But it is certain we shall die, and we shall give up our bodies to the dust from whence they came.

[Second Tablet] Our Souls die not. They are to exist forever. But how shall their experience be? Miserable, unhappy? Could we determine it, we should choose the happy state, but then we ought to be prepared for its enjoyments. And what is necessary to prepare the soul for its happy state, and what will make it fit for its enjoyments? Who ever saw the vicious happy? Even in this gross bodily state they are not so. They can clothe themselves in purple, they can live in palaces, they can own piles of gold. They eat of dainties and become drunk of rich wine. But is this Happiness? Or is it not rather the source of unhappiness? If deprived of those things would they not be miserable. In the grave none of those things follow with them. If they think but on death and futurity, it is agony to them. What then will realization be?

The guide comes suddenly, strikes him on the shoulder and says: Brother, you wish to be accepted as a Master. Come follow me.

Two knocks [at the Lodge door].

Deacon   Who is here?
Guide   A Fellow who wishes to be accepted as a Master.
Deacon   The pass?

[The pass is given.]

Guide   He is five years old and has worked in the second court of the Temple on the smooth stone. He has served his time and his Masters are well pleased with him.
Deacon   Are you worthy to wear this badge?

[Deacon] tears it off [the Candidate].

Address

W.M.   Brother, you are now brought to the inner chamber. When you are passed to the place of which this is an emblem, there no art nor deception can hide any error or any imperfection. The Judge who there presides views the hearts of men and knows their most hidden secrets. Wherefore, in reverence to these solemn truths, be sincere.
   My Brother, we are here assembled to commemorate and to lament the death of our Great Master. His loss we may justly sorrow for, and as justly deplore the cause

of his death, and, deploring them, shun them. He was killed by unfaithful Fellows. No guile was in his heart nor evil in his ways, yet they set his goodness at naught and their ruffian hands murdered him.

Brother Warden, show our Fellow the horrid spectacle before us and watch him well and see if he appears to be one of the conspirators against the Grand Master.

S.W. Our Fellow does not appear to be among the guilty, and is moved at this sight.

W.M. We are glad that you do not appear greatly concerned in this work of death, and we hope you never will join those who are guilty. Bring him on the Masters' path for instruction, that he can join us in seeking the Master.

First Round

Remember death.

That man who has a sense of his own frailty and who has learned to observe his own imperfections has made the first step towards the Light.

Second Round

Remember death. It is unavoidable.

How dangerous it is to venture upon the far distant journey without a knowledge of the way we are going. How foolish to refuse to attend the infallible doctrines which point out the way. Would one who thus ventures, and thus refuses, not easily err and not find the city he sought, but instead thereof faint among the sands of the desert where there is no water to allay the burning thirst, no bread to keep from starving?

Third Round.

Remember death. It is unavoidable. Perhaps it is near at hand.

Let us incline our hearts to instruction and our minds to understanding and learn the way to the habitation of comfort and of rest. Let us seek the way thither with earnestness. Let us knock at its door with confidence and with all humility. Let us seek alms for our wants of the good Master of the house, and, believe me he will not reject our prayer and will even grant us much more than we expected, and more than we can dispose of.

W.M. Let him now ascend the seven steps of the Temple, and bring him with Master's steps to the East.

My Brother, before you can be accepted as a Master, it is required of you to make a solemn covenant with us.

The covenant is read. The covenant is short and much like the others.

W.M. Now, Brother, you are to receive the Word and Grip of this degree, and in future when you use these things, call to mind the situation you were in just before you received them.

Brother Warden, lead our Fellow to the place where we shall all assemble.

Accepts him. Hymn and procession.

W.M. Behold Brethren, the pall covers. The coffin contains a Brother. God give he may henceforth be dead to sin and ever may he bear in mind that he shall die. May he have firm hope of being raised from the Fellow to the Master, from darkness to light, from dust to heaven, from mortality to eternal life, and may this hope cheer him and make you faithful.

Brethren let us seek to find our Master who was slain.

Travel once [around the grave].

O Lord, help the children of the dust!

Here is a sprig of acacia, and this has the appearance of a grave. Let us look into this grave.

Brethren, as the Word was lost at the death of our Master, let is now agree that when the body is raised, the first word spoken shall hereafter be considered as the Master's Word. The flesh is corrupt.[41]

Then raises the body.

(60.1)Address after the Brother Is Raised and Is Preparatory

W.M. You are now about to commence a symbolic journey for the purpose of receiving a full explanation of things pertaining to this degree, closely and intimately connected with the ceremonies through which you have passed, and opening to your view the end, and the object of our rite. It is to be hoped that you have not forgotten anything which this evening has met your view. It will be a journey full of instruction. Therefore, let me ask you to pay attention to those objects which I shall point out for your attentive consideration.

[*Presenting the sword.*] You are now entitled to receive this instrument. Take it, my Brother, and as you have been instructed in its use, never cease to wield it in a proper manner. You must not part with it. There is but one place were you will relinquish this beautiful emblem, and that it will be my business to explain.

When you was made a Mason, and received among us, you commenced in the sight of the Brethren, the erection of an edifice, not of material substances, or with common tools, but within yourself. You were told that the designs of the Master were before you, and if they were carried out according to his directions, the structure would be an enduring one, and would be beautiful indeed.

[*Presenting the trowel.*] Take, then, this instrument to complete it, and as you pass around the structure, which we trust you are building, survey it well, and let no imperfection escape your observation. Spread the cement well and in a manner that time will not destroy it.

---

41. According to the R.E.R. ritual, the "word" *Mak Benak* means, "the body is corrupt," or "the skin separates from the bones." (*Rituel de Loge de Sainte-Jean, 3ᵉ Grade* [Brussels: Grand Loge Régulière de Belgique, n.d.], pp. 36, 42.)

Passes once round the coffin.

Remember, my Brother, that the All Seeing Eye is upon you, that it never slumbers or sleeps. It has witnessed your vows, it pierces the secrets of your soul, and will most surely observe and follow you in the journey you are about to take.

Music while he again travels the second round.

We have now come to the three steps. They are called Faith, Hope and Charity. They may symbolize the three first degrees through which you have passed.

The Entered Apprentice, [or] Disciple,[42] may be called Faith, and is emblematic of youth, or early life, when the passions have full sway and, when indulged, lead the soul away from truth. You there learned the important doctrine, that although man had fallen from his high estate, and strangely deformed himself, yet he could, by using the proper means be restored again to his pristine purity.

The Fellow Crafts Degree is called Hope, and is emblematic of manhood, when the powers of the mind are fully developed, and the character becomes fully formed. It was presumed that your labor in the vestibule of the Temple had so far progressed that you had effected some change for the better in the appearance of the subject on which you commenced the work. And, that it should be more perfectly adorned, your attention was directed to the study of the liberal arts and sciences, by means of which you could add to the perfection of the beauty of the work you were engaged in.

The Masters Degree is called Charity, which is love, and is emblematic of old age—fit season for reflection upon the past, and contemplation upon the future. Happy is the man who has performed his duty faithfully in the vestibule of the Temple, and adorned his labors in its court, by a well ordered life. When he is about to pass to the inner chamber his mind will be filled with Peace. Let us now ascend the steps and pass on our way.

Here is represented a Bee Hive, which is placed there to remind us that we should be industrious, never sitting down contented while our fellow creatures around us are in want. We should never neglect the duties of life. We should remember the wants of the suffering, the needy, and the afflicted, and labor diligently for their relief, thus acting and thus living.

The next emblem, the Pot of Incense, will show fully the state of that man's heart who has been faithful in the performance of the duties, which we have barely hinted at on this occasion. He will be blessed in all his ways, his heart will glow with gratitude to the Master on high, and thanks will constantly ascend for all the blessings and comforts he receives at his hand.

The Anchor and Ark are emblems of a well-grounded hope, and a well spent life. The path through life is variegated with both good and evil. Passion, prejudice and pride lead the man astray, far from the asylum of comfort and of rest, like the tempest tossed barques upon the ocean, without a rudder and without a guide, it drifts over the pathless waste of waters and finally strands upon the hidden rock.

---

42. FM2:60.27. Although this paragraph is in plaintext, the word *Disciple* is in cipher.

Faith in the promises of the Master on high, with a strict adherence to the plan which he has marked out, Hope arising from the crowning blessings we are hourly in receipt of, and Charity for all mankind, will prove a sure anchor to the tempest-tossed soul, and no storm of adversity, however strong it may beat, will destroy the refuge which that anchor makes. The barque will hold its moorings and waft its possessor to a haven of rest.

The Scythe is an emblem of time. While health is blooming upon the cheek, the brittle thread is severed and man takes up his dwelling in the dust.

We have now done with these things. We have arrived at the end of our symbolic journey, and to the place where you will lay down the implement of your work.

[*Candidate lays down the trowel.*]

The strong man boweth himself here and goeth to his long home. The silver cord is loosed the golden bowl is broken. The dust returns to the dust as it was, and the spirit unto God who gave it.

The Address at the Foot of the Coffin

(30.2)Having finished the ceremonial part of the degree we will now turn our attention to that which more particularly deserves our serious consideration.

You now stand symbolically in the inner chamber. When you have passed to the place of which this is a symbol, it is needless for me to tell you that your destiny will be forever fixed. No deception can serve you, for the Judge who here presides is intimately acquainted with all your secret thoughts. Therefore, let me, in reverence to the place and the occasion, ask you to be sincere. For the ceremonies through which you are passing are calculated to make a deep impression upon your mind. It is hoped they may have a lasting effect upon your character.

The wisest statesman, the bravest warrior, the poorest beggar, the rich, the gay, the young, the beautiful, the happy, all travel together in the same pilgrimage, and terminate their wanderings in the same house, appointed for all the living. Here the towering schemes of ambition are forgotten, the burden of oppression and of sorrow is laid aside. The gay laugh and merry jest is hushed to, and the mighty and mean together enter upon that sleep, which to mortals knows no waking.

Surrounded as you may be with prosperity,[43] the rose of health blooming on your cheek, and your eye sparkling with intelligence, the time will come when the battle must be fought and you will be vanquished. Though you will most surely feel his icy hands around you, and although strong ties bind you to the world, those ties must be severed. Though the tear of sympathy may be shed and plead in your behalf, it will be unavailing. The dust must return unto the dust from whence it came, and the spirit unto God who gave it.

---

43. FM2:30.19 reads, "Surrounded are you are <may be> with prosperity."

Committed to the Flames

Figure 2. The Master's carpet reconstructed from Folger's description on FM2.64.

Before you enter this silent mansion you have a work to finish, for there is no work nor device nor repentance here. No man can do this work for you, you must do it for yourself. And it is important for your welfare that this should not only not be forgotten, but entered upon with diligence, for you may full soon take up your dwelling in the dust. Surrounding this solemn [scene][44] as Brethren, let me, in the language of kindness, entreat you to look upon the destiny which awaits you, and bear in your mind the place to which your steps are speedily advancing. Let me ask you in view of these things to pray earnestly, ere you enter the grave that your work may be finished, according to the requirements of the Master, that when you enter here it may be with acceptance. He is full of tender mercies, his ear is ever open to the utterings of the destitute, he gives liberally and does not upbraid, nor will he send you empty away.

(35.2)Generation after generation have felt as we feel, and their fellows were as active as our own. They passed away like a vapor, while nature wore the same aspect of beauty as when her Creator commanded her to be. The heavens shall be as bright over our graves as they are now around our paths. The world will have the same attractions for our offspring yet unborn that she had once for ourselves, and that she has now for our children. Yet a little while and all this will have happened.

The throbbing heart will be stifled and we shall be at rest. Our funeral will wind on its way, and the prayers will be said, and our friends will return, and we shall be left to darkness. And it may be for a short time that we shall be spoken of, but things of life will creep in, and our names will soon be forgotten. Days will continue to run on, and laughter and song will be heard in the place in which we died, and the eye that mourned for us will be dried, and glisten again with joy, and even our children will cease to think of us, and will not remember to lisp our names.

(35.19)It is not an uncommon scene. The passing events of daily life bring it forcibly to our remembrance, and should fill the mind with solemn and holy thoughts in its contemplation. Here, the brave repose who have died in the cause of their country, here the statesman rests who has achieved the victories of peace not less renowned than war. Here, genius finds a home that has sung immortal strains, or has instructed with still diviner eloquence. Here, learning and science, the votaries of inventive art, and the teacher of the philosophy of nature comes. Here, youth and beauty, blighted by premature decay, drop like tender blossoms into the virgin earth, and here, age retires ripened for the harvest. Here the benefactors of mankind, the good, the merciful, the meek, the pure in heart are congregated, to them belongs an undying praise.

(36.9)The sad realities of the present scene apply themselves with equal force to the future. Within the flight of a few years how many of the great, the good, the wise, will be gathered here. How many in the loveliness of infancy, the beauty of youth, the vigor of manhood and the maturity of age will lie down here, and dwell in the bosom of their mother earth. The rich and the poor, the gay and the wretched, the

---

44. FM2:31.7–8 reads, "Surrounding this solemn — as Brethren." The phrase "solemn scene" is used to describe this setting on FM2:36.18.

favorites of thousands, and the forsaken of the world, the stranger in his solitary grave, and the patriarch surrounded by the kindred of a long lineage. Even we ourselves, from the Master, who now directs these simple ceremonies, and the other Brethren who surround the solemn scene and listen to his voice, to the watcher who guards the Temple, when these holy doctrines are taught, from the intrusions of the profane and thoughtless, will alike be numbered among the silent inhabitants in this chamber of "repose." Here will be buried brightest hopes and blasted expectations. How many bitter tears will here be shed? How many agonizing sighs will here be heaved? How many trembling feet will return from scenes like this, and returning leave behind them the dearest objects of their reverence and their love? This scene, then, should bring home to us thoughts full of admonition, of instruction, and of consolation also. It admonishes us by its very silence, of our own frail and transitory being, it instructs us into the true value of life, and in its noble purposes, its duties and its destination, and it spreads around us in the reminiscences of the past sources of pleasing, though melancholy reflection. But let us not despond, for the same voice which has uttered the decree appointing it unto man once to die, has promised unto us a country beyond this vale of tears, where faith shall terminate in sight and hope in fruition. It has described to us a Temple not made with hands, in which are many mansions, a city whose gates are pearl, whose streets are paved with gold, the trees of which are filled with fruit and watered by the river of life. He has told us that sickness and affliction are not there. There, sorrow and crying can never come, no tears are ever known, but all is perfect happiness and peace. It is the dwelling place of the righteous, the eternal home of the virtuous and the good. We see before us the way of entrance to this happy state, a clime where privilege is unknown, where death and time sound like strange words.[45]

(90.2) We can not deprive ourselves of the idea of consciousness in the grave. It is universal, innate, that although the body is dead, and no life and animation there, yet we conceive that the dead are acquainted with its darkness and its silence, its cold and its heat. Hence the desire to be buried in a sunny spot, a dry and oft frequented place. It is this which makes the traveler long to come home and die, and be buried among his kindred. He hates to be thrown by the wayside, or in the sea, and though he often says that he cares not where his body be, yet his heart's best feelings belie the assertion. Even those who have the highest hopes, have been heard to beg in a dying hour, that they might not be buried with the common herd of strangers (Captain Smith, an example).

(65.1) Address Which May Be Used Discretionarily

We shrink from the scorching heat of the sun, or we shiver beneath the blasts that wither us as they pass. The noise of the world is wearying the noise and din of life.

---

45. FM2:37.21–22. The last fourteen words are lightly written in pencil.

The flowers we gather have thorns that pierce us, and the tree under whose boughs we turn for shelter falls to crush us. We take our way along crowded streets, meeting nothing but strange faces that stare coldly as we pass—no smiles, no welcome. We wander through greener paths and perchance some are with us that we love or think we love, but even in green paths there are briars to wound the foot, or the serpent's shining track crosses the road we go, or those with us fall away and utter loneliness is ill to bear. This is life. But the dead have rest. Where ends our path? Taken through dreary crowded streets, or through desolate bye ways, where is our bed at last? For we cannot always wander, struggling, striving, hoping, fearing, for we scarce know what. There must be some place of solace. Where shall we find it?

Oh, weary, weary, spirit, here ends thy toil. Here, where the turf is so cool and green. Here, where the wind whistles mournfully through the long waving grass. Rest thee, rest thee, take thy mantle around thee, lie down upon this ready earth, it will open and give thee rest. Art thou cold? Ask the close sepulcher to take thee to its narrow chamber, thou wilt shiver in the winter wind no more. Doth thy brow ache with all this feverish excitement, this whirlwind of sound and motion? Press it to the cool mantle of the tomb. Let the air grow damp and, chill from passing over graves, fan thy burning cheek. It will woo thee to stillness and to calm. Thou wilt forget the hot turmoil of existence, thy new home shall be so quiet.

Thus reasons the silly world, forgetful of the word of Truth.

It is appointed unto men to die, and after that the judgment, and although to the mortal vision death seem the terminus of the battle and the strife of life, yet the undying spirit there drops or lays aside the material Temple in the grave and passes unshackled into the presence of its Judge.

Deceive not thyself with the language of the world. Remember, it is a fearful thing to fall into the hands of the living God, unwashed, uncleansed, unpardoned. Beware.

(55.14) INSTRUCTION TO THE NEW BROTHER

W.M.   Your being advanced to this degree, the objects of our Order can no longer be strange to you. But permit me to call your attention to some of the things which are inculcated by our symbols and ceremonies, independent of our obligations. Your mind was, at an early period of your connection with our institution, called upon to consider the very important and interesting subjects of time, death, and immortality. And our aim in the course of initiation has been symbolically and directly to point subjects for meditation which could lead men to live virtuously and happily, to meet death with serenity and to cheer the hope of a blissful futurity.

The necessity of mutual confidence in each other must be apparent to all who have wandered from the court of the Temple to its inner chamber. Who would follow on in strange paths, blind, or in darkness, or seeing where the sword point rests against the naked breast, except he had confidence in the directions of those with whom he went? And who would conduct any to the sanctuary of fraternity, and make an indissoluble covenant of friendship with him, unless he had confidence in his honesty and was convinced that he would not betray, and would not become an enemy?

Confidence grows, however, out of the good opinions we may have conceived of others, either arising from a knowledge of their good principles or our observation of their good acts. Thus, if we know men who live blameless lives, who shun covetousness and other vices, who encourage faith and virtue, who protect innocence, who do good, then we should certainly have confidence in these.

If these, at the same time, strive to propagate rules of life or doctrines tending to make men happier than they otherwise would be, then, considering the character of these men, we should at least examine the things they hold out to us. And if we even will not readily admit them, we ought not to neglect trying with them, and if upon a fair trial and proper examination they be found to be useful, as having a salutary effect upon individuals and upon Society in general, if they are in unison with the truth, if they answer the great ends of making men better qualified for the discharge of duties, if they make men really happier, then it would undoubtedly be very contrary to our ideas of duty, if not very foolish, to reject them or even to neglect them. And that, even if they should be a little at variance with our customary thoughts, or be somewhat inconvenient because of our habits, such men and such rules or doctrines as I have alluded to are to be found, and it is believed that every one who has strove to do his task as a Disciple and Fellow will seek and find them.

(31.18)And in order that you may be better acquainted with the nature of your work, as well as with the designs of the matter, we again present you with that great light of Masonry—the Holy Bible.

[*Exhibits Bible*] It should be ever open in a proper Lodge, to the end that we may be reminded of the duty of learning and practicing the excellent principles it contains. And if we, as far as we can, scrupulously examine both the character of those who gave the precepts, and the influence these have had, and still have upon society, if we examine the great ends and views of the doctrines written,[46] and thus become acquainted with that volume, we shall experience that it is an inestimable treasure and should be received as such by all good men. It is in fact the book that contains the rules of life pointing out to man his whole duty.

This book is of great antiquity. The splendid monuments of the ancients have decayed, the nations who peopled the countries where these things were written have vanished, or are scattered over the face of the earth. Their former places of abode are desolate, the languages the book was written in are dead, yet the book survives, and the enemies of order, the opposers of the good precepts this volume contains, have sought with astonishing obduracy and unwearied pains, with jests, with philosophy falsely so-called, with misapplied learning, with every effort of their genius, to bring this volume into contempt. But they have been engaged in a foolish work. All their pains have been taken in vain. It stands deservedly higher now in the estimation of the good than it ever stood before.

---

46. FM2:31.25 reads, "of the Doctrines here written."

Considering the character of the writers of this volume and finding them to be good even inimitably so, examining the doctrines contained in this volume, and observing their unison with truth and their beneficent influence upon society and upon individuals, thinking upon the great antiquity of these writings and the many revolutions which they have survived and their complete victory over the efforts of enemies, therewith continually increasing in the estimation of the world at large and in estimation of the friends of good order and of truth, then it can be said, even if there were no other reasons for so saying, that this volume is not to be neglected, but on the contrary that it ought to be examined and should be made the subject of our attention and study.

And see how correct is its philosophy, how interesting the history, how sublime and beautiful the poetry, how acceptable the doctrines of religion and morality contained in this volume. It is calculated in every point of view to engage our attention, and if attended to, the truths it contains make men better, wiser and happier. And the benefits arising from these sacred truths are not limited to the period of human life. They point not forward to the grave as the boundary of human existence, as the place where man shall cease to be. No, the thick gloom of death is dissipated by Divine truth. A ray of sacred light makes visible to the eye of the faithful a state of existence beyond the grave, a state of existence, at the approach of which all must fear, for it lasts to all eternity. For it is a state of reward and punishments, for it is dependent upon Divine mercy, for no man can claim a place there. Happy indeed is that man who strove to lay aside his prejudices, and is thus fitted for the task of a Fellow, the studying and executing the designs of the Master. [47] Happy is he if he has observed the pattern given him by the Master. With his knowledge he has made the first step toward the light and has thus become more susceptible of the Truth than he was before.

(59.14)By contemplating upon the image of the pillar of beauty, he may have observed his own inability to make his work according to the pattern given him by the Master. If he is sensible of his own incapacity and imperfections, he has in truth made the first step toward the light and has thus become more susceptible of the truth than he was before. Then he will have the trestleboard in his hands and use all proper means to become acquainted with the designs which are drawn, and no doubt he will not only direct others how to execute them, but he will participate in the labor in the erection of a truly noble edifice—a Temple sacred to the name of God—and in this work he will use the implements of the Master.

[*Exhibits compasses*] (33.13)The compasses will remind you to set proper limits to your desires and actions, not to be eccentric in behavior, but to pursue an even line of conduct without irregularities.

---

47. FM2:33.9. Although the words "Now go to (fifty nine again" are superimposed at this point, a line is inserted extending towards a symbol on line 12, which we believe indicates where the text should break. It does, however, bear some similarity to the second maxim delivered to the R.E.R. Candidate during his circuits: "Happy is he who, having well studied himself, knows his faults, perceives his ignorance and feels he requires succour [*sic*], for he has already taken the first step to light." (*Rituel de Loge de Sainte-Jean, 3e Grade* (Brussels: Grand Loge Régulière de Belgique, n.d.), p. 26.

We should, by example and persuasion, try to exact and encourage fraternal love. This is the very cement of the Temple. If it is wanting the whole becomes a heap of rubbish and is of no worth, but on the contrary is an obstacle to those who pass where it lies and a nuisance to them who may have a habitation near it. Where fraternal love is not, there must be many evils. There the ruffian passions are enthroned and virtue is driven out or laughed at, or spurned with contempt, or bound with thorns. There folly divides wisdom, and truth is obliged to hide her fair face. There religion or morality cannot be found. There all is mockery.

[*Exhibits hourglass.*] Here is an emblem of time. I have now turned it, and the sands are rapidly passing away. They will soon be gone. Time we can never recall, but we can and we ought to use that aright which is to come. We should improve the moments as they fly. See the sand. The particles still run rapidly, and, for ought we know, with the passing of one of these you or I shall die. It is uncertain. We should not neglect a moment, but from henceforth do all we can to the great end of being really happy. For we shall surely die. We shall soon go hence to be here no more forever. And in the grave there is no working, no device, no knowledge, no pardon there.

[*Exhibits skull.*] See this emblem, this melancholy memento. It is silent, vacant, dead. Yet it speaks to our minds and it says, "Remember."[48] The good hear the voice, and it often makes them tremble. To some it can be great cause of terror. We have crowned it with a green sprig, for we believe in and hope in, partaking of immortality. We believe that though a man die, yet shall he again live, that the time will come when those who sleep in the dust shall hear the voice of the Son of God,[49] and they that hear shall live. We, therefore, hope for immortality and happiness beyond the grave through faith in the giver of every good and perfect gift.[50]

Let us then earnestly strive to do His will, remembering that man was created in His image and, although deformed and fallen, can be raised again and made fit for blissful enjoyments. Let us not be ashamed of truth and religion for that would make us unfit for fraternity on earth, and disqualify us utterly for the enjoyments of a future state, where Love is a most essential requisite. Let us be charitable and sensible to the wants of our fellow men, for else we are monsters, even here although associated as Brethren, and therefore would be hereafter unfit for lasting Joys. Let us live in love, remembering that we are nearer now to the end of our pilgrimage than we were when we assembled, and hope to meet the presence of the Master with acceptance and with Joy.

(59.20)*Salutation by the Master and by the Brethren.*

---

48. A human skull is sometimes called a *memento mori*, signifying, "remember you must die."
49. FM2:34.13. The words "the Son of" are superimposed.
50. "Every good gift and every perfect gift is from above, and cometh down from the Father of lights, with whom is no variableness, neither shadow of turning." (James 1:17, KJV)

Folger Manuscript 2

Masters Lodge Opening and Closing

W.M.   Your name [and] duty?
S.W.   [*Answers.*]

Lighting [of the tapers]. [Then follows the] Prayer.
[The Master inquires as to the] Time [and the Warden responds.][51]

W.M.   Are you a Master?
S.W.   I am acquainted with the acacia.
W.M.   Where is the Masters Lodge held?
S.W.   In the inner chamber.
W.M.   What is that place?
S.W.   A place of perfect silence.
W.M.   Where is it situated?
S.W.   In a deep valley or under the ground.

Furniture, jewels, lights, ornaments, symbols, numbers, colors, signs, grips, words, bowls in each degree, also the obligation the same as in the English Lodges.

W.M.   From whence come the Masters?
S.W.   From the East.
W.M.   And why?
S.W.   To dispense light and knowledge of the truth.
W.M.   When one of our Brethren is missing where can we hope to find him?
S.W.   In the inner chamber, between the compass and square?

The prayers are all in the other book.
The obligations of all the degrees contain the clause "that I will not communicate the secret of this degree to any person in the world, except to him or them who have been received in a perfect Lodge, such as I am now in, or even converse about the same, with any others, than those who have been thus made."

---

51. FM2:59.22 reads, "your name duty ans lighting prayer time." According to the R.E.R. ritual, the name of a Master Mason is *Gabaon*, which signifies, "exalted." (*Rituel de Loge de Sainte-Jean, 3ᵉ Grade* [Brussels: Grand Loge Régulière de Belgique, n.d.], p. 51.

(72. 1)CONSECRATION

Preliminary

The new Temple will be pompously decorated. The lights of the Master, Wardens, officers, et al., must be all new. The emblem in the East will not be lighted. The Master of Ceremonies, Grand Expert, and Inside Tyler will remain inside of the room with sword in hand, in darkness, the door shut. The Inside Tyler keeps the key in his own hand. Invite all the visitors you can.

The regalia and jewels of the officers of the new Lodge will remain on the throne. At the foot of the throne, a table upon which the jewels of the Senior and Junior Wardens, the square of the Master, one terrestrial globe, and the tie, which should be long enough to surround the room, also a round cake of bread, hollow in the middle, two goblets filled with red wine. On the throne will be the bylaws, charter, Constitution and the General Statutes of the Supreme Council.

Inauguration

At the day and hour appointed between the Supreme Grand Council and the new Lodge, the Master Elect will order the Lodge to meet in an adjoining room, but never in the room to be consecrated. The officers will not wear their regalia.

The Lodge will then open its work in the usual manner. After the Lodge is opened the Master will direct the Secretary to read the edict, or declaration, of the Supreme Grand Council, which authorizes the inauguration of the new Temple, and deliver a lecture, or the Orator will perform that office, in order that the Lodge may proceed as soon as the Supreme Council may be present. The lecture consists in a recapitulation of the forms and ceremonies to be gone through with on the present occasion.

Then the Supreme Council is announced. The Master orders the columns up, and at the due guard and the sword drawn. Then the Grand Expert precedes the two Masters of Ceremony, the Master being at the head, and four other Brothers, those Brothers bearing the lights, they go to the entrance of the Lodge when the Master commands the Arch of Steel, and presents to the Supreme Council his gavel. He takes it and goes to the seat of the Master in the outside room. Then the Installator commands the columns to be seated. Then a salutatory speech. The Installator then opens the work in the first degree. The petition is then read. The decision of the Supreme Council declared and the Orator concludes the speech and announces the same. Then the work is suspended and the procession formed in the following order:—

1st—*The Standard Bearer and the Sword Bearer.*

2^{d}—*The Installator, on his right, the Master, on his left the Senior Warden.*

3^{d}—*The three first officers of every Lodge which assists at the ceremony, according to their numbers.*

4th—*The Orator and Secretary of the new Lodge.*

5th—*Members of the Supreme Council, visiting Brethren of new lodges, and members of new Lodge.*
The procession, going round, stops at the outside door.
Music.
The Installator raps three, loud. The Brother Expert, who is inside, says in a loud voice:
   Brothers, let us be on our watch, there is someone outside of the Temple.
Installator says, "I hear someone talking inside of the Temple."
Gives one knock and says, "Who is this that has penetrated of the Temple, or in the interior of this Temple?"
The Grand Expert answers, "They are workmen who worked at its construction and have been charged to keep it."
Installator says, "Open, I ask you in the name of the Brethren who accompany me."
Inside Tyler puts the key in the lock and opens the door, and says, "What do you wish to do in this Temple?"
Installator: "To finish the work in consecrating it, to the Glory of the Grand Architect of the Universe, and to virtue and truth."
The Tyler throws open the door, and giving him the key says, "As this Temple is to be dedicated to so glorious a purpose, I deliver the key to you and will join and help you in an action so noble and glorious."
Installator says, "My Brethren, the thick darkness which reigns in this Temple will not permit us to penetrate it. Our work will be nothing but disorder and confusion. Let us altogether invoke the Great Architect of the Universe, that He would accord to us a sparkle of His sacred fire, which will dissipate the darkness, enlighten our work, and fill with glory this new Temple that we have erected in His fear and to His name; vowing before we enter the same, that we will only practice the virtues proper to perpetuate the morals, that we will never burn the incense, only upon the altar of wisdom, and that we will teach the essential useful truth, which ought to distinguish the Mason from the profane world."

Prayer

(An appropriate prayer may be made)

   Thou Great and Holy One! Before Thou didst form the Universe Thou didst create the light which ought to enlighten us. Permit us to consecrate to Thee our first work and to draw from this flint a sparkle of that primitive sacred fire which Thou hast spread over all nature.
Lights the match, and the Master of Ceremonies holds the new candle, says, "Fiat Lux! My Brethren, let us all enter into this Temple in order to finish the work we have commenced."
The Installator takes the candle from the Master of Ceremonies, and all go into the Temple and arrive at the foot of the emblem. The Installator gives one rap and says, "On the due guard."

He then opens the emblem and lights it, and says, "Symbol of the star of day, vivify with celestial light all the workmen who will meet together in this sanctuary to labor for the moral perfecting of humanity. Dissipate the darkness of the prejudices of the Neophytes who will enter into this Temple. Light us without ceasing by the clear light in order that we may never err or wander from the way of truth."

The Installator then lights the three lights on the throne and says, "Those three lights in a triangle, which are shining upon the throne, symbolize the three essential luminaries of the Great Architect of the Universe, also His wisdom, his justice and His bounty, and answer the three divine qualities which humanity can experience and possess. We should never deviate from the path of wisdom, and we are unitedly to be kind and just to all the human race."

The Installator then gives the light to the two Masters of Ceremonies, who go to the Senior Warden with the Installator. The Installator then lights the Senior Warden's lights and says, "The flame of this light symbolizes the flame of Virtue. This flame will unceasingly remind us that virtue is the tie which binds society together, that without virtue there is no such thing as happiness in the world, and that she gives us this sweet internal satisfaction, the only reward which is the aspiration of the wise."

The Installator then lights the Junior Warden's and says, "The flame of this light symbolizes the brightness and the dignity of humanity, when inspired by the zeal of charity unfeigned. It fills the heart with a pure love for his fellow men, and urges us to the practice of charity in order to make men happy, and that it is by the happiness of the whole human race that the individual happiness of man depends."

Installator then goes to the Orator, lights his light, and says, "The flame of this light symbolizes the one which has enlightened the mind of the initiate and fortified his reason, in order to preserve him from the dangerous error of fanaticism and superstition."

Then goes to the Secretary, lights, and says, "The flame of this light symbolizes the clearness and the simplicity of the Trestle Board which contains the exact and regular plan of our work. It is a well known fact that without a clearly defined plan the work contemplated will always result in confusion. The plan that we have to follow, consists in the sublime point which Masonry claims for itself, viz., in the justice of the principles which we have, to teach in the explanation of the allegories and symbols which characterize the Order, and in the strict execution of the obligations which we have contracted."

Installator then returns to his place, gives one rap and says, "My Brethren, the light having taken the place of darkness we will soon be able to give ourselves up to our work, and advance with security and pleasure. This is the object of all our meetings. But in order to work, we must have tools, this is indispensable. Therefore, I beg of our Master of Ceremonies to bring us the symbolic tools of Masons."

The Master of Ceremonies presents the Globe to the Installator, who says, "This symbol of the Universe will remind us that it, by the study of nature, and by the contemplation of the wonders of the Divine Omnipotence, that we can arrive to the acknowledgment of the truth. This symbol indicates to us equally that Masonry is cosmopolite, and that its works ought, like the sun, diffuse and spread light over the human race."

The Master of Ceremonies then presents the Compass. Installator says, "It is with this instrument that we examine and compare the diversity of the proportion of the objects which surround us. The compass symbolizes our reason, which ought ever deeply examine the nature of things, in order to the acknowledgment of the truth, and in order to distinguish the good from the bad, the true from the false."

The Master of Ceremonies then presents the Square. The Installator says, "This square has between its two ends a right angle. It is called the perfect angle. It symbolizes the rectitude and perfection of judgment we arrive at when, we are not in our reason and our conscience, subjected to the influence of prejudice and ignorance."

The Master of Ceremonies then gives the Senior Warden's jewel, the Level, "This is a symbol of equality. We meet upon the level here. Worldly distinctions are forgotten and virtue is the only distinguishing quality among us as Brethren. Whatever may be our circumstances in the world, here we come and are reminded that we travel the same road, to the same destiny, and that human distinctions will not avail."

The Master of Ceremonies then presents the Junior Warden's jewel, the Plumb. The Installator says, "My Brethren, let us be constantly following the rectitude which is indicated to us by this beautiful emblem. Let us always endeavor to build up, with order, the materials of the moral and scientific edifice, on which we have to work, in order that a strong and substantial basis prevent it from crumbling down. By observing the perpendicular in our march forward in the way of truth, and in the practice of philanthropy, the passions and vices never could cause in us a deviation from the perfection to which we would attain."

The Master of Ceremonies then gives the Tie. Installator says, "My Brethren, up and under the due guard. Let us form the Chain of Union."

The Installator takes in his hand the Tie, and after that all the Brothers take hold of the same. The Installator then ties it around him (his body) and says, "My Brethren, the tie is the symbol of the union which makes the basis of every durable society. Our union will make our strength. Let us tie the fraternal knot which ought to unite all Masons and, that the fraternal kiss, which we are going to exchange mutually, may be the certain sign of our harmony and peace, and which always ought to rule among all Masons wheresoever scattered over the surface of the earth."

The Installator then gives the Sign and Sacred Word of the First Degree and the Fraternal Kiss to the Master, then the same to the Senior Warden, from then, it passes round the bottom each way, when the Master of Ceremonies takes it, and carries it to the Installator who says, "All is correct; to your places."

The Installator then goes to the throne and gives one rap, the two Wardens repeat. Installator says, "Brother Senior and Junior Warden, announce to your respective columns that this new Temple, which is erected to the Glory of the Grand Architect of the Universe and of truth and virtue, is inaugurated under the name of the Most Respectable Lodge of Saint John, definitive title ———, under the Jurisdiction of the Supreme Grand Council of Sovereign Grand Inspectors General of the 33^d

Degree, Ancient and Accepted Scottish Rite. Invite the Brethren to join us to applaud this Consecration, by three times three."

The Wardens repeat the announcement, after which the Installator commands the Brethren, "Up, and under due guard."

After which, all give the Sign and three times three. After which, the Installator gives three raps, repeated by the Wardens.

Installator says, "Worshipful Master, Senior and Junior Wardens, please to come to my side, and you all, my Brethren, let us form a circle."

Installator comes down and stands up between the throne and the table. When the Circle is formed Installator says, "My Brethren, let us crown the solemnity of this occasion, by eating the same bread and by drinking in the Cup of Friendship, in order to retire the knot which unites us, and to cement the sweet fraternity which distinguishes the members of the Order."

The Installator takes the circular bread, breaks it in two, takes a small piece and gives the rest to the Master. He drinks in the first cup with the Senior Warden. Each Brother does the same at this Mystic Agapé. When the ceremony is finished the Installator says, "To our places. Brethren."

Installator, in the throne, gives one knock and says, "Brother Inside Tyler, advance to the throne."

He then delivers to him the key of the Temple and says, "Brother Inside Tyler, the security of this Temple depends upon your watchfulness. I here deliver the key to you, but you will give entrance here only to the true Mason, and never suffer any of the profane to enter into its bosom."

The Installator then says, "Brother Grand Expert, please to announce at the four cardinal points, in a loud voice, that this Temple is dedicated to the Glory of the Grand Architect of the Universe."

The Expert announces it in the four corners. Now the Orator delivers a Speech.

The Installator then says, "The inauguration is done and the work is suspended."

Then may follow the regular Installation of the officers to their respective posts, if ready. After which ceremony there may be music, etc., then take up a collection and close the Lodge in usual form. When, if a supper, all retire to the same.

(77.1) Opening of a Scottish Lodge (French) —

1st Degree

The Members being in the room and clothed, the Venerable Master says: In order, Brethren. Brother Senior Warden, are you a Mason?
Ans. My Brethren recognize me as such.
W.M. What is the first duty of the Senior Warden in the Lodge?
Ans. To see that the Lodge is tyled outside.
W.M. You will please to perform that duty.
Ans. The Lodge is perfectly tyled outside.
W.M. In order, Brethren. Up, and under the Due Guard.
    Brother Senior Warden, what is the second duty of the Senior Warden in the Lodge?
Ans. It is to assure himself that all present in the Lodge are Masons (*standing up*).
W.M. Are you satisfied that such is the case?
Ans. I am; they are so on both Columns.

The same is passed to the Junior Warden, who replies in the same way.

W.M. They are all Masons in the East.
S.W. (*to the Expert*) You will examine outside.
The Expert goes out, returns and reports to the Senior Warden: We are tyled outside and all is right.

This is said by Junior Warden to Senior Warden, and he to the Master.

W.M. Brother Senior Warden, where do you come from, as a Mason?
Ans. From a respectable Lodge of St. John.
W.M. What were they doing Brother, when you was there?
Ans. They were digging a prison for vice, and they were building a Temple dedicated to virtue.
W.M. What do you come here to do?
Ans. To subdue my prejudices and my will, and to make some progress in Masonry.
W.M. Where does the Master stand in a Lodge?
Ans. In the East.
W.M. Why?
Ans. The example of the sun, which rises in the East and passes toward the West, to his place of rest; like him the Master takes his place there to enlighten the workmen with his light and to help them with his counsels.
W.M. Thank you, Brother.
W.M. Brother Senior Warden, what is your age as an Apprentice?
Ans. Just three years.
W.M. At what hour does the Apprentice Masons begin their work?
Ans. At noon.
W.M. What is the hour, Brother?

Ans.   High noon.

W.M.   As it is time when we are accustomed to open our work, Brother Senior and Junior Wardens, with the Brethren who compose your respective columns, you will unite yourselves with me to open this respectable Lodge, which is duly constituted by the Supreme Council of Sovereign Grand Inspectors General, sitting in the valley of New York, and is by definitive title, Lodge ———, in due form.

The Senior Warden repeats this after the Master, and then the Junior Warden.

W.M.   Up Brethren, and under the Due Guard. Attention, Brethren.

The Sign and Battery, three times, ● ● — ●.

W.M.   Brother Senior and Juniors Wardens, inform the Brethren who compose your respective columns, that this respectable Lodge (name) is open and that it is not allowed to any one of the members to withdraw themselves, nor is it allowed to them to speak without permission from the West.

This is repeated by the two Wardens.

W.M.   Brethren, be seated. The Lodge is open. Give your attention to the minutes of the last meeting, which will now be read.

[*The minutes are read.*]

W.M.   Have you any remarks?
Brother Orator, give your conclusions.

Orator speaks. Master returns thanks.

Work

W.M.   Brethren, it appears by the ballot that you have admitted the profane, Mr. ⸻ to be initiated into our mysteries. If you have any objections, please express them now, and in the proper manner, etc.

The Brethren give the Sign of consent.

W.M.   Brother Conductor, please go to, and place the Candidate in the state required, and bring me his last will and testament, his hat, money, etc.

The Conductor retires, places the Candidate in the Chamber, takes with him the things required and returns to the Lodge, leaves them with the Master in the East. Master then reads the will.[52]

(83.15)Chamber of Reflection

This Chamber must be painted black inside, all over. All its furniture must be black, and it must have no windows, or any means by which the light can be admitted from without. It is properly called the Black Chamber. The entrance to it should be through a massive door, and a person should be obliged to stoop low to enter, or else go down steps. There should be in it a coffin, a table, on which is a black cover, a Bible open, an hourglass, a vase or pitcher of water, a glass, a piece of bread, a plate of salt, another with sulfur, the testament, a pen and ink. All these pieces are black. There should be two chairs, also black. A skeleton is sometimes lade in the open coffin.

In front of the table, and on the wall should be represented a cock, and the hourglass, and under them the two words, "Vigilance—Perseverance."

There should be also painted on black cards, about eighteen inches long, the following sentences, which may be hung around the room on the walls:—

"If curiosity has led thee hither, depart. This is no place for thee."

"If thou art unwilling to be enlightened concerning thy failings, or to be spoken to concerning thy errors and thy sins, thou wilt not meet from us a kind reception. Better for thee to leave in peace."

"If thou art capable of dissimulation, or hypocrisy, tremble; for thou wilt be exposed."

"If thou covetest human distinctions, go not any further, none of these do we acknowledge within our Temple, or encourage them in our associations."

"If thy heart sinks within thee and thou art frightened, do not go any further."

"If thou persevere, thou wilt be purified by the elements, thou wilt emerge from the abyss of darkness, thou wilt see the light."

There should be in the room a hanging lamp, or else a taper on the table. The Candidate is brought to this room by the conductor who, after seating him at the table,

---

52. FM2:78.7. Following this line it reads, "The Ceremonies in the Chamber &c are described in another place— (<8 use first>)." We presume Folger meant FM2:83, where the ceremony is found.

addresses him in a proper manner concerning the object of bringing him there and the emblems, of the place which should engage his attention while there.

Having finished his address, he leaves him to his meditations where he remains for a short time. The Conductor then returns and calls his attention to the will, which is before him on the table, containing a printed form of name, birth place, city, county, state, profession, residence, his religion; under which are printed the following questions, which he must also fill up and answer with his own hand:—

What is a man's duty toward God?
What is a man's duty toward himself?
What is a man's duty toward his fellow men?

After this follows the testament, or disposition of his property, which he must fill up and which being completed is taken to the Lodge, and deposited with the Master.

All these ceremonies, addresses, etc., being completed, the Candidate is then prepared, as in the other rite, to be brought in. His hat, sword, money, watch, rings, etc., are brought into the Lodge, and placed with the Master.[53]

(78.9)*The Candidate having remained in the Chamber a sufficient length of time, and being properly prepared, is brought by the Conductor to the door and makes a very loud and irregular alarm.*

W.M.   See who knocks at the door.
S.D. It is a profane who desires to be a Mason.

The Junior Warden tells it to the Senior Warden, and the Senior Warden to the Master, and the Master to the Lodge.

W.M.   Ask him his name, age, country, occupation, residence, and what he desires from us, and whether he believes in the existence of One True and Living God.

These inquiries are separate, and go to the Senior Warden, then Junior Warden, then Senior Deacon, and replies returned in same way.

W.M.   Introduce the profane and we will see if he is worthy to be initiated as a member of our ancient institution.

They open the door with a loud noise, make obstructions, etc., and then the Conductor says to the Master: The Profane is in the Temple.
W.M.   Bring him to the East.
   Sir, please to lift us your right hand.

He places the sword against his breast.

W.M.   Sir, swear upon your honor that, in case you should not be received, among us, you will never betray to any one under any circumstances whatever, any thing you may have seen or heard.

---

53. FM2:84.16. Immediately following appears a brief overview of the ritual, which would break continuity, and is thus omitted.

CAND.   I swear.

W.M.   Drop your hand, I receive your promise.

Master directs the Candidate to be seated on a chair before the altar.

W.M.   Sir, the first qualifications we require from you, in order to be admitted among us, and without which you could not be initiated to our mysteries, are the pure sincerity, docility and constancy which is unfailing (unflinching).

Your answers will enable us to judge. What are you ideas in coming here? Who or what gave you the first idea of it ? Is it not curiosity? What do you think about Masonry? Answer fully and be true. Are you ready to approve and support all the proofs by which you have to be tried? Who brought you in here? Do you know him to be a Mason? Did he tell you any thing about it beforehand? How do you know any thing you never could prove? Tell me, Sir, under what impressions are you since you left your house to come here? Are you married? Did you tell your wife, or friend, (as the case may be) of your intention to join us? Why did you not tell them? Were you afraid they would prevent you?

Well, Sir, you are right. It is by the practice of virtue you must be known among the profane as well as among Masons.

What reflections did you give to the objects you saw in the chamber? What do you think about your present state? What idea do you have of a society in which they urge the Neophyte to be introduced in such a singular way? Be frank in your answers, because we read your heart. Is not the step you are now taking an inconsiderate one? Have you no fear that we shall abuse the state of weakness and blindness in which you suffer yourself to be placed? You are now unarmed, nearly naked, and in the power of unknown persons.

You are right, Sir. The correctness of your answers, your confidence in us gives us the assurance that if received you will honor the Order, because Masonry, Sir, is an association of virtuous men, whose purpose it is to live in perfect equality and be strongly united under the name of Brother and to excite one another to the practice of virtue. With this explanation, you will perceive that it is the incumbent duty of every Lodge not to admit to the participation of our mysteries any except those which shall be found worthy to partake of these advantages, and able to undergo the trials and attain to the elevated point to which we aim, and such as we shall not be ashamed of before the Masonic world.

After a pause.

W.M.   Now, Sir, it becomes our duty to cause you to submit yourself to the indispensable proofs. I warn you, Sir, that if in the course of these proofs the strength and courage which are necessary to you should fail, you will always be at liberty to retire. These proofs are, all of them, mysterious and emblematic. Give them your best attention. Are you decided to go on?

He answers.

[The Emblematic Voyages]

W.M.   Brother Conductor, make the first voyage. (*One rap.*) Go on.

He makes the first voyage and then is again seated.

W.M.   Well, Sir, what did you remark in that voyage?

Answers.

W.M.   That first voyage is the emblem of human life, the tumult of the passions, the shock of diverse interests, the difficulties of the enterprise, the obstacles that attend your steps, the competitions of interests to rebuke and tire you. Everything is a figure, represented by the noise and fracas which struck your ears and the inequality of the way you have traveled over.

Now address him on the questions of the last will and testament.

W.M.   You know, Sir, that the most virtuous man has always small vices, or at least a principal fault. It is indispensable, Sir, that we know yours. Well, Sir, don't have any false shame. Masonry is a mutual school, in which each member who compose the Order must be willing to be corrected by teaching. Well, Sir, be frank. What is your principle fault? Are you not inclined to be proud? Or Covetousness? Or Anger? Or any other passion? If you are perfect then you need not come here.

W.M.   Well, Sir, are you willing to go on with the indispensable proofs of your initiation?

Answers.

W.M.   (*One rap*) Brother Conductor, seize the profane and guide him in the second voyage. He is under your care, take care that no arms are found about him. Go on.

WATER. Returns to the East and is seated.

W.M.   Well, Sir, what are your reflections during that voyage?

Answers.

W.M.   You found in the second voyage less difficulty and embarrassment than in the first. We wished to render very sensibly to you the effect of your constancy to follow in the way of virtue. The more you follow it the more agreeable it is. The noise that you heard figures the combat of a virtuous man which he is obliged unceasingly to sustain in order to triumph over the attacks of vice. You have been purified by water. You have still some other proofs to sustain. Arm yourself with courage, in order to support them to the end.

   Before you go any further, Sir, I have a question to propose to you. Your answer to this question can decide your rejection or your admission among us. You have promised to us to be true, remember your promise. Tell me, Sir, do you already belong to any society whatever? Religious, political, or philanthropic? And say frankly.

Answers.

W.M.   Well, Sir, what is the one object of that Society? What is the Secret?

If he is disposed to betray, turn him out. If he refuse, the Master says:

It is only a few moments since you have promised to answer with frankness and truth, and now you refuse to tell me the secret. I am sorry, Sir, but you cannot be received a Mason. We have not any secrets from another, and your want of confidence in us does not allow us to initiate you. Then, Sir, you have the resolution to deprive yourself of the privilege of being a Mason?

Answers.

W.M.   Sir, your answer is full of good sense and courage. You have well displayed it on this trial. Your firm and invulnerable will to renounce your initiation, sooner than betray the secret of your society, gives us the measure of your character—upright and loyal—and inspires us with confidence in the principles which you possess, and which are absolutely requisite before you can be made the depository of the secrets of the Order

Brother Conductor, take the profane and lead him on his third voyage. (*One rap*) Go on.

Fire.

W.M.   Sir, you remark that this voyage has been less painful than the preceding. The flame through which you have passed has completed your purification. May the material fire, with which you were surrounded, light up forever in your heart the love of your brethren and fellow men. May charity preside over actions, and never forget that sublime moral precept, which is common to every nation: **"Do ye unto others as you would wish them to do unto you."**

The frankness, with which you have declared what your human weakness was, gives us the hope that you will try to correct it yourself. You have been materially purified by water and fire. It is your duty to carry the work to completion by practicing the precepts and virtues that your Brethren will at all times show to your sight.

The constancy that you have displayed in your three voyages give us the assurance that you will support the same proofs yet unfinished. Do you persist, Sir, to go on?

Answer.

W.M.   Sir, among the virtues that we cherish, and which we most practice, and that which is nearest to our being is charity. The metals that we have been deprived of are the emblems of vices. Can you without reluctance sacrifice those to the profit of the poor and unfortunate that we generally help, the money, and the produce to the metals which belong to you, and which have been delivered to me? Take care, Sir, a numerous society now have their eyes upon you, and they are attentive to the answer that you will give. I claim of you an act of charity, fear not to make any ostentatious display for the sake of doing the act.

After the answer.

The charity that I ask will cease to be a virtue if you exercise it to the prejudice of some more sacred and more binding duty. Perhaps you have some civil engagement to fulfill, a family to support, or parents or unfortunate relations. These are the first duties that nature commands. They are the privileged debts of every man who regulates his conduct on the principles of equity. What opinion would you have of a man who would show himself charitable before thinking of these things? I recall your attention to my first proposition. Can you, without reluctance, deprive yourself of these things without injuring yourself in order to bestow upon the poor, whom we generally support, the whole or a part of the money and the jewels which belong to you, and which have been delivered to me?

Answer.

W.M. Well, Sir, as it may be the case that those jewels are a present from some dear and cherished friend, or the produce of hard labor and saving, and it would probably be attended with pain to deprive you of those things, we wish you to make yourself easy, and at the same time to give a free offering from your heart, which is so well disposed to charity.

I will send a person to you, to whom you will speak very low, the sum that you can spare, in favor of a poor widow who has five young children and whose situation is deserving of the support of Masons. But remember well, Sir, the observations that I made. We are soliciting of you an act of Charity. Do not put in its place an act of ostentation, because, among us, the one who gives very little or nothing when he can not do otherwise is as much respected as the rich giver.

W.M. (*to the Almoner*) Brother Almoner, Minister of Charity, approach the profane and ask him what he is willing to give to the poor, and report to me.

Answers.

W.M. Sir, in the name of all Masons, I thank you. Sir, we will in a moment demand of you an obligation which will guarantee your discretion. This obligation must be signed with your blood. Do you consent to spare a sufficient quantity to sign it?

Answers.

W.M. Brother Surgeon, approach the profane and tell me if he can loose blood without danger.

Your resignation gives us a proof, Sir, that at all times and in all circumstances you will be always ready to fly to the help of your brethren, and if necessary to spill your blood for them.

Brother Master of Ceremonies, give to the profane the Cup of Bitterness.

Sir, swallow that beverage to the last drop, and learn by its bitterness that it is the emblem of sorrow, and inseparable from human life, and that resignation to the Divine Will can alone add any sweetness to that bitter cup.

Sir, before we go any further I must inform you that almost all Masons bear a particular mark. That mark consists in the application of a red hot iron stamping on a part of your body, which you may choose, a sign, characteristic and ineffaceable, in order to constitute you a Mason. Are you willing, Sir, that this mark should be applied to you?

Answers. Upon which past, remarks:

W.M. Brother Conductor, hold him strong.[54]
Sir, the good reports that we have of your morality, and the good opinion that we have of your Introducing Brother, pleases me to let you know that the indispensable proofs which you have passed through are so great a recommendation to us that we will dispense with any other proofs which under ordinary circumstances you would be obliged to submit to but I must inform you, Sir, that you have to take an obligation to bind you to the Order. Do you consent to take it? Sir, the oath that you will take will not affect, *etc.*, nevertheless it is my duty to inform you that it is solemn and sacred, *etc.* Are you willing, *etc.*?

[*Answers.*]

Brother Master of Ceremonies, lead the recipient to the foot of the throne and place him in a proper position, etc.
One knock. All the Brethren up and under Due Guard. Master then says: Repeat with me, *etc.*

The Obligation is same as in the York Rite (love the Brethren and help them, conform to the laws and constitutions, perjury, entrails, heart burnt, etc.).

W.M. Sir, you will remember your Obligation. You will now sign it with your blood.

Remarks. The Test.

Sir, the oath that you have just taken, does it not give you inquietude? Do you feel the resolution to observe it? Will you consent to give it again when the blind is taken off?

Answers. Senior Warden goes behind him. Brethren form a circle.

W.M. Sir, what do you most wish?
*Candidate says:*Light.
W.M. Well, Sir, you will get it. (*Says to the Junior Warden:*) Brother Junior Warden, are you a Mason?
Ans. I am.
W.M. Why did you become a Mason?
Ans. Because I was in darkness and wished for Light.
W.M. What do you wish for the Neophyte?

---

54. This "test" often involved the snuffing of a candle, and the application of its hot wax to the Candidate's breast.

Ans. The same favor.

W.M. (*At the third sound of the gavel*) Let the light be given to the Candidate.

Master raps three (• • — •).

> Sir, the swords around you, which are pointed at your breast, *etc.*
> Brother Master of Ceremonies, lead the Candidate to the throne to repeat his Obligation.

Master places the compass to his breast. Remarks on Justice.

> Brother Conductor, return the Candidate to the Dark Chamber to dress, *etc.*

Candidate returns and is placed in the West. Master calls up the Lodge. Due Guard.

Goes to the Candidate and accepts him: In the name of God, by authority of the Supreme Council and by virtue of the power vested in me by this Respectable Lodge, regularly constituted by the Grand Orient of New York under the distinctive title of ———, I receive and constitute you an Apprentice.

Fraternal kiss, three [times].

W.M. (*To Master of Ceremonies*) You will please lead the Candidate to the throne by the Apprentice Steps.

> *Master then gives the apron to the Candidate and says:* My Brother, this apron which you will always wear in the Lodge, will remind you that man is condemned to work, and that a Mason must lead an active and laborious life.
> *Giving the gloves, he says:* Let these gloves, by their whiteness, remind you that candor reigns in the heart of an honest man, and that his actions must be always pure. The Sword you will always wear in the Lodge. Let it remind you that a Mason should be always ready to protect and succor his Brethren and always ready to punish the perjurer.
> Brother, to be admitted into our retreat and participate in the ties which unite us all over the globe, it is necessary that you be able to recognize and make yourself known as a Mason. I will give you the Sign, Word, Grip, and Token with which we recognize one another, and by the help of which you will be recognized by Masons wherever you may be.

Sign, Grip, Word, and second kiss.

> Brother Master of Ceremonies, lead the Candidate toward the light in the West, in order that he may make himself known as a Mason.

Goes to Junior Warden, Senior Warden, and then to both columns. Instructed by Master of Ceremonies how to enter a Lodge, then instructed to work on the Rough Stone.

W.M. Up, Brethren, and under the Due Guard. Brothers Senior and Junior Wardens, invite the Brethren who compose your respective columns to recognize henceforth Brother ——— forever for an Apprentice Mason, and the members of this Respectable Lodge to join themselves to you, and me to applaud his initiation.

Wardens repeat, then Master of Ceremonies gives thanks. The Candidate is then conducted to the Orator, who delivers an Address or Eulogy.

Closing

W.M.   Brothers Junior and Senior Wardens, you are requested to ask your respective columns if they have any thing to offer, etc.
WARDENS   They are silent, Venerable.
W.M.   As silence reigns, Brothers Junior and Senior Wardens, all the Brethren will give attention to the minutes, etc.

Secretary reads them.

W.M.   Are there any observations?

Orator replies.

W.M.   Up, and under the Due Guard, Brethren. Brother Senior Warden, where stand the Wardens in the Lodge?
ANS.   In the West.
W.M.   Why?
S.W.   As the Sun, *etc.*
W.M.   Are the Brethren satisfied?
S.W. They seem to be.
W.M.   It is the same in the East. Brother Junior Warden, at what time do the Entered Apprentices close their work?
ANS.   At midnight.
W.M.   What is the hour?
ANS.   Full midnight.
W.M.   As it is full midnight, and as it is the hour when Apprentice Masons are in the habit of closing their work, Brothers Senior and Junior Wardens invite the Brethren, who compose your columns, to assist me to close this Respectable Lodge.

Gives the Sign. Wardens repeat. Together: salutation. Secrecy is enjoined. Master informs of the close. Retire in peace and harmony.

(66.1) ANCIENT MYSTERIES

Those who would be initiated into the secrets of the Egyptian priests applied to one of the initiated who knew him well, and by this person was the Candidate made particularly acquainted with the priests, and the priests with him. It was necessary that the request should be in writing, and often times accompanied with a recommendation from the King himself, as was the case with Pythagoras.

After a short delay with the applicant, if he was a foreigner, he was circumcised (Herodotus). Then they prescribed to him a certain form of food as fish and pulse. Even a bare sight of beans, which could never be eaten by other Egyptians, polluted him. He was also forbidden the use of wine until he had attained the higher degrees. Beer and water was his drink.

So prepared, they at last led him to an unearthly or subterranean cavern in their Temple, which he dared not leave for many months. Here he must prove himself. He was required to write down all his thoughts and secret reflections, and this writing they examined to discover the intents or motives of the newcomer.

If they were content with his exercises during this seclusion, then they led him out of the hole into a long subterraneous way, which was adorned on both sides with pillars and moral sentences. He also found upon the floor moral sentences which he must learn by heart. If he continued constant in this proof and fulfilled the required duties, then there was sent to him a Thesmophore, or guide. He held in his hand a strong whip, which he explained as a symbol, the use of which was to drive back with force the uninitiated from the door of the profane. Through this door the Candidate was brought to the Door of Men. If the Candidate continued his request, then they put a thick bandage around his eyes and fastened his hands with a strong linen band.

[First] Degree: [Pastophor]

A heavy thunder was heard to roll, the guide took the Candidate by the hand and led him through the Door of the Profane before the Door of Men. Outside this door stood and old man, of the degree, who kept watch, for the D[isciple] had this office to perform, viz., to keep watch over the Door of Men. As soon as the guide with the Candidate had come before the Door of Men, he struck the watching Brother silently upon the shoulder. Whereupon, the watching Brother made a loud and strong knocking upon the door. The door was soon opened partially and a voice asked, who was there, what the man desired, if he has stood his proofs, and if he believed himself to be sufficiently strong to stand his other trials. If the questions were answered satisfactorily, then they opened with a loud rushing noise, the Door of Men, and the Candidate was led by the guide into the Chamber called Birantha.

The Hierophant, or President, spoke to him in a rough manner. He asked him various questions concerning his way of life, to discover if he understood clearly the object of his reception, and if he was still desirous that the ceremony of reception should proceed. If his answers were to the satisfaction of the Hierophant, then the guide again took the aspirant by the hand, and led him several times around the chamber. By this symbolic journey they again sought to put his courage and constancy to another proof. A fearful and tremendous rushing was heard, the hissing of snakes, dreadful sounds of mourning and lamentation, a heavy wind blew, hard rain, and heavy thunder rolled. By and by all this uproar ceased, the Candidate was again placed at the door of entrance and the Menies, or second in command, read to him the bonds of fellowship and secrecy, which he must take upon himself.

When this was finished they led the Candidate up to the Hierophant in the upper part of the room, when he was seated upon a throne. Here he must fall down upon the naked knee. They placed to his throat the point of a sharp sword and then he took the Disciples oath. Sun, moon and stars were called upon to witness it, that he would never break truth with the fellowship and would forever conceal the secrets of fraternity, and never reveal them to the uninitiated.

Now he was an initiate. They unbound his hands and took the bandage from his eyes. He found himself in a wide and well-lighted hall, surrounded with very numerous initiates. On the throne was the Hierophant. In the lower third of the hall stood two high four-sided pillars, and between these lay a ladder consisting of seven steps.

The Hierophant rose and spoke with a loud voice:

"You have a right to hear me, therefore, hear. Shut the door, and guard and watch it well, that no uninitiated, no unholy, no derider of the sanctuary enter. But you, son of the heavenly labors and heavenly examinations, hear my speech. Great and weighty are the truths which I open unto you."

"Preserve yourself from prejudices. They remove you far distant from the way of happiness. Direct your thoughts before all things upon that Heavenly Being. Let his presence be constantly before your eyes, so shall your heart be prepared for virtue. Reflect and remember that you walk constantly before the eye of the All Powerful, who has made and preserved the world. That is the being who has brought forth all things and still cares for and preserves them. He sees all, but none of woman-born can behold Him, who was from eternity and will be forever. No Disciple can conceal himself from Him."

The Hierophant ceased. A fearful, profound, silence reigned in the assembly.[55] Now there came to him an old priest and explained to him a part of the symbols: the ladder over whose steps he must go was likened to the souls wandering on the earth. They instructed him also over the secret explanation of the name of the Undivided God, which was carefully concealed from the people, (This explanation was partly historical, partly natural, containing some apparent errors but they always insisted upon the doctrine of the Godhead.)

Now they commenced instructing the Disciple upon the doctrine of nature, lightning, thunder and winds. The different appearances of nature were explained with relative doctrines of the agency of the Godhead, which was always carefully concealed from

---

55. FM2:68.1 reads, "A fearful <profound> silence reigned around in the Assembly."

the people. He was also instructed in medicine and anatomy. Then they instructed him in their symbolic language, and the usual Hieroglyphic writings were explained to him.

When the ceremony of reception was over, then they communicated to him the Word by which all the Disciples acknowledged one another: Amoun, it was called; its explanation, "keep silent." Besides this word they had a hand grip as a sign of acknowledgment.

Now they clothed him. They gave him a kind of cap of a pyramidal form. Around his hips they girded an apron. Around the neck he bore a kind of cross, which hung down upon his breast. His whole clothing must consist of linen. His office was always, as often he bore his iron instrument, to watch the Door of Men.

Second Degree: [Neocoris]

They had many opportunities to observe the *Pastophor*, or Disciple. Did he show much strength of character? Had he made himself perfectly acquainted with the science of his degree, and were his natural talents of a kind that they could speak well themselves of him? His tasks were laid the more lightly upon him, and they forthwith commenced instructing him in the mysteries of the second degree (*Neocoris*).

At first they put him upon rigid diet and fasting, and left him again to his own reflections. When the time of his fasting was over the guide led him into a black chamber. What this black chamber had usually been we will not now say, it was called *Endymion*. Here the hardest trials were to be submitted to & many never came from the grotto alive.

The guide left the Disciple, but in his place there entered a most beautiful woman; beautiful as the morning. In her hand she carried a basket filled with excellent and tempting food. Laughing, she tortured him to refresh himself. She herself handed him the pitcher, caressed him on his cheeks, and sought in every possible manner to raise his passion and love. She wearied him to fill his stomach with dainty food. She went out. In her place there came a woman much more beautiful than the first. She brought him more delicate food and a pitcher of refreshment, hung around him kissed him, and by every art tried to raise his desire, etc. So it went on from day to day, the food more delightful, the woman more beautiful and enticing.

If he stood all this manfully, then came the guide to him, whom he had never seen since his introduction, praised his courage, asked him more questions concerning the science in which he had been instructed in a former degree. If the answers were satisfactory then he went to the assembly with them.

All who had been received in the higher degrees were here assembled. The Hierophant sat upon the throne, and at the door stood the *Stolista*, or water bearer, who carried in his hand a great vessel filled with water. The Hierophant asked the Candidate, in a few words, if he had fulfilled all his duties up to the present, and had led a life of constancy, chastity and virtue. If he answered him "yes," then the water carrier raised his vessel and poured the water all over his body, this being a symbol that all moral deformities were now washed away from him. When this had taken place then came the guide before him, holding in his hand a live snake. This he cast upon his body, naked as he was. After suffering the snake to crawl over him and twine about him he was taken away. Sometimes, more than one snake was around and about him. After this new proof was finished, then the ceremony of reception went on. They led him again to the four-sided high pillars, between which a griffin was to be seen, who bore before him a wheel with four spokes. Now he must swear that he would never reveal, either to the profane or to the Disciple, what he had seen in this degree or what he was about to see.

Now they gave to him an explanation of all the symbols. The two pillars were the emblems of the rising and the going down (East and West). The griffin was the image of the sun, the wheel with its four spokes represented the year with its divisions (four) They instructed him in the way of becoming acquainted with the art of leveling, but chiefly was geometry and building the things to which he should apply himself.

The external Sign of this degree was a stick with a snake wound around the top. The Word for this degree was *Heva*, or "Eve," and should remind the Candidate of the first fall of man in the garden. The Sign was to bear both arms, crossing over the breast. The Office of the C[andidate] was to wash the two pillars (a most inexplicable symbol).

Third Degree: Melanophir — The Door Of Death

Diligence, truth, obedience, abstinence, and pure morality were the steps by which the *Neocori* could attain this degree. If found worthy they admitted him thus—

Silently, the guide approached him and led him through a long way, at the extreme end of which was a door, over which was written the "Door of Death." The guide opened the door and suffered the Candidate to enter in. He now found himself in a large chamber and the images and symbols of death surrounded him on every side. There lay beast and men mummies on every side and every kind. There stood coffin upon coffin, arranged around on every side, but in the middle of the chamber was a very large coffin, open, in which was a corpse swimming in blood and full of wounds. This represents the coffin of Osiris. Besides this, many fresh corpses were here exposed and the Brethren were employed in embalming them. Some were cutting the corpses open to take out the bowels. There were one class covering the bodies with balsam, there another wrapping them with clothes, and there were others employed in putting away the corpses, to be placed at last in the final resting place.

The guide turned here to the Candidate and spoke, "Behold here thy slain Lord Osiris. Hast thou taken part in his murder, or are thy hands pure from his blood?"

Although the question was replied to in such a manner as to assure the assembly of the innocence of the Candidate, it did not help him. Two *Tapixeiten* or, Death Laborers, seized him and led him around the chamber, and so out of the door into a great hall, where all of this degree were assembled together. With deep mourning and clothed in black mantles and caps, their faces to the earth, the Brethren were arranged in a ring around the room. Even the King himself was present at these ceremonies. They acted in a friendly manner to the Candidate, praised him for his constancy and steadfastness, manifested in the trying proofs he had passed through, yet afterward they spoke thus to him in a bitter voice thus,

"Let this warn thee to push thyself no deeper into our mysteries. The first, the very first proof thou undergoest might prove fatal to thee. Therefore, beware! Woe unto thee if thou fail. Be content with what thou knowest and receive here a reward for thy labours."

With these words they reached him a golden crown, but the Candidate, who had been previously told by the guide that he would fall into these circumstances and instructed how to act, took the crown, cast it on the floor with contempt and trod upon it with his feet. Then sprang up the King and seized him. Then he cried out "Offence! Revenge!" With these words he seized hold upon the offering axe laying for him, and struck the Candidate with the same lightly upon the head. Then both Tapaxeiten seized him, cast him backwards upon the floor, and the *Pariskeiten* bound him like a mummy with linen bands. During these transactions all the Brethren sung a lament, or song of mourning, and it raised among them weeping and lamentations.

The *Tapixeiten* then seized the so-called dead again and bore him around the room, after this to another door over which was written "The Sanctuary of Spirits." The opening of the door was accompanied with loud blows. The image corpse was then borne down many steps. There he heard the water rush. A boat landed, Charron took the passenger in and set him down on the other side. Here was expected the Unearthly Judge. Pluto sat upon the throne, and at his side stood Rhadamanthus, Minos and Archess. There also appeared here other shades, among whom was Orpheus, who had a great knowledge of the Lyre. Pluto spoke hard to the shade of the new comer. He asked him about his whole course of life, and in the end he condemned the Melanophor to remain hereafter with all of his grade in the unearthly cavern.

The proofs were over and the instruction began. The body was unwrapped and made acquainted with its duties: first, to spare human blood; second, to stand by his Brother in danger under all cases, to assist him in want, and be willing to offer up his life for his Brother's sake; third, never to suffer the dead's rest to be disturbed; fourth, to believe in a future and final resurrection of the dead and expect a future reward.

Now he was obliged to give or devote a portion of his time to the act of painting, in order to be able to adorn the coffins and bands of the mummies. He received also an appointment to a particular kind of writing called *Hiero-Grammatische*. In this writing was contained the history of Egypt, as well as all the principles of astronomy then known. Here, in this unearthly cavern, he was also instructed in the art of eloquence, in order to be able to hold forth in the speech for the dead (funeral eloquence). The Sign of Melanophor consisted in a kind of motion of the hand on the body, through which means the fear or power of death should forever be cast out. The Word was called *Monach Caron Mene*, signifying, "I remember the day of anger."

The Candidate saw the daylight no more, until the priests saw he was capable of receiving the higher degrees. If he was not willing to go farther, if he was cowardly, or

---

56. FM2:71.31. Following this line Folger penned the note, "This extract has an important bearing upon true Masonry."

if he did not perform further trials, then he remained a *Pariskista* or *Heroi*, and never, while he lived came out of this cavern, or was he permitted to see the light of day.[56]

(84.27)FOURTH DEGREE: CHRISTOPHORIS

The time of wrath lasted ordinarily eighteen months. When it was over the *Thesmosphores* came to see the Candidate, saluted him graciously and invited him to follow him, after first having armed him with a sword and shield. They passed through dark galleries. Suddenly, men wearing masks of hideous forms, surrounded by serpents and bearing torches in their hands, attacked the Candidate, crying *Panis*! The *Thesmophores* incited him to dare all danger and bravely to surmount all obstacles. He defends himself with courage, but finally succumbs to numbers, then his eyes are bandaged, a cord is placed around his neck, and by it he is dragged on the ground to the apartment where he is to receive a new degree.

The shades now suddenly flee with loud cries. He was then raised, much fatigued, and hardly able to stand, and introduced into the assembly. Here he was restored to light, and his eyes were dazzled with the brilliancy of the decorations around him. The apartment presented the appearance of a splendid picture. The King himself was seated by the side of the *Demiurgus*. Below these dignitaries were seated the *Stolista*, or purifier by water, the *Hiero Stolista*, or Secretary, wearing a pen or feather in his head dress, the *Zacoris*, or Treasurer, and the *Komastis*, or director of banquets. All wore the *Alydeus*, or "symbol of Truth." The *Odos*, Orator or Singer pronounced a discourse in which he congratulated the newly initiated Candidate on his courage and resolution. He invited him to persevere, for he had only undergone half the trials which it was necessary he should submit, in order to furnish a complete proof of his worthiness. He was presented with a cup, filled with a very bitter beverage, which was called *Circe*. This he was obliged to drink the whole of. After this he was invested with various ornaments. He received the shield of Isis, or that of Minerva. The sandals of *Anubis* (the same as Mercury) were places upon his feet, and he was covered with the mantle of *Orci*, adorned with its hood. He was ordered to seize a scimitar, which was presented to him, and to cut of the head of an individual whom he was informed he would find in the recess of a cavern, not far off, whither he was going and to bring the same to the king. At the same instant all the members cried, "*Niobe*, behold the cavern of the enemy!" On entering he perceived the figure of a beautiful woman, which was composed of very fine skins or bladders, but so artistically constructed that she seemed to be a living creature. The new *Christophoris* approached and, taking hold of the hair, cut off her head, which he presented to the King and *Demiurgus*. After having applauded this heroic action, he was informed that the head which he had cut off represented the head of the *Gorgon*, wife of *Typhon*, who had caused the assassination of Osiris. This circumstance was seized upon to impress upon him the duty of always being the avenger of evil. After this, he was presented with new clothing and received permission to wear them, his name was inscribed on a book which contained those of all the judges in the country. He enjoyed familiar intercourse with the King and received his daily food from the Court. To him was given at the same time, with a code of laws, a decoration which he could only wear at the reception of a *Christophor* in the city of Sais. It represented Isis, or Minerva, in the form of an owl. This symbol was thus explained to him:—Man at his birth is blind as an owl, and becomes enlightened only by teaching and experience. The helmet signified the highest degree of wisdom; head of the *Gorgon*, subjugation of the passions; the buckler, or shield, the legitimate defense against calumny; the column signified firmness; the vase of water, the thirst of science; the quiver of arrows, the power of eloquence; the lance, or pike, persuasion carried to a great length, i.e., that one can by his reputation make a profound impression at a great distance; the palm and olive branch were symbols of peace. He was taught the name of the great lawgiver, which was *Jao*. This also was the Word of the degree.

The members of this assembly occasionally had a reunion, at which no one but *Christophores* were admitted. The Chapter was called *Pixon*, the word in use to express its sittings was *sasychis*, and the study of the Candidate was the *Amounic* tongue. or the mysterious language (see First Degree).

This is the end of the Smaller Mysteries. The remainder is called a knowledge of the sacred doctrines, called the *Manifestation of Light*.

Fifth Degree: Balahate

The *Christophores* held the right to claim this degree, which the *Demiurgus* could not refuse to confer on him. Conducted to the place where the assembly was held, he was received by all the members. He was then introduced into a room arranged for a theatrical performance. Here he was as it were the only spectator for each of the members took part in the performance. A person called *Orus*, accompanied by several *Balahates*, bearing torches, entered the room and appeared as if in search of something. *Orus* draws his sword, on arriving at the entrance of a cavern, from whence issued flames; the murderer *Typhon* was seated therein, wearing a melancholy look. *Orus* approaches, *Typhon* rises and assumes a frightful appearance, a hundred heads erect upon his shoulders, his body covered with scales, and his arms of immeasurable length. Without being discouraged by this frightful aspect, *Orus* advances toward the monster, fells him to the ground and kills him. After having decapitated him, his body was thrown back again into the cavern, from whence the flames ceased not to pour, and without speaking a word, this hideous head was shown to all the spectators. This ceremony was concluded by the instruction which was now given to the new *Balahate*, and which explained to him the true meaning of this allegorical representation. He was told that *Typhon* signified fire, which is a terrible agent and without which, nevertheless, nothing could be done in this world, that *Orus* was the emblem of labor and industry, and by aid of which man performs great and useful enterprises, in subduing the violence of fire, in directing its power, and in appropriating its effects to himself. The *Balahate* learned, in this degree, chemistry, the act of decomposing substances and combining metals. He was at liberty to assist, when he chose, in the researches and experiments which they made in that science . For this reason the Word of this degree was *Chymia*.

Sixth Degree: The Door of the Gods

Some preparation was necessary previous to receiving this degree. The Candidate was put in irons on entering the apartment. The *Thesmophores* conducted him to the "Door of Death," where it was necessary to descend four steps, as the cavern which served for this reception was the same where the initiation into the third degree took place, it being then filled with water to float Charon's boat. The eyes of the Candidate rested upon coffins placed here and there. He was told that they contained the remains of men who had been put to death for having betrayed the society. He was menaced with a similar fate should, he ever happen to commit a like crime.

He was conducted to the center of the assembly there to contract a new obligation. After having pronounced the oath, they explained to him the history and origin of the Gods, the objects of the worship and adoration of the people, and by aid of which their credulity was amused and directed; at the same time he was shown the necessity of conserving polytheism for the people, the vulgar multitude. Then the ideas, which had been presented to him on his reception in the first degree, were developed, on the elements of the doctrine of the One Great Being, who embraced all ages, presided in unity over the admirable regularity of the whole system of the Universe, and who by His nature was above all the comprehension of the human mind.

This degree was consecrated to the instruction of the Neophyte in the practical knowledge of astronomy. He was obliged to be present at their nocturnal observations, and to assist in the works which they required him to perform. Care was taken to warn him to be on his guard against all astrologers, and makers of horoscopes, and to regard them as the authors of idolatry and superstition. The Society held them in aversion. These false teachers had chosen the word *Phoenix* for their Word of Recognition, the word the astronomers turned into derision.

After the reception, the Candidate was conducted before the Door of the Gods, and he was introduced into the Pantheon. He there saw all the Gods represented in magnificent paintings. The *Demiurgus* again retraced to him their history without hiding any thing from him. A list of all the chief inspectors in chronological order was placed before him, as well as the table or register of all the members of the society scattered over the surface of the globe. He was also taught the dance of the priests, the steps of which represented the course of the stars.

The Word of the degree was *Ibis*, which signifies "crane," and was the symbol of vigilance.

Seventh Degree: Propheta, or Sapphenach Pancha.

The Man Who Knows the Mysteries.

This degree was the last and the most eminent. In it was given a detailed and complete explanation of the mysteries. The astronomer could not obtain this degree, which completed his qualifications for all functions, even public or political, without the assent of the King and *Demiurgus*, and the general consent of the interior members of the Order. The reception was followed by a public procession to which was given the name of *Pamylach*. In this procession all the sacred objects were shown to the people. The procession over, all the members of the Order secretly left the city during the night, and went to a neighboring place, where they gathered themselves together in a house of square shape, containing several apartments, ornamented with admirable paintings representing the life of man. These houses were called *Maneras*, because the people believed that the initiated were in correspondence with the Manes of the departed. They were adorned with a great number of columns, between which were placed coffins and sphinx.

Having arrived thither, the new prophet was presented with a beverage named *Ormellas*, and he was told that he had reached the end of all his trials. He then received a cross, which had a certain signification known only to the initiated. He was obliged to have it constantly upon him. He was invested with a very handsome, striped white robe, made very full and called *Etangi*. His head was shaved, and the headdress he wore was of a square shape.

His principal Sign was made by crossing his hands in his sleeves, which were very wide. He was permitted to read all the mysterious books, written in the Ammonic Language, of which the key, which was called "the royal beam," was given to him. The greatest prerogative, attached to the last degree, was the right of contributing in the election of a King.

The Word of the degree was *Adon*. The new prophet could also, after a certain time, attain to an office in the Society, and even to that of *Demiurgus*.

Of the Officers and Their Costumes

1st—The *Demiurgus*, Chief Inspector of the Order, wore a sky blue robe embroidered with stars and a yellow girdle. Suspended from a chain of gold around his neck was a sapphire, surrounded with brilliants. He was the Supreme Judge of the Country.

2d—The *Hierophant* was similarly dressed, with the exception that he wore a cross upon his breast.

3d—The *Stolista*, charged with the duty of purifying the Candidate by water. He wore a striped white robe, and sandals of a peculiar shape. The vestry was confided to his care.

4th—The *Hierostolista* (secretary) wore a plume, or pen, in his headdress, and held in his hand a cylindrical vase, called canonicon, which contained ink.

5th—The *Thesmophores*, director and introducer of Candidates.

6th—The *Zacons* (treasurer).

7th—The *Komastis* had the care of the table and of the banquets. Under his orders were all the Pastophores.

8th—The *Odos*, Orator or Singer.

Banquets

Before seating themselves at table, the members were obliged to wash. The use of wine was not permitted. They drank a beverage resembling the modern beer.

They carried around the table a human skeleton, or a *Butoi* (representation of a coffin).

The *Odos* then chanted the *maneros*, a hymn commencing thus, "O Death! Come at the proper hour." All the members joined in the chorus.

The repast being finished, each one retired, some to attend to their several occupations, others to meditation, the greater number to indulge in sleep, with the exception of those whose turn it was to watch at the door of the Gods, in order to introduce the Candidates for the sixth degree, who were to make their astronomical observations.

They were obliged to spend the whole night in assisting, or rather directing, the astronomical labors of the Candidates.

EXTRACT FROM A SPEECH OF DEWITT CLINTON BEFORE THE GRAND LODGE OF NEW YORK

(113.1)The grandeur and antiquity of the Temple of Solomon has ever been a theme for the pride and boast of Masonry. This great Temple was threescore cubits in length, twenty in breadth and thirty in height. More, if we include the courts with the size and space of all the kings royal palaces. They all united would not amount to anything more than an humble cottage in comparison with the extent, grandeur, magnificence, antiquity and present state of preservation of the ancient temples of Thebes, Apollinopolis, Karnac, Luxor and others recently discovered in Egypt, some of which occupy a space of several miles. These wonderful monuments of the ancient arts and sciences seem to bid defiance not only to the ravages of barbarous nations but even to that of time itself while the boasted pigmy monuments of Solomon. the pretended founder of Masonry, were in the short space of about four hundred years from their commencement leveled to the ground having not even a wreck behind. In defense of the antiquity of Free Masonry and to show at the same time the great veneration in which the Craft have held in all ages nothing is more common than to hear its votaries claiming the relationship of Brotherhood with the great and virtuous personages of ancient times. Among the professed patrons of the art the names of many of the Apostles are by no means the least conspicuous though we deny that there is any proof on record to justify the conclusion that Masonry had an existence in the age in which these exemplary defenders of all that is excellent lived. The names of Archimedes, Pythagoras, Euclid, etc., are also not unfrequently lugged in as promoters of the Royal Art divine. Enthusiastic friends of our institution have done it much injury and covered it with much ridicule by stretching its origin beyond the bounds of credulity. Some have given it an antediluvian origin while others have represented it as coeval with the creations. Some have traced it to the Egyptian Priests, and others have discovered its vestiges in the mystical societies of Greece and Rome, the erection of Solomon's Temple, the retreat of the Druids, and the Crusades to the Holy Land have been at different times specially assigned as the sources of its existence. The order, harmony and wonders of creation, the principle of mathematics; science and the productions of architectural skill have been confounded with Free Masonry. Whenever a great Philosopher has enlightened the ancient world he had been resolved by a species of moral metempsychosis or intellectual chemistry into a Free Mason and in all the secret institutions of antiquity the footsteps of Lodges have been traced by the eye of credulity. Archimedes, Pythagoras, Euclid and Vitruvius were in all probability not Free Masons, and the love of order, the cultivation of science, the embellishments of tastes and the sublime and beautiful works of art have certainly existed in ancient, as they now do in modern, times without the agency of Free Masonry.

(115.1)ADDRESS [AND EXCERPTS, ORDER OF THE RED CROSS DEGREE]

Companion, the Council here assembled represents the Grand Council assembled at Jerusalem in the first year of Darius, King of Persia, to deliberate upon the unhappy situation of their Brethren, and to devise means whereby they could obtain the favor and assistance of their new Sovereign, in rebuilding the House of the Lord.

If you are desirous of joining in our deliberations it is necessary you should assume the name and character of Zerubbabel, one of the princes of the house of Judah, whose hands laid the foundation of the first Temple and whose hands the Lord promised should finish it.

Companions, you will attend to a lesson from the records of our fathers (*Ezra 3ᵈ 8 x 11 – Ezra 4ᵗʰ*)

After the Address, the Conductor replies, then Prelate continues:

Companion Zerubbabel, the Council with great joy accept your noble and generous offer and will invest you with the necessary passports by the means of which you will be able to make yourself known to the friends of our cause wherever you may meet with them, but on entering upon an undertaking of such vast importance to the Craft it is necessary that you take a solemn obligation to be faithful to the trust reposed in you. I will invest you with the sword by the use of which you will be enabled to defend yourself against your enemies. You will kneel at the altar and receive your obligation.

1ˢᵗ—*The usual point.*
2ᵈ—*Due signs and summonses, forty miles, unavoidable accidents or bodily infirmities, etc.*
3ᵈ—*[Not be] present at conferring, unless E.A., F.C., M.M., etc.*
4ᵗʰ—*Forming or opening a Council unless five [members are present], or representatives of three different Encampments, etc.*
5ᵗʰ—*Support and maintain Constitutions, etc.*
6ᵗʰ—*Help, aid and assist, etc.*
7ᵗʰ—*Penalty, etc.*

Companion Zerubbabel, the Master of Infantry will now invest you with the Jewish Pass, by which you will be able to make yourself known to the friends of our cause wherever you may meet with them and which will insure you their protection and friendship.

I now present and invest you with this green sash as a mark of our peculiar friendship and esteem. You will wear it as a constant memorial to stimulate you to the performance of every duty. Its color is green and may remind you that the memory of him which falls in a just and virtuous cause is blessed and will flourish like the green bay tree. Farewell Companion, may success attend your enterprise.

O ye princes and rulers, how exceeding strong is wine. It causeth all men to err that drink it. It maketh the mind of the king and the beggar to be all one, of the bondsman and the freeman, of the poor man and the rich it turneth also every though into jollity and mirth so that a man remembereth neither sorrow nor debt, it changeth and elevateth the spirits and enliveneth the heavy heart of the miserable. It maketh a man forget his Brethren and draw his sword against his best friends. O ye princes and rulers, is not wine the strongest that causeth us to do these things.

It is beyond dispute, princes and rulers, that God has made man master of all things under the sun, to command them, to make use of them and apply them to his service as he pleases, but whereas men have only dominion over other sublunary creatures, Kings have an authority even over men themselves and a right of ruling them at will and pleasure, now he that is master of those who are masters of all things else hath no earthly thing above him.

The Master of Infantry then follows with his reply for Candidate upon women, but most of all Truth.

[EXCERPTS, KNIGHT TEMPLAR DEGREE]

(117.6)Companion you are now seated in the Chamber of Reflection. Before you, upon a table, you will find that great light of Masonry, the Holy Bible. You will also find upon the table a paper containing three questions, to which you are required to make answers in writing, yes or no, as you may see cause, and sign your name in the margin, and you will also find upon the table a bowl of pure water, in which you will wash your hands, and wipe them upon a napkin in token of the purity of your intention in the business you are now engaged with an awful reference to the day of your death and the coming judgment.

QUESTIONS

1st—Should you ever be called upon to draw your sword, will you wield it in defense of the Christian Religion?

2^{d}—Does your conscience upbraid you for any known or overt act unrepented of?

3^{d}—Do you solemnly promise to conform to all the ceremonies, rules, and regulations of this Encampment, as all valiant and magnanimous Sir Knights have done, who have traveled this way before you?

(1.1)ADDRESS

The rules of the Order have required that I should bring you to his place. It is silent, and retired. I beg of you to endeavor to abstract your mind from all worldly considerations for a short space of time and devote this season to thinking of yourself and the things that may here occur to you. To the place of which this is a symbol we must all sooner or later come. The wisest statesmen, the bravest warrior the meanest beggar, the old and decrepit, the gay, the beautiful the happy all travel the same journey and terminate their wanderings in the same house appointed for the living. Here they lay down all their sorrows and the burden of their worldly trouble is removed. Here the gay laugh is changed to silence, here the towering schemes of ambition are forgotten and the mighty and the mean, the rich and the poor enter upon that sleep which to mortal knows no waking. Though you may now be smiling in prosperity and surrounded with the comforts which the world bestows upon its votaries, the ruffian conqueror must be met, the battle fought, and you must be vanquished in the conflict. Though strong ties may bind you to the world they must be broken. Though the language of affection may plead in your behalf it will be unavailing, the dust must return unto dust as it was and the spirit unto God who gave it.

> How loved, how valued once, avails thee not
> To whom related, or by whom begot.

> A heap of dust alone remains of thee
> Tis all thou art, and all the proud will be.

[*Points to the Bible*] But see, here is the only light by which we can learn how to enter this dark and dreary mansion. It is the Book of Wisdom. It contains a revelation of the Divine Will. It is of great antiquity. The splendid monuments of the ancients have decayed, the people who inhabited the countries where these things were written have long since passed away, and their generations are scattered over the face of the earth. Their former places of abode are desolate, the languages in which this book was written have long since become dead, yet the Book still survives, and the enemies of order, the opposers of the good precepts this book contains, have sought with astonishing obduracy and with unwaivered pains, with jests, with philosophy falsely so-called, with misapplied learning, with every effort of their genius, to bring it into contempt. But now stands higher, and deservedly so, in the estimation of the virtuous and the good, than it ever did before, and the result has proved that they have been engaged in a very foolish work. How correct is its history, how beautiful its philosophy, how sublime its poetry, and how divine the doctrines it contains. My Brother, examine it well, you will find it an inestimable treasure, for it will not only be the guide to your feet and the lamp to your wanderings, it will discover to you the evil of your dispositions and point you out the remedy.

Takes the Hour Glass and turns it. Here is an emblem of Time. Behold how rapidly the sands run. They will soon run out, and then if no external power set it in motion, its motions will never be renewed. Let this be deeply impressed upon your mind. Time we can never recall. But we can and we ought to improve the fleeting moments as they pass, for on time, eternity depends.

Points to the Skull. Here is a melancholy memento, the emblem of mortality. It is now silent, vacant, dead. The rose of health once bloomed upon the cheek, the eye sparkled with intelligence and the countenance was perhaps once fair to look upon, but it is now an object of loathing and disgust. As it now is, so you will be, look then at this melancholy memento. Listen, for though silent, it speaks to the mind in a voice which cannot be misunderstood. It says, "Remember."

We have placed a green sprig by its side, for we do not believe that the grave is the final resting place, or death an endless sleep. No, we believe in immortality. We believe that though a man die, yet he shall live again, that the time will come when those who sleep in the earth shall come forth from the grave and meet the Master face to face. How important then, that the moments of life should be properly improved, that the precepts of this sacred volume should be laid to heart, that our labors for improvement and participation should be unceasing . For we shall die, and we shall rise again. We shall behold the Master face to face, and then deception either with him, or with ourselves, will be unavailing. We shall receive our reward or we shall be punished, for so he has decreed.

Questions asked and answered. Washing.

Folger Manuscript 2

Obligation

1st—*Usual point in all the same.*

2d—*Attend to all due signs and summons, if within the distance of forty miles, natural infirmities and unavoidable accidents only preventing.*

3d—*Help, aid and assist, with my counsel, purse and sword, all worthy Sir Knights, their widows and orphans, so far as my ability will allow, or truth, honor and justice will warrant.*

4th—*[Will not be present at] opening, unless there are nine regular Knights present, or the representatives of three different Encampments, acting under the sanction of a legal warrant.*

5th—*Forty miles on foot, or even barefoot on frosty ground, to save the life or relieve the distresses of a Sir Knight.*

6th—*That I will wield my sword in the defense of innocent virgins, helpless orphans, destitute widows and the Christian religion.*

7th—*Constitution, General Grand Encampment, and Bylaws, etc.*

8th—*Not be present at the conferring of this Order, unless the person has previously received E.A., F.C., etc.*

Address.

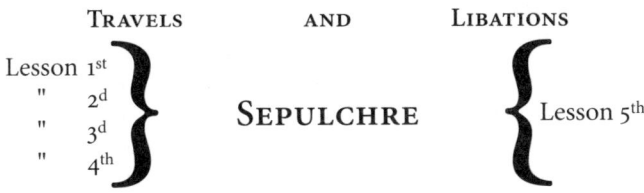

Address

Pilgrim, the scene before you represents the splendid conclusion of that hallowed sacrifice offered by the Redeemer of the world, to open a way for the salvation of men. This sacred volume informs us that He was born of a lowly virgin, that He led an humble and secluded life until He entered upon His ministry, which was attended with self denial, sufferings and privations of no ordinary kind, that He was tempted, buffeted and scoffed at in almost every step He took for the benefit of suffering and degraded humanity. Though He came to benefit them they set His goodness at naught, they derided and insulted Him, they mocked at His pretensions, and although no guile was in His heart, nor evil in His ways, although His nights were often spent in fervent prayer for those who were deriding him, although He never ceased to express His ardent love, and strong desire for the good of those He came to save, His persecutors never rested until a formal accusation was made against Him, for which He was tried and formally condemned, when He was led forth by the mob as a common malefactor and murdered by their ruffian hands. He was despised and rejected of men, a man of sorrows and acquainted with grief. We hid, as it were, our faces from Him. He was despised, and we esteemed him not. He hath borne our grief and carried our sorrows, yet we esteemed Him stricken. Smitten of God and afflicted. All we like sheep have gone astray, we have turned, every one of us, to his own way. And the Lord hath laid on him the iniquity of us all. He was wounded for our transgressions, He was buried for our iniquities, the chastisement of our peace was upon Him, and with His stripes we are healed. He was oppressed, and He was afflicted, yet He opened not his mouth. He is brought as a lamb to the slaughter and as a sheep before his shearers is dumb, so He opened not His mouth, and He made His grave with the wicked, and the rich in His death.

Pilgrim, on the hill of Calvary He bowed His sacred head and died, the fair sun veiled Himself in darkness, the earth shook, the rocks were rent and the dead forsook their graves. They laid Him in a Sepulcher, but the grave could not hold Him. He burst the bars of death, and became the first fruits of them that slept. He ascended with transcendent majesty to heaven, where He now sits at the right hand of God, Mediator and intercessor for all those who have faith in Him.

Pilgrim, I now invest you with an emblem of that faith and the badge of the Order. When you look upon it, it may remind you of those scenes which took place in the Garden, and on the Cross. It may speak to you in the language of inspiration. Is it nothing to you as to pass by, behold and see if thereby any sorrow like unto my sorrow wherewith the Lord hath afflicted me in the day of his fierce anger. It may teach you to imitate the virtues of the immaculate Jesus, who died that you might live.

Pilgrim, the ceremonies through which you are passing are calculated to make a deep impression upon your mind, and I most sincerely hope will have a lasting effect upon your character. You were first, as a trial of your faith and humility, enjoined to perform seven years pilgrimage. It represents the great pilgrimage of human life through which we are all passing. We are all weary pilgrims traveling from afar and anxiously looking forward to an asylum, where we shall rest from our labors. Yet it is dangerous to venture upon this far distant journey without a knowledge of the way we are going, and without this knowledge we shall easily go astray and fail in finding the asylum which we seek, but instead thereof faint among the sands of the desert, where there is no water to allay the burning thirst, no bread to keep from starving. Incline your heart to instruction and your mind to understanding and, in your pilgrimage, learn the way to the habitation of comfort and of rest. Seek it with earnestness and diligence, for this is not your place of rest.

You were next directed, as a trial of your courage and constancy, to perform seven years warfare. It may represent to you the constant warfare that is necessary to be performed with the lying vanities and deceits of this world. The passions of the man lead him astray and sensual enjoyments entice him from the garden of happiness into the wilderness of vice and the labyrinth of error, but presently, often alas too late, it is to be feared he is undeceived or, what it worse, he is satiated. A feeling of duty or of shame rouses him to view his present state, and he sees with remorse that he is far from where he should be, but the ways he has wandered through are so winding and intricate that he can never, perhaps, retrace his steps, and he stands like the fool, not knowing from whence he came and whither he went.

War not with your own welfare, make not yourself miserable, but be wise in time, consider every step of your journey, its end and its intention. Avoid the evil and choose the good, and when you find your strength failing in the contest, or your spirit falter, call upon your Captain, who has led the way and He will give you strength in time of need.

You are now performing penance as a trial of your humility. Of this our blessed Lord and Savior has left us as bright example. For though He was rich, yet for our sakes He became poor, that we through His poverty might be made rich. Though surrounded with the glory of His Father, He laid it aside and humbled Himself to take a human form, subjected himself to the sorrow and the joys, the infirmities and the trials of humanity, in order that He might know how to weep with those wept, and administer consolation and comfort to the tempted and the afflicted.

It is also a trial of that faith which will conduct you safely over the dark gulf of death everlasting, and land your enfranchised spirit in the abodes of the blessed.

Pilgrim, bear ever in mind this solemn truth. You know not how soon you may be called upon to render an account to Him, from whom not even the most minute act of your life is hidden. For although you now stand erect in the pride of beauty, and the strength of manhood, the rose of heath blooming on your cheek, and your eye sparkling with intelligence, the angel may have already received the mandate to cut you off from among the living, and the arrow which is to pierce you be already on its flight, even while I am speaking to you, may prostrate you before us in the arms of death, and the feet of those Companions who surround you, be employed in bearing you from this asylum a lifeless corpse.

Man that is born of a woman is of few days and full of trouble. He cometh forth like a flower and is cut down. He fleeth as a shadow and continueth not. In the midst of life we are in death. Thou changest the countenance of man and sendeth him away. Yet, though a man die, he shall again live. Though he say to corruption, "thou art my mother" and to the worms, "thou art my sister and my Brother", his spirit shall bloom and flourish beyond the shores of time, and be finally united to that spiritual body, either in the abode of wretchedness and despair, or in the beauteous paradise of God.

How important it is then, Pilgrim, that in the journey you are pursuing, your steps should be directed by wisdom which cometh from on high, that your mind should be enlightened by the truth of the Divine, in order that you should have a clear and perfect view, not only of the enemies which beset you in your course, but also of the manner in which you are to resist them "striving unto Blood." How important that in the warfare you are engaged in, you should fight manfully the fight of faith, having your lamp burning and your loins girt about, taking with you the sword of the spirit and the helmet of salvation, and in the thickest of the fray to be familiar with the commands of your Captain, who will always send you assistance and deliverance, if you call upon Him in your hour of need. How important that you should always be on your watch of penitence, that you should be waiting and ready for His approach, in order that you may gladly follow the steps of those who

> Once were mourning here below,
>   And wet their couch with tears,
> And wrestled hard, as we do now,
>   With sin and doubt and fears.
>
> They marked the footsteps which he trod,
>   His zeal inspired their breasts,
> And following their incarnate God,
>   Possessed the promised rest.

The Pilgrim here passes to the Asylum and partakes of the Fifth Libation, when the ceremonies conclude by installation.

Lessons. Closing prayer.

[LECTURE ON TEMPLES]

(38.17)Wherever the Temples of the ancients stood, if the situation of the place would permit, it was so contrived, that the windows being open, they might receive the rays of the rising Sun. The front was placed toward the West and the altars, etc., toward the other end. The doors being opened they should receive the rays of the rising Sun. They were divided into two parts: the sacred and profane, and a vessel of stone or brass filled with holy water with which all those who were admitted to the holy sacrifices were besprinkled and beyond which it was not lawful for any one that was profane to pass. This vessel was at the entrance of the Temple sacred, and in the vicinity of the porch or entrance was a cavern, or as has been termed, a tomb or grave, with monuments, pillars, etc.

(44.10)The first generations of men had neither temples or statues for their gods but worshipped toward heaven in the open air. The Persians even when temples were common in other countries had no Temple as they did not think the gods to be of human shape. The Greeks and most other nations worshipped upon the tops of mountains. The nations which lived near Judea sacrificed also upon the tops of mountains. Balak, king of Moab carried Balaam to the top of Bahal to sacrifice and curse Israel from thence. Abraham was commanded by God to offer Isaac, his son, for a burnt offering upon one of the mountains in the land of Moriah, and in later ages temples were often built upon the summits of mountains.

There is no doubt that temples owe their first original to the reverence and devotion paid by the ancients to the memory of their deceased friends, relations, and benefactors, and monuments were at length converted into temples when it was usual to offer prayers, sacrifices and libations. They were built and adorned with all possible splendor and magnificence, supported by Doric, Ionic and Corinthian pillars, were generally surrounded with groves, always in the most retired place they could find. They were divided into two parts, the sacred and the profane. In the latter part, or near the entrance of the sacred part, stood the laver, or basin vessel of stone or brass, and filled with holy water, with which all those who were admitted were besprinkled and beyond which it was not lawful for the profane to pass. Some conclude that it was placed at the very entrance of the Temple. No sort of idol was more common than the oblong stone erected, and thence termed "pillar." The square stone was black, named Bethel (Baituloi) and signifies, "the house of God."

(46.1)The Adytum was the inmost recess of the Temple, into which none entered but the Priests. In this was placed the *Arceion*, which was a repository. The temples of ancient times were without statues, and their worship was without any visible representation. There was generally an altar at the chancel, and here sacrifices were made, and always a cavern or grave at the entrance, or near it. The form of the altar was either oblong or square, and were adorned with horns. It was the place of suppliants, and it was customary to engrave upon the altar the name of the God they worshipped (*Acts*, Paul speaks of the unknown God, "whom ye ignorantly worship him I declare unto you"). The act of consecration consisted of unction with oil (*see the tabernacle with all its vessels, also the altar and priests themselves. Exodus 11:9–10; Numbers 7:1; Genesis 28:18; 35:14*). It was required that whoever was admitted to the office of Priesthood should be sound and perfect in all his members, neither maimed, lame, or in any way imperfect, no defect or any superfluity. They were stripped naked and examined (*Lev. 21:21–23, for sacred examples*). Nor ought they to be only perfect in body, they should be upright in mind, they therefore lived temperately and chastely. It was their allotment to prepare and make sacrifices for the people, and every person who came to the solemn sacrifices was purified by water, sometimes by sprinkling, to which end, at the entrance stood the basin or laver, full of water, consecrated by putting a burning torch into it, which was lighted from the altar of sacrifice. And the same torch was made use of to besprinkle those who came to the sacrifices. At other times they used a green laurel branch to do this office. The worshippers formed a circle around them, and and sometimes stripped them and washed their bodies all over, at other times the hands and feet. The water must be pure and clean (*see the practices of the Essenes, also Heb. 10:22; Ezekiel 36:25*). They sprinkled thrice, which number was sacred. No incestuous person, or murderer, or adulterer could be present, and those who had been thought dead were obliged to be passed through a woman's lap, or a gown, before they could be present and take a part in the sacrifices, which may explain the foundation of the sacred [?????].[57]

(48.16)This Tabernacle, which was erected by the Children of Israel by the command, and under the direction, of God himself, while they were sojourning in the wilderness, was an image of the Temple that was to be, and being designed as a protection for the Ark, was solemnly consecrated at its erection and sanctified anew every year on the day of expiation. This tent was divided into two apartments, the first called the Sanctuary or Holy place, into which only the clean priests might enter and it contained the Altar of incense, the Golden Candlestick and the Table of Shewbread; the second, separated from this apartment, by a veil of embroidered linen, was called the Most Holy Place or Oracle, where the Ark with its furniture and the cloud of glory overshadowing it, had their residence, into which the High Priest, only might enter on the day of expiation. But before this Tabernacle was made, it had been determined in the councils of infinite wisdom that a more durable and costly residence for the Ark and the Shekinah should be founded in Jerusalem. The privilege of erecting this sacred edifice was denied to David because he was a man of blood, but the Temple was completed by Solomon and, in its construction, resembled perfectly the Tabernacle of the children of Israel. All other temples of ancient date and for sacred purposes bore a most perfect resemblance to the above, and it is perhaps a most singular fact that the external forms of service therein performed bore quite the same similitude. The proofs of this may be found in the various histories of Temple service in all the writers on antiquity, of Egyptians, Greeks, Romans, etc. It is a subject of deep interest, etc.

[LECTURE ON RELIGION]

(50.29)Genuine religion, or that which is termed in revelation *Christianity*, must always appear as an insult on the taste of the public. Yes, its most respectable part in the most important matters. This, it is evident, must be the case so long as she bears for her motto "*That which is highly esteemed among men is abomination in the sight of God*," and while as a proper counterpart to this her favorite topic is to show that the character which was, and still continues to be, disallowed of men, is chosen of God and precious in His sight (yet she is a tree of life to them that lay hold upon her). On this account her presence everywhere awakens aversion and disgust. Yet, she is a tree of life to them that lay hold on her and happy is every one that uttaineth her. And though her enemies will always find cause to despise her, yet she will ever be justified of all her children. Being a stranger from above come to visit the earth for the benefit of men, and having no other errand than to distribute the bounty of heaven among the indigent, she can have no interest of her own to promote by the aid of men. Accordingly, she never makes her court to those who are best capable of introducing her into the good graces of the public. She ever wears a benign aspect to the destitute and with her richest smiles diffuses joy among her dependents, while she looks with an eye of steady neglect and contempt on all who pretend ability to bring her any additional ornaments or importance. She came not to call the righteous, but sinners to repentance. She fills the hungry with good things and sends the rich empty away. Yea, her steady contempt of the latter is highly serviceable to ascertain and enhance her kindly regard to the former. Though she has no reverence for the names of greatest repute in the world, yet she aims not to change or reverse the order wherein the characters of men are ranked in the estimation of the public. She never insinuates that Publicans and Harlots have as good a claim to public esteem as decent and devout Pharisees, she only declares that the former go into the kingdom of heaven before the latter, and that there are many who are at first in this world who shall be last in the next. So that though her language and temper must always be most provoking to those of first repute as bearing hardest on their pretensions as to the kingdom of heaven, yet she never disputes their claims to precedence in the kingdom of this world. Yea, the very nature of her opposition to them rather serves in some respects to support that claim. Having no political scheme to promote, she is no murmurer at the badness of the times, nor joins issue with those who urge the disconcerted inquiry, "what is the cause that the former times were better than these", a sort of discontent ultimately to those in authority. For the same reason she interferes not with the state of religious parties as having any inclination to raise on to the depression of another, nor does she spirit up any faction to rival the established church of any land. As she proposes no benefit to the bodies politic, so she claims no distinguished privilege nor thinks herself any way entitled to particular favor or encouragement from those in power. Yet, as she is far from doing or intending any hurt to such societies, she has a right to tolera-

---

57. FM2:46.29. Unfortunately, the other Hebrew letters are not distinct enough to be understood.

tion and simple protection in quality of a harmless stranger. If she is refused this she rebels not but suffers patiently or peaceably retires.

She is a zealous asserter of Liberty, yet she dogmatizes which the greatest assurance. As she assumes no jurisdiction herself over those who despise her instructions, so neither is she desirous to draw upon them the frown of those in authority. Yea, she frowns with indignation at all who would thus befriend her. Her open declaration on this head runs thus. "If any man hear my words and believe not, I judge him not, for I am come not to judge the world but to save the world. He that rejecteth me and receiveth not my words hath one that judgeth him. The word that I have spoken the same shall judge him in the last day." Thus we see at one view how zealous she is for liberty, and at the same time how positive and preemptory in dictation.

(55.3)As she comes not to offer problems to exercise the wit of man but to declare divine truth, she boldly on the part of heaven denounces her anathemas against all who oppose or corrupt the Truth. Had she brought less strength of evidence and affirmed with less assurance, she would have yielded so much the less comfort to the weak, the foolish and the destitute. For, it is well known that, when the heart of man comes to sink under its proper weakness (and the stoutest heart sooner or later grows weak) nothing less can then support it than the all commanding evidence and authority of Divine, Undeniable Truth. When many of her professed sons began to think of establishing their own importance and preeminence, they affected to imitate her assurance in dogmatizing and uttering anathemas in support of tradition and the decisions of human wisdom. And the effect, at last was their hunting one another's bodies, a striking sign of the spiritual death attending such apostasy, she deserves the dignity of her character both in respect of heaven and earth, while steady to Divine Truth, she shows all meekness toward all men. Ever condescending to the needy, she never fawns on those who look above her, never aims by softening matters to deprecate their displeasure, but, despising them herself, encourages her children to do the same, saying with a determinate voice, "Let them alone, etc." As for all those, who, standing above the level of her dependents, would yet claim kindred to her she addresses them only with spiritual weapons mighty to pull down. In general, as she needs not the applause of multitudes to support her cause, she never affects to gain ground upon men in the way of soothing any of their prejudices by the art of eloquence, yet her adversaries, even by their opposition, are frequently subservient to the progress of her benevolent design. Nothing more naturally haunts the heart of man than the sense of blame of the conviction of guilt. Yet, to nothing does his heart make a more vigorous resistance than to such conviction. Now she, in a way peculiar to herself, testifies to the world that their works are evil. Yea, in such a manner as stings even the men of best repute in the tenderest part. Thus, she awakened the hatred of the world. And the noise thence arising, often serves as an echo to publish and spread her testimony till it reaches the ears of the worthless, to whom it proves indeed to be good tidings of great joy. It may be observed here that the most cautious of her adversaries, the better to secure their own quiet, are commonly the most careful to make little noise with their resentment against her. As her great aim is to convince men of sin and show the necessity of the

Divine Righteousness she reports, men serve her purpose by accusing and exposing one another. For however blind individuals may be to their own faults, they are commonly quick sighted enough to those of others. The same holds true of different religious parties striving for preeminence in the world. Now, however much parties may be agreed in their opposition to the leading views of that wisdom which comes from above, yet they often find her dictates useful to expose the claims, and damp the confidence of each other. It sometimes pleases the Pharisee to hear her put to silence the Sadducees, and the latter no less to hear her repel the high pretensions of the former, though in the main, neither party is well satisfied with the general strain of her opposition to the other, as finding too often the occasion for the murmuring complaint "thus saying, thou reproachest us also." However, while such parties strive and jostle, they frequently prove the happy means of awakening attention to her salutary instruction among some detached and obscure individuals little accounted of any part. So that she is never disconcerted in her grand design, let noisy parties behave as they will. Though she concurs not with any of the parties aspiring after the public leadings in Religion, nor animates any of her children with such emulation, yet she forms a peculiar union among her children altogether upon the maxim of the Kingdom of Heaven, teaching them to love one another and never to dream that their cause can flourish and prevail till the resurrection of the dead. She animates them to maintain with tenacious and inflexible zeal the heavenly truth which ascertains the purity of the divine character, in opposition to all the corruptions of the world, even that truth which is the bond of their union, and the source of their common joy, while she teaches themas to every thing human and selfish or all things within their own disposal to be flexible, gracious and yielding, both among themselves and toward all men, well knowing that the truth which unites them will always expose them to the hatred of the world, she would have them careful, as much as in them lies not to dishonor their grand controversy by giving men any other occasion to reproach them.

(42.14) The elapsed periods of human life acquire importance from the prospect of its continuance. The smallest thing arises into consequence when regards as the commencement of what has advanced or is advancing into magnificence. The little rill near the source of a great river is an interesting object to the traveler who is apprised as he steps across it, or walks a few miles along its bank, that this is the stream which runs so far and which gradually swells into so vast a flood. So, while we anticipate the endless progress of life and wonder through what unknown scenes it is to take its course, its past years lose that character of vanity which would seem to belong to a train of fleeting, perishing moments, and we see them assuming the dignity of a commencing eternity. In them we have begun to be that conscious existence which we are to be through endless duration, and we feel a strange emotion of curiosity about this little life in which we are setting out on such a progress, we cannot be content without an accurate sketch of the windings thus far of a stream which is to bear us on forever. We try to image how it will be to recollect at a far distant point of our era, what we were when here, whether those remembrances will be pleasing or filled with sorrow. How striking then, to observe under what various forms of character men are passing through this introductory season of their being and with what emotions or feelings they will enter upon its greater stage. Wilt thou mourn at the last my Brother?

(120.1)OUR PRINCIPLES

May they be *entered* in the intellect, *passed* to the understanding, *raised* to the heart and conscience and *advanced* to preside over the life of each one invested with the secrets of the Order. (*Reverend Mr. Walker*)

OUR INSTITUTION

Though adverse circumstances have likened it to the broken pillar of our Order with its beautiful capital buried at its base, it is consolatory to us to know that it is not entirely cast down or destroyed. As by the remnant of the pillar that is yet standing we can ascertain to what order it belongs, and determine what its proportions [and] ornaments were, when it was entire may we be enabled by diligence and perseverance to form another pillar in the likeness of the broken one, more perfect and beautiful than that which adverse circumstances has destroyed. (*Anonymous*)

Three strange recumbent shapes in one arose.
Three strange and different shapes laid down, and arose in one.

8

Folger Manuscript 3

THIS CIPHER MANUSCRIPT WAS ALSO KNOWN AS THE *WALGREN BOOK*. It was discovered and purchased in the Midwest by the late Kent L. Walgren, a Salt Lake City attorney, Masonic bibliographer, and bookseller. He listed it in *Catalog 26: Freemasonry & Hermetica* ([Salt Lake City, Ut.: Scallawagiana Books,] 1994), as entry #87:

> (Manuscript Ritual.) [*No title*]. *Manuscript ritual of "Entered Apprentice, Anc. Acc. Rite; Fellow Craft, Anc. Acc. Rite; Master, Anc. Acc. Rite; Consecration, Anc. Acc. Rite; Address—K. Templar at the Resurrection scene; Ad[d]ress-K. Templar, Chamber of Reflection."* October 23, 1884. 74p. 24.5 × 20cm. very good to fine; ¾-leather over boards; lightly lined paper with a bluish cast. **$250.00**
>
> Manuscript ritual, written in a very fine hand, easily legible. Written in a book with the following label on front paste-down: "Sold by E. & L. H. Embree, Booksellers, Stationers, and Blank Book Manufacturers, No. 134 Bowery, New-York." Includes primary lectures, etc., omitting the signs, words and tokens.

Prior to mailing the catalogs, Walgren phoned Arturo de Hoyos and informed him of the manuscript; he also sent a photocopy of the entire document. Upon receiving it, de Hoyos phoned Walgren and stated that he wanted to purchase the manuscript, but Walgren informed him that it had just been sold to the University of Utah in Salt Lake City. When de Hoyos informed Walgren that he had identified the handwriting as Robert Folger's, Walgren remarked that he regretted the sale, but that it could not be undone. Our transcript is from the de Hoyos copy, made prior to the sale, and we have not been able to study the original. However the copy is clear and legible.

Folger Manuscript 3

Index

Entered Apprentice—Anc. Acc. Rite—	Page—	1.
Fellow Craft— " " "	"	35.
Master " " "	"	51. & 52.
Consecration " " "	"	61.
Address— K. Templar—at the Resurrection scene	"	67.
Address— " " Chamber of Reflection	"	70.

October 23 — 1889

[ENTERED APPRENTICE]

Opening

The Worshipful Master strikes one blow with the mallet and says:

W.M. Very Dear Brother Senior Warden, what is the first duty of a Warden in his lodge?
S.W. It is to assure himself that the temple is tiled.
W.M. Will you ascertain that such is the case, my Brother?

The Tiler performs his duty and reports to the Senior Warden.

S.W. Worshipful Master, the temple is tiled.
W.M. What is the second duty of a Senior Warden. in his Lodge?
S.W. It is to ascertain if all the Brethren present are Masons.
W.M. Are they so, my Very Dear Brother?
S.W. They are on both columns, Worshipful Master.

The Master strikes one blow and says:

W.M. Very Dear Brother Junior Deacon, what is your place in the Lodge?
J.D. At the right of the Senior Warden, if he so permits it.
W.M. Why so, my Brother?
J.D. To carry his orders to the Junior Warden, and to see that the Brethren of both columns conduct themselves with propriety. (1.1)
W.M. Where is the Senior Deacon's place?
J.D. Behind the Worshipful Master, or at his right, if he permits it.
W.M. Why so, Very Dear Brother Senior Deacon?
S.D. To bear his orders to the Senior Warden, and to the other officers, in order that the works may be most promptly executed.
W.M. Where is the Senior Warden's place?
S.D. In the South.
W.M. Very Dear Brother Junior Warden, why do you occupy that station?
J.W. The better to observe the sun at its meridian, to set the Craft to labor, to call them from labor to refreshment, that the Worshipful Master may have honor, and glory thereby.
W.M. Where is the Senior Warden's station?
J.W. In the West.
W.M. Why so, Very Dear Brother Senior Warden?
S.W. As the sun sets in the West to close the day, so is the Senior Warden in the West, to open and close the lodge, to pay the Craft their wages, and to dismiss them contented and satisfied.
W.M. Where is the Master's station? (2.1)
S.W. In the East.
W.M. Why, my Brother?

S.W. As the sun rises in the East to commence his journey and open the day, so is the Master in the East, to open the lodge, to direct its labors, and to enlighten it by his wisdom.
W.M. At what hour are Apprentice Masons accustomed to open their works?
S.W. At noon, Worshipful Master.
W.M. What is the hour, Brother Junior Warden?
J.W. Full noon.

The Master then gives three blows of the mallet and, turning towards the Senior Deacon, they both give the Guttural Sign. The Master gives to the Senior Deacon, in a whisper, the Sacred Word to open a Lodge of Apprentice Masons in the Scottish Rite. The Senior Deacon carries it to the Senior Warden, who sends it by the Junior Deacon to the Junior Warden, who having received, it strikes one blow with the mallet and says:

Worshipful Master, all is just and perfect.

The Master takes off his hat and says:

W.M. In the name of God, and of St. John of Scotland, the lodge of Apprentice Masons is open. The Brethren are hereby forbidden to speak or to pass from one column to the other, without having obtained permission, or to entertain political or controversial discussions, under the penalties prescribed by the general statues of the Order. Together Brethren.

All make the Guttural Sign and the battery. The Master says:

(3.1) Take your places, my Brethren.

Very Dear Brother Secretary, will you read the minutes of the labors of the last session.

The Master strikes one blow and says:

Attention, my Brethren.

The reading of the minutes being finished, the Master strikes one blow. The Wardens repeat.

W.M. Brothers Senior and Junior Wardens, announce to your columns that if any of the Brethren wish to make any observations permission is given to them.

The two Wardens strike each one blow. The Senior Warden says:

S.W. Worshipful Master, silence reigns on both columns.

The usual sanction is then given to the conclusions of the Brother Orator.

W.M. Brother Master of Ceremonies, will you retire to the vestibule of the Temple and ascertain if there are any visiting Brethren?

The Master of Ceremonies goes out and, returning between the Wardens, reports, places on the altar the diplomas of the visiting Brethren, and then retires to keep them company. The Master sends the Brother Grand Expert to examine the visitors, and another Expert to obtain their signatures, which is to compare them with the certificates.

W.M. Brother Tiler, inform the Master of Ceremonies that he may introduce the visiting Brethren.

The Master of Ceremonies knocks. The Wardens repeat.

W.M. Permit them to enter the Temple. To order, Brethren.

The Master asks them the following questions:

W.M. From whence come you?
Visitor From the Lodge of John of Scotland, Worshipful.
W.M. What do you bring? (3.1)
Visitor Joy, health and prosperity to all my Brethren.
W.M. Do you bring nothing more?
Visitor The Master of my lodge salutes you by three times three.
W.M. What are they doing there?
Visitor They elevate temples to virtue, and construct dungeons for vice.
W.M. What come you hither to do?
Visitor To conquer my passions, subdue my desires, and make new progress in Masonry.
W.M. What do you desire, my Very Dear Brother?
Visitor A place among you.
W.M. It is granted. Brother Master of Ceremonies, conduct these Brethren to a proper seat.

If the visiting Brother is an officer of a Grand Lodge, a Deputy near it, a Grand Elect of the Sacred Vault, or Sublime Prince of the Royal Secret, he is received at the door of the Temple with five stars, mallets beating, and under the Arch of Steel. If a Master of a Lodge, with three stars. The Worshipful compliments the visitors and salutes them with a "huzza." (5.1)

Chamber of Reflection

This chamber must be painted black. Inside, all over, all its furniture must be black, and it must have no window, or any means by which the light can be admitted from without. It is properly called the "Black Chamber." The entrance to it should be through a massive door, and a person should be obliged to stoop low to enter, or else to go down steps.

There should be in it, a coffin, a table on which is a black cover, a Bible open, an hourglass, a vase or pitcher of water, a goblet or tumbler, a piece of bread, a plate of salt, a blank Will, pen and ink. All these pieces are black. There should be two chairs, also black. A skeleton is sometimes laid in the open coffin. In front of the table and on the wall should be represented a cock, the hourglass, and under them the two words "Vigilance," "Perseverance"

There should also be painted on black cards about eighteen inches long, the following sentences, which may be hung around the room on the walls:

"If Curiosity has led thee hither, depart. This is no place for thee"—

"If thou art unwilling to be enlightened concerning thy failings, or to be spoken to concerning thy errors and thy sins, thou wilt not meet from us a kind reception. Better for thee to leave in peace."

"If thou art capable of dissimulation or hypocrisy, tremble, for thou wilt be exposed."

"If thou covetest human distinction, go not any further. None of these do we acknowledge within our temple, or encourage them in our association."

"If thy heart sinks within thee, and thou are frightened, do not go any further."

"If thou persevere, thou wilt be purified by the elements, thou wilt emerge from the abyss of darkness, thou wilt see the light." (6.1)

There should be in the room a hanging lamp, or else a taper on the table.

The Candidate is brought to this room by the Conductor who, after seating him at the table, addresses him in a proper manner concerning the object of bringing him there, and of the emblems of the place which should engage his attention while there. Having finished his address, he leaves him to his meditation where he remains for a short time.

The Conductor then returns and calls his attention to the Will, which is before him on the table, containing a printed form of name, birth place, city, country, state, profession, residence, his religion, under which are printed the following questions:

What is a man's duty toward God?

What is a man's duty toward himself?

What is a man's duty toward his fellow man?

After these questions follow the Will, or disposition of his property, which he must fill up and which being completed, is taken to the Lodge and deposited with the Master.

For what follows, the ritual will show in its proper place. (7.1)

Reception

W.M. Brother Expert, retire and ascertain if the Profane is in the Chamber of Reflection.

He does so, then returns and reports.
The Worshipful Master knocks, the Wardens repeat.

W.M. My Brethren, the three ballots having been favorable, the Profane N— and his reception being now in order, are disposed to proceed.

All the Brethren extend their hands in token of assent.

W.M. Brother Expert, take pen, ink and paper, and retire to the Profane. Inform him that the trials he has to undergo are dangerous, and that it is prudent for him to make his Will.

The Expert retires, and when he thinks the testament is finished, he goes and gets it, and takes it to the Master, who causes it to be read aloud by the Orator. The Master then asks the Treasurer if he is satisfied, and if he is not, he tells him to "perform his duty." The Treasurer then retires to the Profane and receives the initiation fee and, returning to the Lodge, says, "I am satisfied."

W.M. Brother Expert, return to the Profane, prepare him, and conduct him to the Master of Ceremonies at the door of the temple.

The Expert then goes out, returns with his hat, money, etc., and places them before the Master. He then returns to the Profane, releases him from the Chamber of Reflection, makes bare his left breast and right knee by divesting him of clothing, and the left foot in a slipper. Having blindfolded him and prepared him fully, he commences with the "travel," which may be made long or short, according to circumstances. Having finished the travel, he makes a delivery of the Profane to the Master of Ceremonies, who leads him to the door of the temple, and makes a tremendous alarm. All is confusion, slamming of doors, to keep him out struggling, etc., finally the door is shut in his face and the Senior Warden says:

S.W. Worshipful Master, someone knocks at the door of the temple as a Profane.
W.M. See who it is, my Brother, who dares to interrupt our labors.

The Tiler places the point of his sword to the Candidate's breast gently, so that he may feel the cold steel, and says in a loud voice:

Tiler Who thus dares to enter our temple?
M.C. Hold! Withdraw your sword, it is I, brother Expert, who presents a Profane to this Respectable Lodge.[1]
W.M. Brethren, to your arms. A Profane is at the door of the temple.
Brother Master of Ceremonies, why this indiscretion in thus presenting yourself

---

1. The manuscript reads, "this ~~reppee~~ <respectable> ☐"

here with a Profane? What are you about to do? What do you demand?

M.C.   That he may be admitted among us.

W.M.   How has he dared to expect it?

M.C.   Because he is freeborn and of good report.

W.M.   Since he is freeborn and of good report, ask him his name, place of birth, age, religion, civil quality, and place of residence.

The door must be half open, the Master of Ceremonies and Candidate are without, an Expert within to report the answers, to the Junior Warden, he to the Senior and he to the Master. The Secretary inscribes his answers on the minutes.

W.M.   Let him enter.

As he enters Brother Terrible places the point of his sword to his breast, so that he feels it.

W.M.   What do you feel? What do you see?

PROFANE   I can see nothing, but I feel the point of a weapon.

W.M.   Learn that the weapon of which you feel the point is a symbol of the remorse which shall torture your heart if ever you perjure yourself in regard to the society into which you desire (9.1) to enter, and that the state of blindness, in which you are now, symbolizes that in which all men are plunged, who know not the paths of virtue, those paths which you are now about to tread. What do you ask here?

PROFANE   I wish to be received a Mason.

W.M.   Is it by your own free will, without constraint or suggestion, that you present yourself?

PROFANE   Yes, Sir.

W.M.   Reflect well, Sir, on the demand you make. You have to pass through terrible trials which will require all the courage which the firmest character is susceptible of. Have you decided to undergo them? Do you feel the courage to brave all danger to which your indiscretion may expose you?

PROFANE   I do.

W.M.   Since it is so, I cannot answer for you. Brother Terrible, retire with the Profane from the precincts of the temple. Lead him where must pass all mortals who are daring enough to present themselves within our sacred walls.

The Candidate is led around the anteroom two or three times, the door is then opened, the paper frame is placed, and when the Candidate is one the top of the inclined plane the Master says:

W.M.   Precipitate the Profane into the cavern.

They then give him a hard push through the paper frame, two Brethren receive him in the blanket as he falls, the door is slammed too, and silence is observed for a minute or two. The Brother Terrible conducts the Candidate between the Wardens and remains by his side. The master strike one blow of the mallet and says:

W.M.   Cause the Candidate to kneel. Profane, you will now take part in the prayer which we are about to offer on your behalf. Brethren, let us humble ourselves before the (10.1) Sovereign Architect of the Universe. Let us recognize His power and our weakness. Let us keep our minds and hearts stayed upon Him. He is One. He exists by himself alone. It is to him that all beings owe their existence. He works in all and through all, invisible to mortal eyes, He seeth all things.

Prayer

Deign, Almighty Father, we implore Thee, to protect these workmen of peace. Inflame their zeal, fortify their souls against the war of passions, purify their hearts by the love of virtue, and grant them success. Vouchsafe Thine aid to this Candidate, who desires to participate in our mysteries, and sustain him, by Thy powerful arm, through all the trials of life which he may be destined to undergo. Amen.

W.M. Profane, in whom do you place your trust?
Profane In God.
W.M. Your trust is well founded. Arise, Sir. Follow your leader and let not fear enter your bosom.

The Expert or Terrible conducts the Profane to the East, and the Master says:

W.M. Sir, before this assembly, of which I am but the organ, are willing to admit you to the trials, they wish to sound your heart by interrogating your mind on various subjects. And first, do you believe in the existence of One true, eternal and ever-living God?

He answers.

W.M. This belief does honor to your heart. It is not only the belief of the philosopher, it is also that of the savage. As soon as he perceives that he exists, he feels that he does not exists by himself alone. He asks all nature for his father, and the silence of mute nature is the answer which brings him to the feet of the Maker and Ruler of all Worlds. You will now please to be seated for a few moments.

Sir, the first qualifications we require from you, in order to be admitted among us, and without which you could not be initiated into our mysteries, are the pure sincerity, docility and constancy which is unflinching. You answers will enable us to judge. (11.1)

What are your ideas in coming here? *Answers.*
Who, or what gave you the first ideas of it? *Answers.*
Is it not curiosity? *Answers.*
What do you think about Masonry? Answer fully, and be true.
Are you ready to approve and support all the proofs by which you have to be tried?
Who brought you here?
Do you know him to be a Mason?

Did he tell you anything about it before hand?
How do you know anything you could not prove?
Tell me, Sir. Under what impressions are you since you left your house to come here?
Are you married?
Did you tell your wife, or friend, as the case may be, of your intention to join us?
Why did you not tell him or them? Were you afraid they would prevent you?
Well, Sir, you are right. It is by the practice of virtue you must be known among the profane, as well as among Masons.
What reflections did you give to the objects you saw in the Chamber of Reflection?
What do you think about your present state?
What idea do you have of a society in which they urge the neophyte to be introduced in such a singular way? Be frank in your answers, because we read your heart.
Is not the step you are taking an inconsiderate one?
Have you no fear that we shall abuse the state of weakness and blindness in which you suffer yourself to be placed? You are now unarmed, nearly naked and in the power of unknown persons.
You are right, Sir. The correctness of your answers, your confidence in us gives us the assurance that if received, you will honor the Order, because Masonry, Sir, is an association of virtuous men, whose purpose it is to live in perfect equality, and be strongly united, [under] the name of Brother, and to excite one another to the practice virtue. With this explanation you will perceive that it is the incumbent duty of every Lodge, not to admit to the participation of our mysteries any, except those who shall be found worthy to partake of these advantages, are able to undergo the trials, and attain the elevated point to which we aim, and such as we shall not be ashamed of, before the Masonic world.
What do you understand by the word virtue?

He answers.

W.M.   It is a disposition of the soul which induces a man to do good. What do you understand by the word vice?

He answers.

W.M.   It is the opposite of virtue. It is an unhappy habit which leads to all evil, and it is for this reason that we assemble in this Temple together, to learn to bridle the impetuous springs of cupidity, to elevate ourselves above the vile interests which agitate the profane world, to calm the feverish ardor of our passions. Here we labor without ceasing, to teach our minds to bring forth eternal principles of healthy morality that we can succeed in giving to our souls that just equilibrium of force and sensibility which constitute wisdom, or rather the science of life. This labor is painful, but you will be obliged to perform it, if you persist in the desire which you have expressed to become a Mason. You perhaps have very different ideas. If they are the gross and false ideas of the ignorant and vulgar herd, if to work constantly to perfect yourself morally, seems to you a work above your strength, you are at

liberty to retire. Do you persist in your determination to become a Mason?
PROFANE   I do.
W.M.   Sir, every society has its particular laws, and every member has certain duties to perform. And as it would be imprudent to impose an obligation which you know not, this assembly thinks proper to inform you what will be your future duties.

The first is absolute silence on all that you may have seen or heard among us, as well as all that you may see or hear or know hereafter.

The second duty, and which makes masonry the most sacred of bonds, even if it was not the most noble, imposing and respectable among the institutions of men, this duty which is the very essence of our being, is, as I have already told you, to control the passions which dishonor and render man unhappy, to practice virtues, to aid your Brethren, to smooth their misfortunes, to assist them by your council and by your knowledge, which would be but a rare quality in a Profane, is but the accomplishment of his duty in a Mason. (13.1)

Every occasion to be useful, neglected, is an infidelity, every aid refused to a Brother is a perjury, and if tender and consoling friendship has also her worship in our Temple, it is less because it is a sentiment, than, that being a duty, it may there become a virtue.

Your third duty, the obligation of which you will contract only after having been made a mason, will be to conform to the General Statutes of the Order, to the particular laws of this Lodge, and to submit to everything which may be prescribed to you in the name of this respectable assembly into which you have solicited the favor of being admitted.

And now knowing the principle of a Mason, have you the strength of mind and reason to put the same into practice
PROFANE   Yes, Sir.
W.M.   Before proceeding farther we must exact your oath of honor, but this oath must be taken on a sacred cup. If you are sincere you may drink with confidence, but if falsehood and dissimulation accompany your promise, swear not. Beware the cup, and fear the prompt and terrible effect of the drink. Do you consent to swear?
PROFANE   I consent.
W.M.   Let the Candidate approach the altar.

The Master of Ceremonies conducts to the steps of the altar.

Brother Sacrificer, present the Candidate with the cup, so fatal to perjurers.

A waiting Brother brings a cup of water, and when the master makes him a sign he gives it to the Candidate to drink. He has also some wormwood in a bottle, which he pours into the cup after the Candidate has drank a part of it.

[Obligation]

W.M.   Repeat after me your Obligation:
   I engage myself to the most absolute silence in regard to all kinds of trials to
(14.1) which my courage shall be subjected. If I prove faithless to my oath, and wanting in my duty, if a spirit of curiosity has conducted me hither—(*The Master gives the sign for the cup to be given him*)—I consent that this draught[2]—(*The wormwood is here put into the cup*)—shall be changed to bitterness, and that it may become a subtle poison to me—(*He empties the cup*).

The Master strikes a blow, Wardens repeat.

W.M.   What do I see, Sir? I perceive an alteration in your countenance. Does your conscience give the lie to the assurance of your tongue? Has the draught so soon changed to bitterness? Take away the Profane.

He is conducted between the Wardens and seated.

   Sir, if you here designedly deceived us, you have still a remedy. You have liberty to retire. I, cannot however, imagine that you would render yourself forever unworthy of the good opinion we have conceived of you. I can no longer be silent. To enter our society, and for us to be assumed of the sincerity of your duties and requests, you have still greater trials to undergo.
   You have without doubt heard in the profane world of the severity of our trials. But whatever idea you may have formed of them, those which now await you surpass them still. Reflect, Sir. The moment approaches, and once engaged in those trials you cannot retire from them. If you feel that you have not the strength to support them, ask to retire. Permission will be granted you.

He answers. The Master strikes one blow, Wardens repeat. The Master says in a loud voice:

   Brother Terrible, take this Profane, seat him on the stool of reflection.

The Brother Terrible seizes him with violence, turns him round two or three times, and then seats him on the stool of reflection.

   Give him up to his own conscience. Let the obscurity which veils his eyes and the hour of solitary silence be his only companion.

Strict silence for a moment, when the Master continues:

   Have you reflected, Sir, on the consequences of your demand? I give you notice for the last time, that although our trials are all mysterious, and emblematical, they
(15.1) are nonetheless terrible, and such that many have sunk under them. Therefore, pronounce your own sentence. Will you return to the profane world, or do you persist in being received a Mason?

---

2. The manuscript reads, "draft."

He answers affirmatively. The Master gives a blow, Wardens repeat. Master says:

> Brother Terrible, seize the profane, and cause him to make his first voyage. Try to bring him back without accident.

The Brother Terrible strikes him suddenly on the shoulder, and says, "Up, go forward." He make his first voyage in silence over rugged ways, etc. Inclined planes, tipping boards, circles, genuflections, etc. Brings him opposite the Junior Warden. He strikes the shoulder of the Junior Warden three times, who rises and says:

J.W.   Who goes there?
Terrible   A Profane, who asks to become a Mason.
J.W.   How has he dared to hope it?
Terrible   Because he is freeborn, and of reputed good character.
J.W.   Let him pass. Conduct him to the Venerable Master.

He is conducted and again seated.

S.W.   Worshipful Master, the first voyage is accomplished.
W.M.   Well, Sir, how do you find yourself after this, your first voyage?

He answers as he thinks fit.

W.M.   Sir, our trials, as I have told you, are mysterious and emblematical. What have you remarked in this first voyage? What moral reflections has it caused you? In fact, under (16.1) what emblem has it presented to your imagination?

He answers, and then the Worshipful Master presents the following explanation:

W.M.   This first voyage is the emblem of human life, the tumult of passions, the shock of conflicting interests, the difficulties of enterprises, the obstacles which attend your steps and multiply under your feet, the competitions of interests which weary and tire you. All this is represented by the noise and tumult which struck your ears, and by the rough and rugged road over which you passed.

The Master now addresses him on the subject, and questions of his last Will and Testament, then:

W.M.   You know, Sir, that the most virtuous man has always small vices, or at least a principal fault. It is indispensable, Sir, that we know yours. Well, Sir, don't have any false shame. Masonry is a mutual school, in which each member who compose the Order must be willing to be corrected by teaching. Well, Sir, be frank. What is your principle fault? Are you not inclined to be proud? Or Covetousness? Or Anger? Or any other passion? Women?
   If you are perfect then you need not come here.
   Well, Sir, are you willing to go on with the indispensable proofs of your initiation?
Profane   I am.

W.M.   Brother Terrible, seize the Profane and guide him in the second voyage. He is under your care. See that no arms are found about him. Go on.

Noises, stooping, wind, thunder, silence, and last the water. Then steps at the Senior Warden, when the same questions are asked and answers given as on the first voyage to the Junior Warden. Then seats the Candidate as before, and says:

TERRIBLE   Venerable, he has completed his second voyage.
W.M.   Well, Sir, what are your reflections during this second voyage?

He answers as he thinks fit.

W.M.   You found in the second voyage less difficulty, and embarrassment than in the first. The noise that you have heard figures the strife which a virtuous man is obliged unceasingly (17.1) to maintain, in order to triumph over the attacks of vice. You have been purified by water. You have still other proofs to sustain. Arm yourself with courage, in order to support them to the end.
   Before you go any further, Sir, I have a question to propose to you. Your answer to this question can decide your rejection or your admission among us. You have promised to us to be true, remember your promise. Tell me, Sir, do you already belong to any society whatever? Religious, political, or philanthropic? Tell me frankly.

He answers.

W.M.   Well, Sir, what is the one object of that Society? What is the Secret?

If he is disposed to betray, turn him out. If he refuse, Master says:

   It is only a few moments since you promised to answer with frankness and truth, and now you refuse to tell me the secret. I am sorry, Sir, but you cannot be received a Mason. We have not any secrets one from another, and your want of confidence in us does not allow us to initiate you. Then, Sir, you have the resolution to deprive yourself of the privilege of being a Mason?

He answers.

W.M.   Sir, your answer is full of good sense and courage. You have well displayed it on this trial. Your firmness and unswerving integrity in renouncing your initiation, sooner than betray the secret of your society, gives us the measure of your character—upright and loyal—and inspires us with confidence in the principles which you possess, and which are absolutely requisite before you can be made the depository of the secrets of our Order
   Brother Terrible, cause him to perform his third voyage. (One rap) Go on.

Terrible conducts him. Fire.
They stop before the Master. Terrible says:

   Worshipful Master, his third voyage is accomplished.
W.M.   Sir, you remark that this voyage has been less painful to you than the preced-

ing. The flame through which you have passed has completed your purification. May the material fire, with which you have been surrounded, light up forever in your heart the love of your Brethren and fellow men. May charity preside over your actions, and may you never forget that sublime moral precept, which is our rule and duty: "Do ye unto others as you would wish them to do unto you."

The frankness, with which you have declared what your human weakness was, gives us the hope that you will try to correct it yourself. You have been materially (18.1) purified by water and fire. It is your duty to carry the work to completion by practicing the precepts and virtues that your Brethren will at all times show to your sight.

Your voyages are happily now finished, and I cannot sufficiently praise your courage, but let it not abandon you, Sir. You are not yet at the end of your labors. Those trials which you have yet to pass through, although they are of a different nature, are yet more difficult. The Order into which you have sought admission may perhaps exact from you even to the last drop of your blood. If you feel the courage to offer yourself as a sacrifice, you must give us the assurance otherwise than by mere verbal promises. It is by your life blood, now, that all your promises must be sealed. Do you consent?

PROFANE Yes, Sir, I do.

W.M. In what part of your body do you consent to have a vein opened?

He answers as he pleases. Brother Terrible acts as Surgeon.

W.M. Brother Surgeon, do your office. You will, of course, be careful to measure the quantity by the strength of the Candidate. The Lodge trusts to your wisdom and prudence.

The ceremony of bleeding is then performed, as usual. When finished:

W.M. Your resignation gives us a proof, Sir, that at all times and in all circumstances, you will always be ready to fly to the help of your Brethren, and, if necessary, to spill your blood for them.

Brother Master of Ceremonies, give to the profane the Cup of Bitterness.

Gives it.

Sir, swallow that beverage to the last drop, and learn by its bitterness that it is the emblem of sorrow, and inseparable from human life, and that resignation to the Divine Will can alone add any sweetness to that bitter cup.

Each step you have hitherto taken, in the career you have undertaken, has met (19.1) with success, and you have now triumphed so far over all obstacles. But you are not yet at the end of your trials. A profane, when once received as a Mason, belongs no longer to himself. He belongs to a society which is spread over all parts of the habitable globe. And that a Mason may be recognized as such, in whatever place his steps may lead him, or whatever may be the difference of country or language, there exists in every Lodge of the Universe a seal, marked with hieroglyphic characters, known only by Masons, which seal having been heated red hot, and impressed upon the body, there leaves an imperishable and indelible mark. Do you consent to receive this glorious mark, that you may point to it and say, "And I also, and I am a Mason"?

The seal is applied.

Now, Sir, the time has come when you can put into practice a virtue which is the most cherished among us. We have here, in this Lodge, unfortunate Masons' widows and orphans, whom we daily assist. The metals that we have been deprived of are emblems of vices. Can you, without reluctance, sacrifice those to the profit of the poor and the unfortunate that we generally help, the money and the produce of the metals which belong to you, and which have been delivered to me? Take care, Sir, a numerous society now have their eyes upon you, and are attentive to the answer that you will give. I claim of you an act of charity. Fear not to make any ostentatious display for the sake of doing the act.

He answers.

The charity that I ask will cease to be a virtue, if you exercise to the prejudice of some more sacred and more binding duty. Perhaps you have some civil engagement to fulfill, a family to support, or parents, or unfortunate relations. These are the first duties that nature commands. They are the privileged debts of every man who regulates his conduct on the principles of equity. What opinion would you have of a man who would show himself charitable before thinking of these things? I recall your attention to my first proposition. Can you, without reluctance, deprive yourself of these things without injuring yourself in order to bestow upon the poor, whom we gen- (20.1) erally support, the whole or a part of the money and the jewels which belong to you, and which have been delivered to me?

He answers.

W.M.   Well, Sir, as it may be the case that those jewels are a present from some dear and cherished friend, or the produce of hard labor and saving, and it would probably be attended with pain to deprive you of those things, we wish you to make yourself easy, and at the same time to give a free offering from your heart, which is so well disposed to charity.

I will send a person to you, to whom you will speak very low, the sum that you can spare, in favor of a poor widow who has five young children and whose situation is deserving of the support of Masons. But remember well, Sir, the observations that I made. We are soliciting of you an act of charity. Do not put in its place an act of ostentation, because, among us, the one who gives very little or nothing when he cannot do otherwise is as much respected as the rich giver.

W.M.   Brother Almoner, Minister of Charity, approach the Profane and ask him what he is willing to give to the poor, and report to me. For you must know that a Mason's acts of benevolence, not being acts of ostentation and vanity on the part of the giver, nor of humiliation on the part of him who receives, should always be kept inviolably secret.

He goes to him, asks in a whisper, receives his answer, and reports to Worshipful Master.

If the donation is generous:

W.M.   Sir, I expected no less from your good heart. The Lodge, though me, wishes to testify for gratitude and you may count on the gratitude of all those distressed whose miseries you contribute to alleviate.

If the donation is small:

W.M.   Sir, the widow's mite, given with a free heart to the indigent, is as pleasing to the Grand Architect of the Universe as would be the rich man's gold. Your gift is received and accepted with thankfulness.

W.M.   Sir, the good reports that we have of your morality, and the good opinion that we have of your Introducing Brother, please me to let you know that the indispensable (21.1) which you have passed through are so great a recommendation to us that we will dispose with any further proofs which, under ordinary circumstances, you would be obliged to submit to. But I must inform you, Sir, that you have to take an obligation. Do you consent to take it? Sir, the oath that you will take will not affect your religion or politics, nevertheless, it is my duty to inform you that it is solemn and sacred. Are you willing to take it?

Brother Master of Ceremonies, lead this profane to the foot of the throne, and place him in a proper position.

He does so, and reports.

W.M.   Up, Brethren, and under Due Guard.

Master says, "Repeat with me."

Obligation

Similar to the York Rite, and that will answer.

W.M.   Sir, you will remember your Obligation. You will now sign it with your blood.

He makes a motion to do so.

Sir, will you consent again to take this Obligation, when the blind is taken off?

The Master of Ceremonies now conducts the Candidate from the altar to the anteroom. The lights in the room are then extinguished without noise. Two vases of burning spirits are placed in the East, one on each side.
A Brother lies down in the middle of the floor, as if dead.
All the Brethren draw their swords, form a circle toward the West with their swords pointed towards the Candidate.
The Master descends from his throne, the Candidate is brought in and placed between the Wardens. The Master knocks three times with his gavel. At the third blow the Master of Ceremonies lifts the bandage.

W.M.   This pale and ghastly light is to show the vengeance we reserve for the coward who basely perjures himself. These swords, directed against you, are borne (22.1) by as many deadly foes who are ready to plunge them in your breast, should you ever be so vile as to violate your oath. To whatever place of the earth you may fly for refuge, in none will you find an asylum. You will bear with you the mark of your crime, your sentence will have already gone forth. You will there find Masons who are enemies to perjury, and who await your coming with terrible punishments.
Brother Master of Ceremonies, blindfold him again.

The Candidate is led out of the Lodge. All the lights are re-lit, so as to form a brilliant contrast with the former gloom. The Candidate is then brought in the room, placed as before, swords all put away. Three knocks.

W.M.   Brother Senior Warden, you, upon whom reposes one of the columns of this Temple, do you consider this Candidate worthy of being admitted among us since his courage and devotion have made him victorious in the long struggle between the Profane and Masonic man?
S.W.   I do, Venerable.
W.M.   What do you ask for him?
S.W.   The great light.

Worshipful Master gives a knock, and says:

W.M.   Let there be light!

The bandage drops at his feet.

W.M.   Sic transit gloria mundi! Let the show of weapons no longer alarm you. All is peace and contentment here. We have received your oath and believe it sincere. The happy dawn of confidence and friendship appears. Behold in us your Brethren, your friends whom you have conquered and who are ready to fly to your aid and to defend your life and honor with their swords.
Brother Master of Ceremonies, conduct our new Candidate to the throne to repeat his Obligation. (23.1)

The Candidate is conducted to the throne. Kneels. Master places the Compass to his breast, repeats again the Obligation, and says:

W.M.   Brother Master of Ceremonies, lead the Candidate to the Dark Chamber to dress, and return with him to the Lodge.

The Candidate retires, dresses himself, and returns, and is placed between the two Wardens, when the Worshipful Master says:

W.M.   Up, Brethren, form the circle, and under the Due Guard. ꜟ-ꜟ —ꜟ [three gavels]

The Brethren all rise, and form the circle. The Master descends from the throne and goes to the Candidate, causes him to kneel, lays his sword upon his head, and says:

W.M. To the glory of the Great Architect of the Universe, and under the auspices of ———, and by virtue of the powers in me vested, by this respectable Lodge, I receive and constitute you an Entered Apprentice Mason of the Ancient and Accepted Scottish Rite, and member of this Respectable Lodge.

The Master strikes three blows with the gavel upon the sword, takes the Candidate by the hand, raises him up and salutes him with the fraternal kiss and says.

Brother Master of Ceremonies you will please lead the Candidate to the throne by the proper steps.

He leads him, teaching him the steps. The master then presents him with the apron, and says:

W.M. Receive this apron, which we term "clothing." It gives you the right of sitting with us. You must not present yourself in the Lodge without it. Let it remind you that man is condemned to work, and that a Mason must lead an active and laborious life.

The Master of Ceremonies, after having seen that he is taught how to wear his apron (24.1) *presents him with a pair of men's gloves, white, saying:*

Let these gloves, by their whiteness, remind you that candor reigns in the heart of an honest man, and that his actions must always be true. Never sully their purity by contact with the muddy waters of vice. They are the symbol of your admission to the temple of virtue.

He then presents him with a pair of woman's gloves, and says:

W.M. These are destined for her you love the best. As we are persuaded that a Mason cannot make an unworthy choice.

The sword you will always wear in the Lodge. Let it remind you that a Mason should be always ready to protect and succor his Brethren, and equally ready to punish the perjurer.

To be admitted into our ritual, and participate in the ties which unite us all over the globe, it is necessary that you be able to recognize Brethren, and to make yourself known as a Mason. All Masons recognize each other by certain Signs, Words and Grips or Tokens.

The Sign of the degree is made thus—

He shows him the steps and gives him the Sign, and explains it thus———.

It will remind you of the oath you have taken, and the penalty incurred by its criminal infraction.

The Token is given, and the Master says:

The Token is made thus— (*explains*)

The Sacred Word is—— (*Gives it, and explains to him the manner of giving it*).

My Brother, Masonry is universally known, although it is divided into many rites—as the York, the Modern, the Ancient and Accepted Scottish, and various others. Nevertheless, they remain on the same basis and inculcate the same principles. We work under the Ancient, or Scottish Rite, because it is the purest essence of Masonry, and has been transmitted to us by the earliest founders of the Order. I will give you the Signs, Words, and Tokens of the Modern Rite—

The Master then gives the explanations, then the fraternal kiss, and says:

W.M. Brother Master of Ceremonies, conduct the Candidate to our Brother Expert.
(25.1)
W.M. Brother Expert, you will receive the Sign, Word and token from our new-made Brother.

The Brother Expert receives them, and reports to the Junior Warden, he to the Senior Warden, who says:

S.W. Venerable, the Sign, Word and Token is just and perfect.

The Master then requests the Candidate to retire. Then the Master of Ceremonies instructs him in the alarm on entering the Lodge, learns him the steps, the salutations, etc.

W.M. Up, Brethren, and under the Due Guard. Brothers Senior and Junior Wardens, invite the brethren who compose your respective columns to recognize henceforth Brother ——, forever and Apprentice Mason, and the members of this Respectable Lodge to join themselves to you and me, to applaud his initiation.

The Senior Warden repeats, then the Junior Warden. After which, salute.
The Master of Ceremonies makes a fitting reply for the Candidate, and they salute.

W.M. The Brethren will observe order, while our Brother Master of Ceremonies conducts the new-made Brother to the entrance of the Temple, in order to instruct him in his work as a Mason, upon the Rough Stone.
M.C. My Brother, you are here experimentally to commence your work as an Apprentice upon the Rough Stone.

Teaches him and then makes him do it.
Proper explanations, and the Brethren salute the work.
The Venerable then shows the warrant of a Lodge, with suitable explanations.

[Lecture]

Orator Very Dear Brother, it is a duty laid upon me to give you some reasons for, and explanation of, some of the ceremonies through which you have passed, especially those to which the Venerable has not alluded.

You was first introduced to a black and dark chamber where you was left for a season, to your own reflections, upon subjects to which your attention was particularly called. And it is hoped that your thoughts, while in a place of retirement, was properly occupied. Your hat was taken from you, to be returned to you again, with the instruction that in open Lodge you are always to remain uncovered, the privilege of sitting with the hat on being only given to the Master in the East.

Likewise your sword, for you was about to be introduced to the assembly of the Brethren, who profess and ought to be men of peace. Whatever may be the views of men of the world or their customs, the contrary of the spirit of peace can find no entrance in our asylums. We would endeavor to encourage each other in a work of love.

You have taken back your sword. Receive it with this friendly admonition, use it bravely for the defense of the country, the country in which you live, for the safety of your home and fireside, for the protection of your person when in imminent peril. But beyond this be careful, for remember that it is written, "Thou shalt not kill."

Here you have received back your money, jewelry, etc. Beware of covetousness. Watch carefully against the pernicious influence of this terrible sin.

You was divested of all metallic substances with external clothing. This was done to ascertain that you were a man. For the Order, although it cherishes the virtuous and the good among the other sex, does not admit them among its numbers. You was divested of your money and jewelry that you might learn that worldly distinctions cannot give rank and must not create differences among men. In the Lodge we all meet upon the level. In fact, among the good and impartial nothing but virtue and mental acquirements can give preeminence among men in the world, and nothing less can distinguish Brethren in the Lodge. Of all metallic substances, as a matter of usage, for at the building of the Temple there was not heard the sound of an ax or hammer (27.1) or any tool of iron. As the timber was hewed in the forests of Lebanon the stones were squared in the quarries of Zeredatha, were all conveyed to Jerusalem where they were adjusted to their several places without noise of any kind.

You was neither naked nor clothed, barefoot nor shod.

You was then deprived of the Light. If cast upon the world and exposed to its vicissitudes, you would doubtless soon, in this condition, have perished by the way. Let this remind you to help a falling Brother, and when his cry reaches you never to withhold the helping hand.

You was placed in darkness, that you might be insensible to anything but the voice of the Master. You were about to make an advance toward the Temple, and all who would come within its sacred enclosure must lay aside every thing of a worldly nature, must forget the follies, the pleasures, the allurements and the gaudy trappings of the world, and listen only to the voice of instruction, in order to walk in the right path.

You had pledged yourself to submit to our usages, yet if you thought proper to alter your mind you could have done so. And if that alteration had taken place, being in darkness you would have been again returned to the world without being able to discern the beauties of the place or the faces of the persons who composed the assemblage.

The alarm was given at the door, and was attended with great noise and apparent difficulty. This may remind you of the struggle and the resistance which is made in the mind of a man who has resolved to forsake the path of folly and make his way toward the Light.

The trials and proofs through which you afterward passed have been fully explained to you by the Master himself.

Orator Venerable, my task is done.

W.M. Brother Master of Ceremonies, you will now please conduct our new-made Brother to the Junior Warden, and request that he instruct him in the carpet of the degree.

He conducts him.

J.W. My Brother, a Lodge is constituted by three, five, seven Brethren or more, with a Warrant from some regularly constituted body empowering them to hold meetings for the purpose of forwarding Masonic labor or work. It is not material at what place the Lodge is assembled, so that it is held in a sure place of retirement and secrecy, and all access guarded against by faithful watchers. Our Ancient Brethren selected for their place of meeting a high hill or low valley, in order that the approach of the profane could be the better observed. Of late years custom has made it a law that all regular Lodges shall he held in a room or place properly consecrated and set apart for the purpose.

But the true dimensions of a Lodge are very great. They extend from the North to the South and from East to West. In other words, the whole surface of the earth constitutes the field for the beneficent labors of the Brethren.

Its covering is the cloudy canopy or starry decked heaven, and the supports of this great canopy are three great pillars which are named Wisdom, Strength and Beauty. For Infinite Wisdom could alone contrive so noble an edifice, Infinite Strength could alone support, and Divine Beauty could alone adorn this glorious and stupendous piece of Architecture.

The light given to this edifice you see represented before you, viz., the sun to rule the day and the moon and stars to govern the night, and it is by the medium of these shining lights that man is enabled to pursue his labors.

Although the Master is in heaven and we are upon the earth, and although there appears to be and is in fact a separation between the two, yet by the symbolic ladder which you there see represented, and which is and emblem of that ladder which Jacob saw in the visions of the night, we may by its aid hope to ascend into the immediate presence of the Master like the angels of God. The rounds of that ladder are but three, and are named Faith Hope and Charity. Faith fixed upon the Most High God, a firm belief and practice of the commands which he has given. Hope living on the promises of his Word, and the perfect exercise of Charity or love for the undivided family of man will bring to the mind and heart the assurance that when this tabernacle of flesh is laid aside we shall ascend up on high and dwell with Him for ever more.

The furniture of this Lodge is the Holy Bible the Compass and the Square. (28.1) The Holy Bible, or the Sacred Scriptures, is the revealed will of God and is His inestimable gift to man. It contains all that is important for a man to know. For it shows us our miserable condition by nature, and the manner in which that misery many find a remedy. It reveals to us the Avenger of all sin and the immediate dispenser of all our blessings. It calls upon us for reverence and gratitude in our low estate and not only points out the path that leads to happiness here but also to a home beyond the skies.

The Square is the emblem proper of the Master. It should not only remind him of the duty he owes to the Lodge over which he is called to preside but it should teach all Masons to regulate their conduct by the principles of mortality and virtue.

The Compass may teach you to limit your desires to every station and to set a boundary to passion, for by means of this man is often made to err. By reflecting often upon these things you will be kept in the path of duty and walk in a manner becoming the Order which has just received you.

The ornaments of the Lodge are the Mosaic pavement, the indented tessel and the Blazing Star. The Mosaic pavement is emblematic of human life, checkered with good and evil, the beautiful border which surrounds it, those blessings and comforts man constantly enjoys, and the blazing star which appears in the center may remind you that in every situation of life in which you may be placed, by reflecting on this emblem and looking to Him of whom this star is a type, your courage will be sustained, your weakness made strong, and your life be filled with resignation.

The Rough Ashlar, the Smooth Ashlar, and the Trestle Board have already been explained. The Pillar is here explained pertaining to this degree.
Also read from a Monitor, Brotherly Love, Relief, Truth, Temperance, Fortitude, Prudence, Justice.

    The name of this degree is called "Faith."
J.W.   Venerable, my task is ended and our new-made Brother now awaits your pleasure.
W.M.   Brother Master of Ceremonies, conduct the Brother between the columns.

(30.1)*He conducts him there and places him.*

W.M.   My Very Dear Brother, this day is forever a day of favor. You will take your place at the head of the South column, which is the place you are to occupy in this degree. Merit it by the assiduity of your labors, and by the practice of the Masonic virtues you have imposed upon yourself, and of which your Brethren will set you the first example. Merit also to penetrate deeper into our mysteries, and to receive the favors which the Lodge never refuses to those who are worthy of them.

˥-˥ —˥ [three gavels] *The Wardens repeat.*

Rise, and in order, Brethren, while I proclaim Brother —— in your hearing an Apprentice Mason, and a member of the perfect Lodge ——. I therefore invite you to recognize him henceforward as such, and to help, aid and assist him in all cases where he may need.

The Wardens repeat the proclamation verbatim. After which, the Venerable says:

W.M. Let us rejoice, my Brethren, over the acquisition the Lodge has made of a new Brother and friend.

They make the usual signs and batteries. After which, the Master of Ceremonies, or the Candidate himself, responds to the thanks and answers in the same manner.

The Worshipful Master requests the Orator to gratify the Lodge by some piece of Architecture, if he is prepared to do so.

Having finished, he then causes the Wardens to ask of both columns if any Brother has anything to propose for the good of the Order in general, or of the Lodge in particular.

Then the bag for propositions, etc., and the charity box are passed around, the orator reporting the result.

The Secretary reads the minutes of proceedings.

W.M. Brothers Senior and Junior Wardens, announce to your columns that if any Brother has any observation to make in regard to the minutes, he can do so.

The Wardens make the announcement, and report. (31.1)

W.M. Rise, and in order, Brethren. Let us return thanks to the Great Architect of the Universe for the works and blessings of the day.

Prayer

O Thou, who art from everlasting to everlasting, the same yesterday, today and forever, the source of light, happiness and immortality. We worship and bow before Thee, to return to Thee thanks, and to offer unto Thee praise.

And we humbly ask of Thee to continue unto us Thy protection and Thy guidance, that we may not go astray. Amen.

Brethren And Amen! So may it be forever.

W.M. May friendship and benevolence, the passion of noble and sensible hearts, the delicious enjoyments of delicate and honest heart, ever sustain and ornament this Temple, which we raise.

And may prudence and discretion be the constant companion of the Brethren of this Lodge, and when they have returned into the Civil world, may they be recognized by their discourse, by their conduct, and by their actions, that they are truly the widow's worthy sons.

The Master strikes one blow and proceed to close the Lodge.

The close goes on the same as the opening, beginning at the Senior Deacon sends the Word, etc., same as York Rite.

When the time permits, the catechism or lecture may be recited. It is the same as the York Rite, with the exception of the trials. (34.1)

FELLOW CRAFT

Opening

The Lodge being open in the Entered Apprentices degree, the Master knocks once and says:

W.M.   Brothers Senior and Junior Wardens, announce on your respective columns that the works are suspended in order to pass to those of a Fellow Craft, and invite the Apprentice to retire from the Lodge.

The Wardens repeat, and announce that the Apprentices have retired.

W.M.   Brother Senior Warden, what is the first duty of a Warden in a Fellow Craft's Lodge?
S.W.   Worshipful, it is to be assured that all the Brethren present are Fellow Crafts.

The Master knocks once and says:

W.M.   Rise, and in order, Brethren.

All the Brethren face the West.

Brothers Senior and Junior Wardens, assure yourselves that all the Brethren present are Fellow Crafts.

The Wardens pass along the columns and receive from each Brother the Sign, Word and Grip. When finished, they return to their places. The Senior Warden reports to the Master as follows:

S.W.   All the Brethren present are Fellow Crafts.

The Venerable rises, comes to order as a Fellow Craft, sends the Sacred Word to the Senior Warden, who forwards it to the Junior Warden by the Junior Deacon. Then Junior Warden says:

J.W.   All is just and perfect, Venerable. (35.1)
W.M.   In order, Brethren.

They make the Sign, Battery, and Exclamation, and he says:

In the name of God, and of St. John of Scotland, the Lodge of Fellow Crafts is open. The Brethren are hereby forbidden to speak, or to pass from one column to another without having asked permission.

Brother Secretary, be kind enough to read the minutes of our last Fellow Craft's labors.

After the reading of which, he continues.

Brother Master of Ceremonies, retire into the anteroom, and see if there is any visitors.

The Master of Ceremonies obeys, retires, and when he returns, makes his report as usual.

Reception

W.M.   Brother Master of Ceremonies, go and prepare the Candidate, and bring him here in the required manner.

He goes and returns with the Candidate, who carries a rule in his left hand, one end resting on his left shoulder, the flap of his apron up. He knocks at the door as an Apprentice.

W.M.   See who knocks, Brother Senior Warden.

The Senior Warden asks the Junior, the latter asks the Guardian, who opens the door and asks, "Who knocks?" The Master of Ceremonies answers:

M.C.   It is I, who am conducting an Apprentice, who asks to pass from the Plumb to the Level.

The Junior Warden repeats to the Senior Warden, and he to the Master.

W.M.   Ask him his age, his civil and Masonic qualities.

The questions and answers pass successively from the Guardian to the Junior Warden, from him to the Senior Warden, and from him to the Venerable. The Secretary transcribes them on his minutes.

W.M.   How does he expect to gain admission to this degree?
M.C.   Because he is freeborn and of good report.

The Venerable knocks and says:

W.M.   Let him enter as an Apprentice, and place him between the columns.

When the Candidate enters, he continues.

Brother Junior Warden, Commander of the column of Apprentices, has the Candidate, who asks to pass from the Plumb to the Level, served his time as such, and are the Brethren of his column (37.1) satisfied with him?
M.C.   Yes, Venerable.
W.M.   Do all the Brethren consent to his advancement?

All the members extend their right hand. Master knocks, and addresses the Candidate:

My Brother, you must regard it as a particular favor which this Respectable Lodge[3] shows you, in thus allowing you to pass so rapidly into the second class of workmen. I must inform you that in olden times it was necessary for a Candidate to work for five years without interruption among the Apprentices, but we do not shorten the time for all, and those, who like you, my Brother, have been excused from this probation, must learn to merit by their future conduct all the favors which this Lodge has shown them. We flatter ourselves, my Brother, that you will

---

3. The manuscript reads, "resp ☐"

neglect no means in your power to justify our action in your behalf. What procured the privilege of being received a Mason, my Brother?

Cand.   A wise friend, whom I have since found to be a Brother.

W.M.   In what state were you presented to the Lodge?

Cand.   Neither naked nor clothed.

W.M.   Why so?

Cand.   To teach me that luxury is a vice which imposes only on the vulgar, and that the virtuous man must cast aside all sentiments of vanity and pride.

W.M.   Why were your eyes blindfolded?

Cand.   To teach me how prejudicial to man's happiness are the darkness of ignorance and (38.1) the passions which blind us.

W.M.   Why did they cause you to travel?

Cand.   To teach me that we cannot attain virtue by the first step.

W.M.   What did you see when the bandage was taken from your eyes?

Cand.   All the Brethren, armed with swords, which were presented at me.

W.M.   Why?

Cand.   To show me that they were ready to spill their blood for me, if I was faithful to my obligation, as well as to punish me, should I ever violate it.

W.M.   Why was a Compass placed on your left breast?

Cand.   To show me that the heart of a Mason should be true and just.

[The Emblematic Voyages]

W.M.   My Brother, you have now five voyages to make. Brother Master of ceremonies, let this Apprentice travel on his first voyage.

The Master of Ceremonies puts into the Candidate's left hand a mallet and Chisel, takes him by the right hand, and leads him round the Lodge. Returned between the pillars, he says:

M.C.   Brother Junior Warden, the first voyage is finished.

The Junior repeats to the Senior, and he to the Venerable.

W.M.   My Brother, this first voyage is symbolical of the first year of service of an Apprentice, during which time he is employed in squaring and making perfect the stones, which as an Apprentice, he learned to hew[4] by the aid of the Mallet and Chisel. This emblem demonstrates to you (39.1) that however perfect an Apprentice may be in his work, he is still very far from the end of his labors, that the rough edges of the materials consecrated to the constructed of the Temple, which he elevates to the Great Architect are not yet renewed, that he has yet to labor hard with the mallet and Chisel, and to follow the lines which have been marked out for him by the Master. Give me the Sign of an Apprentice.

---

4. The manuscript reads, "hugh."

W.M. What means this Sign?
Cand. It reminds me of the Obligation I took at my reception, in which I consented to have my throat cut, should I be so vile as to reveal the secrets which have been confided to me.

The Master knocks, and says:

W.M. Brother Master of Ceremonies, let him make his second voyage.

The Candidate takes in his left hand a Compass and Rule, and the Master of Ceremonies conducts him by the right arm once around the Lodge, stopping as before.

W.M. My Brother, this second voyage is emblematical of the second year, during which the aid of the Rule and Compass, a Mason learns the practical elements of Masonry. That is to say, the art of tracing lines upon the materials which he has squared and made perfect. My Brother, give the Token of an Apprentice to our Brother Senior Warden.

He gives it.

S.W. The Token is correct, Venerable.

The Master knocks, and says:

W.M. Brother Master of Ceremonies, let the Apprentice perform his third voyage.

(40.1)*The Candidate takes in his left hand a Rule, and carries on his left shoulder a Pincers. He is conducted as before.*

W.M. My Brother, this third voyage represents the third year of an Apprentice, during which time he is entrusted with the transportation and placing of the material, when finished. This is regulated by the Rule and Pincers. The Pincers, instead of the Compass, is the emblem of the power which knowledge adds to our individual strength, and without which we should be unable to execute our designs. What do you understand, my Brother, by Masonry?
Cand. I understand it to be the study of the sciences and the practice of the virtues.

The Master knocks, and says:

W.M. Brother Master of Ceremonies, let this Apprentice perform his fourth voyage.

The Candidate carries in his left hand a Square and Rule, conducted as before.

W.M. This voyage, my Brother, represents the fourth year of an Apprentice, in which he is directly employed in the elevation of the edifice, to see that the various parts agree, and to verify by the Square the position of the materials brought to finish, the Masonic work. It teaches you that application, zeal and intelligence in the work before you, can alone elevate you above your less instructed and less zealous Brethren. Brother Master of Ceremonies, let this Apprentice perform his fifth and last voyage.

The Candidate has his hands empty. The Master of Ceremonies holds the point of a sword to his heart, which he holds there by his thumb and finger of his right hand, conducted as before.

W.M.   This fifth and last voyage signifies that being sufficiently instructed in manual practice, the Apprentice must employ this last year in the study of theory. Learn from this, my Brother, that it is not sufficient to be in the road to virtue, but to remain in the same powerful, efforts must be made to acquire perfection. Follow then, the route traced for you, and render yourself worthy (41.1) of being admitted to the knowledge of the more elevated Masonic works. Give the Sacred Word of an Apprentice to the Brother Grand Expert.

He gives it and the Expert says:

Expert   The word is correct, Venerable.
W.M.   Brother Master of Ceremonies, let this Candidate perform his last work as an Apprentice.

The Master of Ceremonies puts into his hand a mallet, with which he knocks as an Apprentice, upon the Rough Stone, and when finished, he announces it to the Venerable.

W.M.   Brother Master of Ceremonies, lead the Candidate to the foot of the throne, and cause him to step as an Apprentice.

The Master of Ceremonies obeys, and the Venerable then says:

W.M.   Rise, and to order, Brethren. Repeat after me your Obligation.

Obligation

The Brethren all stand under the Sign.
Having finished, the Venerable places his sword upon the Candidate's head, saying:

> In the name of God, and under the auspices of, etc., and by the powers confided in me by this respectable Lodge, I receive and constitute you a Fellow Craft Mason.

He strikes three blows with his Mallet upon the sword. The Master of Ceremonies raises the Candidate. The Venerable puts down the flap head of his apron, telling him that being now a Fellow Craft, he will wear it henceforth in that manner.

W.M.   Henceforward, my Brother, you will work on the Cubical Pointed Stone, and receive your wages at the column J. This new work will remind you that a Fellow Craft, whose duty it is (42.1) to repair the defects of the edifice, must use all his care, not only in hiding the defects of his Brethren, but also to correct them by his example and council.[5]

I will now give you the Sign, Word, and Grip of a Fellow Craft.

---

5. The manuscript reads, "example & ~~conduct~~ council."

The Sign is made—, the Token—, the Sacred Word—, the Pass Word— is given.

W.M.   Go now, my Brother, and give the Sign, Word and Token to the Grand Expert, accompanied by the Master of Ceremonies, that he may recognize you as a Fellow Craft.

The Expert receives them and announces them as correct.

W.M.   Brother Master of Ceremonies, let this Brother now work as a Companion, and instruct him in the steps of this degree.

The Candidate strikes three blows upon the Cubic Stone, makes the Sign and Step, etc., then retires.
The Candidate dresses, and returns to the Lodge to be conducted. On his return he is led to the Venerable, who says:

W.M.   My Brother, Masonry is progressive. It is necessary in every pursuit of knowledge gradually to advance in order to understand things aright. Wherefore, you was not all made acquainted at once with all the rites of our Order, but are advanced gradually through them.

The degree which you are now taking may be considered partly as a recompense for labors past, but more particularly as a introduction to the Masters Degree. The former degree is well calculated to impress upon the mind the duties of morality, and imprint on the memory the noblest principles which adorn the human mind.

The working tools of this degree are the Plumb, Square and Level. They are made use of by Operative Masons to raise perpendiculars, lay horizontals, and to square their work. Our Order recognizes the Plumb as admonishing us to walk uprightly in our several stations before God and man. The Square, etc.

See Monitor.

(42.1)L E C T U R E

My Brother, we are now about to pass symbolically into the middle chamber of King Solomon's Temple. And previous to our so doing it is necessary that some further explanation of ceremonies should be given, in order that you may properly understand the nature of our ritual.

The Temple, strictly speaking, was composed of only two rooms, viz., the Sanctuary or sacred place, where the children of Israel met to worship and to hear the laws of the Most High proclaimed, and the Sanctum Sanctorum, or Holy of Holies, which was a place of deposit for the Ark of the Testimony, which contained the Divine Writings, the Mercy Seat and the Cherubim, where the Lord manifested Himself, and into which place the High Priest went but once a year, and then to make atonement for the sins of the people.

In front of this Temple stood the Porch, Vestibule, or Outer Court. Here all indiscriminately assembled, but no entrance was found to the so called Middle Chamber unless through the Porch or Vestibule, or Outer Court. And those who entered from the Vestibule must undergo a preparation before they could find admittance there. For it was a place set apart for the service of the Most High, and to the meditation upon subjects which would have a tendency to purify the heart. Hence, no one who would not undergo the preparation was deemed fit for a place there.

The degree of Entered Apprentice, which you have already taken, is emblematic of the primary stage of human life, or its vestibule, and the doctrines taught in that degree, the course of preparation necessary to pass to the middle stage, with acceptance to the Author of your being. You have there been taught the necessity of eradicating from your heart all prejudices and passions, which were contrary to the Divine Law, and encouraged to cultivate all proper dispositions. You have been warned against troublesome and evil dispositions, and persuaded to court a life of peace. You have been instructed that charity, which is love, is the doctrine not only to be first learned, but also practiced in all after life, and many other doctrines of an important nature have been held up to your view. If you have learned these things aright and are, daily and hourly, trying to profit by them, you have undergone the preparation necessary for entering the middle chamber, and I will (44.1) endeavor, as your guide, symbolically to conduct you there.

You have been instructed that it is necessary to rest a part of your time from worldly labor, and to devote that time to the service of your Great Benefactor, the Most High God. For in six days God created the heavens and the earth, and all that in them is, but He rested on the seventh, and hallowed it. In all ages of the world, and among all the people whom He has enlightened, that day has been consecrated and rigidly observed. His bounty permits you to spend six days of the week in worldly labor, during which He surrounds you with blessings of the richest kind. He guards you by day and by night, he preserves you in the house and by the way. How reasonable then, that the seventh part of time should be spent in bringing Him the offering of a grateful heart, and rendering unto Him adoration for all His mercies. And the proper observance of this day of rest will fit you for the proper service of Him in the six days that are to come. Learn then, at the very entrance of the Sacred Temple, to observe the ordinances which He has given, and bear it in mind, that is not well pleased with him who walks contrary to His commands.

At the door of the entrance stood two brazen pillars—the one on the right, the other on the left. They were alike in each other in all respects. The name of the one was Jachin, the other Boaz, signifying, "In strength shall it be established for ever." They were cast by Hiram, the widow's son, on the banks of the river Jordan, in the clay grounds between Succoth and Zarthan, in common with all the other holy vessels. They were hollow, of molten brass, and were eighteen cubits high. They were adorned with two large chapiters, ornamented with net work, lily work, and pomegranates. They also had two large globes, the one celestial, the other terrestrial, which contain on their convex surfaces maps, charts, etc., of the celestial and terrestrial bodies.

These pillars stand at the very entrance of the Temple and, by their uprightness and beauty, admonish us of the character we ought to bear, the integrity which should fill all our purposes, the regularity of life we should lead, and peacefulness of disposition we should cultivate[6] in order to stand as a pillar in the assembly of the Brethren. They are fixed upon a firm foundation, they stand uprightly, and their beauties could be seen afar off. The chapiters, adorned with lily work, net work and pomegranates, denote purity of thought, and unity of purpose, in order to be filled with the abundance of plenty which the Master will bestow on all who cultivate heavenly dispositions.

My Brother, let us disdain the performance of any mean and criminal act, let us discountenance libertinism and all excess, let us encourage charity and benevolence, let (44.1) our manner be unassuming, our conversation chaste, modest, and discreet, and let us from henceforth abstain from all foolish and vain pursuits, and use the time allotted to us, to labor here with diligence, remembering that time flies swiftly, and is irrecoverable, and that we are traveling on to the Master, from whom we hope to receive a reward.

Three, five and seven steps.

The three first steps are emblematic of the Wisdom, which we should constantly seek from above to guide us in all our ways, and without which we shall most certainly go astray, the Strength, which we should constantly pray for to support us in all our trials and sufferings in life, and prevent us from murmuring against the beneficent dispensations of Him, who does all things well, in order that our walk and conversation among the Brethren and the world may be adorned with the Beauty of holiness in every part.

The five are emblematic of the five different orders of architecture, viz., the Tuscan, Doric, Ionic, Corinthian and Composite (see Monitor).

Also, the five different senses, viz., hearing, seeing, feeling, tasting, smelling (Monitor).

The seven allude to the seven liberal arts and sciences (see Monitor).

In conclusion of this part of the instruction, let me say to you that the liberal arts and sciences deserve our encouragement and attention, as these distinguish a polite people from savages, and the capacity for acquiring a knowledge of them leads men to contemplate upon the works and perfections of Deity, and enables them to lead others from many pernicious errors, and to shun them himself. And the study of these things belongs not to the vestibule, of early life, for then first principles occupy the mind. They belong not to the latter period, that should be spent in reflection and improvement. Here is the time and place, viz., the middle age, when the man is clear and vigorous and the body fit to undergo the fatigue accompanying the labor of acquirement, before the golden be broken or the silver cord be loosed, before the wheel be broken at the cistern, and the dust return to the dust.

We will now salute the Junior Warden. (46.1)

---

6. The manuscript reads, "we should ~~inculcate~~ cultivate."

Salutes the Junior with 3 and 2.
He passes through an examination and explanation of the Sign and Word, which represents Plenty, Sheaf of Wheat and Waterfall. History of the Word—York Rite.

We will now salute the Senior Warden.

Sign and lesson. Hypocrisy (Lisping).
Conducts the Candidate to the Master.

W.M.   My Brother, you are now symbolically admitted to the Middle Chamber, on account of that which ought to attract your earnest attention.

Behold this Mysterious Star, and never let it escape your memory. It is the emblem of the genius which elevates itself to great things. It is also the symbol of that sacred fire with which the Great Architect of the Universe has gifted us, and whose light we must learn to discern, live, and practice Truth, Justice and Equity.

Behold the Delta, it contains the sacred name of God.

Though unseen by mortals, His eye is ever upon us. He is intimately acquainted with all our actions, even our most secret thoughts. With Him there is no beginning of days or end of life. He is immutable, unchangeable, past finding out. Yet He is our wise and glorious benefactor, and supplies all our wants. He will guide us in life, and keep us in all our ways, and deserves at our hands constantly the tribute of grateful acknowledgment. Acquaint now thyself with Him, and be at peace. Worship and adore Him, for He is worthy of all thy praise.

The Master of Ceremonies will cause the Candidate to step and kneel.

W.M.   Rise, and in order, Brethren. Repeat after me your Obligation.

Same as in the York Rite.
He rises and is again placed between the columns.

W.M.   Brother Senior and Junior Wardens, announce on your respective columns that we are about to applaud, to testify the pleasure this respectable Lodge feels in counting henceforth Brother ——, among the Fellow Crafts (Companions). (47.1)

The Warden announce, the Master knocks and says:

W.M.   In order. (He makes the Sign, Battery, and Acclamation of a Fellow Craft, together with all the Brethren.)

The Candidate returns thanks and salutation.
The charity box and bag passed as in First Degree.

Closing

The same as in the First Degree, substituting proper Sign, Word, etc. (48.1)

[MASTER MASON]

Introduction

The Chamber of Reflection must be gloomy, the walls being covered with various appropriate maxims. The Preparing Brother should be capable of preparing the mind and imagination of the Candidate by wise and moral discourse relating to the importance of the degree.

The Candidate's hat and sword are taken by the Master of Ceremonies, and given to the Master. The Architect sees that there is placed on the table of the Warden a roll of pasteboard eighteen inches in length, and nine in circumference. The room is lighted by a single yellow taper. It should contain a skeleton, and also some broken tools and rubbish.

The Lodge is hung with black, spread with white deaths heads and crossbones, an hourglass, silver tears are placed by three, five and seven. Nine stars, by three times three, illuminate the room.

The Masters all wear black, hats flapped, white gloves, Masters' apron and scarf. The Master is covered with a pall, embroidered with skulls, crossbones, and tears. Round the coffin, a separation is formed by a moveable screen, representing the Middle Chamber. In one corner of this chamber, in the West, is planted a sprig of Cassia. At the head of the coffin is placed a Square, at the foot, a Compass. (51.1)

Opening

The Master strikes one blow with his mallet, which is repeated by the Wardens.

W.M. Venerable Brother Senior Warden, what is the duty of a Senior Warden before opening a Masters Lodge?
S.W. It is to ascertain if the Temple is duly guarded within and without.
W.M. Satisfy yourself of the same, Venerable Brother.

The Senior Warden sends the Deacon, who returns and informs him that the Temple is well tiled.

S.W. Most Respectable, the Masters Lodge is tyled.
W.M. What is your second duty, Venerable Brother Senior Warden?
S.W. It is to be assured that all the members present are Master Masons.
W.M. Venerable Brothers Senior and Junior Wardens, pass along your respective columns and ascertain if all Brethren present are Master Masons.

The Master then faces the East, all the Brethren do likewise. The Wardens pass along their columns, beginning at the last and ending in the East, receiving from all the Sign, etc. When finished, the Junior Warden reports to the Senior, and he to the Master.

S.W. Most Respectable, all the Brethren present are Master Masons.
W.M. Venerable Brother Junior Deacon, where is your place as a Master Mason in a

Master Mason's Lodge?
J.D. Behind, or at the right of the Senior Warden, if he will permit.
W.M. Why there, Venerable Brother? (52.1)
J.D. To carry the Senior Warden's orders to the Junior Warden, and to see that the Brethren behave with decency on both columns.
W.M. Where is the Senior Deacon's place?
J.D. At the right of the Master.
W.M. Why there, Brother Senior Deacon?
S.D. To carry the orders of the Master to the Senior Warden, and to all the Brethren, that the works may be more promptly executed.
W.M. Where is the Junior Warden's station?
S.D. In the South, Most Respectable.
W.M. Why in the South, Brother Junior Warden?
J.W. The better to observe the sun at meridian, etc.
W.M. Where is the Senior Warden's station?
J.W. In the West, Most Respectable.
W.M. Why so, Brother Senior Warden?
S.W. As the sun sets in the West, etc.
W.M. Where is the Most Respectable Master's station?
S.W. In the East, Most Respectable. (53.1)

The Master knocks three times. Wardens repeat. The Master gives the Word to the Senior Deacon, uncovering and then replacing, his hat. The Senior Deacon bears the Word to the Senior Warden, who sends it to the Junior Warden by the Junior Deacon. The Senior Warden knocks once, and says:

J.W. All is correct and perfect, Most Respectable.

The Master then uncovers, all the Brethren do likewise.

W.M. Venerable Masters and Brethren, in the name of God, and of St. John of Scotland, this Lodge of Master Masons is open. No Brother is permitted to speak, or to pass from one column to the other without having obtained permission from the Venerable wardens. Together, Brethren.

He makes the Sign, with Sign of Horror. All do the same. After which Master says:

Venerable Brothers Senior and Junior Wardens, announce to your respective columns that the labors of the Middle Chamber are opened.

Reception

The reception having been approved by the unanimous vote of the Brethren, the last-received Master places himself in the coffin, feet to the East, forming a square, his right hand on his heart, the left extended along his body, a shroud covering him from his feet to the waist, his apron turned up over his breast, and a bloody cloth covering the upper part of his face. All the lights but one yellow taper, on the Master's table, is extinguished.

W.M.   Venerable Brother Master of Ceremonies, you will retire and prepare the Candidate. (54.1)

Preparation of the Candidate

The Candidate must be barefoot, his arms and left breast bare, divested of all metals, a small Square is fastened to his right arm, a cord three times around his waist, a Fellow Craft's apron, and his hair in disorder.

The Master of Ceremonies knocks at the door as a Fellow Craft, still holding the Candidate by the hand. The Venerable Grand Expert goes immediately to ascertain who knocks. Having reported to the Senior Warden, the latter says:

S.W.   Most Respectable, the Master of Ceremonies presents to this Respectable Lodge a Fellow Craft, who has served his time, and who asks to be initiated into the degree of Master.

The door is slightly opened.

W.M.   (*In a loud voice*) Why does the Master of Ceremonies come thus to trouble our sorrow? Our laments should have taught him to keep away all suspicious persons, and more particularly a Fellow Craft.

    My Brethren, it may perhaps be one of those who have caused our grief. Let us arm ourselves. Who knows, but it may be Divine Justice which gives up the guilty to our just revenge.

    Venerable Brother Grand Expert, take with you the Brother Terrible, and four armed Brethren (raising his voice); go, seize the Fellow Craft, examine him well, look at his hands! Search his clothing! Take away his apron and bring it to me as a testimony of his actions. Finally, see if you can find on or about him any trace of the horrid crime which has been committed.

The Candidate is seized, and his apron taken from him. The Expert enters bearing the apron, having the Candidate and four armed Brethren outside, and the door ajar.

Expert   Most Respectable, I have performed your order, but I have discovered nothing about the Fellow Craft which indicates the commission of a murder. His clothing is white, his hands are pure, and this apron which I bear is without stain.

W.M.   Venerable Brother, may the Grand Architect grant that I may be in error, and that this Fellow Craft may not be one of those whom our revenge pursues. But to receive him among us we must take many precautions, and make the most strict researches. For, my Brethren, if this Fellow Craft be (56.1) innocent, he must assuredly know the cause of our grief. Would he have chosen so dangerous a moment to present himself before us if he were guilty? The artifice would have been ridiculous, for he must have feared that our suspicions would have fallen upon him. Venerable Brethren, in introducing him within the walls, we will interrogate him and, from his ancestors, we may learn what we are to think of him. Are you of one accord? Venerable Brethren, if so, you will manifest it.

The Brethren raise their hands.

Venerable Brother Expert, Guardian of the Door, since this respectable assembly are in favor of the introduction of the Companion, you will ask him how he expects to gain admission among us.

The demand is made as usual, and the answer returned by the Guardian to the Junior Warden, by him to the Senior Warden, and by him to the Master. The Candidate answers, "By the Pass Word."

W.M. By the Pass Word! This bold answer confirms my suspicion. How can he know it? This is without doubt a consequence of his crime. Here, Venerable Masters, you see a proof of his audacity and his crime.

Brother Senior Warden, retire and scrupulously examine the Candidate.

After having examined him, he enters and says:

S.W. Most Respectable, his audacity is extreme. His manners show a refinement of crime. He comes, I am sure, to spy out our actions or to deceive our good faith, under the mask of hypocrisy.

He then examines him more closely. He looks at his right hand and, pushing it from him, exclaims:

Heavens! It is he!

Then, seizing him by the collar, crying in a menacing tone:

Speak, wretched man! How can you give the Pass Word? Who has committed it to you?

The Candidate answers.

CAND. My Conductor will give it for me, for I know it not.

The Senior Warden says: (56.1)

S.W. Most Respectable, the Companion[7] confesses that he is ignorant of the Pass Word, but that his Conductor will give it for him.

W.M. You will receive it, Venerable Brother Senior Warden.

The Conductor gives the word to the Senior Warden, who answers:

S.W. Most Respectable, the Pass Word is correct.

---

7. *Companion* is the French Masonic term for *Fellow Craft*.

W.M.   Let the Candidate enter.

The Master of Ceremonies leads him in backwards.

Let those who guard him abandon him not for one instant. Let them place themselves with him in the West.

They take their places with him, the Brother Terrible holding the cord.

Companion, you must be very rash and indiscreet to present yourself here, at a moment when all your comrades are suspected for just reasons. The traces of grief and consternation which you see on our countances, the mourning which surrounds us, these sorrowful remains enclosed in that coffin, all must speak to you of death, and if this death was but the effect of a cause of nature we should without doubt lament it, but we should not have, as now, a crime to punish and a friend to avenge. Tell me, Companion, are you accessory to this dreadful crime? Are you of the number of those infamous Fellow Crafts who committed? Behold the work!

The corpse is showed him. He answers, "No." The Candidate is turned towards the Master, when the Brother who is in the coffin gently gets up so as not to be seen by the Candidate.

Tis well. Let the Companion travel.

The Master of Ceremonies takes the Candidate by the hand, Terrible holds him from behind by the cord, and the four armed Brethren escort him, two on each side. In this manner he passes around the Middle Chamber, and is then led to the side of the Master. The Master of Ceremonies takes the hand of the Candidate and with it knocks on the shoulder of the Master., who turns around, places his mallet on the Candidate's heart, and says:

W.M.   Who comes here?
M.C.   A Companion, who has served his time, and who asks admission to the Middle Chamber. (57.1)
W.M.   How does he expect to gain admission?
M.C.   By the Pass Word.
W.M.   How can he give it, if he has it not?
M.C.   I will give it for him. (Gives it.)
W.M.   Pass, T—.

He is conducted to the West.

W.M.   Venerable Brother Senior Warden, let the Candidate advance to the altar, three, two, one.

He makes the three Steps and Sign of an Apprentice, then two for a fellow Craft, and one, for a Master. He kneels on both knees, right hand on the Bible, the extended points of the Compass on his breast. The Master descends from his throne, all the Brethren rise and place themselves in order.

Obligation

After which the Master takes him by the hand, interrogates him as usual, bids him rise and says:

W.M.   Companion, you will now represent the greatest man of the Masonic world, our Respectable Master, Hiram, who was assassinated before the completion of the Temple, as I will now inform you.

The Brethren all form around the coffin. The Junior Warden is in the South, armed with twenty-four inch Gauge, the Senior Warden in the West, armed with a Square, and the Master, with his Mallet, in the East. The Candidate is placed at the foot of the coffin.

Historical Discourse (58.1)

When the history arrives at the escape by the South, the Candidate is led to the Junior (ruffian), who goes through the usual ceremony, then to the Senior Warden, and the Master continues. When he relates the act of Jubelo, the Senior Warden goes through with it as usual, and the Candidate is conducted to the Master, who continues the history until Jubelum, when he gives him a light blow upon the forehead with the instrument. Two Brethren then lay him in the coffin. He is covered with the pall, and the lights are lit. The Master continues the history. When he comes to the search, they go through with that. History continues, procession, sprig, etc. The raising at the proper place in the history.

W.M.   Brother Master of Ceremonies, conduct the Candidate to the altar, to renew his obligation. Rise, and to order, Brethren, the new Master is about to reiterate his oath.

The Wardens repeat. Master of Ceremonies conducts the Candidate to the altar, etc. Reiterates.

Accepts Him as Master

Gives him Signs, with explanations, Words, with explanations, and Grips, etc. Distress, Amazement, Five Points, etc.

Salutation as in Other Degrees

Address of the Orator

Address of the Master

Salutation of Brethren

Closing—as in Other Degrees

(60.1)CONSECRATION OF A LODGE IN THE SCOTTISH RITE

Preliminary

The new Temple will be pompously decorated. The lights of the Master, Wardens, officers, et al., must be all new. The emblem in the East will not be lighted. The Master of Ceremonies, Grand Expert, and Inside Tyler will remain inside of the room with sword in hand, in darkness, the door shut. The Inside Tyler keeps the key in his own hand. Invite all the visitors you can.

The regalia and jewels of the new Lodge will remain on the throne. At the foot of the throne, a table, upon which the jewels of the Senior and Junior Wardens, the square of the Master, one terrestrial globe, and the tie, which should be long enough to surround the room, also a round cake of bread, hollow in the middle, two goblets filled with red wine. On the throne will be the bylaws, charter, Constitution and the General Statutes of the Supreme Council.

Inauguration

At the day and hour appointed between the Supreme Grand Council and the new Lodge, the Master Elect will order the Lodge to meet in an adjoining room, but never in the room to be consecrated. The officers will not wear their regalia.

The Lodge will then open its work in the usual manner. After the Lodge is opened the Master will direct the Secretary to read the edict, or declaration, of the Supreme Grand Council, which authorizes the inauguration of the new Temple, and deliver a lecture, or the Orator will perform that office, in order that the Lodge may proceed as soon as the Supreme Council may be present. The lecture consists in a recapitulation of the forms and ceremonies to be gone through with on the present occasion.

Then the Supreme Council is announced. The Master orders the columns up, and at the due guard and the sword drawn. Then the Grand Expert (61.1) precedes the two Masters of Ceremony, the Master being at the head, and four other Brothers, those Brothers bearing the lights, they go to the entrance of the Lodge when the Master commands the Arch of Steel, and presents to the Supreme Council his gavel. He takes it and goes to the seat of the Master in the outer room. Then the Installator commands the columns to be seated. Then a salutatory speech. The Installator then opens the work in the first degree. The petition is then read. The decision of the Supreme Council declared and the Orator concludes the speech and announces the same. Then the work is suspended and the procession formed in the following order:—

1ˢᵗ—The Standard Bearer and the Sword Bearer.

2ᵈ—The Installator, on his right, the Master, on his left the Senior Warden.

3ᵈ—The three first officers of every Lodge which assists at the ceremony, according to their numbers.

4th—*The Orator and Secretary of the new Lodge.*
5th—*Members of the Supreme Council, visiting Brethren of new lodges, and members of new Lodge.*
The procession, going round, stops at the outside door.
Music.
The Installator raps three, loud. The Brother Expert, who is inside, says in a loud voice:
Brothers, let us be on our watch, there is someone outside of the Temple.
Installator says, "I hear someone talking inside of the Temple."
Gives one knock and says, "Who is this that has penetrated of the Temple, or in the interior of this Temple?"
The Grand Expert answers, "They are workmen who worked at its construction and have been charged to keep it."
Installator says, "Open, I ask you in the name of the Brethren who accompany me."
Inside Tyler puts the key in the lock and opens the door, and says, "What do you wish to do in this Temple?"
Installator: "To finish the work in consecrating it, to the Glory of the Grand Architect of the Universe, and to virtue and truth."
The Tyler throws open the door, and giving him the key says, "As this Temple is to be dedicated to so glorious a purpose, I deliver the key to you and will join and help you in an action so noble and glorious."
Installator says, "My Brethren, the thick darkness which reigns in this Temple will not permit us to penetrate it. Our work will be nothing but disorder and confusion. Let us altogether invoke the Great Architect of the Universe, that He would accord to us a sparkle of His sacred fire, which will dissipate the darkness, enlighten our work, and fill with glory this new Temple that we have erected in His fear and to His name; vowing before we enter the same, that we will only practice the virtues proper to perpetuate the morals, that we will never burn the incense, only upon the altar of wisdom, and that we will teach the essential useful truth, which ought to distinguish the Mason from the (62.1) profane world."

Prayer

This, or an appropriate prayer may be made.

Thou Great and Holy One! Before Thou didst form the Universe Thou didst create the light which ought to enlighten us. Permit us to consecrate to Thee our first work and to draw from this flint a sparkle of that primitive sacred fire which Thou hast spread over all nature.

Lights the match, and the Master of Ceremonies holds the new candle, says, "Fiat Lux! My Brethren, let us all enter into this Temple in order to finish the work we have commenced."
The Installator takes the candle from the Master of Ceremonies, and all go into the Tem-

ple and arrive at the foot of the emblem—★[8]

The Installator gives one rap and says, "On the due guard."

He then opens the emblem and lights it, and says, "Symbol of the star of day, vivify with celestial light all the workmen who will meet together in this sanctuary to labor for the moral perfecting of humanity. Dissipate the darkness of the prejudices of the Neophytes who will enter into this Temple. Light us without ceasing by the clear light in order that we may never err or wander from the way of truth."

The Installator then lights the three lights on the throne and says, "Those three lights in a triangle, which are shining upon the throne, symbolize the three essential luminaries of the Great Architect of the Universe, also His wisdom, his justice and His bounty, and answer the three divine qualities which humanity can experience and possess. We should never deviate from the path of wisdom, and we are unitedly to be kind and just to all the human race."

The Installator then gives the light to the two Masters of Ceremonies, who go to the Senior Warden with the Installator. The Installator then lights the Senior Warden's lights and says, "The flame of this light symbolizes the flame of Virtue. This flame will unceasingly remind us that virtue is the tie which binds society together, that without virtue there is no such thing as happiness in the world, and that she gives us this sweet internal satisfaction, the only reward which is the aspiration of the wise."

The Installator then lights the Junior Warden's and says, "The flame of this light symbolizes the brightness and the dignity of humanity, when inspired by the zeal of charity unfeigned. It fills the heart with a pure love for his fellow men, and urges us to (63.1) the practice of charity in order to make men happy, and that it is by the happiness of the whole human race that the individual happiness of man depends."

Installator then goes to the Orator, lights his light, and says, "The flame of this light symbolizes the one which has enlightened the mind of the initiate and fortified his reason, in order to preserve him from the dangerous error of fanaticism and superstition."

Then goes to the Secretary, lights, and says, "The flame of this light symbolizes the clearness and the simplicity of the Trestle Board which contains the exact and regular plan of our work. It is a well known fact that without a clearly defined plan the work contemplated will always result in confusion. The plan that we have to follow, consists in the sublime point which Masonry claims for itself, viz., in the justice of the principles which we have, to teach in the explanation of the allegories and symbols which characterize the Order, and in the strict execution of the obligations which we have contracted."

Installator then returns to his place, gives one rap and says, "My Brethren, the light having taken the place of darkness we will soon be able to give ourselves up to our work, and advance with security and pleasure. This is the object of all our meetings. But in order to work, we must have tools, this is indispensable. Therefore, I beg of our Master of Ceremonies to bring us the symbolic tools of Masons."

★**Bible, The Great Light,** *see at the end.*

---

8. This is a symbol for the Blazing Star.

The Master of Ceremonies presents the Globe to the Installator, who says, "This symbol of the Universe will remind us that it, by the study of nature, and by the contemplation of the wonders of the Divine Omnipotence, that we can arrive to the acknowledgment of the truth. This symbol indicates to us equally that Masonry is cosmopolite, and that its works ought, like the sun, diffuse and spread light over the human race."

The Master of Ceremonies then presents the Compass. Installator says, "It is with this instrument that we examine and compare the diversity of the proportion of the objects which surround us. The compass symbolizes our reason, which ought ever deeply examine the nature of things, in order to the acknowledgment of the truth, and in order to distinguish the good from the bad, the true from the false."

The Master of Ceremonies then presents the Square. The Installator says, "This square has between its two ends a right angle. It is called the perfect angle. It symbolizes the rectitude and perfection of judgment we arrive at when, we are not in our reason and our conscience, subjected to the influence of prejudice and ignorance."

(64.1)*The Master of Ceremonies then gives the Senior Warden's jewel, the Level,* "This is a symbol of equality. We meet upon the level here. Worldly distinctions are forgotten and virtue is the only distinguishing quality among us as Brethren. Whatever may be our circumstances in the world, here we come and are reminded that we travel the same road, to the same destiny, and that human distinctions will not avail."

The Master of Ceremonies then presents the Junior Warden's jewel, the Plumb. The Installator says, "My Brethren, let us be constantly following the rectitude which is indicated to us by this beautiful emblem. Let us always endeavor to build up, with order, the materials of the moral and scientific edifice, on which we have to work, in order that a strong and substantial basis prevent it from crumbling down. By observing the perpendicular in our march forward in the way of truth, and in the practice of philanthropy, the passions and vices never could cause in us a deviation from the perfection to which we would attain."

The Master of Ceremonies then gives the Tie. Installator says, "My Brethren, up and under the due guard. Let us form the Chain of Union."

He takes in his hand the Tie, and after that all the Brothers take hold of the same. The Installator then ties it around his body and says, "My Brethren, the tie is the symbol of the union which makes the basis of every durable society. Our union will make our strength. Let us tie the fraternal knot which ought to unite all Masons and, that the fraternal kiss, which we are going to exchange mutually, may be the certain sign of our harmony and peace, and which always ought to rule among all Masons wheresoever scattered over the surface of the earth."

The Installator then gives the Sign and Sacred Word of the First Degree and the Fraternal Kiss to the Master, then the same to the Senior Warden, from them, it passes round the bottom each way, when the Master of Ceremonies takes it, and carries it to the Installator who says, "All is correct; to your places."

The Installator then goes to the throne and gives one rap, the two Wardens repeat. Installator says, "Brother Senior and Junior Warden, announce to your respective columns that this new Temple, which is erected to the Glory of the Grand Architect of the Universe and of truth and virtue, is inaugurated under the name of the Most Respectable Lodge of Saint John (definitive title), under the Jurisdiction of the Supreme Grand Council of Sovereign Grand Inspectors General of the 33d Degree, Ancient and Accepted Rite. Invite the Brethren to join us to applaud this Consecration, by three times three."

The Wardens repeat the announcement, after which the Installator commands the Brethren, "Up, and under the Due Guard."

After which, all give the Sign and three times three. After which, the Installator gives three raps, repeated by the Wardens. (65.1)

Installator says, "Worshipful Master, Senior and Junior Wardens, please to come to my side, and you all, my Brethren, let us form a circle."

Installator comes down and stands up between the throne and the table. When the Circle is formed Installator says, "My Brethren, let us crown the solemnity of this occasion, by eating the same bread and by drinking in the Cup of Friendship, in order to retire the knot which unites us, and to cement the sweet fraternity which distinguishes the members of the Order."

The Installator takes the circular bread, breaks it in two, takes a small piece and gives the rest to the Master. He drinks in the first cup with the Senior Warden. Each Brother does the same at this Mystic Agapé. When the ceremony is finished the Installator says, "To our places. Brethren."

Installator, in the throne, gives one knock and says, "Brother Inside Tyler, advance to the throne."

He then delivers to him the key of the Temple and says, "Brother Inside Tyler, the security of this Temple depends upon your watchfulness. I here deliver the key to you, but you will give entrance here only to the true Mason, and never suffer any of the profane to enter into its bosom."

The Installator then says, "Brother Grand Expert, please to announce at the four cardinal points, in a loud voice, that this Temple is dedicated to the Glory of the Grand Architect of the Universe."

The Expert announces it in the four corners.

Now the Orator delivers a Speech.

The Installator then says, "The inauguration is done, and the work is suspended."

Then may follow the regular Installation of the officers to their respective posts, if ready. After which ceremony there may be music, etc., then take up a collection and close the Lodge in usual form. When, if a supper, all retire to the same.

★ *The French Brethren have banished the altar and the Bible from* their *Lodges, and have omitted in their ritual any mention of them. In the German Lodges these are retained. It is here given from the original, and comes in at the above sign, which see. The altar is the throne. On it is placed an open Bible. The Master of Ceremonies presents the Installator with this bible, closed. The Installator opens it and says:*

My Brethren, behold this great light. It should ever be open in a proper Lodge, that we may be reminded of the duty of learning and practicing the excellent precepts it contains. It is the book that contains the rules of life, pointing out to man his whole duty. It contains the designs of the Master. It is of great antiquity, and is calculated to engage our earnest attention, and if attended to will make men better, (66.1) wiser, and happier. And the benefits arising from these sacred truths are not limited to the period of human life. They point not forward to the grave as the boundary of human existence, as the place where man shall cease to be. They reveal a state of existence beyond the grave, that lasts to all eternity. Happy is that Brother who has studied it faithfully and has treasured up its truths in his heart.

[KNIGHT TEMPLAR DEGREE]

(70.1)Address — Chamber of Reflection

The rules of the Order have required that I should bring you to his place. It is silent, and retired. I beg of you to endeavor to abstract your mind from all worldly considerations for a short space of time, and devote this season to thinking of yourself and the things that may here occur to you.

To the place of which this is a symbol we must all sooner or later come. The wisest statesmen, the bravest warrior the meanest beggar, the old and decrepit, the gay, the beautiful the happy all travel the same journey and terminate their wanderings in the same house appointed for the living. Here they lay down all their sorrows and the burden of their worldly trouble is removed. Here the gay laugh is changed to silence, here the towering schemes of ambition are forgotten and the mighty and the mean, the rich and the poor enter upon that sleep which to mortal knows no waking.

Though you may now be smiling in prosperity and surrounded with the comforts which the world bestows upon its votaries, the ruffian conqueror must be met, the battle fought, and you must be vanquished in the conflict. Though strong ties may bind you to the world they must be broken. Though the language of affection may plead in your behalf it will be unavailing, the dust must return unto dust as it was and the spirit unto God who gave it.

[*Points to the Bible*] But see, here is the only light by which we can learn how to enter this dark and dreary mansion. It is the Book of Wisdom. It contains a revelation of the Divine Will.

Calls his attention particularly to the Scriptures open before him, on which is placed the skull surmounted with a green wreath.

Here is an emblem of Time (*the hourglass*). Behold, how rapidly the sands run. They will soon run out, and then if no external power set it in motion, its motions will never be renewed. Let this be deeply impressed upon your mind. Time we can never recall. But we can and we ought to improve the fleeting moments as they pass, for on time, eternity depends.

Points to the Skull. Here is a melancholy memento, the emblem of mortality. It is now silent, vacant, dead. The rose of health once bloomed upon the cheek, the eye sparkled with intelligence and the countenance perhaps was once fair to look upon, but it is now an object of loathing and disgust. As it now is, so you will be. Look, then, at this melancholy memento. Listen, for though silent, it speaks to the mind in a voice which cannot be misunderstood. It says, "Remember." (70.1)

We have placed a green sprig by its side, for we do not believe that the grave is the final resting place, or death an endless sleep. No, we believe in immortality.

We believe that though a man die, yet he shall live again, that the time will come when those who sleep in the earth shall come forth from the grave and meet the Master face to face.

How important then, that the moments of life should be properly improved, that the precepts of this sacred volume should be laid to heart, that our labors for improvement and participation should be unceasing. For we shall die, and we shall rise again. We shall behold the Master face to face, and then deception either with him, or with ourselves, will be unavailing. We shall receive our reward or we shall be punished, for so he has decreed.

Questions asked and answered.
Washing.

Obligation

1st—Usual point in all, the same.

2d—Attend to all due signs and summons, if within the distance of forty miles, natural infirmities and unavoidable accidents only preventing.

3d—Help, aid and assist, with my counsel, purse and sword, all worthy Sir Knights, their widows and orphans, so far as my ability will allow, or truth, honor and justice will warrant.

4th—Will not be present at opening, unless there are nine regular Knights present, or the representatives of three different Encampments, acting under the sanction of a legal warrant.

5th—Will go forty miles on foot, or even barefoot on frosty ground, to save the life or relieve the distresses of a worthy Sir Knight.

6th—That I will wield my sword in the defense of innocent virgins, helpless orphans, destitute widows and the Christian religion.

7th—Will support the Constitution of the General Grand Encampment, and Bylaws, etc.

8th—Will not be present at the conferring of this Order, unless the person has previously received the E.A., F.C., M.M., Mark M., P.M., M.E.M., R.A.M., and Red+K.

9th—Penalty, etc.
Address, explanatory.

(67.5)*Commencement of the ritual—placed here by mistake.*

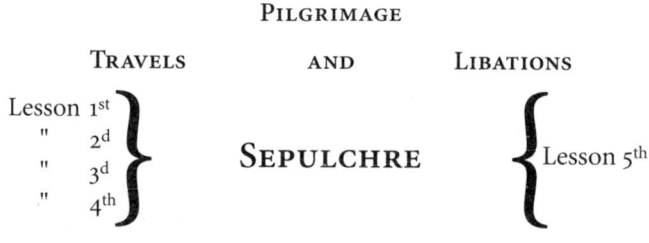

Hymn and Prayer

When brought before the Transparency of the Resurrection Hymn—"The rising God forsakes the Tomb."

Address

(Resurrection and Ascension)

Pilgrim, the scene before you represents the splendid conclusion of that hallowed sacrifice offered by the Redeemer of the world, to open a way for the salvation of men. This sacred volume informs us that He was born of a lowly virgin, that He led an humble and secluded life until He entered upon His ministry, which was attended with self-denial, sufferings and privations of no common kind, that He was tempted, buffeted and scoffed at in almost every step He took for the benefit of suffering and degraded humanity. Though He came to benefit them they set His goodness at naught, they derided and insulted Him, they mocked at His pretensions, and although no guile was in His heart, nor evil in His ways, although His nights were often spent in fervent prayer for those who were deriding him, although He never ceased to express His ardent love, and strong desire for the good of those He came to save, His persecutors never rested until a formal accusation was made against Him, for which He was tried and formally condemned, when He was led forth by the mob as a common malefactor and murdered by their ruffian hands.[9] (67.1)

(72.1)He was despised and rejected of men, a man of sorrows and acquainted with grief. We hid, as it were, our faces from Him. He was despised, and we esteemed him not. He hath borne our grief and carried our sorrows, yet we esteemed Him stricken. Smitten of God and afflicted. All we like sheep have gone astray, we have turned, every one of us, to his own way. And the Lord hath laid on him the iniquity of us all. He was wounded for our transgressions, He was buried for our iniquities, the chastisement of our peace was upon Him, and with His stripes we are healed. He was oppressed, and He was afflicted, yet He opened not his mouth. He is brought as a lamb to the slaughter and as a sheep before his shearers is dumb, so He opened not His mouth, and He made His grave with the wicked, and the rich in His death.

Pilgrim, on the hill of Calvary He bowed His sacred head and died. The fair sun veiled himself in darkness, the earth shook, the rocks were rent and the dead forsook their graves. They laid Him in a Sepulcher, but the grave could not hold Him. He burst the bars of death, and became the first fruits of them that slept. He ascended with transcendent majesty to heaven, where He now sits at the right hand of God, Mediator and intercessor for all those who have faith in Him.

Pilgrim, I now invest you with an emblem of that faith and the badge of the Order. When you look upon it, it may remind you of those scenes which took place in the Garden, and on the Cross. It may speak to you in the language of inspiration. Is it nothing to you as to pass by? Behold and see if thereby any sorrow like unto my sor-

---

9. Following this is a line which reads, "Now turn 5 pages forward for continuation of Address. / Page 72."

row wherewith the Lord hath afflicted me in the day of his fierce anger. It may teach you to imitate the virtues of the immaculate Jesus, who died that you might live.

Pilgrim, the ceremonies through which you are passing are calculated to make a deep impression upon your mind, and I most sincerely hope will have a lasting effect upon your character. You were first, as a trial of your faith and humility, enjoined to perform seven years pilgrimage. It represents the great pilgrimage of human life through which we are all passing. We are all weary pilgrims traveling from afar and anxiously looking forward to an asylum, where we shall rest from our labors. Yet it is dangerous to venture upon this far distant journey without a knowledge of the way we are going, and without this knowledge we shall easily go astray and fail in finding the asylum which we seek, but instead thereof faint among the sands of the desert, where there is no water to allay the burning thirst, no bread (72.1) to keep from starving. Incline your heart to instruction and your mind to understanding and, in your pilgrimage, learn the way to the habitation of comfort and of rest. Seek it with earnestness and diligence, for this is not your place of rest.

You were next directed, as a trial of your courage and constancy, to perform seven years warfare. It may represent to you the constant warfare that is necessary to be performed with the lying vanities and deceits of this world. The passions of the man lead him astray and sensual enjoyments entice him from the garden of happiness into the wilderness of vice and the labyrinth of error, but presently, often alas too late, it is to be feared he is undeceived or, what it worse, he is satiated. A feeling of duty or of shame rouses him to view his present state, and he sees with remorse that he is far from where he should be, but the ways he has wandered through are so winding and intricate that he can never, perhaps, retrace his steps, and he stands like the fool, not knowing from whence he came and whither he went. War not with your own welfare, make not yourself miserable, but be wise in time, consider every step of your journey, its end and its intention. Avoid the evil and choose the good, and when you find your strength failing in the contest, or your spirit falter, call upon your Captain, who has led the way and He will give you strength in time of need.

You are now performing penance as a trial of your humility. Of this our blessed Lord and Savior has left us as bright example. For though He was rich, yet for our sakes He became poor, that we through His poverty might be made rich. Though surrounded with the glory of His Father, He laid it aside and humbled Himself to take a human form, subjected himself to the sorrow and the joys, the infirmities and the trials of humanity, in order that He might know how to weep with those wept, and administer consolation and comfort to the tempted and the afflicted. It is also a trial of that faith which will conduct you safely over the dark gulf of death everlasting, and land your enfranchised spirit in the abodes of the blessed.

Pilgrim, bear ever in mind this solemn truth. You know not how soon you may be called upon to render an account to Him, from whom not even the most minute act of your life is hidden. For although you now stand erect in the pride of beauty, and the strength of manhood, the rose of heath blooming on your cheek, and your eye sparkling with intelligence, the angel may have already received the mandate to cut you off from among the living, and the arrow which is to pierce you be already on its flight, even while I am (73.1) speaking to you, may prostrate you before us in the arms of death, and the feet of those Companions who surround you, be employed in bearing you from this asylum a lifeless corpse.

Man that is born of a woman is of few days and full of trouble. He cometh forth like a flower and is cut down. He fleeth as a shadow and continueth not. In the midst of life we are in death. Thou changest the countenance of man and sendeth him away. Yet, though a man die, he shall again live. Though he say to corruption, "thou art my mother" and to the worms, "thou art my sister and my Brother", his spirit shall bloom and flourish beyond the shores of time, and be finally united to that spiritual body, either in the abode of wretchedness and despair, or in the beauteous paradise of God.

How important it is then, Pilgrim, that in the journey you are pursuing, your steps should be directed by wisdom which cometh from on high, that your mind should be enlightened by the truth of the Divine, in order that you should have a clear and perfect view, not only of the enemies which beset you in your course, but also of the manner in which you are to resist them "striving unto Blood." How important that in the warfare you are engaged in, you should fight manfully the fight of faith, having your lamp burning and your loins girt about, taking with you the sword of the spirit and the helmet of salvation, and in the thickest of the fray to be familiar with the commands of your Captain, who will always send you assistance and deliverance, if you call upon Him in your hour of need. How important that you should always be on your watch of penitence, that you should be waiting and ready for His approach, in order that you may gladly follow the steps of those who

Once they[10] were mourning here below,
    And wet their couch with tears,

And wrestled hard, as we do now,
    With sin and doubt and fears.

They marked the footsteps which he trod,
    His zeal inspired their breasts,

And following their incarnate God,
    Possessed the promised rest.

The Pilgrim here passes to the Asylum and partakes of the Fifth Libation, when the ceremonies conclude by installation.
Lessons, and closing prayer.

---

10. The word *they* is superimposed.

NOTES

CHAPTER 1: INTRODUCTION

1. Henry W. Coil, et al., eds., *Coil's Masonic Encyclopedia* (New York: Macoy Masonic Publishing and Supply Co., 1961), s.v. "New York."
2. Dorothy Ann Lipson, *Freemasonry in Federalist Connecticut, 1789-1835* (Princeton: Princeton University Press, 1977), p. 238.
3. Robert Freke Gould, et al., *The History of Freemasonry*, 3 vols. (New York: John C. Yorston & Co., 1889), vol. 3, p. 339.
4. Coil, s.v. "Scottish Rite Masonry," "Stephen Morin."
5. Samuel H. Baynard, Jr., *History of the Supreme Council, 33°*, 2 vols. (Boston: Supreme Council, 33; N.M.J., 1938), p. 152.
6. Baynard, pp. 155-56; Joseph Cerneau, Patent of Authority, July 15, 1806, Baracoa, Cuba, Manuscript in the hand of Mathieu Dupotet(?), Archives, Supreme Council, 33°, S.J., Washington, D.C
7. Baynard, pp. 181-83.
8. Baynard, p. 183.
9. Baynard, pp. 155-56.
10. Coil, s.v. "Morgan Affair."
11. Lipson, p. 268.
12. William Preston Vaughn, *The Antimasonic Party in the United States* (Lexington, Ky.: University Press of Kentucky, 1983), p. 14.
13. Paul Goodman, *Towards a Christian Republic* (New York: Oxford Univ. Press, 1988), p. 4.
14. Vaughn, p. 16.
15. Coil, s.v. "Anti-Masonry."

CHAPTER 2: THE MYSTERY OF THE FOLGER MANUSCRIPTS

1. Robert Folger, "Recollections of a Masonic Veteran," part 11, *New York Dispatch*, Sept. 28, 1873.
2. *Columbia University Alumni Register: 1754-1931*, (New York: Columbia University Press, 1932), p. 285.
3. "The Late Dr. Gram," *The Homeopathic Examiner*, vol. 1, no. 2, Feb. 1840, p. 101; "Hans B. Gram, M.D.," *The U.S. Medical and Surgical Journal*, vol. 2, July 1867, pp. 449-52.
4. Wil Baden, Decryption of the Folger Manuscript, ca. 1955, Typescript, Archives, Macoy Publishing ant Masonic Supply Co., Inc., Richmond, Va.
5. R. A. Gilbert, "The Masonic Career of A. E. Waite," *Ars Quatuor Coronatorum*, vol. 99 (1986), pp. 96, 97; William G. Peacher, M.D., Great Prior, C.B.C.S., Riverside Calif., Jan. 15, 1991,

to S. Brent Morris, Columbia, Md., Typescript, In the possession of the author.

6. Henry C. Atwood] to [James Foulhouze], New Orleans, [ca. July, 1853], Transcript in the hand of Robert B. Folger, Archives, Supreme Council, A.A.S.R., N.M.J., Lexington, Mass.

7. *Rituel de Loge de Saint-Jean, 3e Grade* (Brussels: Grande Loge Régulière de Belgique, n.d.), p. 61.

8. *Rituel, 3ᵉ Grade*, p. 62; F. Amez-Droz trans., "Ritual of the Second Degree (Companion), Decreed at the Convent General of the Order in 5782 [1782]," n.d., p. 1, Archives, Iowa Masonic Library, Cedar Rapids.

9. *Rituel, 3ᵉ Grade*, p. 63; F. Amez-Droz trans., "Ritual of the Third Degree (Master Mason), Decreed at the Convent General of the Order in 5782 [1782]," n.d., p. 1, Archives, Iowa Masonic Library, Cedar Rapids.

10. *Rituel, 3ᵉ Grade*, p. 63; F. Amez-Droz, trans., "Third Degree," p. 1.

11. Heinrich Lachmann, *Geschichte und Gebrauche der maurerischen Hochgrade und Hochgrad-Systeme* (Braunschweig: Herzoglich Waisenhaus-Buchdrukerei, 1866), p. 36.

12. Albert Gallatin Mackey and William R. Singleton, *The History of Freemasonry* (New York: The Masonic History Co., 1906), vol. 2, p. 293.

13. [Carl Friedich Eber], *Sarsena oder der vollkommene Baumeister* (Bamberg: Kunz, 1817).

14. Folger, "Recollections," part 3, May 18, 1873, and part 8, Aug. 17, 1873.

15. "Scottish Rite Testimony," *Masonic Chronicle*, vol. 15, no. 7, Jun., 1893, p. 196.

16. Robert Folger, "Recollections," Part 3, May 18, 1873.

17. Norman D. Peterson, "Broad Characteristics of the A.&A.S.R. Blue Degrees" (typescript, Portland, Oreg., N. D. Peterson, Aug. 1990 draft), p. 3; N. D. Peterson, *A Documentary Notebook on the Latin Craft* (Portland, Oreg.: N. D. Peterson, 1975), passim.

18. Henry M. Smith, "Homeopathic Directory: New York Historical Sketch," *The New England Medical Gazette*, vol. 6, no. 2, Feb. 1871, pp. 91-94.

19. Jørgen Vagn Jørgensen, Præses, Den Danske Frimurerorden Informationsdirektoriet, Copenhagen, to S. Brent Morris, Columbia, Md., Nov. 8, 1990, Typescript, In the possession of the author.

20. *Transactions of the Grand Lodge of Free and Accepted Masons of New York, 1816-1827* (New York: Masonic Publishing and Furnishing Co., 1880], p. 477.

21. Vagn Jørgensen, to Morris, Nov. 8, 1990. Typescript, In the possession of the Author.

22. Robert B. Folger, "Recollections ," Part 4, June 1, 1873.

23. *Minutes, Supreme Council in and for the Sovereign and Independent State of New York*, [Second Atwood Supreme Council] Mar. 8, 1853, Transcript in the hand of Robert B. Folger, Collection Number SC012, Archives, Supreme Council, A.A.S.R., N.M.J., Lexington, Mass.

24. Robert B. Folger, "Recollections," part 34, July 19, 1874.

25. [E. Diterle], *Précis Historique de La Sincérité No. 373*, ([New York]: [1955]), p. 26.

26. James Foulhonze, *Memoire à Consulter sur l'Origine du Rite Ecossais Ancien Accepté*, New Orleans: L. Marchand & Co., 1858.

Chapter 4: The Coadjutors of Robert B. Folger

1. Henry M. Smith, "Homeopathic Directory: New York Historical Sketch," *The New England Medical Gazette*, vol. 6, no. 2 (Feb. 1871), pp. 91-94; Jørgen Vagn Jørgensen, Præses, Den Danske Frimurerorden Informationsdirektoriet, Copenhagen, to S. Brent Morris, Columbia, Md., Nov. 8, 1990, Typescript, In the possession of the author.

2. Thomas Bradford, *The Pioneers of Homeopathy* (Philadelphia: Boericke & Tafel, 1897),

p. 289; "The Late Dr. Gram," *The Homeopathic Examiner*, vol. 1, no. 2 (Feb. 1840), p. 101; "An Historical Note of Dr. Gram," *The Hahnemannian Monthly*, vol. 7 (1871), no. 1, p. 84.

3. Vagn Jørgensen to Morris.

4. William H. King, *History of Homeopathy*, 4 vols. (New York: Lewis Publishing Co., 1905), vol. 1, pp. 60–61; Bradford, *The Pioneers of Homeopathy*.

5. Robert B. Folger, "Recollections of a Masonic Veteran," part 11, *New York Dispatch*, Sept. 28, 1873; King, *History of Homeopathy*, vol. 1, p. 61.

6. *Transactions of the Grand Lodge of Free and Accepted Masons of New York, 1816–1827* (New York: Masonic Publishing and Furnishing Co., 1880), p. 477.

7. Smith, "New York Historical Sketch"; S.B. Barlow, "Miscellaneous: Dr. Gram," *The American Homeopathic Review*, vol. 3, no. 4 (Oct. 1862), p. 185; Bradford, *The Pioneers of Homeopathy*; Folger, "Recollections," part 11; King, *History of Homeopathy*, vol. 1, p. 61.

8. Barlow, "Dr. Gram"; "Obituary: Hans B. Gram," *The United States Medical and Surgical Journal*, vol. 2, July 1867, pp. 449–52; "The Late Dr. Gram."

9. Allan Boudreau, [Librarian, Grand Lodge of New York, F.&A.M.], N.Y., to S. Brent Morris, [Columbia, Md.], June 7, 1990, Typescript, In the possession of the author.

10. Smith, "New York Historical Sketch."

11. "Obituary, Ferdinand L. Wilsey," *The American Homeopathic Review*, vol. 2, no. 9 (Jun. & Jul. 1860), pp. 431–32.

12. Boudreau to Morris; William L. Gardner, *Historical Reminiscences of Morton Commandery, No. 4, Knights Templar* (New York: John W. Keeler, 1891), p. 24.

13. Boudreau to Morris; "Obituary, Ferdinand L. Wilsey."

14. "Obituary: Ferdinand L. Wilsey."

15. Harold V. B. Voorhis, "Henry Clinton Atwood—A Connecticut Yankee in New York," *Transactions of the American Lodge of Research* [New York], vol. 3 (1960), no. 1, pp. 89–96.

16. Folger, "Recollections," part 4.

17. Folger, "Recollections," part 4, and part 5, June 29, 1873.

18. Abraham Jacobs, "Register, Rules & Status. of the Sublime Degrees of Masonry," ca. 1809], Archives, Supreme Council, 33°, N.M.J., U.S.A., Lexington, Mass.; Folger, "Recollections," part 6, June 29, 1873.

19. Folger, "Recollections," part 6, June 29, 1873.

20. Folger, "Recollections," part 5; Jacobs, "Register"; Edmund B. Hays, "Hays Register," Archives, Supreme Council, 33°, N.M.J., U.S.A., Lexington, Mass.; Henry W. Coil, et al., eds. *Coil's Masonic Encyclopedia* (New York: Macoy Masonic Publishing and Supply Co., Inc., 1961), s.v. "Henry Clinton Atwood," by Edward R. Cusick.

21. Voorhis, "Henry Clinton Atwood"; Cusick, "Henry Clinton Atwood."

22. *Coil's Masonic Encyclopedia*, s.v. "Anti-Masonry"; Folger, "Recollections," part 14, Nov. 9, 1873.

23. Folger, "Recollections," part 14 and part 17, Dec. 14, 1873.

24. Folger, "Recollections," part 4 and part 15, Nov. 23, 1873.

25. Folger, "Recollections," part 15.

26. Folger, "Recollections," parts 17 & 4.

27. Voorhis, "Henry Clinton Atwood" p. 92.

28. Supreme Council for the United States, their Territories and Dependencies [Thompson-Folger Cerneau Supreme Council revived], *Official Manifesto*, (New York: Isley & Marx, 1881), p. 15; Samuel H. Baynard, Jr., *History of the Supreme Council, 33°*, 2 vols. (Boston: Supreme Council, 33°, N.M.J., 1938), vol. 1, pp. 244–46, 251; Josiah H. Drummond, "Ancient and Accepted

Scottish Rite of Freemasonry," in *History of Freemasonry and Concordant Orders*, H. L. Stillson et al., eds., (Boston: Fraternity Publishing Co.,1912), p. 819.

29. Folger, "Recollections," part 16, Dec. 7, 1873, part 18, Jan. 4, 1874, and part 30, May 24, 1874.
30. Folger, "Recollections," part 30.
31. Folger, "Recollections," part 29, May 10, 1874, and part 4.
32. Folger, "Recollections," part 30; Samuel Oppenheim, *The Jews and Masonry in the United States* (Bronx, N.Y.: S. Oppenheim, 1910), p. 36.
33. Baynard, *History*, pp. 253–54; Folger, "Recollections," part 31, May 31, 1874.
34. Folger, "Recollections," part 31; Enoch T. Carson, "History of Ancient and Accepted Scottish Rite Masonry in the United States," in *The History of Freemasonry*, R. F. Gould et al., eds., 4 vols. (New York: John C. Yorston, 1889), vol. 4, p. 674.
35. William Sewall Gardiner, *A History of the Spurious Supreme Councils in the Northern Jurisdiction of the United States* (Washington: Pearson's Steam Press, 1884), p. 52.
36. Carson, "History of Ancient and Accepted Scottish Rite Masonry," p. 675.
37. Gardiner, *A History of the Spurious Supreme Councils*, p. 54.
38. Carson, "History of Ancient ant Accepted Scottish Rite Masonry," p. 675.
39. "The Spurious Council 33d, New York," *The Freemason's Monthly Magazine*, vol. 12, no. 8 (Jun. 1, 1853), p. 240.
40. Carson, "History of Ancient and Accepted Scottish Rite Masonry," p. 675.
41. [Henry C. Atwood], "The Supreme Grand Council of the Northern Masonic Jurisdiction," no. 9, *The Masonic Sentinel*, Oct. 11, 1851, pp. 34–36.
42. *Minutes of the Cerneau Supreme Council* [Second Atwood Council], Mar. 8, 1853, Transcript in the hand of Robert B. Folger, Collection Number SC012, Archives, Supreme Council, A.A.S.R., N.M.J., U.S.A., Lexington, Mass.
43. "Recollections," part 34, July 19, 1874.
44. *Transaction of the Grand Lodge of New York, F. & A.M., from July 8th, A.L. 5852 to June 11th, A1. 5853* (New York: Robert Macoy, Printer, 1853), pp. 65–66, 237.
45. Peter Ross, *A Standard History of Freemasonry in the State of New York* (New York: Lewis Publishing Co., 1899), p. 445; *Statement of Proceedings Relative to Grievances Existing in the Grand Lodge of the State of New York, and the Reasons for Reviving St. John's Grand Lodge* (New York: Charles Shields, 1853), p. 28.
46. Joseph D. Evans, Deputy Grand Master, Edict, Aug. 12, 1853, Archives, Grand Lodge of New York, F. & A.M.; *Transactions of the Grand Lodge of New York, F. & A.M., from August 16th A.L. 5853 to June 10th A.L. 5854* (New York: Robert Macoy, Printer, 1854), pp. 10, 18.
47. Robert B. Folger, New York, to James M. Austin, [Grand Secretary], Sept. 26, 1853, Typescript, Archives, Grand Lodge of New York, F.&A.M.; Transactions of the Grand Lodge of New York, A.L. 5854 [1854], p. 14.
48. Folger, "Recollections," part 34.
49. [Henry C. Atwood] to [James Foulhouze], New Orleans, [ca. July, 1853], Transcript in the hand of Robert B. Folger, Archives, Supreme Council, 33°, N.M.J., U.S.A., Lexington, Mass.
50. [Atwood] to [Foulhouze]. The "Gourgas, Moore & Mackey imposition" refers to the Northern Supreme Council started by J. J. J. Gourgas. Charles W. Moore was its Grand Secretary General from 1844 to 1862, and Albert G. Mackey was the Grand Secretary General of the Southern Supreme Council which supported Gourgas and Moore. The "Willard Power" is the Grand Lodge of New York, the "Phillips Power" is the Past Masters' Grand Lodge, and the "Pythagoras or Hamburg power" is the German-speaking Pythagoras Lodge illegally chartered by the Grand Lodge of Hamburg.

51. [Albert Pike], *Beauties of Cerneauism. No. 1*, [Washington, D.C.: Supreme Council, 33°, S.J., 188–], p. 4.
52. *Proceedings of the Grand Lodge of Alabama* (Montgomery, Ala.: Masonic Signet Office, 1853), p. 19.
53. *Transactions of the Grand Lodge of New York, A.L. 5854* [1854], p. 200; Carson, "History of Ancient and Accepted Scottish Rite Masonry," p. 675.
54. Folger, "Recollections," part 35; Folger, "A History of the Ancient & Accepted Scottish Rite in the U.S.," 1877, Typescript, Collection No. SC087, Archives, Supreme Council, 33°, N.M.J., Lexington, Mass, p. 221.
55. La Sincérité Lodge No. 2, New York City, to the Grand Master of the Grand Lodge of New York, February 20, 1855, Transcript, Archives, Grand Lodge of New York.
56. Drummond, "Ancient ant Accepted Scottish Rite," p. 820; Folger, "Recollections," part 35, July 26, 1874; *Minutes of the Cerneau Supreme Council*, Apr. 4, 1853, and Mar. 1, 1854.
57. Folger, "Recollections," part 35.
58. Folger, "Recollections," part 36, Aug. 2, 1874; Drummond, "Ancient and Accepted Scottish Rite," p. 820.
59. Robert B. Folger, New York, to Enoch. T. Carson, [Past Lt. Grand Commander], [Ohio], Nov. 9, 1881, Typescript, Archives, Supreme Council, 33°, N.M.J., U.S.A., Lexington, Mass.
60. F. G. Tisdall, Charges of Unmasonic Conduct against Robert B. Folger, [ca. June 1853], Typescript, Archives, Grand Lodge of New York.
61. Robert B. Folger, [New York City], to the Grand Lodge of New York, June 2, 1857, Typescript, Archives, Grand Lodge of New York.
62. Carson, "History of Ancient and Accepted Scottish Rite Masonry," p. 674; Folger, "Recollections," parts 26 & 37; Voorhis, "Henry Clinton Atwood," p. 95.
63. Folger, Recollections, part 39, Sep. 6, 1874; Peter Ross, *A Standard History of Freemasonry in the State of New York* (New York: Lewis Publishing Co., 1899), p. 463.
64. Ross, *A Standard History*, p. 463.
65. Gardiner, *A History of the Spurious Supreme Councils*, p. 56.
66. "The Late Henry C. Atwood," *The Masonic Messenger*, vol. 5, no. 12, Sept. 15, 1860, pp. 110–11; Voorhis, "Henry Clinton Atwood," p. 94.
67. "The Late Henry C. Atwood."
68. *Transactions of the Grand Lodge of New York, F. & A.M., at its Annual Communication Commencing June 4, A.L. 5861* [1861] (New York: T. Holman, Printer, 1861), p. 171.

Chapter 5: The Biography of a Remarkable Mason

1. *Proceedings of the Supreme Council, 33°, for the U.S.A., their Territories and Dependencies* [Thompson-Folger Revived Cerneau Supreme Council] (New York: Masonic Publishing Co., 1892), p. 65.
2. *Proceedings of the Supreme Council, 33°, for the U.S.A., their Territories and Dependencies*, p. 65; *Columbia University Alumni Register: 1754–1931* (New York: Columbia University Press, 1932), p. 285.
3. "Return of New York Lodge No.368, from December 27, 1825, to December 27, 1826," Manuscript, Archives, Grand Lodge of New York, F. & A.M.; Robert Folger, "Recollections of a Masonic Veteran," *New York Dispatch*, part 1, Apr. 20, 1873.
4. Folger, "Recollections," part 3, May 18, 1873, and part 8, Aug. 17, 1873.
5. Folger, "Recollections," part 11, Sept. 28, 1873; Robert B. Folger, "A History of the Ancient &

Accepted Scottish Rite in the United States," 1877, Typescript, Collection No. SC087, Archives, Supreme Council, 33° N.M.J., Lexington, Mass.; Peter Ross, *A Standard History of Freemasonry in the State of New York* (New York: Lewis Publishing Co., 1899), p. 805; "Recollections," part 4, Jun. 1, 1873; *Proceedings of the Supreme Council, 33°, for the U.S.A., their Territories and Dependencies*, p. 65.

6. Folger, "Recollections," part 6, June 29, 1873; *Proceedings of the Supreme Council, 33°, for the U.S.A., their Territories and Dependencies*, p. 65; Robert B. Folger, *The Ancient and Accepted Scottish Rite*, 2nd ed. (New York: by the Author, 1881), Appendix, p. 69.

7. Robert B. Folger, "Reply to John D. Caldwell," in *Rites and Supreme Councils* (Cincinnati: Masonic Review, Oct. 1885), p. 68.

8. Edmund B. Hays, "Hays Register," Archives, Supreme Council, 33°, N.M.J., Lexington, Mass., Folger, "Recollections," part 7, July 20, 1873, "Pen Pictures of the Active Members of the Ancient Council, A∴ & A∴S∴. Rite," *Masonic Chronicle*, vol. 6, no. 10 (Sept. 1884), p. 147; Samuel H. Baynard, Jr., *History of the Supreme Council, 33°*, 2 vols. (Boston: Supreme Council, 33°, N.M.J., 1938), p. 103; "Scottish Rite Testimony," *Masonic Chronicle*, vol. 15, no. 7 (Jun. 1893), p. 199.

9. William Harvey King, *History of Homeopathy*, 2 vols. (New York: Lewis Publishing Co., 1905), vol. 1, p. 62.

10. Jørgen Vagn Jørgensen, Præses, Den Danske Frimurerorden Informationsdirektoriet, Copenhagen, To S. Brent Morris, Columbia, Md., Nov. 8, 1990, Typescript, In the possession of the Author; Henry M. Smith, "Homeopathic Directory: New York Historical Sketch," *The New England Medica1 Gazette*, vol. 6, no. 2 (Feb. 1871), pp. 91–94.

11. Robert B. Folger, "Cipher Manuscript" [FM1, the "Macoy Book"], July 12, 1827, Transcript in the hand of R. B. Folger, Archives, Macoy Publishing and Masonic Supply Co., Richmond, Va.

12. Smith, "New York Historical Sketch."

13. Gardner, *Historical Reminiscences of Morton Commandery No. 4*, p. 24; William J. Duncan, *History of Independent Royal Arch Lodge No. 2, F. & A.M.* New York: Charles S. Bloom, 1904), p. 268.

14. Duncan, p. 126.

15. Charles T. McClenachan, *History of Free and Accepted Masons in New York*, 4 vols. (New York: Masonic Publishing Co., 1892), vol. 3, pp. 58–60, *Transactions of the Grand Lodge of New York, F. & A M., 1841*, pp. 4–45.

16. [Wendall K. Walker, Librarian, Grand Lodge of New York, F. & A.M.], to the Grand Secretary, [Charles H. Johnson], Sept. 1, 1937, Typescript, "Memorandum, Subject: Robert B. Folger," Archives, Grand Lodge of New York, F. & A.M.

17. Folger, "Recollections," part 20, Jan. 25, 1874.

18. [Walker] to [Johnson].

19. Smith, "New York Historical Sketch"; Robert B. Folger, *Folger's Hygeiangelos* [Advertising Booklet] (New York: N.p., 1845).

20. Folger, "Recollections," part 30, May 24, 1874.

21. Folger, "Recollections," part 30, May 24, 1874.

22. Folger, "Recollections," part 30.

23. Folger, "Recollections," part 31, May 31, 1874.

24. Minutes, Supreme Council in and for the Sovereign and Independent State of New York [Second Atwood Supreme Council, Cerneau], Mar. 8, 1853, Transcript in the hand of R. B. Folger, Collection No. SC012, Archives, Supreme Council, 33°, N.M.J., Lexington, Mass.; Folger, "A History of the Ancient & Accepted Scottish Rite," 1877, p. 219.

25. Folger, "Recollections," part 34, July 19, 1874.

26. *Transactions of the Grand Lodge of New York, F. & A.M., from July 8th, A.L. 5852 to June 11th A.L. 5853* (New York: Robert Macoy, Printer, 1853), pp. 65–66.

27. Peter Ross, *A Standard History of Freemasonry in the State of New York* (New York: The Lewis Publishing Co., 1899), p. 445; *Statement of Proceedings Relative to Grievances Existing in the Grand Lodge of the State of New York, and the Reasons for Reviving St. John's Grand Lodge* (New York: Charles Shields, 1853), p. 28.

28. F. G. Tisdall, New York, to the Grand Lodge of New York, F. & A.M., [1853], Typescript, Archives, Grand Lodge of New York, F. & A.M.

29. Robert B. Folger, 27 Suffolk St., to James M. Austin, [Grand Secretary], Sept. 26, 1853, Typescript, Archives, Grand Lodge of New York, F. & A.M.

30. Gardner, *Historical Reminiscences of Morton Commandery No. 4*, p. 24; *Proceedings and Constitution of the Grand Encampment of Knights Templar of the State of New York, Feb. 10, 1854* (New York: McSpedon & Baker, Printer, 1854), pp. 2–24.

31. Folger, "Recollections," part 39, Sept. 6, 1874.

32. Robert B. Folger, New York, to the M.W. Grand Lodge, State of New York, June 2, 1857, Typescript, Archives, Grand Lodge of New York, F. & A.M.

33. Committee on Grievances, "Report," *Proceedings, Grand Lodge of New York, F. & A.M., 1857*, p. 168.

34. Robert B. Folger, *Information for Members of the Ancient Accepted Scottish Rite* (New York: Edward O. Jenkins' Sons, [1884]), p. 38.

35. Folger, "Recollections," part 36, Aug. 2, 1874; Josiah H. Drummond, "Ancient and Accepted Scottish Rite of Freemasonry," in *History of Freemasonry and Concordant Orders*, H. L. Stillson et al., eds. (Boston: Fraternity Publishing Co., 1912), p. 820; Folger, "A History of the Ancient & Accepted Scottish Rite," 1877, p. 233.

36. Folger, "Recollections," part 36.

37. Robert B. Folger, New York, to Enoch T. Carson, [Past Lt. Grand Commander], [Ohio], Nov. 9, 1881, Typescript, Archives, Supreme Council, 33°, N.M.J., Lexington, Mass.

38. Folger, "A History of the Ancient & Accepted Scottish Rite," 1877, p. i.

39. Folger, *The Ancient and Accepted Scottish Rite*, pp. 332–33, 19.

40. Robert B. Folger, New York, to Enoch T. Carson, [Past Lt. Grand Commander], Nov. 17, 1881, Transcript in the hand of R. B. Folger, Archives, Supreme Council, 33°, N.M.J., Lexington, Mass.

41. Folger, "Recollections," part 38, Aug 16, 1874.

42. Robert B. Folger, New York, to Enoch T. Carson, Lt. Grand Commander, July 18, 1873, Typescript, Archives, Supreme Council, 33°, N.M.J., Lexington, Mass.

43. *The Masonic Chronicle*, vol. 6, no. 9 (Aug. 1884), p. 137.

44. Charles T. McClenachan, "A Synoptical History of all of the Supreme Councils that have Ever Existed, and the manner of their Formation in Chronological Order," *Proceedings of the Supreme Council, 33°, N.M.J., 1881*, pp. 128, 4; Folger to Carson, Nov. 17, 1881.

45. *Proceedings of the Supreme Council, 33°, N.M.J., 1881*, pp. 8–84.

46. Folger, *The Ancient and Accepted Scottish Rite*, p. 324.

47. "Scottish Rite Testimony," *Masonic Chronicle*, vol. 15, no. 5, Apr. 1893, p. 137.

48. *Proceedings of the Supreme Council, 33°, for the U.S.A., their Territories and Dependencies* [Thompson-Folger revived Cerneau Supreme Council] (New York: Masonic Publishing Co., 1892), pp. 12–14; "Anna C. Folger," *Masonic Chronicle*, vol. XV, no. 1, Dec. 1892, p. 25.

INDEX

A

"Ad hoc stat" 22
"Adhuc stat," R.E.R. motto (Thus far it stands) 22
Agreement of the People, Leveler document, English Civil War 28
Agrippa, Heinrich Cornelius 45, 46
Aiq Beker 45, 46
Albany, N.Y. 10
All-Healing Balsam. *See* Folger's Hygeiangelos (patent medicine)
Altar 24
American Metropolitan College of the Grand Professed 21
Ancient and Accepted Scottish Rite in Thirty-Three Degrees, The, R. B. Folger (1862, 1881) 89
Ancient and Primitive Rite 11, 91
Ancient Chapter No. 1, R.A.M., N.Y. 78
Andrew in the East Lodge, N.Y. 82
anti-Masonry, American 12–13
Atwood, Edward W. 92
Atwood, Henry C. 21, 31
    appoints E. Hays to succeed him as Gr. Com. 71
    biography 57–73
    condemned by G.M. of Alabama 69
    expelled from G.L., 1837 61
    expelled from Masonry, 1853 67
    Grand Commander, Supreme Council in and for the Sovereign and Independent State of New York 31
    objects to R. H. Walworth's election as G.M. 33
    opinion of Folger 61, 63
    portrait 58
    publishes Masonic Sentinel 64
    receives 32° from A. Jacobs 59
    receives 33° from J. Cushman 59
    requests Craft rituals from J. Foulhouze 32
    revives Cerneau Supreme Council 62
    revives St. John's G.L. 84
    studied ritual under J. L. Cross 57
    supports St. John's Grand Lodge 61
Atwood Lodge No. 208, N.Y. (later Cyrus Lodge) 69
Atwood Supreme Council
    first 65
Austin, James M. 67

B

Baden, Wil 20, 35, 38
Baltimore Lodge of Perfection 10
Barker, John 78
Barthe, Dr. 69
Batavia, N.Y. 12
Bayliss, M. W. 12
Baynard, Samuel H., Jr. 79
Benevolent Lodge, N.Y. 60
Bennett, Donald H. 20, 38
Benschoten, James Van 60
Beyerlé', Jean-Pierre-Louis 47, 49
Bideaud, Antoine 8, 10
    Sublime Grand Consistory, N.Y. 11
Bideaud Supreme Council 10, 11, 78
Blitz, Edouard 21
Boaz, pillar 24
broken pillar (R.E.R. emblem) 22
Brown, William Moseley 21

C

C.B.C.S.. *See* Chevalier Bienfaisant de la Cité Sainte
Canandaigua, N.Y. 12, 56
Carson, Enoch Terry 71, 88, 89, 90
Cassard, Andres 70
Catéchisme des Francs-Maçons (1744), L. Gabanon (L. Travenol) 24
Cerneau, Joseph 8, 10, 11, 12
    Sovereign Grand Consistory, N.Y. 10, 11
Cerneauism 31. *See* Cerneau, Joseph
Cerneau Supreme Council
    divides funds and disbands, 1846 62
Charleston Lodge of Perfection 10
Chevalier Bienfaisant de la Cité Sainte 21
cipher, Masonic. *See* Masonic cipher
Clay, Henry 13
Clay, M. 133

INDEX

Clinton, De Witt 8, 10, 11, 59, 212
Cohen, Moses 59
Colden, Cadwallader D. 10, 11
College of Physicians and Surgeons, Columbia Univ., N.Y. 20, 54, 56, 77
Columbia Council No. 1, R.&S.M., N.Y. 78
Columbian Encampment No. 1, K.T., N.Y. 78
Columbia University, N.Y. 20, 56, 77
Constitutions of 1786 10
Copenhagen, Denmark 19, 29, 31, 33, 52, 79, 80
cord, knotted 24
Coxe, Daniel 7
Crata Repoa (1770) 134
    title page 135
Cromwell, Oliver 28
    theory he originated Freemasonry 24, 27, 34
Cross, Jeremy Ladd 31, 59, 63, 64, 66, 79
    Gr. Comm. of revived Cerneau Supreme Council 63, 83
    ritual as taught by 57–58, 61, 78
Cryptographia, J. B. Friderici's (1684) 45, 46
Cryptologia magazine 38
cubical stone 20
    R.E.R. emblem 22
Cushman, James 59–60, 78, 79
Cyrus Lodge No. 208, N.Y. (formerlly Atwood Lodge) 69

D

"D O". *See* "Dirigit Obliqua"
de Grasse, Count 90
de Hoyos, Arturo 227
de la Motta, Emmanuel 11
"Deponens aliena ascendit unus" 23
Desolation des Entrepreneurs Modernes, La (1747), L. Gabanon (L. Travenol) 24
Deszelus 32, 66, 70
"Dirigit Obliqua" 22
dismasted ship (R.E.R. emblem) 22
Drummond, Josiah H. 90
Dutcher, Benjamin C. 81

E

Eber, Carl Friedrich 27
Ellis, William H. 64
Elmira Consistory, N.Y. 30, 32, 34
Elmira Daily Advertiser, N.Y, newspaper. 30
Emperors of the East and West, France 9
Essai sur la Franc-Maçonnerie, J.-P.-L. Beyerle (1788) 47, 49
Eureka Chapter No. 22, R.A.M., Conn. 59, 60
Evans, Joseph D. 67

Explication de la Pierre Cubique, A. G. Chérau (1806) 46
exposés of Masonic rituals 12, 24

F

Fenger, Dr. 52
Fireman's Lodge No. 368, N.Y. (later New York Lodge) 20, 33, 77
First Lodge, Boston (now St. John's) 7
Folger, Anna C., wife of R. Folger 93
Folger, Robert B.
    affiliates with I.R.A. Lodge No. 2 80
    becomes a Mason 77–79
    biography 75–93
    conclusions about from cipher 48
    Grand Secretary General, Supreme Council in and for the Sovereign and Independent State of New York 31
    history of Scottish Rite, 1862 89
        proposes revision, 1873 90
        reprinted and authorship denied, 1881 91
    initiated through 4° Scottish Master, R.E.R. 33
    introduced F. H. Wilsey to H. B. Gram 29, 33
    officer of Morton No. 4, K.T. 82
    opinion of H. C. Atwood 61, 63
    opinion of A. Pike 89, 92
    opinion of E. Hays 71, 88–89
    opinion of W. Willis 81–82
    portrait 76
    prepared cipher manuscripts 79–80
    publishes "Recollections of a Masonic Veteran," 1873–74 91
    receives 32° from A. Jacobs 59, 78
    receives 33° from H. C. Atwood 79
    revives Cerneau Supreme Council with H. C. Atwood and J. L. Cross 83
    revives Cerneau Supreme Council with H. Thompson 92
    revokes preface to FM1 33, 34
    S.W., Zorobabel Lodge No. 498, N.Y.C. 31
    served in New York State Assembly, 1849 82
    suspended from Masonry, 1841 81
    suspended from Masonry, 1853 85
    W.M. of lodge chartered by Scottish Rite 84
Folger, Robert B., Jr. 93
Folger's Hygeiangelos (patent medicine) 82
Folger Manuscript, The, S. B. Morris (1993) 95
Folger Manuscript 1 (*Macoy Book*) 95–132
    Disciple's Grade 97–110
        Catechism 109–10
        Closing 108
        Lecture 104–6

Index

Obligation 100
Opening 107
Fellow's Grade 111–21
    Closing 119–20
    Covenant or Vow 114
    Lecture 116–17
    Opening 118
History of Freemasonry 130–32
Master's Grade 121–278
    Lecture 123–26
    Opening or Closing 127
Prayers 128
Preface 33, 34, 48, 56, 86, 87, 95
"Scottish" obligations 129
Folger Manuscript 2 (*Supreme Council Book*) 133–226
    Ancient Mysteries 202–11
        1st Degree: Pastophor 202–4
        2nd Degree: Neocoris 204–5
        3rd Degree: Melanophir 205–6
        4th Degree: Christophoris 207–8
        5th Degree: Balahate 208
        6th Degree: The Door of the Gods 209
        7th Degree: Propheta, or Sapphenach Pancha 209–10
    Officers and Their Costume 211
    Clinton, De Witt, extract from a speech of 212
    Consecration of a Lodge 186–90
    Disciple's Grade 137–59
        Address or Lecture 146–55
        Apron and glove presentation 143–44
        Catechism 158–59
        Closing 157
        Lodge diagram 151
        Obligation 142
        Obligation, preliminary 138
        Opening 156
    Fellow's Grade 160–72
        Closing 169
        Covenant 165
        Lecture 166
        Middle Chamber Lecture 170–72
        Opening 160
    First Degree Scottish Lodge (French)
        Closing 201
        Opening 191–92
        Work 193–200
    Knight Templar Degree 215–20
        Obligation 217
    Masters Grade 173–85
        Address 175–84
        carpet 226

    Opening and Closing 185
    Red Cross, Order of 213–14
    Religion, Lecture on 223–26
    Temples, Lecture on 221–22
Folger Manuscript 3 (*Walgren Book*) 227–77
    Consecration of a lodge in the Scottish Rite 267–72
    Entered Apprentice Degree 230–51
        Lecture 247–49
        Obligation 239
        Opening 230–32
    Fellow Craft Degree 252–60
        Opening 252
    Knight Templar Degree 273–77
        Obligation 274
    Master Mason Degree 261–66
        Historical Discourse 266
        Opening 261–62
Fort Masonic, N.Y. 8
Foulhouze, James 21, 32, 64, 65, 66, 68, 69, 71
Francken, Henry Andrew 10
Francs-Maçons Ecrasés, Les, (1747), Abbé Larudan(?) 24, 34
Frederick of the Crowned Hope Lodge, Copenhagen (Frederik til det kronede Håb) 31, 52
French Modern Rite 23, 24
Friderici, Johannes Balthasar 45, 46

G

George Washington Lodge No. 287, N.Y. 20
German Union Lodge, N.Y. 78
Geschichte und Gebrauche der maurerischen Hochgrade und Hochgrad-Systeme, H. Lachmann (1866) 23
glossary of Masonic terms 14–17
Gourgas, J. J. J. 10, 63, 69
Gourgas Supreme Council, N.Y.C. 57, 69
Gram, Dr. Hans B. 29, 33
    admitted to the Royal Academy of Surgery, Copenhagen 52
    became a Mason Nov. 3, 1819 52
    biography 51–55
    born in Boston, July 13, 1786 or 1787 52
    Father of American homeopathy 20, 79
    influence on R. B. Folger 79
    introduced to F. L. Wilsey by R. B. Folger 29, 33
    moves to Copenhagen, 1806 or 1807 52
    moves to New York City, 1825 52
    pioneer of homeopathy in America 51
    portrait 53
    source of Folger's rituals 28–30, 33–34
    W.M., Zorobabel Lodge No. 498, N.Y.C. 31

Gram, Neils B., brother of H. B. Gram 52
Grand Lodge of Massachusetts
    membership, 1830 & 1840 13
Grand Lodge of New York 7
    membership, 1826 8
    membership, 1835 13
Grand Lodge of Vermont 13
Grand Orient of France
    model for H. C. Atwood's grand lodge 68
    Scottish Rite, origin of, claims R. B. Folger 90
Grasse, Count de 90
Gray, Dr. John F. 55, 56

H

Hahnemann, Samuel 20, 33, 54
Hamburg, Grand Lodge of 69, 70
Hanson, Mrs. Vee 95
Harmony Council No. 8, R.&S.M., Conn. 57
Haswell, Nathan B. 64
hauts grades 9, 21
Hays, Edmund B. 71, 72, 88, 89
Henry Clay Lodge No. 277, N.Y. 20
Hermitage Hall, N.Y.C. 72
Herring, James 60, 61, 78
Hibernia Lodge, N.Y. 60
Hicks, Elias 79
Hiram Lodge No.10, N.Y. 55
Historical Reminiscences of Morton Commandery No. 4, W. L. Gardner (1891) 80
History of Freemasonry, A. Mackey (1906) 27
History of the Ancient Accepted Scottish Rite in the United States, A, R. B. Folger (unpublished) 91
homeopathy 20, 33, 51, 52, 54, 56, 79
Hund, Baron 22
Hygeiangelos, Folger's (patent medicine). *See* Folger's Hygeiangelos (patent medicine)

I

I.R.A. Lodge No. 2, N.Y.. *See* Independent Royal Arch Lodge No. 2, N.Y.
Independent Lodge No. 7, N.Y. (now No. 185) 61, 62
Independent Royal Arch Lodge No. 2, N.Y. 7, 77, 80, 81, 88
Ineffable Degrees (4°–14°) 57, 66
"In silentio et spe fortitudo mea" 22

J

Jachin, pillar 24
Jackson, Andrew 13, 71
Jacobs, Abraham 57, 59, 63, 78
Jerusalem Chapter No. 8, R.A.M., N.Y. 20, 29, 33, 52, 54, 78, 79

Jews, admission of to S.R., attacked by R. Folger 89
John the Forerunner Lodge No. 1, N.Y., chartered by first Atwood Supreme Council 31–32, 33, 34, 66, 69, 84

K

Keystone Hotel, N.Y.C. 72
Kloß, George B. 27
Knights Templar (Masonic) 8
Knight Templar Degree 215–20, 273–77
    Obligation 217, 274
Kohlo Masonic congress, 1772 22

L

Lafayette Chapter of Rose Croix, N.Y. 62, 78
Larudan, Abbé 27, 28, 34
Lenox, Mass. 20, 77
Levelers 27, 28
"Libre B," St. John's Lodge, Philadelphia 7
Libri tres de occulta philosophia, H. C. Agrippa (1531) 45, 46
lion, sleeping 28
lodge floor plan
    Disciple Lodge, FM1 25
    Disciple Lodge, FM2 151
    Master's carpet, FM2 226
    R.E.R. 2nd Degree 26
Lowndes, Oliver 59
Lyons Masonic congress, 1773 22

M

Mackey, Albert G. 27, 69
Maçon Démasqué, Le, T. Wolson(?), (1751) 24
Macoy Publishing and Masonic Supply Co. 20, 35, 79, 95
Marshall, George E. 65
Masonic cipher 45
Masonic Publishing Co., N.Y.C. 34, 95
Masonic Sentinel, N.Y., H. C. Atwood, ed. 64
McClenachan, Charles T. 91, 92
Memphis, Rite of 11
Minerva Lodge No. 371, N.Y. 33, 54, 55, 56, 79
mirror ceremony 23
Moore, Charles W. 69
Morgan, William 12–13, 56, 60
Morin, Stephen 9–10, 59
    actions illegal, R. Folger 89
Morning Star Lodge No. 47, Conn. 57, 59, 60
Morris, S. Brent 38, 95, 133
Morton Commandery, No. 4, K.T., N.Y. 55, 56, 78, 80, 82, 85, 86
Mosquera, Gen. Tomás Cipriano de 70

INDEX

Mulligan, John W. 10, 11
Mystic Lodge No. 389, N.Y.C. 57, 59

N

New England Medical Gazette 29
New York City Lodge of Perfection 10
New York Dispatch, newspaper 91
New York Lodge No. 386, N.Y. (formerly Fireman's Lodge) 77, 80
New York Medical and Philosophical Society 54
Nivelleurs 27

O

Old City Hotel, N.Y.C. 77
Olosaonian (patent medicine). *See* Folger's Hygeiangelos (patent medicine)
Order of St. John 55
Order of the Royal Secret (incorrectly the Rite of Perfection) 9
L'Ordre des Francs-Maçons Trahi, anon. (1745) 24, 45, 47
Orient Chapter No. 1, R.A.M., N.Y. (now No. 128) 61, 62
Osborne, George L. 84
Oxford, Conn. 57, 59

P, Q

Palestine Commandery No. 1, K.T., N.Y. (now No. 18) 61, 62
La Parfait Union Lodge, N.Y.C. 7
Peckham, William H. 91
Peckham Supreme Council 92
Pennell, Richard 81
Pentwater, Mich. 21
Perfection, Rite of 8, 9, 90. *See also* Royal Secret, Order of
Philadelphia, St. John's Lodge 7
Philadelphia Lodge of Perfection 10
Phillips Grand Lodge, N.Y. 68, 69, 72
Piatt, William F. 61
Pike, Gen. Albert 71, 89, 92
Ploquin 32, 66
Pythagoras Lodge, N.Y. 69
  requests charter from G.L. of N.Y. 70

R

"Recollections of a Masonic Veteran," *New York Dispatch*, R. B. Folger 28, 91
R.E.R.. *See* Rite Ecossais Rectifié (R.E.R.)
Rainsborough, Gen. Thomas 28
Raleigh, N.C. 21
Ramsay, Chev. Andrew Michael, Oration, 1737 9

Randall, Nelson 66
Rectified Scottish Rite 19, 20, 22, 23, 24, 32, 33, 52, 54, 55, 79, 84. *See also* Rite Ecossais Rectifié (R.E.R.)
  emblems of the degrees 22–24
Red Cross, Order of 213–14
Religion, Lecture on 223–26
Riker, Richard 10, 11
Rising Sun Chapter No. 16, R.A.M., N.Y. 57, 59
Rite Ecossais Rectifié (R.E.R.) 21, 22, 23, 24, 27, 28, 29, 30, 31, 32, 33, 34, 52, 79, 84. *See also* Rectified Scottish Rite
Rite of Strict Observance 23, 27
  transformed into the Rectified Scottish Rite 22
Roullier 32, 66
Royal and Select Masters (Cryptic Masonry) 8
Royal Arch Masonry 8
Royal Secret, Order of 8

S

St. Clair, Ward K. 21
St. John's, Boston (formerly First Lodge) 7
St. John's Grand Lodge, N.Y. 61, 62, 83
  reactivated after R. H. Walworth elected G.M. 33, 67, 67–68, 69, 71, 72, 84, 85, 86
St. John's Hall, N.Y.C. 57
St. John's Lodge No. 1, N.Y.C. 7, 85, 86
Sarsena oder der vollkommne Baumeister, C. F. Eber (1817) 27, 28
Saynisch, Lewis 31, 34, 54, 80
Sceau Rompu, Le, anon. (1745) 45
"Scotticism" 72
Scottish Rite, Ancient and Accepted 8–9
  Craft Degrees 29
  Mother Supreme Council, Charleston, 1801 10
Scottish Rite, Rectified. *See* Rite Ecossais Rectifié (R.E.R.)
Seymour, Harry 11, 91
Shakespeare Hotel, N.Y.C. 81
Shute, J. Raymond II 21
Sickels, Daniel 65
Silentia Lodge No. 198, N.Y. 55, 60, 93
Simons, John W. 65, 66, 72
Simson, Sampson 10, 11
La Sincérité Lodge, N.Y., chartered by first Atwood Supreme Council 32, 66, 69, 70
  requests a charter from G.L. of N.Y. 70
Smith, Dr. Henry M. 29, 80
Solomon Chapter No. 3, R.A.M., Conn. 57
Sovereign Grand Consistory, N.Y.C. (Cerneau) 10, 11, 78, 90
Supreme Council, Connecticut 71

Index

Supreme Council, Northern Hemisphere 64, 83
Supreme Council, Sovereign, Free, and Independent State of New York, 64
Supreme Council, United States of America, their Territories and Dependencies 69, 71
Supreme Council, Western Hemisphere 79
Supreme Council, Sovereign and Independent State of New York 31
Supreme Grand Council, Sovereign and Independent State of Louisiana 21

T

Tardy, John Gabriel 59
Temple Chapter, R.A.M., N.Y. 78
Temple Lodge, N.Y.C. 7
Temples, Lecture on 221–22
"Ternario formatur, novenario dissolvitur" 23
Thompson, Hopkins 92
Three Books of Occult Philosophy, H. C. Agrippa (1531) 45, 46
Tisdall, Fitz Gerald 85, 86
toast, Folger's at Elmira Consistory 30, 34
Tollerton Hall, N.Y.C. 67
Tompkins, Daniel D. 10, 11
Town, Rev. Salem 64
Trenton, N.J. 59, 78
"Tria formant alienum deponent et ascendit in unum" 22
triangular monument (R.E.R. emblem) 22
Tyler, John 71

U, V

L'Union Française Lodge, N.Y.C. 32, 77
test of fire, air, earth, and water 28–29
University of Utah 227
Unkart, Edward 70
Van Buren, Martin 71
Vatet, Eugene 32, 66, 70
von Hund, Baron 22
Voorhis, Harold Van Buren 35, 95, 133

W

Walgren, Kent L. 227
Walworth, Reuben H. 33, 67, 69, 84, 85
War of 1812 8
Warren Hall, N.Y.C. 60
Washington, George 75
Webb, Thomas Smith 57
Wilhelmsbad Masonic congress, 1782 22
Willard Grand Lodge 68, 69
Willets, Charles W. 84
Willis, William 81
    R. B. Folger's opinion of 81–82
Wilsey, Ferdinand L. 29, 33
    biography 55–56
    introduced to H. B. Gram by R. B. Folger 29, 33
    name obliterated in FM1 preface 33, 34, 56, 86
Wirt, William 13

X, Y, Z

York Lodge No. 367, N.Y. 60, 61
Zerubbabel and Frederick of the Crowned Hope Lodge, Copenhagen (Zorobabel og Frederik til det kronede Håb) 29, 31, 52
Zerubbabel of the North Star Lodge, Copenhagen (Zorobabel til Nordstjernen) 31, 33, 52, 79
Zinnendorf, Johann Wilhelm Kellner von 27
Zorobabel Lodge No. 498, N.Y. 31, 33, 34, 54, 80